A RELIGIOUS HISTORY of the AMERICAN GI in WORLD WAR II

A RELIGIOUS HISTORY

of the AMERICAN GI

in WORLD WAR II

G. KURT PIEHLER

University of Nebraska Press | Lincoln

"Praise the Lord and Pass the Ammunition!" words and music
by Frank Loesser. Copyright (©) 1942 Sony Music Publishing
LLC. Copyright renewed. All rights adminstered by Sony Music
Publishing LLC, 424 Church Street, Suite 1200, Nashville TN,
37219. International copyright secured. All rights reserved.
Reprinted by permission of Hal Leonard LLC.

Library of Congress Cataloging-in-Publication Data
Names: Piehler, G. Kurt, author.
Title: A religious history of the American GI in World War II /
G. Kurt Piehler.
Description: [Lincoln]: [University of Nebraska Press], [2021] |
Series: Studies in war, society, and the military | Includes
bibliographical references and index.
Identifiers: LCCN 2021015298
ISBN 9781496226839 (hardback)
ISBN 9781496229991 (epub)
ISBN 9781496230003 (pdf)
Subjects: LCSH: World War, 1939–1945—Religious aspects. |
United States—Armed Forces—Religion. | World War,
1939–1945—Chaplains—United States. | BISAC: HISTORY /
Military / World War II | RELIGION / History
Classification: LCC D744.5.U6 P54 2021 | DDC
940.54/780973—dc23
LC record available at https://lccn.loc.gov/2021015298

Set in Minion Pro by Laura Buis.

For Kathryn Gallitano, an unparalleled teacher formerly at Roxbury High School, New Jersey, who provided the foundation for my career as a historian,

and

the Rutgers College Class of 1942, for their pivotal role in founding the Rutgers Oral History Archives, which opened up new scholarly horizons,

and

Stella Danielle Contente and Aaron Roosevelt Contente: May they live in a world that embraces religious pluralism and tolerance

CONTENTS

ILLUSTRATIONS

ACKNOWLEDGMENTS

No book is possible without good teachers, and I am fortunate to have been mentored by several remarkable ones, beginning with Kathryn Gallitano. Although a generation has passed since I sat in her classroom in a suburban high school in Morris County, New Jersey, I still benefit from the solid grounding she provided in how to study history. Having earned a master's from Columbia University in the 1950s, when it was the preeminent institution in the nation for the study of history, Ms. Gallitano set high expectations. She required students in her advanced placement American history class to not only understand the historical narrative but to be able to grapple with historiography in our essay assignments. Her reading list was demanding and, even more importantly, she stressed honing our analytical writing abilities, a skill set I have used throughout my academic career. Above all she imparted to me, as a first-generation college student, the confidence in my abilities to thrive in academe.

This project has deep roots intellectually. As an undergraduate student at Drew University, I had the good fortune to take several courses with the late Donald G. Jones, a pioneering scholar in the field of American civil religion. William D. Stroker's course in the Hebrew Bible was my first exposure to the critical reading of religious texts. J. Perry Leavell, my undergraduate advisor, and Thomas R. Christofferson taught me a great deal not only about history but also about the practice and profession of teaching when I became an adjunct assistant professor at Drew.

In 1994 the Rutgers College Class of 1942 provided funding that led me to serve as the founding director of the Rutgers Oral History Archives from 1994 through 1998. What was initially conceived as a two-year project focusing on World War II will soon celebrate its thirtieth anniversary.

In embarking on this project, I conducted life-course interviews, including questions about religious practices and observances. I quickly learned from these interviews that, while World War II can be considered a morally necessary war, it was certainly not a "good war" for those in the infantry and other combat arms. Two months into conducting interviews, I realized that the Rutgers Class of 1942 had given me an intellectual gold mine. I will always be indebted to them and other supporters of the Rutgers Oral History project, especially the late Carl Heyer, Class of 1925, for their generosity through financial gifts and sharing so much about their lives in oral histories.

I continue to benefit from the mentorship of my graduate advisor, John Chambers, who played a pivotal role in the creation of the Rutgers Oral History Archives. My second return to Rutgers afforded me the opportunity to work closely with John on several projects and, even more importantly, solidified our friendship. Few could ask for a better and more generous *doktorvater*.

This project emerged as a phoenix from the ashes of an overly ambitious book that I intended to write examining the American response to Nazi Germany. A grant from the Roosevelt Institute allowed me to conduct two weeks of research at Franklin D. Roosevelt Library in the winter of 2005. A series of Rosh Hashanah greetings offered by President Roosevelt from 1933 to 1944 were among the first documents I read.

These greetings by Roosevelt intrigued me in several ways, beginning with the fact that they represented the standard stock-in-trade of any American politician eager to curry favor with constituents. Elected officials traditionally have welcomed opportunities to issue statements marking religious and secular holidays, recognizing historical anniversaries, applauding the work of nonprofit organizations, and celebrating the achievements of individual Americans on major milestones. FDR set no precedents in sending out holiday greetings to Jewish congregations and organizations that requested them; Herbert Hoover had issued similar ones as had other chief executives. At the same time, the reading of these Rosh

Hashanah greetings was quite poignant when I considered the context of world events unfolding in the 1930s and 1940s. While German Jews were persecuted by their government, with anti-Semitic legislation depriving them of basic human rights, followed by Kristallnacht, deportation, and eventual murder, American Jews could count on receiving Rosh Hashanah greetings from the president of the United States of America.

I also became intrigued by FDR's speeches and statements promoting religious pluralism and wondered how this shaped federal policy during the New Deal and World War II. I am very grateful for the support of the Roosevelt Institute and am pleased to express my gratitude.

In spring 2008 I began work on this book while holding a position as a visiting Fulbright lecturer in American Studies at Kobe University and Kyoto University. Teaching American history to Japanese students made me rethink the nature of American society, especially the role of religion. I began asking myself a question my wife raised while we were in Japan: Am I religious because I am American?

Ryo Yokoyama and Masugi Shimada were generous Fulbright hosts, and I learned much from them about understanding American history from a comparative perspective. I am also grateful for the friendship of Yutaka and Masae Sasaki, which has endured.

Seminars and conferences remain essential to scholarship. An NEH Faculty seminar examining "Religious Diversity and the Common Good," held at Boston College in 2009 and led by Alan Wolfe, offered me an opportunity to grapple with current trends in religious studies. The comments of seminar participants on a prospectus I presented for a project titled "A Religious History of the New Deal and World War II" proved critical in my reformulating my work on this book. I can still hear the voice of seminar participant Maureen Fitzgerald, who told me bluntly, "You need to narrow this project's focus on what you know best and center it on the GI experience or you will be spending the rest of your life researching this book."

Due to ten years overseeing an archive as part of my duties at Florida State University, I have developed a deeper understanding and appreciation of the invaluable work archivists perform, which makes historical scholarship possible. Several institutions provided significant financial support to use their holdings, and I am pleased to publicly acknowledge grants from the Cushwa Center for the Study of Catholicism at the University of Notre Dame, the Mary Baker Eddy Library, the Presbyterian Historical Society, the Rockefeller Archives Center, and the Schlesinger Library at Harvard University. I am grateful to have received the Eva R. Dave Fellowship, from the Jacob Rader Marcus Center of the American Jewish Archives, and the Bordin/Gillette Fellowship, from the Bentley Library at the University of Michigan. Judy Litoff's invitation to speak at Bryant University in Rhode Island provided me the chance to consult her rich holdings of women's correspondence from World War II. A summer award from the Office of Research at Florida State University funded a research trip to use the National Archives in Washington DC.

I also want to acknowledge the generosity of Ann Pfau in providing me a copy of the 201 file of Beverly Ward from the National Archives. Over my tenure at Florida State, Anne Marsh has rendered invaluable service in numerous ways. Jordan Bolan served as an undergraduate researcher for this book during her first year at Florida State, and Beatrice Dain more recently assisted on this project. I appreciate several colleagues, Erica Fugger, Houston Johnson, Keara Sebold, Gregory Urwin, and Juliana Witt, who graciously double-checked references that were unavailable at my library as a result of the covid-19 pandemic.

I am especially grateful to Susan Contente, Michael Creswell, Rachel Duke, Marion "Molly" Dorsey, and Ronit Stahl for reading the entire manuscript of this text and making a number of invaluable suggestions for revisions. This book also benefited from comments on portions of the manuscript by Scott H. Bennett, Edward Gitre, Michael Kasper, Gabriela Maduro, and Amanda Porterfield. Portions of this manuscript were presented at annual meetings of the American Historical Association, Society for Military History, and I offered lectures at the Arnstein Jewish Community Center in Knoxville, Tennessee, Florida Atlantic University, Georgian Court University, Gordon State College, Murray State University, and Virginia Tech.

Kara Vuic's enthusiasm for this project proved crucial in bringing this work to the attention of the University of Nebraska Press. One of the leading historians of war and society of her generation, Kara offered invaluable comments that improved this book. The professionalism of the University of Nebraska Press has earned this author's deep appreciation. Bridget Berry, senior acquisitions editor, secured two excellent outside reviewers that not only offered a strong endorsement for publication but provided excellent suggestions for revisions. Emily Wendell, assistant editor for acquisitions, and Ann Baker, senior project editor, have paid careful attention to the many details necessary to bring a book to press. Stephanie Marshall Ward is one of the best copyeditors I have had the privilege of working with during my career.

My daughter, Stella Danielle Contente, took the lead in locating images for this book, including sorting through archival boxes and searching digital collections. Both Stella and her twin brother, Aaron Roosevelt Contente, along with my wife, Susan, joined me on several of my research trips, including one delightful week in Sleepy Hollow, New York, followed by another in Boston.

In writing this book I gained a better understanding of why my late mother, Isolde Clark, embraced the United States after a childhood spent in Nazi Germany and living through World War II and why my late stepfather, Vincent Clark, developed a lifelong adoration of Franklin D. Roosevelt. I will never forget my dad telling me the story of how the Ku Klux Klan burned crosses near his home in the 1920s to drive him and his family out of his community because they were Roman Catholic. In writing this book it is my hope that Aaron and Stella will live in an America that continues to strive to further the vision of religious pluralism espoused by Franklin D. Roosevelt.

A RELIGIOUS HISTORY of the AMERICAN GI in WORLD WAR II

Introduction

Promoting the Free Exercise of Religion

W ith a few notable exceptions, Hollywood combat films seldom dwell on the religious lives of GIs. Occasionally, they show men praying prior to entering combat or at a funeral. With the possible exception of *God Is My Co-Pilot*, chaplains are generally given only small cameo roles, typically leading services before soldiers enter battle or presiding over funerals. Hollywood's reticence about centering stories on chaplains makes the War Department film *For God and Country*, produced in 1943 by the First Production Unit of the U.S. Army Air Force, intriguing; it offers a fictional account of the role and heroism of army chaplains. Captain Ronald Reagan stars as the gregarious Father Michael O'Keefe, U.S. Army chaplain, who makes the ultimate sacrifice and dies on a New Guinea battlefield tending to a wounded soldier.

Classified as a training film, *For God and Country* has the feel and aesthetics of a Hollywood short with simplistic didactic lessons showing how the U.S. Army envisioned chaplains promoting the free exercise of religion by those in uniform. Through imagery and dialogue, the forty-four-minute film portrays religion in the army as an entity that embraces tolerance and religious pluralism. The film underscores the equality among Protestantism, Roman Catholicism, and Judaism by having a Protestant minister, Rev. Tom Manning, and a rabbi, Arnold Miller, join O'Keefe on screen. Offscreen, Walter Huston narrates a story of the friendship that develops among these three chaplains when they meet at chaplain school at Harvard University.

In a semidocumentary format *For God and Country* follows the three chaplains through training at Harvard, their first deploy-

1. Ronald Reagan portraying an army chaplain in *For God and Country* (1943). Ronald Reagan Library.

ment to army camps stateside, and subsequent service with combat units. In providing an overview of their time in training, it emphasizes that they are made into soldiers, undergoing physical conditioning and studying such diverse topics as map reading and military courtesy. Not only do these three chaplains form strong bonds with each other; when deployed, they embrace the adage imparted by the senior chaplain at their graduation ceremony to serve all men irrespective of "race or creed" or station in life and to tackle problems they face, no matter how small.[1]

The chaplains depicted in *For God and Country* embody masculinity. O'Keefe played football in college, and his Protestant counterpart is a Phi Beta Kappa Olympic boxer. At his first assignment, at an unnamed camp in Georgia, Manning is seen playing football, boxing, and tossing horseshoes. Far from putting on airs, Chaplains O'Keefe and Miller, who serve together, take an interest in organizing shows for their men. To underscore the need for chaplains to serve all, Manning—during his visit to the base hospital—finds a soldier holding the rosary and offering prayers. When the chaplain offers to help, the young man asks, "Where is Father O'Neill?" Manning tells the troubled patient that, unfortunately, there is no priest available, but he declares confidently that, while he is not a Catholic priest, Father O'Neill has told him what prayer should be offered in such a situation. Manning pulls out his prayer book and begins reciting the prayer of contrition.

Throughout the film there is a remarkable sensitivity toward avoiding narrow sectarianism. For instance, the senior chaplain, at the graduation ceremony for chaplain school, offers a prayer after his address evoking the Heavenly Father but avoiding any Christological references. The motion picture portrays Roman Catholic, Protestant, and Jewish chapel services and gives equal billing to these three faiths. At Catholic services depicted in the film, Father O'Keefe intones the Mass in Latin and Rabbi Miller offers prayers in Hebrew. Two religious flags are displayed at several points in the picture, one with the Latin cross and the other with an image of the tablets of the Torah.

The final third of the film focuses on deployment and combat, reinforcing the image of chaplains as masculine role models able to inspire men to fight. The film shows Manning jumping with his fellow paratroopers into battle in Europe. O'Keefe and Miller are part of an infantry unit that has to fight its way out after being cut off from its supply lines. In counseling a paratrooper afraid of jumping into combat, Manning assures him that this is a normal reaction to danger that he shares. Manning insists that fear can be overcome, and he sets the example himself.

Underscoring the bravery and sacrifice of chaplains, a shell kills O'Keefe as he attends to a wounded soldier on the battlefield. His death will be mourned by the man he reformed and by his friend and fellow chaplain, Miller. The cemetery where O'Keefe is buried contains graves with crude wooden Latin crosses and stars of David to signify the service and sacrifice of soldiers from the three religions portrayed. Walter Houston offers the final narration, underscoring the dual role the army expected chaplains to perform. They were to serve the religious needs of soldiers anywhere they went, but they were also soldiers, who played an important role in inspiring men to fight.

For God and Country is a heavy-handed example of the way the federal government used the power of the state in World War II to mobilize American society to achieve victory. World War II is not the first time that civilian and military leaders, even in the United

States, used religious values and rhetoric to inspire soldiers to fight. But what made World War II different is the fact that Pres. Franklin D. Roosevelt and the U.S. Army devoted unprecedented resources to promoting the free exercise of religion. Through an expansion of the chaplaincy, the construction of chapels at army bases, the distribution of scriptures to GIs at government expense, and public relations efforts that stressed the value of spiritual engagement, the military inspired citizen soldiers to fight. This promotion of religion reflected the belief among many national and army leaders, most notably Roosevelt and army chief of staff Gen. George Marshall, that citizen soldiers should be able to practice their religious faiths freely while in uniform. This not only entailed a mobilization of clergy into service; the emphasis on chaplains tapped into religious ideals and values to inspire and comfort citizen soldiers. The structuring of religious life in the U.S. Army left an important legacy of ensuring soldiers could worship in an atmosphere that reflected tolerance and pluralism.

This official embrace of religiosity by FDR and his commanders represented a combination of idealism and pragmatism. Roosevelt drew on religious discourse as part of his campaign to convince the entire nation and the citizen soldiers who served in the armed forces of the ideological justness of the struggle against Nazi Germany, fascist Italy, and Imperial Japan. He and General Marshall believed in providing access to religious services and assured soldiers' families that young men and women in the armed forces would not be corrupted by military life. As part of their regular duties, army chaplains were required to deliver monthly lectures on sexual morality to the troops in their units in the hope that moral suasion would reduce high rates of venereal diseases. Roosevelt and military leaders joined with several faith-based organizations to create a quasi-public agency—the United Service Organizations (USO)—tasked with offering wholesome recreational outlets to counter the lure of gin joints, gambling dens, and brothels. In contrast to earlier wars, the armed forces limited the role of the USO and other service organizations on army bases. For instance, unlike in France during World War I, no independent YMCA chaplains ministered to American troops deployed overseas in World

War II. In order to receive partial federal funding, the USO had to deliver services on a nonsectarian basis.

Official policies adopted by the armed forces privileged a religious pluralism promoting tri-faith tolerance and equality among Protestantism, Roman Catholicism, and Judaism. Many chaplains and GIs embraced this tri-faith pluralism, and the lived religion of the GI often shunned narrow sectarianism, especially on the battlefield. But the promotion of tri-faith tolerance engendered significant tensions and divisions. The Roman Catholic hierarchy, as well as many priests serving as chaplains, feared a push for ecumenicalism by some Protestant chaplains and military commanders that would threaten the orthodoxy of faithful Catholics. Protestants and Jews chafed at significant divisions among different faith traditions being submerged. For example a minister was expected to deliver a service acceptable to all Protestants, whether a Southern Baptist, a high-church Episcopalian, or a Christian Scientist. Similarly, a rabbi was expected to offer a service acceptable to Orthodox, Conservative, and Reform Jews. Faiths outside of the tri-faith trinity were marginalized. For instance, the U.S. Army never commissioned a Buddhist chaplain to serve the needs of the Japanese American combat units. Traditional Native American faiths received no recognition by the army or navy chaplaincy. Even fundamentalist Protestant leaders protested they were marginalized by a number of official policies related to commissioning chaplains and the embrace of tri-faith pluralism.

The clergy commissioned to serve as chaplains in the U.S. Army were selected in proportion to the religious demographic makeup of the armed forces. This effort entailed an unprecedented increase in the number of Roman Catholic priests and rabbis commissioned as chaplains. The armed forces printed and distributed, at government expense, Protestant, Roman Catholic, and Jewish translations of the Bible. At the behest of the U.S. Army, Congress—for the first time—funded the systematic construction of chapels for training camps across the United States. To reflect the increased stature of the chaplaincy, the U.S. Army chief of chaplains rose to the rank of major general before the conflict ended. Despite resistance in the navy hierarchy, and over the opposition of some fundamentalists, the U.S. Navy chief of chaplains received flag rank by v-j Day.[2]

The mobilization of religion in support of the war effort is remarkable on several counts. There existed significant pacifist sentiment during the interwar years among many clergy, especially in mainline Protestant denominations. In contrast to other men, who were eligible for conscription, clergy were exempt, on the basis of their occupation, from military service. As a result chaplains who served in the war were all volunteers.

This study will offer more than an institutional history of the establishment and execution of official policies on the free exercise of religion. It aims to offer a bottom-up account of the lived religion of GIs. Religious ideals and values motivated GIs to fight and sustained them while in combat. Prayer and a host of other rituals provided succor to those facing danger, especially on the battlefield, the grievously wounded, and those held prisoner by the Germans and Japanese. Religion served as an essential marker of identity for individual servicemen and servicewomen, a signifier reflected in the "dog tags" they wore around their necks, stamped with a *P* for Protestant, *C* for Roman Catholic, or *H* for Hebrew (Jewish). For citizen soldiers who bristled at the inexorable push by the armed forces to turn them into "government issue," participating in religious services offered an opportunity for GIs to assert their individualism and remember their ties to home. Although the armed services proclaimed that each GI could worship according to the dictates of his conscience, the structuring of religious life fostered a civil religion that promoted pluralism and tolerance.

This institutional and cultural framework, established during World War II, had enduring consequences for midcentury religious practices and beliefs. It further solidified a growing movement toward religious tolerance, promoted by such organizations as the National Conference of Christians and Jews and such symbolic acts as the memorialization of the four chaplains. Through the Character Education Program, U.S. Army chaplains indoctrinated soldiers about the ideological struggles they faced in the Cold War. The tensions that had existed during World War II continued, especially between mainline and evangelical Protestants.

During the war President Roosevelt and military leaders actively fostered religiosity. Over twenty thousand clergymen served in the armed forces to meet the spiritual needs of the over fifteen million men and women in uniform. Never before or since have as many men and women served in uniform as in World War II. Moreover, most GIs served for the duration of the conflict, and many were deployed overseas for years. In World War I, most units first arrived in France in 1918 and returned home the following year.

Institutionally, the U.S. Navy differed in how it implemented the Rooseveltian vision of the free exercise of religion. It was slower in commissioning rabbis to serve as chaplains and only appointed two Black ministers as chaplains before V-J Day. The navy limited the autonomy of the chief of chaplains and remained reluctant to promote him to flag rank. Under naval regulations chaplains could be assigned ancillary duties, and the navy received criticism for not assigning enough chaplains to naval vessels. In contrast to the army, it did not underwrite the cost of distributing Protestant, Roman Catholic, and Jewish scriptures to sailors and marines but relied on the American Bible Society and other private organizations to meet this need.

The navy's divergence from policies adopted by the army reflected the insular culture of this branch of the service. As one scholar has observed, the army often sought to be the willing servant when tasked by civilian leaders with implementing change. In contrast, the navy believed what was good for the navy was good for the country. The leaders of the navy and marines remained less willing to cater to the citizen soldier, and both were reluctant to open their ranks to draftees.

Religion and the Case for War

The institutional support given to buttressing the religious life of the American GI aligned with Franklin Roosevelt's vision of what made American society distinctive. FDR stressed that religious faith remained central to sustaining American democracy. Throughout his presidency Roosevelt drew heavily on rhetoric that stressed religious pluralism and endorsed the tri-faith movement, which instilled mutual understanding and respect among Protestants, Roman Catholics, and Jews. The ways the armed forces structured religious life for the American GI served to foster this tri-faith vision, which ultimately diminished traditional Protestant political and cultural dominance of American society.[3]

Roosevelt's response to the rise of Nazi Germany was influenced by his religious worldview. After Germany's victory over France in June 1940, FDR embarked on a controversial and contested effort to both rearm the United States and provide substantial material aid to nations fighting the Third Reich. He argued not only that Nazi Germany posed a national security threat to the Western Hemisphere but that this regime threatened to destroy religious institutions and values globally. FDR faced significant opposition to his polices from a diverse coalition that opposed foreign intervention. This included such prominent conservatives as Republican senator Robert Taft and the aviator Charles Lindbergh. But this movement, which coalesced around the America First Committee, also included as members the labor leader John L. Lewis and the socialist Norman Thomas. Opponents of FDR's interventionist actions also included much of the Roman Catholic hierarchy in the United States and many mainline Protestant ministers and theologians belonging to churches affiliated with the Federal Council of Churches.[4]

Americans, prior to the attack on Pearl Harbor, remained divided over whether the United States should enter another world war, as low morale among the draftees mobilized in the first peacetime draft, in 1940, caused concern among army leaders. Even though a significant share of the public, by late 1941, supported supplying material aid, through Lend-Lease, to Great Britain and the Soviet Union, there remained significant ambivalence in many quarters about American boys dying in another foreign war.

Nonetheless the devastating loss at Pearl Harbor ended the acrimonious debate over intervention, and the war fostered little overt opposition. Although the cry for vengeance—combined with racial animosity—united Americans in the struggle against Japan, support for the war against Germany proved lackluster. Even after the United States entered World War II, American military leaders continued to fret over whether the draftees who filled the ranks of the U.S. Army were motivated to fight. General Marshall was not alone in identifying the lack of overt ideological commitment among GIS revealed by many journalists and social commentators. Senior military leaders expressed concern that the average foot soldier did not understand why he was fighting Nazi Germany and lacked sufficient hatred of the enemy. When the United States began mobilizing a citizen soldier army, raised through the peacetime draft of 1940, Marshall recognized the need to adhere to democratic values. Traditional military discipline had its limit, and the American GI would need sufficient indoctrination to convince him that the war was worth fighting.[5] Hollywood was enlisted in this effort, and it produced such noted propaganda films as Frank Capra's *Why We Fight* series.[6]

The idea of American GIs fighting together as a "band of brothers," devoid of overt expressions of patriotism, has deep intellectual roots. Journalistic accounts bolstered the findings of Stouffer's group of social scientists that GIs seldom fought for the noble ideals expressed by President Roosevelt and Prime Minister Winston Churchill in the Atlantic Charter. They fought so they wouldn't let their buddies down. An entire genre of wartime journalism, pioneered by Ernie Pyle, sought to understand and interpret the experience of rank-and-file GIs for the home front.[7] Some of the most influential and widely read memoirs produced by GIs reflect this goal, most notably E. B. Sledge's grim *With the Old Breed* and William Manchester's *Goodbye Darkness*.[8] The World War II veteran and literary critic Paul Fussell declared that even the ideals of the Four Freedoms sentiment, "set forth on the Norman Rockwell poster 'Ours to Fight For,' didn't seem to grab the heart, let alone the mind."[9]

By considering the religious life of the GI, this book modifies the current scholarly and popular perception of the American GI as a nonideological warrior who fought only to get the job done and support his brothers-in-arms. Protestant, Roman Catholic, and Jewish chaplains played a key role in explaining to the American GIs why they were fighting and assuring them, when they were wounded or burying lost comrades, that these sacrifices were not in vain. In opinion surveys conducted by a team of social scientists led by Samuel Stouffer, GIs who entered the army after America's declaration of war expressed strong sentiments regarding the religious nature of this conflict and the threat posed not only to Jews but to all religions if the Nazis conquered America.

Scholars seeking to recover the social history of the American GI in World War II are fortunate that few generations of soldiers have been as well studied. Stouffer's team of social scientists determined that comradeship served as one of the essential glues that kept soldiers motivated to fight.[10] Most military historians have often emphasized this theme as essential to understanding the American GI's experience of combat.[11] But when asked in surveys about what kept them going on the battlefield, GIs listed prayer as the single most important thing that sustained them when in harm's way, even more than comradeship.[12]

Historians and Hollywood have gotten one thing correct about the religious life of the American GI—white servicemen and servicewomen served in ethnically, religiously, and geographically diverse units. Despite the armed forces maintaining a rigid system of racial apartheid, dividing Black and white GIs, they did not segregate servicemen or servicewomen based on their religion. Except for Japanese Americans, army units were not segregated based on national origin. All branches of the services welcomed the children of the wave of immigrants from Southern and Eastern Europe—disproportionally Roman Catholics and Jews—who had flocked to the nation's shores from the 1890s through the early 1920s. Men from Manhattan's predominantly Jewish Lower East Side and the Roman Catholic enclave of South Boston lived in barracks alongside Baptists from Appalachia and Lutherans from the upper Midwest. This intermingling of men and women of different ethnicities and religions was celebrated by American propaganda, especially in the countless Hollywood productions made during and after the war.[13]

This celebration of the ethnically diverse platoon during the war stands in contrast to the fierce ethnic and religious sectarianism that marked the interwar years. Discrimination on the basis of race, religion, and national origin remained perfectly legal and commonly practiced. Religious bigotry, exacerbated by racism, led the U.S. Congress, in 1921 and 1924, to enact a quota system that restricted immigration from Southern and Eastern Europe in order to reduce the influx of predominantly Roman Catholic and Jewish immigrants.[14] A soldier entering the army at the age of twenty-one in 1940, under the peacetime draft, would have witnessed as an adolescent the flowering of the second incarnation of the Ku Klux Klan, which strived to define the United States as a White Anglo-Saxon Protestant nation and viewed Roman Catholics and Jews as threats to the body politic.[15] As a teenager in the late 1930s, he probably heard Fr. Charles Coughlin—the radio priest from the Church of the Little Flower outside Detroit, Michigan—lamenting, in his national radio address, the threat posed by Jews and Communists to the American way of life. And if a soldier was Jewish or African American, real estate covenants would have barred him and his parents from buying a home in certain neighborhoods.

Significant voices offered a more tolerant vision of American society, even as the Ku Klux Klan marched by the thousands down Pennsylvania Avenue in Washington DC. In 1923 the Federal Council of Churches fostered the formation of the National Conference of Christians and Jews, which sought to foster interfaith understanding. Uniting Protestants, Roman Catholics, and Jews, the National Council evolved into an independent organization promoting religious tolerance. Sponsoring annual Brotherhood Days and a host of other public programs, the National Council countered the venomous voices of bigotry.[16] As president, FDR lent his voice in support of the National Council, even speaking on a national radio broadcast, in 1936, to mark National Brotherhood Day.

Continuity and Change

The armed forces have always had their share of nativists and bigots, but the fact that the U.S. Constitution explicitly bars a religious test to hold public office militated against efforts to exclude individuals from serving in the military based on their faith. Although the officer corps of the armed services remained heavily dominated by White Anglo-Saxon Protestants into the twentieth century, more recent immigrants often dominated the enlisted ranks and brought religious diversity to the armed forces, especially in peacetime.[17]

In considering the place of religion in World War II, it is important to highlight the continuity and differences between World War II and earlier wars and also what made this conflict distinctive. Prior to 1940 federal support of religion in the military had been lackluster at best, especially for the small regular army that performed constabulary duty in the West and later in Asia in the opening decades of the twentieth century. During the early 1800s the regular army had for a time no chaplains in the service, except at the U.S. Military Academy at West Point. Until the early twentieth century, Congress limited the number of naval chaplains to twenty-four, even in wartime. Then Congress enacted a series of measures to enhance the professional status of chaplains.[18]

World War I witnessed a mobilization of American society that would set many precedents followed in World War II, especially in providing for religious life in the armed services. Abandoning the volunteer tradition, President Woodrow Wilson and the U.S. Congress raised a conscript army that led to an influx of new immigrants from Southern and Eastern Europe into the ranks of the army, which further increased religious diversity.[19] Although a clique of officers who had strong nativist views expressed misgivings, the army implemented a series of programs to integrate these new Americans into the ranks.[20]

When the United States entered World War I, in April 1917, the number of chaplains on active duty in the army was fewer than one hundred, and there existed no system for training clergy once they were inducted into the service. In the early 1900s American religious denominations had responded to the call for clergy to serve as chaplains, and a system had been created for these denominations to certify prospective chaplains. However, the army did not establish a school to indoctrinate new chaplains, before deploying them to serve with their units, until March 1918.[21] To serve the growing religious diversity within its ranks, the army made provisions for commissioning rabbis as chaplains. The army had commissioned Black chaplains to serve segregated African American units since the American Civil War, but the War Department grudgingly increased the number of Black clergymen accepted into the chaplaincy only after pressure from the NAACP.[22]

Gen. John J. Pershing's appointment of his friend Episcopal bishop Charles Brent as chief of chaplains for the Army Expeditionary Force (AEF) in France proved to be pivotal in creating an organizational ethos for the chaplaincy that responded to the growing religious pluralism in the ranks. Brent brought to his position a strong record of ecumenicalism. As missionary to the Philippines, Brent broke with many Protestant missionaries in not seeking to find converts among Roman Catholic Filipinos. As chief of chaplains, he promoted a tri-faith pluralism for the AEF chaplaincy and mandated that chaplains must meet the spiritual needs of all doughboys in their units.[23]

Following the precedent established in earlier conflicts, religious organizations played a vital role in meeting soldiers' religious and humanitarian needs by partnering with the Commission on Training Camp Activities (CTCA). This civilian agency, staffed by progressives, received broad authority to establish recreational programs for army soldiers on American military camps. However, it also possessed the authority to regulate sexuality in the interest of preventing outbreaks of venereal disease among doughboys. The CTCA played a pivotal role in suppressing red light districts throughout the United States and imprisoning women caught within restricted zones near army camps.

To provide wholesome recreation for doughboys in training camps, the army relied on a network of private religious and secular organizations, whose work would be coordinated by the CTCA. To fulfill its mission, the CTCA partnered with a number of religious and other nonprofit organizations. Initially, the CTCA favored the Protestant YMCA in establishing soldier clubs and, later, huts at army camps to provide doughboys a place to relax in home-like settings, attend musical and theatrical performances, watch movies, and attend religious services. With some reluctance the Catholic-affiliated Knights of Columbus was able to establish its own soldier clubs and huts on army bases.

The United States raised an army for the "war to end all wars" that numbered over four million men. After the guns fell silent on November 11, 1918, the country followed the pattern established after earlier conflicts: rapidly demobilizing and maintaining a small regular army supplemented by National Guard units. Peace brought the dissolution of the CTCA, and military leaders determined that one of the lessons learned from the conflict was that the U.S. Army should avoid using private organizations to meet the religious and recreational needs of soldiers. Although significant interfaith cooperation had existed during the war, there had also been considerable tension among the constituent elements of the CTCA. Both Roman Catholic and Jewish leaders resented the dominant position of the YMCA and the tendency of this organization to proselytize.[24]

Despite demobilization, efforts by the armed forces, especially within the U.S. Army, to professionalize the chaplaincy continued. The National Defense Bill of 1920 created a chaplain corps for both the army and the navy with each headed by a chief. During the interwar years, the chaplain corps shrank, along with the rest of the armed forces, but the institutional changes stayed in place. However, although the chaplaincy of the armed forces made significant strides toward professionalization during the interwar period, it still faced significant headwinds. For instance, the regular army had no rabbi serving on active duty, although several held reserve commissions.[25]

In contrast to World War I, the United States began mobilizing for entrance into World War II over eighteen months before the Japanese attack on Pearl Harbor. After the fall of France, in May 1940, FDR federalized the National Guard and convinced Congress to enact peacetime conscription. To meet the needs of the influx of recruits, the army and navy expanded the ranks of the chaplaincy.[26] In contrast to the unbridled exuberance witnessed in World War I, in many quarters, in support of the war, one historian of Protestantism notes the dominant sentiment in World War II was a "cautious patriotism."[27]

Most GIs were draftees, not volunteers. In 1943 the Roosevelt administration prevented men of draft age from volunteering because too many of them opted for elite branches of the armed forces or those deemed safer than the infantry. Conscription compelled men to enlist in the armed forces if drafted, but Congress provided an alternative service for religious pacifists. Although the process of securing conscientious objector status was arduous, over thirty thousand draftees were granted exemption from conscription and, in place of military service, were required to participate in the Civilian Public Service (CPS) program. An unknown number of conscientious objectors, who refused to bear arms but were willing to join the armed forces, were given alternate service, frequently as medics or corpsmen.[28] Allowing men with religious objections, in World War II, to avoid military service can help explain why relatively few GIs had ethical qualms about taking part in the work of killing.

In writing a religious history of the American GI, it is tempting to make it a history of the chaplaincy. Chaplains often left significant paper trails, in the form of official reports not only to their army superiors but also to their religious denominations. We can learn a great deal about the lived religion of GIs through the chaplains' observations of military life, for they were college educated and granted a great deal of professional autonomy by the armed services. Chaplains were subject to the military chain of command, but they were granted freedom of the pulpit. Under military law chaplains could not be compelled to divulge individual communications with GIs, a right not even guaranteed to physicians. This often resulted in chaplains gaining the trust of GIs, who spoke with them more candidly.

Chaplains performed an important role in the shaping of the lived religion of the American GI.[29] At the same time, the lived religion of GIs frequently diverged from the religious orthodoxies chaplains sought to uphold. For instance, soldiers often attended the services of any chaplain present on the battlefield irrespective of their faith. To the consternation of Catholic chaplains and their ecclesiastical superiors, Catholics attended services led by Protestant and Jewish chaplains. Similarly, Protestants and Jews attended Mass and even took communion when it was offered by Catholic chaplains. While the full extent of this will never be known, many GIs embraced amulets and other magical objects designed to keep them out of harm's way. Aircrews often followed a host of rituals and adhered to beliefs that can best be characterized as evoking magical protections. For instance, some aviators wore particular items of clothing for every mission, believing it helped ensure their survival.

The armed forces faced difficulties in forging official policies that provided for the free exercise of religion while bolstering religious pluralism. Considerable tension emerged, especially between Roman Catholic and Protestant leaders, on a range of issues. Protestant chaplains in the army bristled at being under the authority of the Roman Catholic monsignor who served as chief of chaplains throughout much of the war. Roman Catholic chaplains feared their Protestant counterparts would lead their flock astray as they believed YMCA workers had done in World War I.

The army and navy's desire for simplicity and standardization placed every chaplain and GI into only one of three religious categories: Roman Catholic, Protestant, and Jewish. As a result Protestant and Jewish chaplains and GIs had to make compromises. A Protestant chaplain, whether a high-church Episcopalian or a fundamentalist Baptist, was expected to offer a general service in which all Protestants could take part. Despite significant theological differences with both mainline and fundamentalist Protestants, members of the Church of Christ, Scientist and the Church of Jesus Christ of Latter-day Saints were classified as Protestant denominations. Most Jewish GIs were Orthodox, but most chaplains were Reform. Many Jews embraced the common prayer book forged by the Jewish Welfare Board (JWB); however, there were dissenters, especially among some Orthodox Jews unwilling to recognize the authority of Reform rabbis.

Despite significant divisions there were important points of agreement among the three faiths. The Roosevelt administration, together with Protestant, Roman Catholic, and Jewish leaders, supported efforts to promote sexual morality among GIs. Chaplains from all these traditions preached a message that called for sexual abstinence outside of marriage. Despite moral suasion from chaplains, scores of GIs engaged in premarital and extramarital sex. The armed forces overruled the protests of Roman Catholic leaders and fundamentalist ministers and continued to distribute condoms to male soldiers to prevent the spread of venereal diseases. Despite going against official policy some overseas commanders, to the ire of their unit chaplains, established regulated brothels for their men to patronize.

The Journey of a GI

After considering the debates surrounding the American entrance into the war and the recruitment and training of chaplains, this book will follow the religious life of the GI from induction into the armed forces to discharge from service. The structure of religious life varied significantly as the GI transitioned from training to overseas deployment and combat. In training camp most GIs had regular access to chaplains and the opportunity to attend chapel or religious service in local communities. For many GIs training camp was a disorienting experience, not only because they had to acculturate to military life but also because they found themselves in environments that brought them in contact with individuals from different religious, ethnic, educational, and socioeconomic backgrounds. While training camps unmoored many GIs, who were disoriented and homesick, they also emboldened them to try new things since they were freed from the social constraints of family and community.

Most GIs journeyed to war in crowded troopships that provided scant opportunity to attend religious services or find the space for quiet contemplation. The specter of death stalked GIs as they sailed the high seas with the ever-present threat of attack by enemy submarines. Few GIs, prior to the war, had traveled abroad, and deployment overseas created opportunities to encounter people very different from themselves. GIs deployed to North Africa and Asia encountered societies where Christians were a distinct minority. In Italy and France, Protestants found themselves living in predominantly Catholic nations.

Combat tested men physically and mentally, and religion helped to ease their woes. Those who fought in the ground forces, especially in the infantry, lived in a world where the chances of escaping unscathed were slim. Frontline soldiers lived in foxholes they had dug out of the earth, seldom received hot meals, and at times went weeks, even months, without a chance to shower or change their clothing. Often they prayed, and a good many hoped the Bibles they carried in their breast pockets, near their hearts, would shield them from death. Chaplains and many journalists, even many GIs, echoed the slogan, "There are no atheists in foxholes."

However, there were atheists in foxholes, and for some GIs faith proved insufficient to sustain them in the grim conditions they endured. Psychiatric casualties were staggering, and many GIs did not trust the promise made explicit, especially in Christianity, regarding immortality for those true to their faith. Even some chaplains failed to demonstrate sufficient courage in the face of enemy bullets.

Extended combat challenged religious teachings in another way: it hardened the hearts of many GIs and even chaplains toward the enemy. GIs and many chaplains accepted the break in traditional boundaries in waging war and supported the growing escalation of violence. For example, most aviators recognized they might kill civilians and even destroy sacred religious sites during their missions. For many GIs the fact that most Japanese soldiers were not Christian fostered an attitude that led to the further dehumanization of the enemy.

While the war provided a common experience for many soldiers, any understanding of the lived religion of the American GI must also take into account the varied experiences of those in uniform. Most GIs did not fight on the front lines, and a significant number never even left the United States. Many GIs received extensive training, especially as aviators, but the army—desperate for replacements at different stages of the war—sped up the training of infantrymen to fill gaps in the front lines.

The U.S. Army and the U.S. Navy structured religious life differently due to their institutional cultures. Army chaplains had far more autonomy than their counterparts in the navy, who met the needs of sailors and the U.S. Marines. A naval chaplain out to sea had no right to hold services aboard the ship and needed to ask permission of the captain to use a suitable space. Permission was not always granted, as some ship commanders were hostile toward organized religion.

Other differences fell along racial lines. The navy made few concessions to racial diversity; it appointed only two Black chaplains during the entire war. The army compiled a better record; it commissioned several hundred Black chaplains to meet the needs of African American troops. But the army adopted an unwritten policy of trying to prevent nonwhite chaplains from serving the religious needs of white GIs.

For Black GIs religion offered one of the few officially sanctioned opportunities for autonomy and mutual support in the face of pervasive institutional racism. Many Black soldiers sought solace in prayer and found comfort in singing traditional spirituals. In the army the presence of several hundred Black chaplains played a vital role in not only meeting the spiritual needs of Black soldiers but also protecting them from the worst instances of Jim Crow discrimination. African American chaplains were frequently put in untenable positions by the contradiction between official policies that mandated segregation and wartime ideals that declared the fight against fascism to be a struggle against racism. A significant number of Black chaplains ran into trouble with their white superiors when they sought to use their authority as commissioned officers and the freedom of the pulpit to challenge injustices. Due to the paucity of Black chaplains in the navy, Black sailors and marines had to depend on white chaplains or draw on lay leadership for their religious needs.

Differences in wartime experiences also broke along gender lines. Female GIs' service during World War II remained distinctive in several ways. Legally they were barred from combat and were usually assigned military occupations that conformed to prevailing notions of suitable female employment—secretarial work, food preparation, and cleaning. Gender lines were exceptionally rigid regarding the appointment of women as chaplains. All services banned women from the chaplaincy, even though several Protestant denominations ordained women as ministers.

Women, like chaplains, were true volunteers in the war, since they were not subject to the draft, by virtue of their gender. Military women endured significant discrimination and harassment. In the army a widespread whispering campaign among male GIs and the general public deemed women in the Women's Army Corps (WAC) as either prostitutes or lesbians. For the leadership of the armed forces, providing for the religious needs of female GIs silenced critics who claimed that the armed forces morally debased servicewomen. Chaplains' messages to female GIs underscored the need to adhere to the double standard that mandated women avoid premarital and extramarital sex. In contrast to male GIs, women were denied access to free contraception, and pregnancy, inside or outside of marriage, meant an automatic discharge from the service.

Historically, there existed a close connection between medicine and religion, but medical advances beginning in the late nineteenth century fostered a growing divergence between the two. The treatment of the wounded can be portrayed as a clear case where modern medicine limited the domain of religious authority and promoted secularization. Advances in military medicine ensured that most American GIs wounded in battle survived and recovered.[30] In army chaplain school, clerics were advised to defer to the judgment of military physicians in the treatment of psychiatric casualties. But not all accepted the growing influence of modern medicine. Christian Scientists rejected the claims of military medicine, and their practitioners continued to rely on faith healing. Roman Catholic leaders raised questions regarding the psychiatric examinations based on Freudian psychology.

For the wounded and the dying, prayer and access to clergy took on an added importance. Despite the resources devoted to the chaplaincy, GIs frequently lacked access to chaplains of their faith in moments of extreme distress. Catholic leaders and Catholic GIs expressed dismay that a shortage of priests prevented the dying from receiving absolution and last rites. In other cases chaplains assigned to military hospitals took advantage of their captive audiences, confined to hospital beds, to proselytize.

Examining the religious life of American prisoners of war (POWs) underscores one of the successes of the laws of war in bringing a measure of humanity to a dreadful conflict. Both the United States government and the Nazi regime adhered to the Geneva Convention with regard to the treatment of German and American POWs. As a result Americans had freedom of worship and received humanitarian aid from the YMCA movement to support religious life in the camps. American Jewish POWs, with some important exceptions, were accorded the same treatment as their Gentile counterparts. Part of this stemmed from the fact that international law clearly granted Jewish GIs protected status, but there were also protests from Gentile POWs who challenged anti-Semitic measures.

One measure of the ideological commitment of American GIs is found in the experiences of those held as POWs by the Nazi regime. In contrast to the POWs of several other nations, including the Soviet Union, the Nazis never recruited a legion of Americans to fight for them. An American postwar report on Stalag Luft III observed that most interrogations of American POWs were handled by German air force intelligence officers, but among those singled out for interrogation were those who expressed anti-Bolshevik or anti-Semitic sentiments. In the closing months of the war, the Nazis issued an appeal to prisoners in one prison camp calling on Americans to fight against the Bolshevik threat. Strikingly, this appeal was devoid of the usual anti-Semitic tropes. The appeals, no doubt, fell on deaf ears with American resolve strengthened by how inevitable Allied victory seemed in 1945.[31]

Religious Discourse

During the U.S. Civil War, soldiers on both the Union and Confederate sides believed sinful actions, such as the failure to keep the Sabbath, caused defeat on the battlefield.[32] The literary critic Paul Fussell, in his book *Wartime*, is correct in noting there were no mass revivals in the American army during World War II like the ones that took place in the Civil War.[33] American GIs wrote fewer diaries and letters in which they grappled with issues of sin, salvation, and morality than their counterparts in the Civil War. Even in World War I, doughboys had been much more overt in expressing their religiosity.[34] By World War II the nature of religious discourse had changed, and many GIs lacked the vocabulary or desire to express such sentiments. George Eugene Schwend, a Roman Catholic from Verona, New Jersey, kept a diary that is fairly typical of many of the personal writings of American GIs. Reading his diary one learns that Schwend was an avid moviegoer—he even took in a French film when on leave in Paris in 1944—and he often commented on films in his writings. But we also learn from Schwend's entries that he regularly attended Mass over the course of the war, especially on such key holidays as Easter. However, Schwend's diary offers little reflection on religious ideas, and we can only speculate on the degree to which this faith offered him reassurance and comfort. If there were spiritual or moral conflicts, he did not dwell on them.[35]

The lack of overt expressions of religiosity by Schwend can be traced partly to the growing pluralism of the armed forces. The Protestants who had dominated the army of the nineteenth century gave way to the tri-faith armed force of Protestants, Roman Catholics, and Jews. The ethos of Roman Catholics and Jews did not emphasize the same degree of self-reflection as many Protestant traditions. Mainline or liberal Protestant denominations during World War II did not stress the importance of introspection that would lead to a conversion experience. There are important exceptions to this pattern. There were fundamentalists in the ranks, and they wrote letters filled with discussion of faith, sin, and salvation.

In seeking to grapple with lived religion and spirituality, this study recognizes that claims of faith cannot be fully interrogated by scholars. The war dead cannot speak, and we cannot ask them about their passage from life to what many believed to be immortality. But we can understand the rituals and beliefs of the living regarding the fallen. Mourning the dead was one of the most important duties of chaplains and a crucial part of the lived religion of the GI. The lack of enough grave-registration personnel meant combat units, on occasion, had to bury their dead. Chaplains had to comfort the comrades of the fallen and offer messages of condolence to the families of the deceased. Most strived to give meaning to deaths from illness, accidents, or enemy action, asserting these soldiers had died for a just and worthy cause.

Death proved no barrier to duty, as the armed forces continued to enlist the war dead in service of their country. With the consent of their families, many of the war dead received permanent burial in overseas national cemeteries established and maintained by the American Battle Monument Commission (AMBC). In creating grave markers for the fallen, the AMBC did not use the nonsectarian grave markers used by the army for the fallen whose religious identities could not be determined. By default, the war dead buried in overseas cemeteries received either a cross or star of David. Although this decision negated the rights of atheists and Buddhists in the ranks, it nonetheless gave testimony in stone to the tri-faith religion. In an age when returning Jewish veterans still faced discrimination in employment and housing, overseas cemeteries symbolized their incorporation into the body politic.

Before beginning the story, it is necessary to offer a definition of religion and to consider the permeable boundaries that make it difficult to precisely delineate. During World War II most GIs deemed religion to be a set of beliefs and rituals that centered on a faith in a monotheistic God. Both the army and navy stressed the preeminent role of the clergy, endorsed by their respective denominations, as principal sources of authority on religious dogma and rituals. Not all pious GIs embraced monotheism, especially significant numbers of Native Americans, Chinese Americans, and Japanese Americans, but the military largely ignored these distinctive faith traditions. In seeking to understand the lived religion of GIs, the lines between religion and magic proved quite permeable. Many GIs, especially in army air crews, embraced objects and rituals that they hoped would bring them luck and forestall any harm from befalling them. As this work will underscore, religious beliefs—even under the wings of the tri-faith tradition—remained remarkably heterodox.[36]

ONE

Mobilizing a Faithful Nation for War

It is tempting to begin the story of the religious life of the American GI on December 7, 1941. On this day the naval forces of the Empire of Japan attacked the Pacific Fleet at Pearl Harbor and the surrounding army airfields, effectively ending the long debate among Americans over whether the United States should enter World War II. Although dissent did not completely disappear, most former opponents of intervention supported the call to arms against the Empire of Japan. With only one dissenting vote, in the House of Representatives, the next day Congress declared war on Japan. Three days later the German declaration of war against the United States meant the country would fight in Europe as well as Asia.

Early in the attack on Pearl Harbor, an American naval chaplain aboard one of the warships in the harbor exhorted the sailors, on that Sunday morning, to "Praise the Lord and Pass the Ammunition." The fact that a chaplain is credited with coining one of the first bellicose American slogans of the war is ironic given that a significant number of Protestant and Roman Catholic leaders prior to Pearl Harbor had opposed America's intervention in another world war. During the interwar years, the peace movement had enjoyed considerable support in Protestant circles, with several denominations even debating whether they should withdraw their support of the army and navy chaplaincy. Many mainline Protestant denominations pondered how, in the event of another war, they would support the faithful who embraced pacifism and sought conscientious objector status. Although the Roman Catholic Church's adherence to the "just war" tradition held sway among the hierarchy, weakening support for pacifism among the laity, most bishops remained opposed to entering the war against Nazi Germany. Even among American Jews, pacifist and anti-interventionist sentiments were not completely absent.[1] Although most religious leaders who opposed American entry into the war came to support it after December 7, 1941, their embrace remained cautious. Many Protestants expressed a reluctance to fall prey to the jingoism and uncritical support churches and synagogues had offered to Pres. Woodrow Wilson's crusade, in 1917, to make the world "safe for democracy."[2]

After the fall of France, in June 1940, Pres. Franklin D. Roosevelt faced the daunting task of trying to persuade a reluctant American public to enter another foreign war in less than a generation. Even Americans who were fearful of Germany and Japan wanted to avoid full-scale intervention. In making the case for providing aid to Great Britain and, later, the Soviet Union, FDR offered a broad indictment of the dangers the German and Japanese regimes posed to American national security. FDR's rhetoric targeted the antireligious nature of Nazi Germany and the threat it posed to the values of Western civilization. As this chapter will demonstrate, FDR sought to counter the argument, made by religious leaders, that America should avoid this fight by declaring that the peril remained too great. Equally important, Roosevelt's critique of the Nazi regime should also be understood as reflecting his deep-seated beliefs regarding religion and its place in promoting a good and just society. Roosevelt's portrayal of the enemy would be highly influential, shaping the way many soldiers viewed the threat posed by Nazi ideology with regard to religion.

One of the continuing debates is whether Roosevelt saw America's entry into the war as inevitable. Without FDR's leadership it is unlikely Congress would have supported rearmament or initiated America's first peacetime draft. As commander in chief, FDR took a range of unilateral actions that included waging undeclared naval war against Germany, in the fall of 1941, and cutting off American oil exports to Japan in response to its occupation of French Indochina. During a summit meeting with Prime Minister Churchill in August 1941, FDR signed the Atlantic Charter and made it clear the United States wished for the destruction of Nazi tyranny.[3]

Power politics certainly entered FDR's calculus when he opposed the Axis powers in 1941. FDR's use of rhetoric, grounded in religious ideals and values, made the case for opposing the Axis powers—partly as an effort to draw on a common vocabulary of religious themes, symbols, and images shared by a majority of Americans. A pragmatic leader, Roosevelt has confounded contemporaries and historians. He left us no revelatory diary and often remained guarded about his emotions and decision-making process. Despite these caveats his religious values and ideals, especially his embrace of the social gospel and strong belief in religious pluralism, remained a constant in FDR's life and profoundly shaped the New Deal. The policies adopted by the armed forces to meet the religious needs of American GIs in World War II bear the imprint of the commander in chief. As chief executive, FDR increased the power of the federal government to meet the challenges of the Great Depression and the threat posed by the Axis powers.

The Assured Religion of FDR

A lifelong Episcopalian, Roosevelt did not envision a secularized public life devoid of religious values. Religion mattered to Roosevelt; his most inspiring influence at the Groton School had been an Episcopalian priest and headmaster, Endicott Peabody. FDR continued to be an active member of the vestry of his parish church in Hyde Park throughout his presidency, and he frequently confided to friends how his faith inspired and sustained him.[4] Specially organized church services marked his inauguration and other significant events of his presidency. FDR granted regular access to a number of religious leaders, favoring mainline Protestant leaders associated with the Federal Council of Churches, members of the Roman Catholic hierarchy supportive of the New Deal, and Jewish leaders from the Reform movement. Evangelical Protestants and Orthodox Jewish leaders were seldom afforded a presidential audience. In terms of public policy, there existed significant concessions to the autonomy of religious organizations. For instance, the Social Security Act of 1935, which established a national retirement system for wage earners, made participation of clergy completely voluntary.[5]

During his presidency Roosevelt exhibited considerable sensitivity to issues surrounding the relationship between church and state. Religious leaders continued to exercise considerable influence on public life, and cultural norms regarding the Christian Sabbath were widely observed. On September 19, 1934, press secretary Stephen Early wrote a confidential memo to Marguerite "Missy" LeHand, FDR's secretary and confidant, expressing concern about a series of stories that depicted the president as engaged in a range of activities on Sunday that did not include attending church services. Several Sundays previously, newspapers had run stories of the president attending a game, at his Hyde Park home, between two rival teams of journalists and actively participating as a coach for one of the teams. More recently, news reports had reported him fishing off a speedboat in the vicinity of Newport, Rhode Island, on a Sunday. Early observed to LeHand that "there are many, perhaps too many, people through the country who still take Sunday observance seriously," and these stories about the president's activities on this day of rest had serious political implications.[6]

There were religious leaders—some prominent, like Norman Vincent Peale—who blamed FDR's lack of overt piety for his policy shortcomings regarding the New Deal. There were other sources of tension. Many Protestants, especially fundamentalists, believed that FDR's repeal of prohibition had been a grievous mistake and made him morally suspect. Although a minority, a group of fundamentalists crafted an eschatology that saw the New Deal's centralization of federal power as a sign of the end times. Surveying the world scene, they viewed the reconstitution of the Roman Empire under Benito Mussolini, the persecution of the Jews by the Nazis and the Jewish people's resettlement in Palestine, and the emergence of Communist Russia as further pointing to the coming rapture and impending conflict between the forces of good and evil at Armageddon.[7]

Fundamentalists were not alone in challenging FDR. Perhaps the most significant religious critic was the Roman Catholic priest Fr. Charles Coughlin. Rector of the Church of the Little Flower in suburban Detroit, Coughlin regularly spoke to a radio audience that numbered in the millions. Though an early supporter of the New Deal, Coughlin later turned into FDR's fiercest critic. Supported by his local bishop, to the dismay of many Roman Catholic leaders, Coughlin preached an anti-Semitic message that painted FDR as beholden to international Jewry over the interests of the American people.[8]

Throughout his presidency Roosevelt frequently spoke out on behalf of religious and ethnic tolerance. Perhaps Roosevelt's most noteworthy intervention along these lines was the endorsement he offered to the National Conference of Christians and Jews in support of Brotherhood Day. In 1934 he publicly supported the organization's work and Brotherhood Day, declaring that the "occasion presents an opportunity for concerted thinking on a vital problem of national welfare; it should help us all in our efforts to rise above ancient and harmful suspicions and prejudices and to work together as citizens of American democracy."[9] In a 1936 national radio address marking Brotherhood Day, FDR emphasized that tolerance did not mean erasing religious differences among Americans: "There are honest differences of religious belief among the citizens of your town as there are among citizens of mine. It is a part of the spirit of Brotherhood Day, as it is a part of our American heritage, to respect those differences. And it is well for us to remember that this America of ours is the product of no single race or creed or class."[10]

One of the fiercest debates regarding Roosevelt is the question of whether he held anti-Semitic views that impacted his policies, especially with regard to his response to the Holocaust. While it is beyond the scope of this study to fully document the Holocaust, this work will argue that the preponderance of evidence suggests that, on balance, FDR embraced religious tolerance and rejected bigotry. On a personal level, Roosevelt developed a network of Jewish friends and advisors that included the first Jewish justice of the Supreme Court, Louis Brandeis; Harvard Law Professor Felix Frankfurter; and his Dutchess County neighbor, Henry Morgenthau, who served as treasury secretary from 1934 to 1945.[11] He had a particularly close working relationship with New York judge and speechwriter Samuel Rosenman, who coauthored some of Roosevelt's most important speeches in the late 1930s and 1940s. Often Rosenman joined FDR and other advisors in spending long hours drafting some of FDR's most important speeches on the question of war and peace. On one occasion FDR invited Rosenman and his wife to come to Washington for the weekend to sail with him on the presidential yacht. FDR trusted Rosenman with editing his public papers and shared with him the royalties from their publication.[12]

Roosevelt's statements on religious tolerance can, by today's standards, appear innocuous and even be dismissed as tepid and not forceful enough in denouncing anti-Semitism. However, Roosevelt and the leadership of the chaplaincy celebrated religious pluralism and hailed cooperation among Protestants, Roman Catholics, and Jews. At the same time, Roosevelt's embrace of religious pluralism, especially with regards to challenging anti-Semitism, should not be minimized. Scores of anti-Semites wrote to FDR during his presidency protesting what they viewed as pro-Jewish policies. Many of these letters were faithfully filed alongside presidential greetings for Rosh Hashanah, the endorsement of Jewish philanthropic work, and the condemnation of German policies toward the German Jews and, later, European Jewry.[13]

The Road to War

Roosevelt took office only a few weeks after Adolf Hitler assumed power in Germany, in January 1933. Initially, FDR deliberately turned inward and focused on reviving the American economy, taking only limited diplomatic initiatives. Overall, most Americans remained cool to measures that would engage the United States internationally, rejecting Roosevelt's effort to have the country join the World Court. Roosevelt, in his second term, would more forcefully engage the United States in world affairs. In 1937 FDR delivered a major public address, in Chicago, in which he argued that unnamed countries engaging in aggressive wars of conquest should be quarantined to stop the threat they posed to the world order. Likening the problem of aggression to a communicable disease, FDR's vagueness in the quarantine speech alarmed critics who feared possible involvement in an overseas conflict.[14] The following year the proposed Ludlow Amendment to the U.S. Constitution called for a public referendum before the United States declared war. It nearly won a majority of votes in the U.S. House of Representatives. Widespread anti-Semitism certainly constrained FDR's foreign policy initiatives in his first two terms in office with regard to the refugee crisis. Responding to public pressure, the U.S. Congress rejected efforts to liberalize immigration to take in German Jews and others fleeing Germany after Hitler came to power in January 1933.[15]

Prior to the Japanese attack on Pearl Harbor, on December 7, 1941, the fierce debate over whether the United States should join the fight crossed political lines. Many on the left and right joined forces, in the America First Committee in 1940, to oppose American intervention in the struggle against Nazi Germany. While many Republicans joined Ohio senator Robert Taft's opposition to Roosevelt's strategy of providing Britain all-out aid, short of war, the internationalist wing within the GOP embraced Roosevelt's internationalism. Two prominent Republicans joined his administration in 1940. Henry Stimson, secretary of state under Herbert Hoover, took charge of the War Department, and newspaper publisher Frank Knox, who had run for vice president on the Republican party ticket in 1936, took over the helm at the Navy Department.

Anti-interventionist sentiment remained the strongest in the historic peace churches, Society of Friends (Quakers), Brethren, and Mennonites, who had maintained their pacifist stance even after the declaration of war against Germany in World War I. But considerable opposition also existed among many mainline Protestant denominations that had, in World War I, offered fervid rhetoric in support of war. Until Pearl Harbor, Americans were deeply divided over the question of war and peace, with many determined to avoid the mistake of entering another world war. The most prominent organization for mainline Protestants, the Federal Council of Churches, opposed intervention and remained wary of providing aid for Great Britain.[16] The *Christian Century* served as the most important forum for mainline Protestants in this era, and it maintained that war undermined Christian and democratic values. This periodical endorsed Wendell Willkie for president and even suggested that Roosevelt enacted conscription not out of legitimate national security needs but as a way to inculcate the values of Americanism in youth.[17] The *Christian Century* also defended Charles Lindbergh, the most prominent leader of the noninterventionist movement. An August 21, 1940, editorial denounced a savage attack against Lindbergh that tarnished the aviator "as a coward, a fool, a leader of a fascist fifth column and a parrot for Goebbels."[18]

A significant fissure over the question of American belligerency developed within the mainline Protestant establishment. Reinhold Niebuhr, the most important theologian to embrace intervention, sought to rally support for interventionism by establishing a new journal, *Christianity and Crisis*. Niebuhr's embrace of what came to be termed Christian realism accepted the necessity of using force to counter the evil represented by the Nazi regime. Niebuhr earned the bitter enmity of many fellow theologians and church leaders for turning his back on his belief in pacifism. But he was not alone; there were other Protestant leaders who supported him, most notably John Mott and Henry Sloane Coffin.[19]

Among the Roman Catholic hierarchy, theologians continued to embrace just war theology and had fewer qualms about state-sponsored violence as long as it met certain conditions. At the same time, Roman Catholic leaders and their flocks were divided over America's entry into a war. With a hierarchy and pews filled with Irish Americans, they viewed Great Britain with suspicion, even after the fall of France, and as the island nation clung to survival in late 1940 and early 1941, Joseph P. Kennedy, one of the most prominent Irish Americans and ambassador to the Court of St. James, doubted Britain's chances of survival and thought the United States should recognize the inevitability of German victory.[20]

Other topics confronted religious organizations in even more stark terms. Deeper and more significant theological issues centered on the atheism inherent in the regime of Joseph Stalin and the international Communist movement. In opposing intervention many prelates were following the lead of the Vatican. Pius XI had raised concerns about the Nazi regime in *Mitt Brennender Sorge* (1937), but this document was restrained compared to *Divini Redemptoris*, an encyclical issued a few days later, which explicitly condemned Communist ideology. His successor, Pius XII, denounced the Moscow regime even more strongly. With important exceptions American Roman Catholics supported Francisco Franco's overthrow of the Republican government in Spain. Pius

XII was much more cautious than his predecessor in his relations with Nazi Germany and Fascist Italy. Amid total war Pius XII sought to promote peace and reconciliation and was hesitant to protest against Nazi atrocities. For Pius XII the survival of the Roman Catholic Church and safeguarding the Eternal City of Rome remained the paramount diplomatic objectives.[21]

Roosevelt, in calling Americans to meet the threat posed by aggressor nations, did not cede the moral ground to religious opponents of American intervention. While cautious about getting too far ahead of public opinion, FDR promoted a worldview that saw religion, democracy, and a stable world order as intertwined. When surveying the international scene in his State of the Union address of January 1939, FDR made oblique references to the recent international crisis in Europe over the Sudetenland, which had almost led to war. Roosevelt and his fellow Americans had no hand in the Munich Pact of 1938, where Great Britain, Italy, and France agreed to allow Germany to annex the Sudetenland of Czechoslovakia, an agreement that the British prime minister believed would secure a peaceful Europe. Roosevelt insisted that "religion, democracy, and international good faith complement and support each other." Without naming specific nations, FDR said that where "religion and democracy have vanished, good faith and reason in international affairs have given way to strident ambition and brute force." Roosevelt proclaimed, "The defense of religion, of democracy and of good faith among nations is all the same fight. To save one we must now make up our minds to save all."[22]

After the outbreak of war in Europe in September 1939, FDR's rhetoric turned more forceful as he made a series of speeches arguing that in order to defend democratic values and religion it was essential to oppose Nazi Germany. Following the fall of France, FDR increasingly articulated why the United States must oppose German actions and advocated a strategy of military preparedness and aiding regimes halting Nazi aggression. In making the case for war in 1940 and 1941, Roosevelt stressed the imminent threat posed by Nazi Germany through the growing expansion of German influence in Latin America and the role played by fifth-column activity (internal subversion) by Nazi sympathizers in the United States. For Roosevelt, Germany had to be stopped from waging aggressive war against America's neighbors and from destroying all that was decent in Western civilization.[23] Roosevelt advocated U.S. intervention by defining the values America would—and should—defend in opposing Hitler's regime. In his 1941 State of the Union address, FDR argued that the United States must promote four essential freedoms—freedom of speech, freedom of religion, freedom from want, and freedom from fear.[24]

Even before Pearl Harbor, FDR made it clear that compromise was impossible with Nazi Germany. In August 1941 Roosevelt secretly boarded the USS *Augusta* and set off for the North Atlantic to meet with Winston Churchill. Not only did FDR leave behind the White House press corps, but even key members of his administration were unaware of his planned summit with the beleaguered British leader. FDR rendezvoused, off the coast of Newfoundland, with the HMS *Prince of Wales*, and he, Churchill, and their principal military advisors met for several days. The two leaders concluded their first of many wartime summits by issuing a broad statement of war aims that would soon be termed the Atlantic Charter. In this statement both leaders looked to the final defeat of the scourge of Nazi tyranny and declared for a new world order that promoted freedom from fear and want.

Churchill sought to court FDR and bolster support for the British war effort. One tool at his disposal was the Sunday church service he mandated aboard the *Prince of Wales*. Churchill went to great lengths to plan a service that highlighted the common religious and cultural bonds between Great Britain and the United States. He picked several hymns that underscored the need for the United States to come to the aid of their British brethren. The first hymn, "For Those in Peril on the Sea," certainly was apt given the close ties these two men had with their respective nations' navies. Churchill had served twice as the First Sea Lord, and FDR had been assistant secretary of the navy in the First World War. FDR was especially moved by the singing of "Onward, Christian Soldiers." After the service he commented to his son that even if nothing else happened at the summit, this service had forged bonds between the two nations. "We *are*, and we *will* go on, with God's help," Roosevelt declared.[25]

Returning home, Roosevelt reflected on the "very remarkable

2. Morning services aboard the HMS *Prince of Wales* at the Atlantic Conference, Placentia Bay, August 1941. Franklin D. Roosevelt Library 48–22:3713 (60).

religious services on the quarterdeck of the *Prince of Wales*," led by a U.S. Navy and a Royal Navy chaplain with several hundred American and British sailors worshiping before an altar decorated with British and American flags. FDR recalled that all of the attendees recognized they had participated in one of the great historic events of their lifetimes.[26]

It is unsurprising that Churchill and Roosevelt sought comfort from the divine in August 1941, given the perilous circumstances they faced. Great Britain and the British Empire had been at war with Germany for nearly two years and, after the fall of France, had fought alone until Hitler decided to launch an invasion of the Soviet Union in June 1941. Military advisors and pundits on both sides of the Atlantic expressed deep skepticism that this officially atheistic regime would withstand the Nazi blitzkrieg. Meanwhile, in the United States, Roosevelt faced a divided nation that still sought to avoid entering a land war in Europe. Roosevelt had prodded Congress and the American public to expand the armed forces and adopt peacetime conscription, but the military buildup was incomplete. Although the United States had started providing significant aid to Britain through Lend-Lease, Roosevelt faced significant opposition to his policies with regard to providing all-out aid short of war.

In the fall of 1941 U.S. rhetoric against Nazi Germany became even more strident. Borrowing British manufactured propaganda, FDR warned Americans via radio address that he had received a copy of a secret plan issued by the Nazis that called for the destruction of all religion:

> Your Government has in its possession another document, made in Germany by Hitler's Government. It is a detailed plan, which, for obvious reasons, the Nazis did not wish and do not wish to publicize just yet, but which they are ready to impose, a little later, on a dominated world—if Hitler wins. It is a plan to abolish all existing religions—Catholic, Protestant, Mohammedan, Hindu, Buddhist, and Jewish alike. The property of all churches will be seized by the Reich and its puppets. The cross and all other symbols of religion are to be forbidden. The clergy are to be forever liquidated, silenced under penalty of the concentration camps, where even now so many fearless men are being tortured because they have placed God above Hitler.[27]

On November 3, 1941 New York Mayor Fiorello LaGuardia, in his capacity as U.S. director of civil defense, sent a circular to American churches and synagogues urging them to take part in Civilian Defense Week from November 11–16, 1941. Specifically, he called on them to commemorate Sunday, November 16 as "Freedom Day." This letter outlined a sermon that LaGuardia hoped would be delivered in every church and synagogue, which emphasized the "powerful part religion played in the formation of this Nation, its cleansing influence throughout our history, and its importance in the present crisis." It would, ideally, focus on three interconnected themes, beginning with an examination of how "religion is the source of democracy" and continuing on to how "democracy gives religion its most satisfactory opportunity." The sermon highlighted the importance of religious leaders. "In countries where "tyrants have enslaved the people, the boldest voices opposing them have been those of bishops and pastors and rabbis." It singled out the German Lutheran pastor Martin Niemöller and the Swiss-born Karl Barth for their "unfettered faith" and said: "In the midst of persecution the rabbis of Israel have tended their people as shepherds their flocks." The ideal sermon should conclude with an examination of how "democracy and religion can together build the good society."[28]

Despite an official push from prominent politicians, this call for religious leaders to preach military preparedness sermons met with dissent. The Rev. Dr. Charles Clayton Morrison, editor of the *Christian Century*, lambasted the call for sermons on democracy. In a front-page story, the *New York Times* covered the controversy, publishing Morrison's full statement denouncing this act as an instance of totalitarianism taking hold in the United States: "Who would have imagined that an agency of the American Government would go so far as to tell Preachers what to preach and actually to provide the outline of a model sermon for them to follow?" He stressed that Protestant, Catholic, and Jewish clergy would defy this call and would be roused to the realization that totalitarianism had actually happened here.[29]

Of course, Roosevelt did have allies among religious leaders. On the eve of the 1940 election, FDR joined his secretary of war, Henry L. Stimson, as numbers were pulled from glass containers, conscripting young men into the army. Addressing a national radio audience, FDR not only spoke of the vital need for this step but also read letters of support from religious leaders for this unprecedented action. He read excerpts from correspondence from the presidents of the Federal Council of Churches and the Synagogue Council of America and Cardinal Francis J. Spellman, who served as military bishop for Roman Catholic chaplains in addition to heading the diocese of New York. All three leaders expressed their hope for peace even while endorsing conscription. Dr. George Buttrick, who headed the Federal Council, applauded the protection accorded conscientious objectors and promised to establish ministries for those of the Christian faith serving in the army and navy. Dr. Edward L. Israel of the Synagogue Council lauded selective service as an "extraordinary measure" to preserve democracy that would inculcate these values among the young people called into service. Cardinal Spellman offered the most bellicose remarks, declaring "Americans want peace and we shall prepare for peace, but not for a peace whose definition is slavery or death."[30]

Framing the war with Germany as a struggle with significant religious overtones reflected a conscious effort by FDR and his administration to court the large portion of the American public that still embraced religious values and institutions. However, this rhetoric did not go unchallenged by noninterventionists and pacifists.[31] Even among those who viewed Germany as a threat, some expressed even greater fears about the Soviet Union. Indeed, American Catholics—leaders in both the hierarchy and the laity— questioned American dealings with the Soviet Union.[32]

Despite the fact that many Christians and even a smattering of Jews supported the America First Committee and other noninterventionist organizations, they failed to prevent a series of provocative actions by the Roosevelt administration that inched the United States closer to intervention in 1940 and 1941. The administration persuaded Congress to modify neutrality legislation to allow trade with Germany's adversaries and provide direct and open aid to Britain by 1941. Not only did the administration mobilize the National Guard, drastically increasing spending on rearmament, but it managed to convince the American public to accept the first peacetime draft.[33]

Enacted on September 16, 1940, the peacetime draft was without precedent. Only twice before, in wartime, had the federal government directly conscripted individuals to fight. Despite significant opposition from peace groups and noninterventionists, it was passed. The call-ups were limited to men over twenty years of age. Despite the controversies surrounding conscription, most men reported for induction and served, although many were unenthusiastic soldiers and morale remained low until the attack at Pearl Harbor.

In the Selective Service and Training Act of 1940, Congress set important policies with regard to the religious life of the American GI in World War II. Specifically, Congress affirmed that conscientious objectors would be granted greater protection from being forced to violate their consciences and carry arms. It also exempted clerics from conscription, and this required the country to rely on volunteers to fill the ranks of the chaplaincy.

Conscientious Objectors and the "Good War"

The peacetime draft bore the strong imprint of the peace movement, especially the historic peace churches. Major Protestant denominations took an important role in ensuring that conscientious objectors did not endure the harassment and imprisonment often visited on them in the First World War. Draft boards in 1917 frequently refused to accept the claims of objectors as legitimate and inducted them into the military. In army camps many conscientious objectors refused to participate in training, and many commanders were unsympathetic and took punitive action against them.[34]

The military, during World War II, did require a religious test for those who claimed conscientious objector status. One of the great contributions of peace churches, but also several mainline denominations and Protestant leaders, was to prod the Roosevelt administration and Congress to include a more humane system for conscientious objectors in the 1940 peacetime draft. In contrast to the 1917 draft, conscientious objection, under the 1940 peacetime conscription act, was extended to individuals of all religious faiths and denominations and not simply members of the historic peace churches. Moreover, conscientious objectors and the organizations that supported them had an ally in Gen. Lewis Hershey, who assumed control of the selective service system prior to Pearl Harbor. Hershey, who personally had little affinity for organized religion, had a Mennonite heritage that made him sensitive to those with religious scruples about state-sanctioned violence. Although he had no tolerance for absolutist pacifists—who refused to abide by selective service policies—and rejected dissenters who objected to war on secular grounds, throughout the war Hershey remained committed to protecting the status of conscientious objectors motivated by religious principles.[35]

Those claiming this status had to complete a lengthy form detailing their religious background and demonstrate a long-term commitment to principles of conscientious objection. The initial decision to grant an exemption rested with a local draft board, which could—and sometimes did—reject the claim. Congress also established an appeal process that technically reached as high as the president of the United States. The decisions of draft boards were, on many occasions, reversed upon review.

Conscientious objectors had an opportunity to avoid military service completely. Working with the historic peace churches, they could perform alternate services in the Civilian Public Service (CPS). The CPS camps were an interesting amalgamation of the religious and the military. With a few exceptions, all were funded and staffed by one of the historic peace churches. Chapel, especially in Mennonite and Brethren camps, remained a regular part of CPS camp.[36] Most conscientious objectors who remained on the home front were assigned to CPS camps, where they worked on a range of conservation and other projects. In addition 2,000 staffed mental hospitals, 240 enlisted in forest-fire battalions, and 500 heroically subjected themselves to medical experiments.[37]

Not all who sought conscientious objector status wanted to avoid military service. The number of conscientious objectors who served in support functions that did not directly lead them to take part in violence numbered between 25,000–50,000. Scores served as medical personnel, many as frontline medics with the army or corpsmen with the navy and marines.[38] It would be difficult to overstate the heroism of frontline medics and corpsmen. Unarmed, they were highly visible as they dashed through the combat zone coming to the aid of those wounded in battle. In North Africa and later Europe, medics openly displayed their Red Cross emblems on their helmets, and German troops generally recognized their noncombatant status. In contrast, Japanese forces in the Pacific offered no such deference, and many medics gave up their Red Cross helmets and armbands.[39]

Whether or not to seek conscientious objector status was a difficult choice for many young men. The chapel director at Dartmouth, writing to a recent graduate who had just begun his ministry, dwelled at length on the moral dilemma faced by "Bud," who had decided not to continue his seminary education in order to engage in a community life project to aid Vermont farmers. After receiving his draft notice, "Bud" started "vagabonding for a week or so, trying to clear up his fogs and mists" to ponder his conscience and his decision. While it was certain Bud would not carry guns, it was unclear whether he might elect to do noncombatant work in the medical corps or "some kind of Quaker-workcamp project." But since Bud was "not quite an out-and-outer" it made it a "mighty tough problem."[40]

Conscientious objection required a religious test and involved established principles that clashed with the beliefs of some conscientious objectors. The Rev. Howard Schomer objected to the blanket exemption accorded to all clergy. To begin with Schomer protested the fact that he would have to register for conscription in order to receive the exemption accorded clergy and would not be required to perform alternative service. Moreover, the very act of registering provided "tacit assent and compliance to the militarization of this country."

By Schomer's interpretation the blanket exemption violated the constitution of the Congregational Church and, "since the supreme law of the land guarantees freedom of religion and equality of treatment, a violation also of the Constitution of the United States." Schomer insisted that his church made no distinction between a minister and a layman, except "in function." By granting ministers a blanket exemption, the government unfairly separated him from "his people on precisely the most important issue of the present day."[41]

Schomer was arrested but eventually released and, ultimately, he was able to gain classification as a conscientious objector and perform service in a CPS camp. Others would not be able to meet the religious test for the exemption. Thousands of Jehovah's Witnesses ran afoul of the selective service system, not because they were pacifists but because they asserted they should be exempted from service based on their expansive view of who held the status of minister in their church. Many draft-eligible males registered with the selective service system and filed paperwork claiming ministerial exemptions only to have them rejected by draft boards and appeal boards. Hundreds would ultimately be imprisoned for failing to comply with the selective service system. But the question of who was a minister, entitled to an exemption, could be quite problematic, especially for clergy who were Jehovah's Witnesses.[42] The claim of Elijah Muhammad and his followers in the Nation of Islam that they were entitled to exemptions from the draft because they could not bear arms unless ordered by Allah was also rejected by selective service. Prosecuted and convicted of draft evasion, Muhammad and his followers would be sentenced to serve time in federal prison.[43]

Even after the United States entered the war, there existed significant tolerance for the right of the conscientious objector to abstain from killing or serving in the armed forces. But there were limits to religious dissent—in the charged atmosphere of 1940 and 1941—on the part of both the federal government and many segments of the public. In 1940 the U.S. Supreme Court rejected the refusal of Jehovah's Witnesses to salute the American flag and recite the Pledge of Allegiance, on religious principles, in *Minersville School District v. Gobitis*. Not only did the court rule against the Witnesses, but mobs in several communities attacked individual members, and scores of the church's Kingdom Halls were destroyed.[44]

Even with these limits on dissent, there were many stark contrasts between Nazi Germany and the United States in World War II, but among the most significant in terms of religion was the treatment each society accorded to conscientious objectors. Those who refused military service in Germany and the Soviet Union were routinely imprisoned and often executed.[45]

Pacifist sentiments remained strong among many clergy, especially prior to World War II.[46] Writing to his friend who had recently been ordained an Episcopal priest, E. Clarendon Hyde expressed his misgivings regarding the righteousness of war and criticized nonpacifists for not understanding "that their lack of pacifism is lack of Christianity." Hyde did not claim he was an "absolute pacifist" and, as a result, could not claim to be an "absolute Christian."[47]

Opinion shifted over time, and some individuals who embraced pacifism changed their views as events unfolded in the late 1930s and 1940s. In a radio forum on questions of war and peace, organized in November 1939 by a University of Michigan counselor on religious education, graduate student Cal Kresin railed against what he believed was a drift toward war. While not praising Germany, he argued that Americans should not demonize either side in the war and must avoid falling into the First World War psychology. Ken Leisenring, another graduate student, insisted that he did not espouse pacifism but stressed that several of his fellow students were "outright Pacifists," most objecting to war on religious grounds. He spoke of the need to protect these men, who declared that their "allegiance to God and their conscience is above their allegiance to the powers of human government." Another student on the panel, Jim Vicary, observed that—when polled—two-thirds of the Michigan campus favored an Allied victory, but only 18 percent would want the United States to declare war "if Germany appears to [be] defeating England and France."[48]

The Rev. Carl Knudsen had served as an army chaplain in World War I, but by the 1920s he had become a pacifist. In 1924 Knudsen resigned his reserve commission in protest of the Defense Day Program, authorized by President Calvin Coolidge. Knudsen's attitudes would change as a result of the rise of Adolf Hitler and the persecution of German Jewry by the Nazi regime. In response to Kristallnacht, in November 1938 Knudsen, as pastor of the Congregational Church in Plymouth, Massachusetts, played a pivotal role in seeing that the town's Protestant Council of Churches condemned anti-Semitism and showed their support for their Jewish brethren. For the first time in 317 years, a rabbi delivered the annual Thanksgiving Day address at the church as "our answer to Anti-Semitism." Speaking at the church, which traced its lineage to the Pilgrims, garnered both Rabbi Samuel A. Friedman and Knudson national attention.[49]

In 1940 Knudson sought to return to the army chaplaincy and received the necessary endorsement from the appropriate ecclesiastical authorities. The Office of Chief of Chaplains remained opposed to his return to the ranks, however, citing as a factor that he was forty-two years of age at the time of his application. Besides this, his resignation and his previous statement on pacifism made it unlikely that he would regain his commission as a reserve chaplain.[50] Although the army chaplaincy would be closed to Knudson, he would find a place with the navy chaplaincy, going on to serve in the Solomon Islands campaign and a stint ministering to the navy contingent at Harvard.

In many ways Knudsen's path mirrored those of other religious leaders after Pearl Harbor. But misgivings over the cost of war endured, and one military chaplain recounted to a colleague a dispute he had with a civilian pastor over using ministerial influence to convince men of military age to volunteer for service. In recalling this conflict, the chaplain insisted that a minister should only use his influence if he was willing to go to war himself as a chaplain. Learning about the terrible cost of war in lives lost only served to confirm this view.[51]

One historian has characterized the attitude of Protestant churches as having embraced a cautious patriotism during the Second World War.[52] Compared with the hyperpatriotism embraced by the Roman Catholic and Protestant churches in the First World War, there existed a much greater skepticism about reconciling war and the tenets of faith. At the same time, the support rendered by churches and synagogues was substantial and played a significant role in achieving victory, through their ability to mobilize over ten thousand clerics to voluntarily serve as chaplains.

Did Roosevelt's argument regarding the religious nature of World War II convince anyone? Even after the United States entered the war, Army chief of staff George Marshall worried about the lackluster ideological commitment American GIs brought to the fight and their lack of hatred of the enemy. The anti-interventionist sentiment, so prominent in the interwar years, lingered even after Pearl Harbor. To foster greater ideological commitment to the cause, the army commissioned the filmmaker Frank Capra to make the *Why We Fight* documentaries to explain the war to new GIs. Religion is a central theme of the first of these documentaries, and *Prelude to War* starts off with themes that echo the Rooseveltian emphasis on religious pluralism. The film begins by emphasizing the central role that religion played in the formation of civilization and opens with quotes from several of the world's major religious figures: Moses, Confucius, Mohammed, and Jesus. Later in the documentary, it stresses in stark terms the Nazi war on all religion and the Japanese establishment of state-sponsored Shintoism, which made Hirohito a god-emperor. In the film Capra underscores, with dramatic visual images, the loss of religious freedom by those living under the rule of the Axis and contrasts that with the freedom of religion enjoyed by Americans. Images show Americans freely worshiping, including a scene where a boys' choir sings "Onward, Christian Soldiers."

In many ways Marshall's fears should have been allayed when

he read the report, prepared by a team of army social scientists in 1943, evaluating the effectiveness of *Prelude to War* in indoctrinating recruits with the proper motivation to fight. In November 1942 soldiers at three replacement training camps had been given an anonymous survey with a range of factual and opinion questions centered on the events leading up to the outbreak of war and on the military threat posed by the Axis. The social scientists were surprised by some of the answers, noting that even among those in the control group, who had not viewed the film, 70 percent of GIs thought that Germany and Japan were intent on world domination and must be stopped by the United States. With regard to religion, 75 percent of this group believed that if Germany occupied the United States, they would shut down American churches, echoing the point FDR had made in his October 1941 national address. An even higher percentage, 82 percent, agreed that if Hitler conquered America he would "persecute and torture Jews and other minority groups."[53] Only a small minority thought the United States should have intervened against Germany for actions it had taken within its own borders, but a slight majority of 53 percent believed the country should have intervened in the war even before the Japanese attack on Pearl Harbor, to protect religious minorities in other European countries.[54] These statistics suggest that Roosevelt's case for going to war had convinced many who would ultimately do the fighting. This message would be embraced by many clergy who volunteered to serve as chaplains, and the story of their recruitment and training will be told in the next chapter.

TWO

Mobilizing Chaplains and Building Chapels

Conscription brought millions of Americans into the armed forces, so many that by v-j Day over fifteen million men and women were in uniform. Meeting the religious needs of these GIs required the U.S. Army and Navy to recruit thousands of Roman Catholic priests, Protestant ministers, and rabbis, who were exempted from the draft. Not only did the armed forces need to find men to volunteer, but the professionalization of the chaplaincy in the early 1900s meant that each cleric's religious body had to consent to his appointment and certify his status.

Without the presence of ordained clergy, many GIs serving with the armed forces would not have been able to remain faithful to the tenets of their religious faiths. The Roman Catholic Church mandated that only a priest could say Mass or offer the seven sacraments vital to salvation. Many Protestant denominations with strong liturgical traditions, such as the Episcopal and Lutheran churches, permitted only clerics to give Holy Communion. Even in Protestant denominations with a strong role for the laity, clergy played a vital role in promoting religiosity. Ministers organized services that usually included sermons, comforted the sick, and counseled the distressed. Judaism did not require a rabbi to lead services; only a minyan of ten male Jews was essential to say the requisite morning, afternoon, and evening prayers. But rabbis, especially in the Orthodox and Conservative movements, were central to interpreting the Torah. Some Reform Jews lacked the Hebrew language skills and the confidence to lead a service without a rabbi. In fact, in the absence of a rabbi, Jews at times turned to a Catholic priest or Protestant minister to lead services.

To recruit chaplains, the armed forces—especially the army—made considerable concessions in structuring the service of chaplains. In contrast to the nineteenth century, when the military could appoint chaplains without consent from a religious body, the professionalization of the chaplaincy during the early twentieth century required the army and navy to obtain an ecclesiastical endorsement from a recognized religious institution before commissioning a clergyman as chaplain. Given the hierarchical structure of the Roman Catholic Church, an individual priest could not volunteer to serve in the armed forces without the consent of his bishop.

Official policies granted chaplains freedom of the pulpit and permitted them to adhere to their own religious doctrines and precepts. Both services commissioned chaplains as officers, and this induced some clergy from modest financial backgrounds to volunteer. The regular salary freed them from dependence on the offering plate. But for other clergy, the military chaplaincy meant a pay cut.

Despite these important concessions, the armed forces required chaplains who joined the military to give up significant autonomy and, in the words of one scholar, "answer to two masters."[1] A chaplain was required to adhere to military discipline, which included wearing a uniform that offered few concessions to his religious status aside from a small insignia. He could voluntarily enlist, but once commissioned, he served at the pleasure of the armed forces and could leave the service only when granted a discharge. Service regulations stressed that each chaplain must abide by the rules of the religious denomination that endorsed his candidacy for an appointment. Denominational bodies withdrew ecclesiastical endorsements of chaplains for misconduct. In both branches chaplains were required to make monthly reports to Washington and received direction from command chaplains. But chaplains in both services were in the chain of command and considered staff officers, reporting to the senior commanders of their units.

Officially, army and navy policies asserted that the armed forces, in supporting the chaplaincy, adhered to constitutional strictures regarding the separation of church and state. But as this chapter illustrates, in the practice of recruiting and training the chaplaincy, these boundaries remained permeable and fostered a distinctive civil religion in several important areas. For instance, clerical status did not automatically warrant appointment to the chaplaincy. A quota system maintained by both services declared that clergy from denominations with too few adherents in the armed forces would not be commissioned as chaplains. Gender exclusion prevented female clergy from serving, and educational requirements disqualified even more potential candidates, particularly among African American ministers, fundamentalist ministers, and Orthodox rabbis.

Although both armed services stressed the freedom of the pulpit, they also emphasized the importance of a chaplain meeting the needs of all GIs. Promoting religious pluralism enjoyed widespread support in the chaplaincy, but tensions arose, especially over calls for chaplains to embrace ecumenical activities. In meeting the spiritual needs of GIs, the armed forces hoped to assist in reducing the incidence of sexual immorality. Most chaplains embraced this task, but tensions emerged when the armed forces adopted policies that included distributing condoms. Although chaplains were tasked with meeting the spiritual needs of the GIs, they had learned in chaplain school that they were also there to bolster GI morale in more than one area of life.

Filling the ranks of the chaplaincy was difficult even though the armed forces, especially the army, strived to make it match the religious diversity found in the ranks. Before World War II, the chaplaincy did not represent the religious composition of the armed forces. Only in World War I had rabbis become part of the chaplain corps, and during the interwar years none remained on active duty as part of the regular army. The number of Roman Catholic priests serving as chaplains was unrepresentative of the number of Catholics in the ranks and general population before the mobilization of 1917. Mainline denominations tended to be overrepresented, and the first U.S. Army chief of chaplains was an Episcopalian. One of the major shifts in the Second World War, along with the dramatic expansion of the chaplaincy, was building one that matched the religious diversity of the armed forces. This quest for diversity was carried out, in part, through quotas. This posed difficulties for the army, especially in filling slots allotted to Roman Catholic priests and African American ministers.[2]

Army and Navy Culture

Significant differences between the institutional cultures of the U.S. Army and U.S. Navy were reflected in how both services recruited and trained chaplains to serve GIs in the Second World War.[3] The U.S. Army has been characterized as the "willing servant" and has remained more responsive than the U.S. Navy to following the direction of civilian leaders. Under the leadership of Monsignor William R. Arnold, the army sought to fulfill the mandate to recruit a chaplaincy that reflected the religious diversity of the United States. In training chaplains, chief of chaplains Arnold and his senior staff stressed the vital importance of chaplains serving all GIs while remaining faithful to their own religious traditions.

The U.S. Navy has traditionally been a far more insular culture than the U.S. Army. In the view of many naval officers, "What was good for the navy was good for the country." In contrast to the army, the naval chaplaincy struggled to match the religious diversity of those serving in the ranks. Rabbis and Roman Catholic priests were in short supply during the war, with many capital ships lacking chaplains from these faiths. The navy proved less accommodating in commissioning chaplains from Protestant denominations without established clergy and made only two token appointments of African American chaplains.[4] There were other important institutional differences, especially regarding the autonomy of chaplains in the two services.

Although the army and navy shared some features, as branches of the same military establishment, differences defined how they mobilized for war and received support from Congress. In the case of the U.S. Army, the senior leadership proved much more supportive of chief of chaplains Arnold's efforts to not only bolster the size of the chaplaincy but also to build chapels and obtain the necessary funds to properly equip chaplains. Arnold, a Roman Catholic priest, had been the longest serving chaplain in the army when appointed chief of chaplains in 1939. Prior to becoming chief of chaplains, he had served in the Philippines, the Pacific Northwest, and Fort Leavenworth. While at Fort Bliss, Texas, with the

3. *Franklin D. Roosevelt talks with Chaplain Crawford W. Brown at Camp T. Robinson, Arkansas* (1943). Franklin D. Roosevelt Library 80–118 (488).

First Cavalry Division, he oversaw the religious affairs of Civilian Conservation Corps (ccc) camps in the region.[5]

Arnold was the first Roman Catholic priest to serve as U.S. Army chief of chaplains, and his appointment caused murmurings of dissent among many Protestant church leaders and outright protest from private citizens. Arnold was sensitive to real and perceived discrimination against Protestants. In replying to an aggrieved Reginald H. Hover of Oneonta, New York, regarding a Roman Catholic serving as chief of chaplains, Arnold began his letter by saying, "I am sorry that you seem to be disturbed by the fact the present Chief of Chaplains is a Catholic." Hover had written FDR about concerns of the leadership of the chaplain corps. Arnold assured him that he was "deeply interested in the religious welfare of every man in the army and the efficiency of every chaplain no matter what his denomination." Moreover, Arnold noted that the previous four chaplains had all been Protestants and that his successor would be Protestant.[6]

During Arnold's tenure the army chaplain corps implemented policies that accommodated the needs of such minority faiths as Christian Science and the Church of Jesus Christ of Latter-day Saints, which lacked ordained clergy. This stood in marked contrast to the navy. Arnold was politically astute; his personal correspondence hints at an ability to cultivate friends in Congress favorable to the chaplaincy. While Arnold received the rank of brigadier general, parallel efforts to make the navy chief of chaplains a rear admiral floundered. In the U.S. Senate, the sponsor of the legislation authorizing the chief of chaplains to hold the rank of brigadier general was a member of the Latter-day Saints from Utah. Before the war ended, Arnold would be promoted to the rank of major general.[7]

Arnold came from a family of modest means, and he held a union card gained from working as a cigar maker.[8] Having spent most of his life in army service, he had only a short stint in a civilian parish and later was a traveling chaplain with a professional circus. His correspondence conveys a genuine desire to comfort the sick and offer suitable penance to the sinner and demonstrates an appreciation of the friends and family who had remained in touch with him from his youth, seminary days, and early career as a freshly commissioned chaplain.[9] His serving as chief of chaplains, twenty years before Vatican II, would open the Roman Catholic Church to ecumenical cooperation with Protestants, Jews, and members of other faiths. Arnold navigated the need, as a priest, to adhere to church doctrine while demonstrating a remarkable effort to support religious pluralism within the army.[10]

Robert Workman, a Presbyterian minister, was appointed to the naval chaplaincy in 1915 and rose to the rank of chief of chaplains in 1937. In contrast to many naval officers, Workman had served in the ranks as a marine sergeant before entering seminary. He no doubt gained some insights into the workings of Washington DC by serving as a messenger for Pres. Theodore Roosevelt. In contrast to Arnold, Workman's personal papers do not survive and many of his professional papers were destroyed, making it more difficult to get a measure of the man.[11] Jacob Goldberg—who worked closely with Workman, as a chaplain with the Third Naval District, during the war—recounted fond memories of him in a postwar oral history interview. He described Workman as having little tolerance for vice and immoral conduct and fighting against efforts by the navy to sanction it. During the war Workman remained committed to promoting religious tolerance and ecumenicalism. In 1944 Workman organized and led an overseas tour to visit American troops, which included Goldberg and a Roman Catholic priest. Not only did the three chaplains appear together at public events, but they also participated jointly in services.[12]

Unlike the U.S. Navy, the U.S. Army gained a Congressional appropriation, in 1941, to systematically build chapels at new and existing bases across the country.[13] In February of that year, chief of chaplains Arnold testified in support of an appropriation of nearly 13 million dollars to build 604 chapels at army posts at $21,220 each.[14] After gaining the support of the chair of the appropriations subcommittee, J. Buell Snyder of Pennsylvania, the army received the money by the summer of 1941.[15] Arnold, along with army chief of staff George Marshall, personally dedicated the first chapel built with these Congressional funds in November 1941.[16]

Securing this appropriation was without precedent. Traditionally, army or navy chapels had been built with either special appropriations or with private funds. As a result many army and navy bases lacked any type of chapel, and worship services often took place in auditoriums, libraries, and other facilities converted for use for religious purposes. In writing to the commandant of the Ninth Naval District about his desire for a chapel for the Great Lakes Naval Training Station, navy chief of chaplains Robert Workman described a Congressional reluctance to pay for a chapel when it was intended for the "professional soldier, sailor, and Marine." The influx of draftees, "who represents the youth of America, compelled to serve his country, has brought about a change of attitude."[17]

The navy did not join in the bounty of money for chapels enjoyed by the army. As the official history of the navy chaplain corps recorded, Congress appropriated funds, in 1941, for only one permanent chapel. In part the evidence suggests that neither the navy leadership nor Workman placed a high priority on seeking such funds. Instead, chaplains at many established and newer bases had to content themselves with makeshift settings for their services. Aboard ships, mess desks often served as sites for religious services.[18]

The lack of chapels reflected the more marginal status of Workman and the naval chaplaincy. In contrast to the army, which granted its chief of chaplains considerable institutional autonomy, Workman and the chaplain division remained part of the U.S. Navy Bureau of Navigation. There were critics of this organizational structure and the navy's level of commitment to the chaplaincy. Bishop John O' Hara of the military ordinariate for the Roman Catholic Church argued for granting greater autonomy to the chief of chaplains and his promotion to the rank of rear admiral, and he observed that the process of appointing chaplains to the navy lagged far behind that of the army. In the army it took an average of only three months to induct a prospective chaplain, and he had to spend only one month in chaplaincy school. In contrast, the navy's induction of a new chaplain took five months, and chaplaincy school ran for two months. Moreover, new chaplains in the navy were always assigned to shore positions before being sent out to sea, limiting the number serving aboard ships.[19]

Criticism of Workman reached Roosevelt's desk in 1943 and led to a presidential inquiry. In one of his typically terse memoranda to his navy secretary, Roosevelt stated he was "inclined to agree with Bishop O'Hara . . . that we have too few Navy Chaplains on board ship or at the front." He also endorsed the need for systemic improvement and wondered whether a "two year or four year head to the Corps [would] make for [a] better selection of Chaplains and a better esprit de corps."[20] Secretary of Navy Frank Knox inquired whether FDR had decided in favor of granting the navy chief of chaplains the rank of rear admiral. In Knox's view the promotion of the chief of chaplains would make little difference in bringing greater efficiency to the running of the chaplain corps. At the same time, Knox agreed that he would raise the issue of the deployment of chaplains with Adm. Randall Jacobs, who headed the Bureau of Naval Personnel.[21] After receiving detailed memoranda from Jacobs and Workman, Knox—in a subsequent letter—agreed that more chaplains needed to be redeployed, noting that of the 942 chaplains on active duty only 260 were either at sea or serving outside the continental United States.[22] The report confirmed not only that the majority of chaplains were not assigned to either forward battle areas or warships but also that Workman's embrace of religious pluralism was limited. Most striking is the fact that only nine Jewish chaplains were in the service.[23]

In a circular sent to all chaplains, Arnold reminded senior chaplains that they did not exercise the right of command over other chaplains. Only the chaplain's commanding officer held this power. Although Arnold's office stressed that a chaplain equaled a staff officer in the army hierarchy, they also emphasized that their responsibilities were primarily to attend to the religious needs of GIs. General orders and circulars to chaplains reminded them they should not serve as recreational officers or librarians, bear arms, or perform other duties that detracted from their spiritual role.[24]

Although chaplains were generally not expected to serve as combatants, under naval regulations they could be assigned a host of ancillary duties. They could be tasked by the ship's captain or unit commander to serve as recreational officers, fill the role of librarians, or administer the navy relief fund. A chaplain at a naval air station, Abbot Peterson Jr., a Unitarian minister, described in a letter to the American Unitarian Association how, in addition to serving as a pastor to two thousand officers and enlisted men, he was responsible for "the station library, nightly motion pictures, stage shows at least twice a week, investigation and case work for the Navy Relief Society." While flattered to be asked to write the pamphlet "A Letter to the Sick Soldier" for the Unitarian Association, for eventual distribution to wounded and ill GIs, he wondered if he could find the time to perform his multitude of duties, which also included supervising the publication of the weekly station magazine.[25]

In making a plea, during a small conference organized by the Congregational Church to consider the "Ministers and Chaplains," Col. Earl Weed, of the Fourth Armory Western Command, looked to the future regarding the vital role chaplains would play in postwar years as the "American way of life" was being tested. In his talk before church leaders, in the Park Hotel in Los Angeles, he noted that a "non-Christian nation" was the only one thus far that had "stood up against Hitler." He asked, "What will Christianity have to offer the world in view of that fact after the war?" In his view the chaplains' overcoming the "fifty-seven varieties of sectarianism" would help forge a dynamic message.[26]

Recruiting True Volunteers

The army and navy deferred to religious institutions regarding the theological and professional qualifications of clergy serving as chaplains. As a result clergy could not be appointed to the military without the endorsement of a recognized religious authority. Roman Catholic priests needed the consent of their bishops. Once this had been granted, they came under the authority of the military bishop, who served as the point of contact between the church and the armed forces. For rabbis, the Jewish Welfare Board (JWB), an autonomous organization comprised of rabbis representing the three strands of Judaism—Orthodox, Conservative, and Reform—endorsed candidates for the chaplaincy. In the case of Protestants, it proved much more complicated because a range of faith traditions were arbitrarily lumped together under the umbrella of "Protestant." The General Committee (later Commission) of Army and Navy Chaplains, organized during World War I by the Federal Council of Churches, operated as the most important clearinghouse for Protestant chaplains. Largely autonomous from the Federal Council, the committee relied on member denominations to provide endorsements of their clergy seeking appointments as chaplains. With a small budget and minimal staff, the General Committee limited support to the chaplains it endorsed, and many chaplains turned to their own denominations once in the military. But the committee did see itself as an advocate for Protestant clergy within the military and sought to promote favorable publicity for their work.

Several larger denominations and smaller Protestant denominations bypassed the General Committee. Despite their theological affinity for the Federal Council, both the Methodist and Episcopal churches elected to deal directly with the army and navy in endorsing candidates for the chaplaincy. Protestants never united during the war. Although a substantial number of Protestant churches belonged to the Federal Council of Churches, there were conspicuous exceptions. Several fundamentalist churches rejected the leadership of the Federal Council and the General Committee on theological grounds. Organized in 1942 the American Council of Christian Churches sought and gained official recognition to appoint chaplains, and the National Association of Evangelicals—a more moderate evangelical group—organized shortly thereafter.

Smaller denominations, often splintered from larger mainline denominations, sought official recognition from the army and the navy for the right to endorse chaplains. Not all of them received recognition, despite the military's professed policies promoting pluralism. Demographic factors often came into play. Army officials stressed that there had to be a statistically significant number of adherents in the armed forces before a chaplain could be commissioned. Some smaller faiths protested vigorously against their exclusion. The International Church of the Foursquare Gospel, founded by Aimee Semple McPherson, protested that their seminary had not been recognized by the U.S. Army as a legitimate seminary, resulting in their theological students being ineligible for deferment from conscription. It also deemed their exclusion from the chaplaincy as running contrary to the "Four Freedoms" and President Roosevelt's call to "return to the faith of our Fathers." By 1944 the army had relented and granted Four Square Church a quota of thirteen chaplains.[27]

But those seeking to serve as chaplains had to meet a range of requirements that often had significant implications theologically and in terms of religious practice. Gender lines were quite clearly demarcated in terms of the appointment of chaplains. Put simply, women were barred even if they belonged to denominations that ordained women as clergy. Norma C. Brown, who held a pastorate with a Disciples of Christ congregation and served as a chaplain in the Illinois state senate, sought an appointment. The chair of the Disciples of Christ Chaplaincy Endorsement Committee gave her application a ringing endorsement, noting that she had been heavily involved with the Flying Squadron and had been associated with such Protestant luminaries as Raymond Robins, Daniel Poling, and Oliver Stewart. The chief of chaplains passed on her application.[28]

Both the army and navy required chaplains to have a college education and theological training. Although this requirement was relaxed over the course of the war, it worked against the appointment of clergy from several religious traditions. Orthodox rabbis educated at European yeshivas were often disqualified, as were ministers from fundamentalist denominations ordained without a college or seminary education, as well as African American ministers, who often lacked the educational requirements. In fact, the army's desire for more Black chaplains over the course of the war relaxed the educational requirement until they no longer required both college and theological training.

Age disqualified many who wanted to serve, even those who had previous military service. As army chief of chaplains William R. Arnold once observed to a line officer, the War Department remained adamantly tied to age limits, even though many older clergy in good health could render valuable service.[29] Others could not pass the physical examination, leading the army chief of chaplains to bemoan to an old friend from seminary days, in a private letter from October 1940, that recently thirteen out of fifteen priests under thirty-four years of age had failed to pass the army physical. He wondered if the problem centered on a new generation of priests who had gone "soft" and were too fond of "Fords, movies, and poker-parties."[30]

A more significant barrier existed for denominations that did not have an ordained clergy. In the case of larger denominations, such as Christian Science and the Church of Latter-day Saints, the army made provisions for the appointment of chaplains. In both cases candidates for the chaplaincy had to meet the educational requirements and demonstrate several years of experience serving in a capacity similar to that of an ordained minister. In contrast to chaplains from denominations with clergy, candidates from the Christian Scientists and the Church of Latter-day Saints had to also pass a theological examination to demonstrate their qualifications.[31] The army commissioned Christian Scientists as chaplains after the mother church selected practitioners as candidates for the chaplaincy. But the barring of women decisively limited the number of viable candidates, as women made up the majority of practitioners in the 1940s.[32]

For males considered for the chaplaincy, gender played a role as well, for the Church of Christ, Scientist's selection committee was eager to weed out candidates who were not deemed sufficiently "manly." It is unclear if they were seeking to ensure gay men were excluded from appointment. The issue of homosexuality was never directly raised, but the committee's concerns often point in this direction, as they gathered in-depth information on candidates they deemed lacking in sufficient masculinity. For instance, one chaplain from California almost had his appointment canceled after the church leaders received reports that he was "effeminate" and would not fit the necessary qualification of being "manly" enough to appeal to those in the service.[33] One "college boy" who attended a reading group he had organized for young people had no confidence in anything this individual said, "for he was just a sissy." This perception led the local church to not appoint him as an "attendant in the Service Men's Room . . . because it was felt he was not a representative type of man to talk to those visiting the rooms."[34]

While the army welcomed Christian Scientists as practitioners of the chaplaincy, the U.S. Navy did not. Over the course of the war, only one Christian Scientist was appointed to the ranks. The navy chief of chaplains was quite blunt in stating that if more were appointed, more commissions would be forthcoming if the Christian Scientists got around to ordaining clergy.[35]

Although the navy was reluctant to appoint Christian Scientists, it differed from the army in developing a program to train prospective chaplains for the service. Men desiring to be chaplains could apply to attend college and theological school under the navy's v-12 program.[36] When the navy announced the creation of the program in 1943, it initially sparked substantial opposition from mainline churches, including an editorial in the *Christian Century* raising concerns regarding the separation of church and state.[37] Opposition was not uniform and, as the official history observes, many churches and seminaries affiliated with the Federal Council of Churches embraced these programs. Several seminaries, most notably Harvard, Princeton, and Union Theological Seminary, hosted v-12 units and educated prospective clergy who, upon graduation and ordination by their respective denominations, became navy chaplains.

No Roman Catholic seminary or fundamentalist seminary participated in the program. Carl McIntire, president of the fundamentalist American Council of Christian Churches, cautioned a seaman inquiring about the program against entering it. McIntire advised Ernest Fisk to wait until the war ended before pursuing a seminary degree, since every seminary participating in the v-12 program was pro-Federal [Council of Churches] and this meant it was either "modernistic or compromising as to the historic faith."[38]

The army had no such program and, despite protests from the Methodists and the Federal Council of Churches, the army refused to do away with the mandated educational credential and the requirement of three years of prior pastoral care. Even when they relaxed the educational requirements over the course of the war, they still insisted that prospective chaplains have three years of experience as practicing clergymen before being commissioned.[39]

The Federal Council of Churches, the General Committee, and many chaplains bemoaned the shortage of volunteers. By 1945 Protestant chaplains who had put in several years of service, working long hours, could not be relieved of duty or even given suitable rest breaks, because there were no ready replacements.[40] William D. Cameron complained to the head of the Federal Council of Churches about the inability of a young man serving in France in late 1944 to find a Protestant minister. His mother advised him to attend Catholic services. Cameron lashed out about the failure of young ministers "preaching 'duty' and 'sacrifice' from the comfortable security of a pulpit." He lambasted the Protestant churches as "infested with an unwholesome form of pacifism that is as un-Christian as it is unsound."[41]

Protestant leaders often envied the influx of Roman Catholic priests who applied and the overall quality of those who served in the chaplaincy. There existed the inaccurate perception that the Roman Catholic quota had been exceeded. In fact, the army and navy, throughout the war, begged for more clergy. The exponential growth of the armed forces, beginning in 1940, meant the army and navy scrambled for more chaplains. For instance, in a March 1943 meeting with a Christian Science official, Dr. S. Arthur Devan observed that in midsummer 1942, the Roman Catholics had a burst of success finding chaplains for the army and came within 2 to 3 percent of reaching their assigned quota. He observed that the Protestant groups were at about the same percentage as the

Roman Catholic Church, but the "rapid expansion of the Army" meant "all groups are short of the number of appointments to which they are entitled."[42]

A Roman Catholic priest seeking to serve in an army or navy position needed the consent of his bishop or religious order. This also meant a bishop, if so inclined, could mandate priests in his diocese serve as chaplains. Four days after Pearl Harbor, Arnold pleaded with the bishop of Monterrey-Fresno on the need for priests. Without priests "men and boys in the army have no Mass, No Sacraments, no priestly counsel."[43] The situation was not much better in 1943, when one priest from Wisconsin expressed his dismay to the chief of chaplains that his diocese would not let him serve as a chaplain. He asked Arnold if there was any way he "might get under, over, or around authority."[44] Arnold wrote him, noting that he was not the first priest who had written expressing a wish to volunteer, pointing out that these letters were important since they helped him defend priests against those who were "questioning their loyalty and spirit of sacrifice."[45]

There were also diocesan officials who considered the chaplaincy a good place for priests with shortcomings. The administrator of the Diocese of Amarillo, Texas, thought the army was ideal for a "good priest" with a weakness for drink. Since this priest did not get drunk when in the company of others, the army would presumably be perfect for him because he would not be alone.[46] Arnold argued such a man was totally unfit for the army, in part because he would not receive the protection of "clerical garb" and he would be "removed from the watchful eye of his Bishop and fellow priests."[47]

Protestant chaplains faced some of the biggest challenges in ministering to their flocks. Theologically, organizationally, and culturally, there existed wide variation in the denominations considered Protestant. These included those with strong liturgical and clerical leadership, such as the Episcopal and Lutheran churches; those with diffuse leadership, such as the various Baptist churches; and still others, such as the Church of Latter-day Saints and the Christian Science church, which had hierarchies but lacked professional clergy. Some denominations embraced infant baptism while others maintained that the sacrament of baptism should only be dispensed to those who had a conversion experience. Conceptions of the Eucharist—or Lord's Supper—varied greatly, with Episcopalian and Lutheran traditions being closer to the Catholic position on the sacrament than Baptists and Methodists.[48]

Why did clergy volunteer? Patriotism combined with a desire to minister to GIs certainly played a big part. Roger Warren Barney, an Episcopal priest serving his first parish in North Conway, New Hampshire, explained to his father, in a letter in early 1943, that most people in the area had either gone into the service or found jobs in major defense centers, so "there is scarcely a man left in this village between the ages of 20 to 45." To effectively build and serve a church in the region required the use of so many rationed tires and gallons of gas that, despite a dispensation from the rations board, he had grown uncomfortable going on pastoral calls using his automobile. Although Barney recognized he could move to another parish, he believed that he must respond to the "crying need" for more chaplains and "nowhere can there be so great a potential receptivity to the Gospel as among men who are living in the actual crisis of battle."[49]

For a clergyman who depended on the voluntary contributions of believers to pay his salary, service with the armed forces might offer a steady income and officer status. Serving as officers afforded chaplains not only a higher salary than enlisted personnel but an array of other benefits: access to officers' clubs, a more regular supply of liquor, usually comfortable quarters on troopships, easier access to passes, and often the services of assistants.

There were other intangibles that weighed in the decision to join and take part in one of the defining events of their generation. One Congregational minister wrote to a friend that he hoped for a bigger church, but if this were not to develop, he would consider taking the plunge. He looked with some envy at the experiences of a passing acquaintance who had joined the army chaplaincy and found himself leading Good Friday services for two thousand men at his camp and did not have to deal with a "Woman's Auxiliary."[50]

Several factors discouraged clerics from volunteering to serve as chaplains. Many were simply too old, and both the army and navy remained firm regarding age restrictions. Others felt compelled to continue to serve their congregations or obey their bishops. Those with families did not want to leave behind wives and young children. One army officer complained, after the war, about the mediocre quality of Protestant chaplains in comparison to their Catholic counterparts. He lambasted the failure of more ministers to volunteer, believed they had shunned service "because they were isolationists," and expressed the "feeling that some hated Roosevelt more than the Nazis!"[51]

Although some faiths were too small to warrant the appointment of a chaplain, for many clergy from established churches or synagogues, finances limited their commitment. Serving a junior office could mean a substantial pay cut and the loss of a home, as many ministers still lived in parsonages. For those who supported spouses and young children, volunteering for the chaplaincy entailed less money and long separations from their families. Although some families followed chaplains to their assignments in the United States, dependents were forbidden to travel overseas. For clergy who served in denominations with decentralized governance and strong congregations, there was no guarantee that they would have positions available to them when the war ended. There was also the nagging issue of preserving their participation in denominational pension systems that required continued contributions. Many chaplains who volunteered relied on their denominations maintaining them on their pension rolls.

Thousands joined the army and navy chaplaincy and, like other officers, they received specialized training—they were sent to chaplain school. Chaplain schools maintained by the U.S. Army and Navy played a pivotal role in inculcating clergy from a diverse range of religious traditions into the unique ethos of the armed forces. In examining the curricula of chaplain schools and the experiences of clergymen attending them, we can gain important insights as to what army and navy leaders hoped chaplains would accomplish.

Training Chaplains

In his welcome letter to new chaplains, U.S. Army chief of chaplains Arnold stressed the important role chaplains would play in the lives of those they would serve, due to the "alarming increase in the number of young men who have no knowledge of God and His eternal law, of the necessity of religious worship and discipline."

Chaplains should provide spiritual sustenance, Arnold argued, that could "establish convictions" and "train consciences," and also "strengthen and comfort them every hour of the day, in daylight or in darkness, when alone or in a crowd." Arnold sought to impress upon new chaplains how religious and military life could complement one another, stressing that "spiritual discipline can sanctify and perfect military discipline."[52]

Although chaplains were volunteers, once in the armed forces they were subject to military discipline and the lawful orders of their superiors. After settling their affairs, most made the journey to either the U.S. Army's chaplain school, located for much of the war at Harvard University, or the U.S. Navy's program at the College of William and Mary. Chaplains learned how to salute, wear their uniforms correctly, stand for roll call in the morning, and march and drill in formation. To prepare them for possible combat conditions, one chaplain recalled that his group had to learn how to use their gas masks by sitting in a room filled with gas and even briefly taking off their masks.[53] Courses on military organization, military law, and first aid were offered. Since chaplains were noncombatants, they did not learn marksmanship or small-unit tactics. Compared with training for line officers, chaplain school was far less physically rigorous.

One young Lutheran pastor recalled in his memoir the dressing-down he received, upon arriving at chaplain school, from the unit commander for the absence of lieutenant bars and a chaplain's insignia from his otherwise complete uniform. He also observed that a chaplain's entire day was regulated and failure to adhere to the schedule could mean no weekend pass.[54] Their inspections were decidedly low-key affairs compared with the spit and polish at many officer candidate schools and midshipman schools. Chaplains were not humiliated like one marine corps officer candidate who so repeatedly confused the difference between his gun and his rifle that the drill instructor made him stand half naked in the barracks for several hours while he alternated between pointing at his penis, indicating this was his gun, and then pointing to his rifle.[55] In contrast to the conscious effort of the army air force to winnow the numbers in pilot training, to ensure only the qualified could become aviators, most chaplains completed their training.

4. *African American Minister and His Colleagues Standing at Model at Army Show in Nation's Capital.* Schomburg Center for Research in Black Culture, Photographs and Print Division, New York Public Library.

Chaplain school was a unique experience for most who attended. Many relished the opportunity to reside at Harvard or the College of William and Mary. Some chaplains, prior to joining the service, had been involved in ecumenical organizations, especially if they came from Protestant denominations affiliated with the Federal Council of Churches, but others came from parochial worlds with little significant contact with clergy from other religious traditions. For instance, the Jesuit priest Fr. Joseph T. O'Callahan, whose heroism as a naval chaplain aboard the USS *Franklin* earned him the Medal of Honor, came from a world with only peripheral contact with Protestants or Jews. Born into an Irish Boston neighborhood, O'Callahan's entire education, from elementary school through graduate school, was spent at Catholic schools. Before receiving permission to serve as a naval chaplain, O'Callahan taught at a small Catholic college and participated only in Roman Catholic Church–affiliated scholarly societies.[56]

Chaplain school proved a rude awakening to some clergy who reported for duty and learned what was expected of them. One chaplain did not know how he could possibly prepare a weekly sermon given the many demands on his time as chaplain. Prior to joining the armed forces, a Baptist chaplain had offered the Lord's Supper to a close circle of believers; how would he now conform to the massive expectations of the army?[57]

By design both the army and navy chaplain schools encouraged, even forced, all chaplains to engage with clergy from other religious traditions. At both schools Jews, Catholics, and Protestants were thrown together as roommates. Although the military was racially segregated, officers' schools were integrated, and several hundred African Americans attended the army's chaplain school. Many chaplains composed letters home, entered into diaries, and reflected in memoirs how much they enjoyed the ecumenical atmosphere and the friendships that developed. Misconceptions and falsehoods could be confronted and corrected. For instance, one Christian Scientist expressed dismay that his Presbyterian roommate initially thought "we engaged in the practice of blessing handkerchiefs and other material articles at our church services." This misconception had occurred although this minister was a "conscientious individual, quite well read, and has desire to know what goes on."[58] One rabbi, in writing to his wife, expressed his admiration for the Catholic priests he had gotten to know. He enjoyed their humorous bantering, declaring that they were regular guys who, despite their vows of celibacy, could on occasion take part in leering at women walking through Harvard Yard. He also observed that the Roman Catholic hierarchy looked after their priests and described the top-notch dinner and drinks they enjoyed one evening when the military bishop came by the school. In contrast, when representatives from the JWB came to Cambridge, dinner for the rabbis was fish and ginger ale.[59]

The curriculum provided a significant amount of information on practical theology from an army and navy perspective. They learned how to organize and lead chapel services, provide pastoral care, perform marriage ceremonies, and bury the dead. Chaplains filled notebooks with not only information about Roman Catholicism, Protestant faiths, and Judaism but also rudimentary information about Islam, Buddhism, and Hinduism. They were admonished that "every man has the right to worship in the army . . . in the manner of his own faith. Do all you can for him, and get him to his own spiritual leader either military or civilian." Rev. Howard Wilson, a Presbyterian minister, kept notes that included an outline for how to structure a general Protestant and Catholic service. For one of his assignments, he was tasked as the "only chaplain on duty with your unit," stationed on a post with chaplains of other faiths for him to draw upon, and required to "prepare for week-day and Sunday a religious program for November 1942 to meet the religious needs of all your unit—Protestant, Jewish and Catholic. Note Holidays."[60]

There was a high degree of sophistication in the indoctrination of chaplains. Although instructors at the army chaplain school emphasized that chaplains were, first and foremost, religious leaders, they had other responsibilities to fulfill, most notably working to promote good morale in the commands they would serve. Chaplains were told they must be careful in how they interacted with GIs, since most of them had little tolerance for holy rollers.

There were some subtle differences between chaplain schools in the two services. Perhaps the most significant was that naval chaplain candidates were sent to nearby navy or marine bases, in the vicinity of Williamsburg, Virginia, for practical application of their duties. Under the guidance of a senior chaplain, they delivered their first sermons in uniform, counseled GIs, and learned the protocols of an operating naval or marine base. Roger Warren Barney, an Episcopal priest attending the naval chaplain school, kept a log of some of the cases he encountered when stationed at the Naval Training Station in Norfolk and, later, behind a desk at the YMCA. Many inquiries were ones that a social worker or even a volunteer host or hostess from the community could have handled. For instance, a group of British merchant sailors was looking to make some extra money as agricultural workers while their ship was in port. There were wives searching for their husbands and parents seeking sons. One parent was unsure of where to find the automobile left behind by a son who had shipped out.

There were issues that lent themselves to pastoral care, such as sailors seeking hardship leave to be with ill family members and those dealing with marital discord. Barney could not grant these men's requests and could merely counsel them and send them on

5. Army chaplain William Knight Thompson in his field office. William Knight Thompson Collection, Institute on World War II and the Human Experience.

to the right part of the naval bureaucracy or to a private relief organization that might be able to assist them. One sailor confessed to Barney that he had cheated on his examinations at gunnery school and feared with deployment his lapse would catch up to him. Barney counseled him that he had probably absorbed enough information to get him started aboard ship and he would be working along with a team. In a follow-up by a permanent base chaplain, Barney learned that a subsequent visit had led to an assessment of the man as "not much good."[61]

With over eight thousand chaplains serving, there were—in the words of one chaplain—a fair share of "intellectual pygmies, psychopathic personalities, and men whose poor digestive tone made them incurable misanthropes" among their ranks. The opportunities and burdens of meeting the spiritual needs of over fifteen million men and women were daunting. Moreover, the haste of the mobilization meant the war years can be best characterized as organized chaos, as the United States struggled to train, arm, and deploy a vast force of citizen soldiers. One struggle concerned the question of religious tolerance. Pockets of religious bigotry existed within the armed forces, but the official policies on religious tolerance made a significant difference, beginning with training. Both services required each chaplain, after he left for his first assignment, to file an official monthly report and indicate how he had served men of Protestant, Roman Catholic, and Jewish faiths. The official expectation was that chaplains must accept the religious pluralism of the armed forces and see to the spiritual needs of individuals outside their own traditions.[62]

THREE

Turning Civilians into GIs

One of the institutional lessons learned by the U.S. Army from World War I centered on limiting the role of private organizations on army camps. The dominant role played by the YMCA provoked significant controversy, especially among many doughboys who resented being proselytized by Y secretaries. In their place, the army deployed chaplains and supplemented their efforts with recreational and educational opportunities overseen by the Morale Branch, later renamed the Information and Education Division. When civilian clergy and private organizations were called upon to offer services on army bases, the chaplains and commanding officers exercised much greater oversight of their work.

Equally significant, the mobilization for World War II was initially much more gradual than that which occurred in 1917. For instance, in World War I conscription was debated and implemented only after declaring war against Germany. In contrast, the effort to meet the threat posed by the Axis powers began in earnest in 1940, with the federalization of the National Guard and implementation of peacetime conscription. During this time the army deployed chaplains to the growing number of military bases and started building chapels for them. This chapter will assess how effective these chaplains were in meeting the religious needs of GIs and the nature of religious life for citizen soldiers.

Few individuals who entered the military in those years ever forgot their initiation into the armed services. Military service required that multiple accommodations be made by the millions of citizen soldiers drafted into the armed forces. The loss of autonomy was considerable, especially in training camps, where virtually every aspect of the day was regulated. GIs were told where to sleep, what to eat, when to shower, and how to pack their personal possessions, and they had to master a new language distinctive to the individual culture of their service. Many GIs also experienced diminished ties to their hometowns, states, and regions.

In the nineteenth century the army, in wartime, raised regiments from local communities; thus, most soldiers served with friends and neighbors. Even in World War I the army clustered men into regionally based units. In World War II the armed forces sought to create units that clustered men and women together from across the country. Although each National Guard unit had a distinctive regional character, after the National Guard was federalized in 1940, over the course of World War II, the influx of replacements made each unit more heterogeneous. Most draftee divisions, especially marine corps divisions, were composed of men drawn from every region of the country. Religious diversity became the norm in virtually all units, with most including Protestants, Roman Catholics, and Jews in varying numbers.

During peacetime the fact that soldiers, sailors, and marines had a reputation for engaging in gambling, whoring, and drinking fostered little public anxiety. But the expansion of gin joints, gambling dens, and brothels surrounding military facilities in 1940 and 1941 represented a public relations problem for the Roosevelt administration and the armed forces. Providing access to chaplains and the moral suasion they could provide was seen as one way to maintain the innocence of the young draftees joining the ranks. Armed with the support of the Roosevelt administration, in 1941 Protestant, Roman Catholic and Jewish faith-based organizations established the USO to provide wholesome recreational opportunities for GIs. The coalition of organizations that formed the USO stressed the spiritual dimension of their mission to servicemen and servicewomen.

This chapter will underscore a tension between the high ideals and official policies with which the armed forces promoted the free exercise of religion and the sharp constraints pious GIs faced in following the precepts of their faiths. The military training schedule played havoc with those seeking to observe religious holidays and made it difficult to adhere to faith-based dietary restrictions. Defining a GI as either Protestant, Roman Catholic, or Jewish caused dismay for those who felt core beliefs and practices were not being fully recognized. Despite the expansion of the chaplaincy, the chaplains on many bases were strained by the sheer number of recruits.

Chaplains' and the USO's impact on diminishing vice is debatable, and this chapter will underscore the limits of promoting religiosity to foster conduct desired by the armed forces. But this chapter will also underscore how chaplains and the network of USO clubs, staffed by civilian workers, helped bolster morale among GIs, especially as they struggled to become acclimated to military life. Chapel services often offered messages of comfort, but they also sought to inspire men to fight. Religion sustained many GIs as they struggled to adjust to the rigors of indoctrination and training in their first weeks in the armed forces. It also served as an important link to maintaining their prewar identities in an institution that sought to diminish individuality.

From Civilian to GI: Barracks Religion

Most Americans pride themselves on their individuality, but GIs—when entering the armed forces—were stripped of their identities. To underscore the complete control the armed forces exercised over an individual, male inductees endured physical examinations that were generally carried out en masse. Joseph Katz, who had been drafted into the navy, reported to Grand Central Station in New York for induction, was transported to an office in lower Manhattan, and took his physical with 149 other recruits. In a postwar interview, he recounted how he and his fellow draftees formed a circle. "Your rear faced toward the middle and the doctor stood in the middle, and he said, spread your cheeks, and he checked everybody for hemorrhoids, 150 people."[1] This was certainly no place for modesty or prudishness.

A sense of disorientation was another part of the process. An inductee was often required to undertake a long journey in an overcrowded train to his first base. Men arrived tired, hungry, and dirty, often wearing their civilian clothes. Additional intrusions into their personal space greeted them. During their first days in uniform, inductees waited in long lines while they were poked, prodded, and given a series of vaccinations. Barbers sheared heads and removed facial hair, and quartermasters issued regulation clothing. Men were housed in barracks that afforded no privacy even when discharging bodily fluids. The very term given to the World War II combatant GI reflected the ethos, felt by many who served, that they were simply "government issue" and treated the same way by the armed forces as one might a piece of equipment.[2]

The military did permit each inductee to preserve two aspects of his identity—his name and religious affiliation—when he was issued special tags to be worn around his neck. These "dog tags" ensured that a GI killed in battle could be identified and his grave properly marked. While the dog tags allowed a GI to signify his religious identity, it gave him only four choices: Roman Catholic, Protestant, Jewish or, by default, no religious preference. The broad category of "Protestant" (P) placed under one group such diverse religious traditions as Baptists, Christian Scientists, members of the Church of Latter-day Saints, and Episcopalians. Other religious traditions were given no recognition, notably Buddhists and Orthodox Christians.[3] As one Protestant leader observed, the army's lack of theological sophistication meant that inductees were classified at some bases as Catholics while at others they were deemed Protestants. Since the army did not maintain distinctive records of the number of Orthodox Christians who enlisted, this reinforced the army chief of chaplains' perception that there were too few Orthodox men in the ranks to warrant appointing chaplains for this faith. Christian Science church leaders urged their members to identify themselves as adherents to this faith in order to raise their profile.[4]

GIs had little time to reflect on this, or other issues, as basic training was rigorous and consumed almost every waking hour. Reveille came before dawn, and inductees' early routine included making bunks, shaving, dressing, and marching quickly to the mess hall for breakfast. All branches stressed physical conditioning and close-order drill, even those in the navy. This Spartan regime presented special challenges to religiously devout GIs, especially enlisted men, who lived in environments where profanity was not only tolerated but spewed from the mouths of those in authority. Banter about sexual exploits and crude humor was a mainstay of discussion in the barracks. Gambling was usually ubiquitous. The lack of privacy meant that outward signs of piety, such as kneeling for prayer before sleep, would be seen by all the men in a barracks. Showering in a group meant that crosses, mezuzahs, and other religious symbols were visible. In his letter to a friend, J.E. Tilford remarked on his good fortune in being posted to an army training program filled with college graduates, located at Harvard, where he would be able to avoid the "Great Trinity of barrack-room conversation: Defecation, Urination, and Fornication."[5]

Thousands of GIs trained at one time at such large bases as the army's Fort Dix, the navy's Great Lakes, and the marine corps' Camp Pendleton. At processing centers and ports of embarkation, the influx of GIs passing through could be staggering. Army lieutenant Richard G. Shea, a Roman Catholic chaplain serving at Camp Patrick Henry in Newport News, Virginia, had over 4353 GIs attend his Sunday Masses and 2784 attend his weekly Masses in just one month. He also reported that he offered general absolution to 605 GIs and heard 1352 individual confessions. In preparing men to embark for the war in North Africa, Shea stressed to his superiors that these numbers were not exaggerated and that his post could desperately use another Roman Catholic chaplain, since only half of the "opportunities for preparing men for the battle of the Atlantic can be grasped by a lone priest in this large camp."[6]

Religious services were offered at training camps on Sunday mornings but also on other days of the week. The services conducted by chaplains followed many of the same forms as those in civilian churches and synagogues. Latin remained the language of the Mass, Protestant services featured the singing of hymns, and Jewish services followed a prayer book with a series of liturgical prayers in Hebrew and English. Chaplains and their GI congregants could use the official army and navy hymnal, which included Protestant, Roman Catholic, and a few Jewish hymns, but chaplains also found other methods to distribute hymns to worshiping GIs.

Despite the regulations regarding freedom of conscience, the application of them could be inconsistent. Periodically, the War and Navy Departments reissued standing orders reminding commanders that GIs could not be compelled to attend religious services. The navy departed from the army and mandated that sailors

6. Morning services for Seabees outside training center in Norfolk, Virginia, 1944. Nancy Moses-Stern Collection, Institute on World War II and the Human Experience.

in boot camp or officer candidate school attend chapel services of their choice. The choices offered to candidates required compromises, especially for Protestants and Jews. Examples of these compromises can be gleaned from Rabbi Joshua Goldberg's description of how, while serving as chaplain for the Third Naval District, he also ministered to the needs of those attending a midshipmen's school (junior officers' training program) based at Columbia University. Goldberg recalled with pride that Protestant, Roman Catholic, and Jewish candidates all marched into Riverside Church for Sunday chapel services. Riverside Church, the nondenominational Protestant house of worship founded by the Rockefellers, had modified one of their chapels to make it an appropriate place to hold Jewish services. On most Sundays Goldberg led separate services in this chapel while Protestants worshiped in the main sanctuary.[7]

Every sixth Sunday Goldberg and the Jewish cadets would join the Protestant service. Goldberg would take his place at the pulpit with the Protestant chaplain and deliver a sermon. For Goldberg this move to ecumenicalism furthered mutual understanding between Protestants and Jews. From Goldberg's perspective attending the Protestant service would broaden the perspective of Jewish midshipmen and also foster greater group harmony among all future junior officers. As he recounted, there were parents of midshipmen who were incredulous that such a worship service could take place, and some visited in order to witness it.

As a Reform rabbi, Goldberg is silent as to how the Jewish services he organized differed from Conservative and Orthodox traditions. These traditions embrace praying three times a day, every day, and both give precedence to holding services on the Sabbath, beginning Friday at sundown and ending at sundown on Saturday. Both traditions stress the importance of saying the requisite prayers during services, something that would not have taken place during the general Protestant service.

Goldberg's embrace of ecumenical services was not unique, especially his quest for cooperation among the three strands of Judaism managed through the JWB. In addition to appointing military chaplains, the JWB established a Responsa legal committee that offered rabbinical rulings on the applicability of Jewish law for those serving in the armed forces. For example, this committee ruled that military chaplains should avoid granting conversions, determined when the Sabbath began when stationed near the Arctic Circle, and described how Jewish burial practices should be applied in combat zones. They also developed a uniform prayer book that drew upon all three major strands of Judaism.[8]

Not all Jews welcomed the unity sought by the armed forces and the JWB. Tensions occasionally flared up. In a letter to another rabbi about his wartime experiences, one Reform rabbi recalled making concessions to the Orthodox and Conservative traditions, especially with regard to rituals. Bringing Jews together in prayer was not always easy, and this naval chaplain recalled a controversy over the use of a shofar (ram's horn) for the High Holidays services at Bainbridge, Maryland. A delegation of Orthodox sailors protested that the shofar he planned to use for the service was not kosher, even after he offered to place a metal mouthpiece over it. When the Reform chaplain asked the delegation how to solve this problem, they provided an acceptable shofar that would be sounded

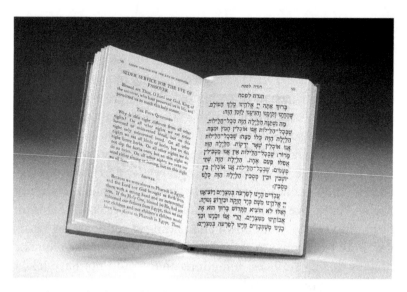

7. Jewish prayer book issued by the Jewish Welfare Board. Leon Lindauer Collection, Institute on World War II and the Human Experience.

during the services by the grandson of a prominent Orthodox leader. Although a small group of Orthodox sailors held an earlier separate service, he was pleased that most Orthodox Jews joined him in the much larger service, where 1500 attended.[9]

Orthodox Jews were not the only ones to express misgivings over forced ecumenicalism. Fundamentalists bristled at the liberal theology espoused by some Protestant chaplains. Edward H. Bohn Jr., attending midshipmen's school in New York City, complained to the fundamentalist leader Carl McIntire about his "contact with Riverside and Dr. Fosdick's teaching." Even worse his chaplain was a Union Theological School graduate and "staunch Fosdick admirer," and Bohn noted that he was "still waiting for him to present a sermon on Christ."[10]

There were also Roman Catholic chaplains and laity who rejected ecumenicalism, especially when they were pressured, even ordered, to attend Protestant-based services under the guise that they were for all Christians. Roman Catholic army chaplain John R. Bradstreet, stationed at Camp White, Oregon, in March 1943, expressed his resentment at calls for his men to attend the Easter Sunrise Service. When asked by Catholic soldiers whether they could attend,

Bradstreet admonished them not to miss Easter Sunday Mass and to attend the joint Protestant service only to satisfy their curiosity. When one GI reported his commander had ordered him to go, Bradstreet told him he should tell his commander, "Your chaplain forbade you to go to it . . . as a substitute for Mass." In considering this unpleasant incident, Bradstreet reflected that "the word proselytizing is a smelly word, and I think in army circles it smells with a vulgar stink. I'm saving that word for my arsenal if I get a few kick-backs within the next couple of days."[11] Another letter heaped praise on a young officer not only because he "complimented me on my sermons, which he did, and which I liked, but . . . because [he] is such a sterling Catholic. He refused to take part in the Easter sunrise service, and when he refused it he said, I'll stand Court Martial first."[12]

Other Catholic chaplains had more positive experiences with the religious pluralism promoted by the armed services. As Chaplain George J. Flanigen informed the military delegate Bishop William T. McCarty, there were non-Catholics who, for the first time in their lives, were coming into "close contact with Catholics and things Catholic." Friendship and comradeship between Catholics and non-Catholics were being nurtured by army service. When deployed in the field, non-Catholics saw him celebrating Mass and in the military hospital administering last rites to gravely ill Catholic soldiers. Flanigen was required to serve all, and some GIs went to him "with their troubles" only to find out he was a Catholic priest. They often concluded that Roman Catholic priests were "not such bad people after all." Flanigen described how one "intelligent boy" was so completely ignorant about Roman Catholicism that he did not know that a priest could not marry, yet he had become a frequent visitor to his tent to talk. In another instance, after Flanigen had written a letter for an "illiterate lad from North Georgia" to the young man's mother, this GI started going with him when he held services and meetings at other units.[13]

Some commanders in the armed forces did not support their chaplains and were skeptical about the value of organized religion. One chaplain ran afoul of his executive officer because the latter was "definitely anti-religious, admittedly so by his Commanding Officer, and it was reported to me that he is antagonistic to Chaplains, having stated that he thought that there was no place in the Army for Chaplains or Religion."[14] Other commanders displayed bigotry toward chaplains of certain faiths. Chaplain Willard Walter Janes's commander, a Roman Catholic lieutenant colonel, pressured him to request a transfer to another unit citing the lack of Christian Scientists available for him to serve. The lieutenant colonel asserted that a Christian Scientist chaplain was not in a "position to minister to other Protestant men in giving Holy Communion." Janes expressed reluctance, to church officials, to accept a transfer, since it would give credence to the allegation that he did not meet the spiritual needs of all Protestants. In fact, Janes maintained that he could, and did, offer Holy Communion.[15]

Army-sponsored services led some GIs to see their own religious traditions in a new light. Sam Zipkin, in a letter to his training camp rabbi, Phineas Smoller, expressed his appreciation that Smoller had recast Judaism, making it more relevant to his experiences. Like others of his generation, Zipkin had drifted away from his faith, in part because of the long drawn-out rituals of some Jewish holidays. In Zipkin's view, Smoller's sermons were so compelling that he could no longer think of attending services as superfluous. He found in Smoller "an intellectual liberal who at the same time had sense enough to keep his feet on the ground."[16]

It disturbed many Protestant chaplains and their civilian church officials that Roman Catholics tended to be more faithful about attending Mass. One Congregational minister observed that the blame could not rest with "any inherent quality in the Catholic faith beyond that possessed by the Protestant" or the "lack of facilities in the Army for such attendance." Instead, there existed a deeper problem with Protestantism that stemmed from the fact that the average layman did not believe that the "failure to attend church services and actively participate in the work of the church whenever possible is [a] sin."[17]

There were more benign reasons why chapel attendance suffered. As one Presbyterian minister reported, Protestants preferred to go into town to worship at their denominational churches. In fact, one of the activities he oversaw as chaplain, on an army air force base in Oklahoma, was organizing transportation to weekday social evenings held in area churches. At the same time, this chaplain reported that many of those who attended "never went to church at home" which meant he was required to "preach in the simplest of terms and use non-religious phraseology."[18] One GI who spent the war in stateside assignments gave several explanations for why he did not attend services. In letters home this Buffalo, New York, native observed that the absence of his family dulled his desire to attend chapel services and, in another instance, he missed a service because he had overslept because of guard duty the night before.[19]

The availability of religious services was not enough to sustain some GIs. As one army GI reflected, in a postwar letter to a friend, "The Congregationalism of my childhood didn't stand the stress of the service." He and his wife, a marine officer during the war, would only return to religion in a serious way as civilians in the 1950s.[20] For others, army religion called into question earlier religious beliefs. While serving as a chaplain's assistant in the U.S. Army, Carl Montgomery wrestled with both his sexual orientation and his religiosity. Montgomery served with a Pennsylvania National Guard unit mobilized prior to Pearl Harbor and relished his role in assisting chaplains as they provided for the religious needs of men in the army. In a letter to a friend, he contemplated becoming an army chaplain, in part because he believed the essential cornerstone of faith was belief in God. "How you worship or think of God is of practically no importance." In his own mind, he tried to serve the needs of "Protestant, Catholic, Jew or atheist." This Presbyterian observed to a close friend that he had done more for a Catholic chaplain he had served under because "he was such a vivid personality and did such splendid work while our Protestant Chaplains were so lax and indifferent."[21]

But there is also the question of the religiosity of the GIs when they entered the service. In a research study conducted by army social scientists in 1944, seeking to understand what caused incidences of mental breakdown, they explored whether there was any correlation between church attendance and adjustment to army life. Among those the study deemed the "best adjusted" GIs, they found that 39 percent frequently attended church (once or twice a week), with another 18 percent declaring they went two or three times a month. In this anonymous survey, 14 percent noted that they only went several times a year, with another 17 percent indicating they never went to services. Researchers did not find a significant difference between soldiers described as "well-adjusted" and those deemed "psychoneurotic," but one pattern stood out: younger recruits were more likely than older ones to have regularly gone to worship services. Among soldiers under twenty years of age, 71 percent reported going to church two or three times a month, while among those over thirty years of age, only 45 percent had this degree of religiosity.[22]

Military imperatives in training played havoc with the spiritual calendar, but the armed services, with the support of the JWB, tried to ensure that Jews, even in isolated training facilities, could attend Yom Kippur and Rosh Hashanah services and participate in seders. In places with large Jewish communities, like Great Lakes Training Center in North Chicago, passes were liberally distributed to Jewish GIs to allow them to attend services or participate in seders with local families. Chaplains were often aided by the USO and Jewish community organizations in placing Jewish GIs into people's homes on holidays, but invitations could come spontaneously. Robert Fishkin, a native of Perth Amboy, New Jersey, recalled how—while training at the Great Lakes Naval Station—an encounter on Chicago's elevated train platform led to an unexpected invitation from a complete stranger to attend a Passover seder with his family.[23]

Just like in the civilian world, Christmas was among the most widely celebrated holidays on military camps and bases. Usually special dinners were planned complete with printed menus featuring a host of holiday mainstays. GIs often sent Christmas cards that emphasized their newfound ties to the military. They relished receiving Christmas cards and presents from home. Close behind Christmas was the widespread observance of Easter at chapel services, often in sunrise services. Like Christmas, Easter—along with Thanksgiving—invariably featured special dinners germane to the holiday.

Food also played an important role in soldiers' religious identities. In the pre–Vatican II Roman Catholic Church, the liturgical calendar designated days when a devout Catholic would either abstain from meat or fast. On those days meat was frequently

8. *Just before Santa Claus leaves his 'jeep-sleigh' the guard of honor stands on
each side. Presenting arms to the Christmas visitor, Camp Lee, Quartermaster
Replacement Center* (December 1941). Still Picture Branch, U.S. National Archives
(111-SC-126777).

served in the mess halls despite the presence of a large number of
Roman Catholics. Before receiving communion Roman Catholics were required to fast for several hours to prepare themselves
for the sacrament. Although a papal dispensation provided GIS
in harm's way the opportunity to forgo many of these restrictions,
some priests and lay Catholics attached great importance to the
church's dietary mandates.

Observant Jews faced greater dilemmas. Although the JWB distributed some kosher meat to Jewish chaplains, this reached relatively few Jews. Some observant Jews ate nonkosher food for
the duration of their time in the service. To serve as guidance,
Responsa rabbinical rulings, issued through the JWB, suggested
rabbis urge Jewish GIS to avoid clearly nonkosher, or *treif,* foods
such as pork and shellfish. It recognized that, out of necessity, GIS
may need to eat meats that had not been slaughtered under Jewish law and eat dishes that combined meat and milk. Despite this

rabbinical guidance, some Jewish GIs simply could not abide by calls from the military and the rabbinate to abandon the dietary strictures. In one tragic case, Chaplain Albert Baum described a young sailor at Bainbridge who was so inhibited that, even with the intervention of an Orthodox rabbi, he could not bring himself to eat nonkosher food and went hungry. As Baum recalled there were deeper reasons at play, and this sailor became a mental patient since he "could not face a non-Jewish environment."[24]

GIs carried Bibles with them but also a host of other material objects to strengthen their faith. Rosary beads were common among Catholic GIs, along with religious medals and images of the Madonna, frequently referred to as Catholic pin-ups by chaplains. Our Lady of Mount Carmel in Hoboken, New Jersey, gave each departing GI a scapula "to shield them in time of danger, and to ensure if they died they would be saved."[25] Some Protestant leaders wondered if they should emulate Roman Catholics and distribute material objects to fortify the faith of their men. Joseph Hunter, President of Bloomfield College and Seminary, endorsed the recommendation of William Woodman, a recent graduate serving as a navy chaplain, that the Protestant church establish a religious medal similar to the one used by Roman Catholics. In a letter to the chief Presbyterian official in charge of chaplaincy affairs, Hunter argued that the Episcopal church had a medal that was popular with servicemen. But when these medals were not available, they clamored for Catholic ones. In Woodman's assessment, "a man needs more than a thought to fasten on to . . . a medal is a stimulus to thought and can be of very great service."[26]

In addition to Bibles, GIs were flooded with literature put out by religious groups. Competition contributed to this abundance, as some chaplains prodded their denominations to match the efforts of other groups. One Universalist chaplain, writing from Fort McClellan, Alabama, observed that his chapel was "cluttered" with printed matter by the Lutherans, Roman Catholics, and Southern Baptists that lacked "real value" and contained "rotten theology." This chaplain was pleased to get some new booklets from his denomination and eager to read and disseminate them."[27] The military ordinariate cautioned Catholic priests to look to the imprimatur as the test of whether a publication was suitable for their

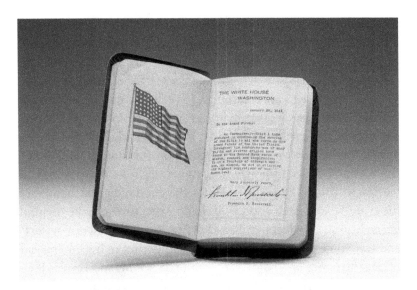

9. New Testament printed for soldiers by the U.S. government during World War II. Charles Stripling Collection, Institute on World War II and the Human Experience.

troops and singled out a clearly unsuitable work titled "Chaplains' Spiritual Ministry for All Faiths in War Emergency."[28]

The role of counselor was the most distinctive role that chaplains played at training and boot camps in the States. During their office hours, and on other occasions, they counseled dozens, even hundreds, of GIS over the course of a week. Countless GIS turned to chaplains, not so much for guidance on fine points of theology but to help them with marital problems, difficulties in adjusting to military life, discrimination, and a host of other problems. Some men were lonely or troubled by the health of their parents or fretted over the problems that beset their siblings. Wives and girlfriends were unfaithful. Jewish chaplains were asked to investigate cases of sons marrying outside the faith and converting to Christianity. Most chaplains, when reporting on their role as counselor, insisted that it made "little difference whether a man is Protestant, Catholic, or Jew, when he is in trouble or if he just wants a sympathetic ear."[29]

In counseling GIS, chaplains, at times, aggressively attempted to assist them in working out their personal problems. In counseling a man whose marriage was troubled, Rabbi David Eichhorn wrote a letter to the soldier's wife reporting that her husband, stationed at Camp Croft, South Carolina, was still in love with her and had "expressed a keen desire" to continue the marriage. He chastised her for objecting to her husband sending five dollars of his monthly pay to his grandmother, maintaining that "any religious and ethical person" would agree with his decision. He further admonished her for having "broken up housekeeping, stored the furniture . . . and joined the WACS." Insisting that traditional gender roles that reinforced patriarchy should be maintained for the good of her husband and the army, he told her a good wife would make sure to write "helpful letters instead of letters that cause him no end of mental discomfort" and try "to help him through this trying period of his life instead of causing worry and pain." Neither the GI nor his spouse was Jewish, and Eichhorn called for her to visit an unbiased person, "preferably your family minister," who had presided over her marriage.[30]

Other chaplains also took a proactive role in intervening in the personal affairs of GIs and enforcing moral precepts. Chaplain Edward Elson, in December 1942, received a detailed letter from a fellow Presbyterian minister, Andrew MacCormick, who headed a congregation in San Pedro, California. MacCormick informed him of the extramarital affair of a Presbyterian layman who served as a captain in the finance department at Fort MacArthur. This captain was engaged in a torrid affair with a much younger woman, who worked in his department, and had moved in with her and her mother. MacCormick noted that this captain had, at one point, made a full confession to his wife, breaking down and sobbing while admitting to "his inability to break free" from the young woman. Could a transfer be arranged to free this captain from "being made a fool of by some unscrupulous women, a species that seems to abound in San Pedro?"[31] In fact, Elson did take action pretty quickly, going directly to the chief of the finance branch at this base, who was "much discomfited at the news of such a situation." Elson reported to MacCormick that this adulterous captain would soon be transferred "to duty outside the United States with an air force mission." Although Elson acknowledged that this transfer would keep him "more remote from his wife and children, we trust that time will have its redeeming quality."[32]

One chaplain's efforts to cleanse the officer's club of pictures of nude women led to a severe reprimand from his commander. William E. Chapple, serving as depot chaplain at Camp Sutton, North Carolina, decided that it was his duty to remove "all such literature and posters that are destructive to the morals of this Command." In defending his action, he described how he had "requested" that the officers' club's attendant remove the posters depicting "vulgar scenes" that served as "poison to the mind and soul of mankind." When the attendant did not follow his direction, he personally removed them, unaware that they were the property of the officers' club. In protesting to the commander of the 12th Replacement Depot, Chapple said he thought it repellent to "replace these obscene posters which are contrary to my Christian ideals."[33]

Chaplains themselves were not immune to temptation. An acting post chaplain at Fort Bragg wrote in confidence to a Baptist state superintendent expressing his concern about the conduct of one Baptist chaplain whose efforts to become a permanent chaplain failed because of a low efficiency rating from his senior officer. This Baptist minister "leaves the impression that he is not married and conducts himself accordingly."[34]

The USO: Recreation and Religion to Keep Men Moral

One perplexing question for military authorities was how could they discourage men from engaging in illicit sex, gambling, and drinking when off duty? Official propaganda continued to preach a message of abstinence, laced with fear of disease, to discourage sex outside of marriage. At the army chaplain's school, clergy had to write and deliver a "practice sexual hygiene" lecture.[35] At training camps chaplains faithfully delivered this lecture, but they often recognized it was a futile proposition given the armed forces' willingness to widely distribute condoms to male GIs going on leave and provide prophylactic stations for men to cleanse themselves after sexual relations. One chaplain recalled that his lecture on sexual morality was preceded by a demonstration of how to use a condom.

A GI recalled attending the sexual morality lectures offered by his unit's chaplains, when deployed overseas, and how the Catholic chaplain reminded them to keep in mind their spouses: "When you go to town and you have to pick up a condom before you can go into town, make sure you pick up two, one for your wife, and send it home to her—get the message? "[36]

Even before the United States entered the war, the War and Navy Departments and civilian agencies began to consider creating opportunities for wholesome activities. At the same time, religious organizations that had participated in the World War I War Camps Commission also began to plot out the formation of a new organization. The most active leaders in this effort were initially Frank Weil, representing the JWB, and representatives of the YMCA and the Knights of Columbus. Out of these efforts would emerge the USO, the JWB, the YMCA, the YWCA, the Salvation Army, National Catholic Community Services (NCCS), and the Travelers Aid Society, which would be charged by the Roosevelt administration with providing wholesome activities to GIs.

The decision to allow a "faith based" public-private organization to provide recreational services to GIs was a deliberate choice by FDR. New Dealers believed reliance on a private religious organization to provide for the recreational needs of World War I soldiers had been a mistake. New Dealers wanted responsibility lodged with a government agency such as the Works Projects Administration or the Federal Security Agency. In contrast, the War Department, under the leadership of Henry Stimson, wanted the task placed with a network of religious organizations and supported the quest of the recently formed USO to gain government recognition and financial support for their efforts. Frederick Osborn, who served as chair of the Joint Army and Navy Committee on Welfare and Recreation (and later as major general in World War II and head of the army's morale division) recounted, in his unpublished memoir, a crucial meeting in which FDR declared his support of the USO over vesting this role in the Federal Security Agency (FSA), headed by Paul McNutt. To soften the blow Roosevelt observed to McNutt, "Paul, if you do this you'll have a large staff and when the war is over you will have to fire them all, and that would break your heart. I wouldn't have that happen to you for anything. We'll have the USO do it."[37]

Since the USO melded together six existing organizations, many of the institutional structures were already in place to quickly begin

establishing clubs around the country. These clubs, staffed by professional workers and volunteers, provided a range of services
that usually included a comfortable place to sit and write letters
home and places to read a book, attend a dance, and seek advice
on a range of problems. The promotion of religiosity remained
an important part of the uso, most notably through the distribution of religious literature at its clubs. Religious services, especially for Jewish and Roman Catholic troops, were held in these
clubs in areas of the country that contained small or nonexistent
communities reflecting their faith.[38]

The uso signified one of the high points of ecumenical cooperation. In speeches, press releases, and fundraising campaigns,
uso leadership extolled the virtues of the organization for bringing
together the great religious traditions of the West—Protestantism,
Roman Catholicism, and Judaism—behind a common cause. The
uso provided a crucial service that was appreciated by GIs, especially young servicemen homesick and yearning for some small
creature comforts or the chance to dance with a female hostess
for the evening. Moreover, the uso pointed with pride to the fact
that any uso club must serve all GIs, irrespective of their religious beliefs. A club was frequently sponsored and staffed by a
single agency (i.e., the JWB), but the uso promised to promote
greater ecumenical cooperation and more efficient use of resources
through jointly sponsored clubs.

In order to receive official recognition as the principal voluntary
organization to meet the recreational needs of American GIs, the
uso was required to deliver services in a nonsectarian manner.
There were tensions between the federal government and the uso,
primarily because the federal government pushed for more efficiency in the delivery of recreational services. In fall 1942 Fowler
V. Harper, retiring chair of the Joint Army and Navy Committee
on Welfare and Recreation, called for more consolidation in the
delivery of services, noting petty jealousies and lack of cooperation in many communities. Harper observed that in Starke, Florida, the new uso building, which housed the YMCA and JWB,
could certainly meet the needs of all-white troops stationed at
Camp Blanding. But he observed the NCCS had decided to maintain four small buildings on this base and the YMCA had started a

new operation at the local public library. He also noted that even when two constituent agencies were housed in a federal building, to deliver services to GIs, the two organizations often sought to isolate themselves in different parts of the building [39]

Chester Barnard, the second leader of the USO, defended the continuation of separate institutional identities for USO clubs and insisted that the organization had "never proposed to abandon operations by agencies." He maintained that the religious differences among the constituent members of the USO were crucial ones since "emphasis was placed first on the religious motivation." Affirming the ecumenical and cooperative nature of the USO, Barnard stressed that the agencies coordinated their efforts through a common management structure "to make all welcome regardless of race or creed and to refrain from proselytizing. We regard this as fundamental to the services we agreed to perform and are rendering, and as essential to [the] carrying out of our proper purposes."[40]

Protestant leaders, during the war, frequently looked with envy on the perceived unity that existed between Roman Catholics and Jews. For Roman Catholics and Jews, the point of tension surfaced with efforts by the JWB and the NCCS to serve Jewish and Roman Catholic GIs in parts of the country with few Jews or Catholics, especially in the Deep South. The NCCS and JWB sponsored clubs that sparked what can be interpreted as anti-Semitic, nativist, and anti-Catholic opposition in some quarters of the general public. In Fayetteville, North Carolina, a group of Protestant ministers objected to the USO leasing facilities from the Roman Catholic church for a clubhouse.[41] It appears the effort to create policies that, on the surface, were intended to foster ecumenicalism were tinged by an effort to minimize displays of Roman Catholic and Jewish identity (i.e., restrictions on the display of religious imagery and requirements regarding the display of religious literature). The USO proved wary of using organizational funds to pay Roman Catholic priests and rabbis to provide religious services. It proved more willing in the case of Jews, in part because Jews serving in isolated locations frequently did not have access to a rabbi, either military or civilian, in many parts of the country.[42]

Religious sectarianism did not derail the USO, and advocates of this organization saw it as promoting wholesome recreational opportunities that would diminish vice. But the evidence is, at best, anecdotal that the USO, along with the expanded chaplaincy, correlated to an increase in GIs embracing abstinence or marital fidelity. The USO leadership maintained that their organization promoted religiosity, but Raymond Fosdick, head of the World War I Commission on Training Camps, when tasked with reviewing the organization's activities, raised concerns over sectarianism inherent in the organization's structure. He argued that the army and navy chaplaincy should be the ones tasked with promoting religiosity among GIs. Moreover, most GIs and their commanders did not believe recreational services had to be delivered by a Protestant-, Catholic-, or Jewish-run agency. After all, Fosdick maintained: "A dance is a dance and a bowling alley is a bowling alley regardless of auspices, and when a soldier talks to a girl, he is not interested in what church she goes to."[43]

Religion and Motivating Men to Fight

Ultimately, the goal of military training is to prepare GIs for battle or support those on the tip of the spear. There were those who had not claimed conscientious objector status when drafted but, once inducted, realized they had moral reservations about bearing arms. One soldier at the Army Air Force Training Center in Fresno, California, told the chaplain that he "earnestly and consistently refuses to bear arms" but did not seek release from the service because he was "enthusiastic about the principal objective for which we are fighting." He requested "non-combat duty under any conditions regardless of danger." Another soldier, from a Lutheran background, had a "mental quirk rather than sincere religious conviction" in the view of his chaplain, who reported to the army chief of chaplains that this individual "conscientiously objects to the taking of orders from any man, basing his position on private interpretations of the Bible, especially Acts 5:29, 'We ought to obey God rather than man.'"[44]

There certainly were men who had religious qualms against participating in war who had their concerns assuaged by chaplains and other religious leaders. In a general letter to all Christian Scientist chaplains, the Camp Welfare Committee described the case of an army air force cadet who could not contemplate using his "machine guns and cannon on his fellowmen and could not reconcile this military demand with what he had been taught in Sunday School." If faced with an encounter with an enemy plane, this cadet contemplated deliberately aiming away from it. Although the specifics are not given, the Christian Scientists allayed this cadet's moral qualms and helped him develop a "clear sense of his duty to God and man." This airman was reminded "that this was not a war on man, but on evil for the liberation of man, and that David was obliged to kill the Philistine who embodied evil."[45]

Chaplains generally embraced the war and saw it as part of a broader religious struggle. Their connections to this mission varied. In training, army chaplains were discouraged from becoming "political commissars," but their role in sustaining morale was important. While the army emphasized that chaplains were to follow the dictates of conscience, many were glad to impart ideological messages urging men to fight. Naval chaplain Harvey Swanson, a Universalist minister serving marines in Camp Elliott, wanted the general assembly of his church to understand that the "real issue of this war is the liberal spirit as opposed to the spirit of totalitarianism." He went on to stress the importance of not just winning the war against foreign enemies but also of making sure the "battle for religious freedom" was not lost "by our own indifference to our liberal churches."[46]

The prayers offered and the sermons delivered could be less than subtle in terms of encouraging men to be good soldiers. A Memorial Day service intended for an entire regiment of National Guardsmen, mobilized prior to the attack at Pearl Harbor, included a prayer that would have made a devout evangelical Christian, and even a mainline Protestant, wince as it conflated the secular and profane and showed insensitivity to those of the Jewish and Islamic faiths. It declared, "We need not go to Mecca or Palestine to find the Holy Land" and noted "the soul of man can transfigure earth and make it holy ground." What were the sacred places that should be considered holy? "They included the Mount of Olives and Garden of Gethsemane; sacred are Plymouth Rock and Bunker Hill, sacred the field of Thermopylae and the Town Common at Lexington."[47] Another chaplain prayed, "Spirit of all life: May

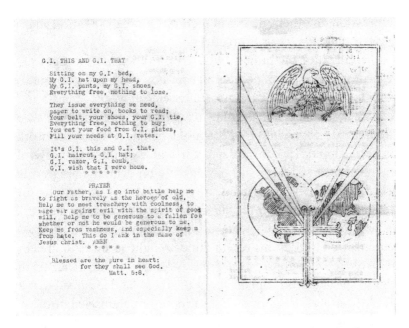

10. Service bulletin (*front and back*), Camp Swift, 1945. Thomas David Bell Collection, Institute on World War II and the Human Experience.

I remember this day the brave and courageous people who have lived in the past. May their sacrifices made in hours of danger and peril give me a greater sense of my responsibility of the present."[48]

Efforts to indoctrinate soldiers could be quite overt. The pamphlets for soldiers issued by religious denominations offered reassurance about the morality of killing in wartime and advice on how to cope with fear and how to conduct themselves with proper values.[49] In one pamphlet, developed by the Unitarian Church, a range of quotes defined American values and beliefs.[50]

Of course, chaplains risked alienating GIs if they tried too hard to indoctrinate them. In a postwar interview, one veteran recalled a chaplain who had been booed for trying to appease a group of soldiers who had thought they would attend college under the Army Specialized Training Program only to find themselves cut from the program and sent to an infantry division. They found no comfort in this chaplain's constant referral to this branch of the army as the "Queen of the Battlefield."[51] While some soldiers found military sermons alienating, these services seem to have made little impression on others. Scores of memoirs scarcely mention chaplains or religious ideas or practices.

The failure of the military to live up to the ideals it espoused regarding the freedom of religion could be profoundly demoralizing for some GIs. For example, after eleven weeks of basic and four weeks of maneuver training, one private—stationed in Camp Beauregard—found his morale sapped when he was forced to work on Yom Kippur. He considered it particularly galling that several men had received three-day passes to go on drinking binges. He asked the civilian rabbi in a nearby town, "Aren't we fighting for Religious Freedom and for our Democratic form of existence?" In fact, this local rabbi—who later became a military chaplain— had inspired him, in his recent Sunday night sermon, to greater observance. In response to the private's complaints, the rabbi urged him to speak to his chaplain about the incident. He agreed that it was "distasteful" to work on Yom Kippur but counseled him "we cannot lose sight of the fact that in fighting the Fascists, we must give up many privileges that we used to enjoy in civilian life."[52]

FOUR

Pilgrims to the Four Corners of the World

W orld War II resulted in millions of Americans, many for the first time, leaving the United States and living abroad. By the end of the war, American GIs had been deployed to six of the seven continents and all but a handful of neutral countries. They manned weather stations in Greenland, drove trucks across Iran to the Soviet Union, stormed ashore the beaches of France, served on ground crews on airfields in Brazil and West Africa that brought supplies to the European theater, staffed quarter-master depots in India, deployed to bomber bases in China, and endured monsoon rains in New Guinea. Both the army and navy faced challenges meeting the spiritual needs of the GIs deployed throughout the globe.

Several factors made religious practices distinctive for GIs deployed overseas. As this chapter will underscore, both the army and navy struggled to deploy enough chaplains abroad. As a result many chaplains and GIs took part in a lived religion that fostered ecumenicalism. It meant that chaplains found themselves offici-ating at services outside of their own traditions.

Except on the most desolate islands in the Pacific, GIs often came into contact with other religions and cultures, especially if they fought in ground forces. At times this interaction with others was fleeting, but for cosmopolitan Christian and Jewish GIs, there were opportunities to seek out co-religionists and to attend local churches and synagogues. Some GIs gained new insights into the global nature of their faith by attending a Latin Mass offered by a Filipino Roman Catholic priest in Manila, participating in a seder with French Jews, or attending a service in a small parish of the

Church of England. For Roman Catholics stationed in Italy, there were opportunities to have a papal audience. Some Christians stationed in the Middle East were fortunate enough to arrange special transportation to take part in pilgrimages to the Holy Land. Other GIs, especially those deployed to Africa and Asia, lived and fought in places where Christians were a decided minority. Chaplains and devout Christians in the ranks often made special efforts to come to the aid of missionaries and their followers, especially in the Pacific.

For other GIs contact with other cultures reinforced parochialism and a strong sense of American sectarianism. Many GIs responded to their exposure to "the other" with condescension and a sense of superiority, often reinforced by the poverty many encountered across the globe. Most American GIs sought to neither proselytize nor gain an understanding of those who adhered to Islam, Hinduism, Buddhism, Shintoism, or other faiths. The only significant contact many GIs craved was the companionship of women. GIs stationed abroad were even further from the strictures of parents and community that regulated their religiosity. Some responded by avoiding chapel services and, in the eyes of chaplains, engaging in a range of vices.

Being deployed abroad made the ties to home more tenuous than being stationed at a stateside training camp. Spouses were not permitted overseas, and leave was seldom granted to GIs deployed overseas. Even making a telephone call to a loved one, difficult in the continental United States, was unavailable to those serving abroad. Letters and packages became the primary ways GIs communicated with friends, family, and others at home. Attending religious services while stationed abroad evoked, for many GIs, fond memories of home.

The availability of military chaplains meant GIs who were not so inclined had little reason to seek out foreign congregations or clerics. Sailors serving aboard naval ships out to sea for weeks, even months, were even more dependent on chaplains to help sustain their faith. The navy faced unique challenges brought on by the vast expansion of the fleet, including the fact that many vessels and transport ships, especially smaller ones, lacked chaplains. Even when a chaplain was assigned a vessel, his ability to meet the spiritual needs of all sailors was limited.

Religious Life on the High Seas

Naval vessels, especially larger ones, were self-contained worlds. Many remained at sea for months and their crews lived together in quarters that were, especially for enlisted personnel, claustrophobic. On naval vessels, especially capital ships, a firm demarcation separated officers' country and the crew's quarters. Even in a battle zone, officers ate in an officers' mess, often waited on by African American ship stewards. Although he generally bunked with another officer, a man holding a commissioned rank usually lived in a cabin with a door that afforded some privacy. Enlisted men enjoyed none of these advantages. Their meals, while they compared favorably to food served to infantrymen on the front lines, usually did not match those served to officers. Their sleeping quarters tended to feature bunks piled so high that dozens, even hundreds, served as roommates with no door to close. In the tropics one sailor recalled how the stench of men sweating and trying to sleep could be overpowering.[1]

All branches of the armed services were hierarchical, but the role of a vessel's commander was striking. In their reports, memoirs, and letters home, army chaplains often told about their ability to roam, even in combat zones, counsel men, organize ad hoc services, and visit aid stations. At the same time, a naval chaplain was under more direct supervision, from a vessel commander and his executive officer, than his army counterpart. In combat, chaplains were often assigned battle stations, albeit as noncombatants. A naval vessel lacked a designated chapel, and this required chaplains to request, from the vessel commander, space to hold services.

Most chaplains serving in the navy were reserve officers, and this put them at a disadvantage with the brass ringers—graduates of the U.S. Naval Academy, who held most of the senior ranks in this service, including most senior officers' positions. Chaplain John David Zimmerman, an Episcopal priest, alluded to the skepticism of many vessel commanders toward chaplains. To develop a rapport with them, he mentioned that he had been a bilger of the naval class of 1929. Zimmerman, who joined the reserves in 1933, had failed mathematics his plebe year at the academy. Invariably, his superior officer would recollect a fellow officer who knew him from this class, and Zimmerman found this connection useful in fulfilling his duties. But this tie to Annapolis did little to persuade the captain or executive officer of his first ship, the USS *Miami*, to attend any of the shipboard services he held. Throughout his chaplaincy aboard the *Miami*, Zimmerman noted that attendance at chapel services was lackluster, even on Christmas.[2]

Even if a chaplain was provided a space for services, he often faced difficulties turning it into a sacred space. Roman Catholic naval chaplain John P. Foley remembered that on the first ship he served aboard, a group of white Southerners would heckle him and the sailors attending Sunday Mass. One of his acolytes asked the hecklers to quiet down and earned the retort, "If you were paying attention to the service you wouldn't hear it." This acolyte challenged the hecklers to join him in a round of boxing after the service—he received no takers. But later, aboard ship, a lapsed Catholic opened a valve to flood the portion of the deck where the services were being held. To halt this behavior, Foley confronted the sailor and threatened to see him reported and court martialed.[3]

Chaplain Francis J. McGarry vented to the military ordinariate about the executive officer of the USS *Steamer Bay* refusing to allow him to announce daily Mass over the ship's public address system. McGarry did not accept the justification that too many announcements were made over the ship's intercom. In seeking "suggestions or advice" from the military bishop on how to deal with the situation, McGarry noted there were relatively few Catholics aboard the *Steamer Bay* and public announcements boosted attendance.[4]

Chaplains were among the few members of the crew who could fraternize with both officers and sailors. Some chaplains reveled in the opportunity to dine with the officers, have coffee with chief petty officers, and visit crewmen in their stations. Father John O'Callahan, who later earned the Congressional Medal of Honor when posted on his first warship, the USS *Ranger*, made it a point to eat at least one meal a day in the enlisted mess.[5] Other chaplains were aloof figures who could be reached only in officers' country, which required special permission to enter.[6]

In contrast to their army counterparts, naval chaplains could be tapped by commanders to perform a range of duties, from running the ship's library to serving as the ship's recreation officer. The roles chaplains could play were idiosyncratic. Hansel Tower, a freshly minted naval chaplain assigned to serve a marine outfit, hitched a ride aboard a destroyer in route to Cuba. The ship's commander decided to send the chaplain to assist in the infirmary since there were no medical personnel aboard ship. Tower spent most of the time taking temperatures and dispensing aspirin and fruit juice to men running high fevers. For the GI suffering from what appeared to be acute appendicitis, he saw to it that ice packs were applied to the "throbbing lower right quadrant." To round out his time at sick bay, he assisted in giving an enema to a marine who needed it.[7]

Many chaplains assigned to these auxiliary duties had no problem organizing dances, purchasing food and soft drinks, and ensuring their crews engaged in wholesome activities. Despite Methodists' embrace of prohibitionist sentiments, Chaplain George K. Davies, of this denomination, purchased and distributed alcohol to his men at parties he was charged with organizing. But other Protestant chaplains objected to having to purchase and distribute beer. One naval chaplain called on the Presbyterian leaders to intervene and use their influence to end the practice. In his view, too many chaplains were spending their time searching out beer when their ships were docked because, in the words of one commanding officer, "Beer is more essential to morale than having a chapel."[8]

The chief of chaplains, Robert Workman, a Presbyterian minister, was on a first-name basis with William B. Pugh, the Presbyterian official who passed on this private protest regarding the requirement that chaplains sell beer. Workman urged this chaplain to speak with his commander and make it clear that purchasing alcohol violated his conscience. In the fifteen to twenty cases brought to Workman's attention, commanders almost universally allowed chaplains to avoid this duty. Moreover, Workman noted that sometimes commanders assigned chaplains to supervise the distribution of liquor because they believed it might "deter the men from drinking" if the chaplain issued the liquor ration tickets.[9]

GIs stationed in the United States often had the option of attending a local church if displeased with their options on a base, but a naval vessel on the high seas left no alternatives; where else could one go on the high seas? As a concession to the shortage of chaplains, the military ordinariate directed priests to offer a general service for Protestants if no other chaplain was available to do it. Although they could lead Protestants in singing hymns, recite the Lord's Prayer, read the Epistles and Gospel, and deliver a sermon, the ordinariate mandated that they could not offer Communion or any other sacraments. Many Catholic priests were less than enthusiastic about officiating at these watered-down services. One priest declared that he did not "relish the job" and sought visiting Protestant chaplains to lead services aboard ship so he did not have to undertake this "unpleasant task."[10] The military ordinariate had to caution their priests that they should, when necessary, embrace this task with diligence to avoid casting the church in a bad light. At the same time, the general service could not replace the obligation to attend Mass, and Catholic GIs were instructed to avoid them. Not all sailors understood this sectarian distinction. One priest serving aboard a naval ship reported to the military ordinariate that many of his Catholic GIs avoided attending Mass because of his presiding over a general service for Protestants. Even after he explained to these sailors that attending a Protestant service was no substitute for the Mass, several Catholics refused to return to the fold.[11]

Many smaller vessels did not qualify to have chaplains stationed aboard them. Organized religious life rested upon the initiative of members of the crew. Donald Mackay, a naval chaplain who had only recently graduated from seminary, described how two enlisted men took charge of organizing services when a chaplain was not on board the vessel transporting them to their post in the Philippines. A Methodist, "undoubtedly one of the important vertebra in the backbone of his church back home," along with an "able Catholic boy," organized "informal interdenominational church services" attended by both Protestants and Catholics. They included "hymns, scripture, and prayer," but they eschewed a sermon.[12] For the military ordinariate the lack of the rosary would have brought misgiving, but even more disconcerting would have been bringing together Protestants and Catholics for a worship service that would have resulted in the watering down of Catholic doctrine.

On troops transport, chaplains traveling with their units or as individual replacements were called upon to offer services. Many GIs, especially those heading directly into combat, took the time to attend to their spiritual affairs. One Roman Catholic priest reported to the military ordinariate that while ashore he had relatively low attendance at Mass and few took the opportunity to make confessions, but aboard ship his attendance averaged sixty, with thirty-five taking communion daily. Sailing to North Africa in late 1942, he was especially gratified by the "number of 'long termers' or 'big fish' who have come back to the Sacraments."[13]

There were those who prayed. William Francis Lewellyn described, in an oral history interview, how a fellow officer, a devout Roman Catholic from Kansas City, Missouri, prayed every night while they bunked together on an infantry landing craft journeying across the Pacific. As Lewellyn recounted, "I had the lower bunk, and he had the upper one . . . I'd be laying there, smoking a cigarette, and he'd be kneeling by my bunk, saying his [prayer]."[14] Others took the opportunity to read the Hebrew Bible, New Testament, and other religious works.

Naval vessels, especially troopships, were traditionally masculine environments, reflected by the embrace of such sports as boxing. On board the *Marine Robin*, boxing matches between officers entertained the 5500 GIs heading to Europe in spring 1945. Chaplain Eugene Lipman agreed to fight an inexperienced young lieutenant who proved to be a quick study and gave him a thorough beating in the ring. Lipman was applauded for his efforts and told that the status of the chaplain corps had been greatly increased, but he reflected in his memoir that he had thought of more painless ways to this same end.[15]

Larry Abbott, a Unitarian army chaplain, described the opportunities and limitations of serving on an army transport. In writing to the Unitarian headquarters in Boston, Abbott stressed that "chaplains are not permitted to sell any ism'" and the army expected them to offer a "general service for Cath[olics], Prot[estants], & Jews." At the same time, Abbott stressed the need for more literature from the Unitarian church to distribute to men he encountered and that "while we cannot label ourselves as Unitarians" in offering services for them "I will normally & naturally be exposing the troops on our ships to Unitarian services."[16]

Encountering the New

After experiencing the miserable conditions of a troopship, many soldiers, aviators, and marines welcomed arriving at their final destination. In many cases GIs arrived at an American military base, like their counterparts at home, and chaplains attempted to take care of virtually all the needs of GIs stationed overseas. In terms of religion American GIs at any base of significant size had access to chaplains and usually at least a crude chapel. In isolated locations, especially in the Pacific, religious services were among the few diversions available on a regular basis. For troops on the battle line, access to chaplains and chapels remained problematic, but in the rear, men and women seeking religious succor could often find it.

Veterans offered varied responses when answering the question, "How and to what extent were religious convictions expressed in your unit?" in a postwar "Army Service Experiences Questionnaire" distributed by the U.S. Army Military History Institute. A staff sergeant who served with the 89th Division had a "feeling" that "all the men were Religious."[17] One army captain who served with GIs reported that while most in his unit were reserved about expressing their religious convictions, "most seemed to become better believers." He reported that church attendance was high during the war.[18] Another junior officer from the same division reported that he thought religious convictions were seldom expressed except by chaplains.[19] A noncommissioned officer from this division echoed this sentiment: "We didn't have time to think much about religion."[20]

In isolated locations, soldiers often had limited access to clergy. Chaplains and the military often went to great lengths to try to compensate, especially for those stationed in isolated atolls and scattered bases in the China-Burma-India theater. Dario Antonucci, a Roman Catholic soldier, remembered only occasionally having the opportunity to attend Mass while serving in an isolated communications unit in Burma. Occasionally, the army airlifted him to a larger base for this opportunity, but a chaplain regularly visited his small unit and gave a general service for all soldiers stationed with him. As Antonucci noted, the chaplains gave the same basic message, centered on the goodness of God, and often gave no hint of their sectarian affiliations. Antonucci recalled how he discovered that one of these itinerant chaplains was, in fact, a rabbi: "And it was almost a year later, and I got close to this chaplain, I think he was a captain, he was an elder man, and I says, 'Father that's a funny cross you have on your lapel.' And he says, 'Son, that's not a cross, that's a Star of David . . . I'm a rabbi.'"[21]

Accommodating Jewish soldiers often proved more difficult, especially if they served in units without enough Jews to make a minyan (the ten-man prayer quorum). Many Protestant and Catholic chaplains even took it upon themselves to preside over Jewish services. One Christian Scientist chaplain, writing home to his wife while deployed to England, recorded how much he "enjoyed and profited" from holding his first Jewish service, "conducting it throughout, and preaching from a text in the Old Testament." When he was invited back, he wrote that he would lead these services the following week.[22] Samuel Frankel, who served with the U.S. Navy in the Pacific, recalled in an oral history being the only Jewish GI in his naval unit, based on an island outpost. His commanding officer still made sure he was able to attend Yom Kippur services. Frankel's commander made special arrangements to transport him to a nearby marine air group base, where a Protestant chaplain led services for him and other Jewish GIs in Hebrew. Frankel recounted an incident that highlights efforts to serve all GIs:

> We went into a Quonset hut, and there was . . . a chaplain there, and there were maybe twenty or thirty men sitting down. It was hot as hell, but, I'll never forget it, because he had a pulpit, and in the front of the pulpit was a cross, and one of the officers, at that time, went up to him and said, "Excuse me, sir, but, maybe some of the men might take offense at this. Would you mind, you know, removing that?" and he looked at me, he said, "Oh, my God, please, excuse me. Men, I apologize. I'm sorry. Please, excuse me," and . . . he picked up the pulpit, and turned it 180 degrees, and there was a Star of David. [laughter] Isn't that a riot? And then, he conducted the service in Hebrew as good as any rabbi.[23]

William E. Capron, a Roman Catholic priest serving as an army chaplain, wrote to Chief of Chaplains William Arnold (also a Catholic priest), expressing satisfaction at not only ministering to Catholics but also presiding over Friday night services for Jewish troops. In reply, Arnold admonished this enthusiastic priest that while Capron could encourage the holding of Jewish services, and even speak at them to offer moral instruction, he threatened his clerical standing within the Roman Catholic Church if he continued to lead Jewish services as an acting rabbi.[24]

Some chaplains actively sought converts and experienced instances of success. Many Christian chaplains recorded in official reports and in private correspondence their success in bringing men to Christ. But efforts to evangelize were complicated by several factors, beginning with the rejection of the message by those whom a chaplain sought to win over to his faith. In the Army Service Experience Questionnaire, Daniel M. Ogden recalled that many in his unit were served by a fundamentalist Baptist preacher who was "washed in the blood of the lamb," so they decided to forgo his services. But this minister's strong positions on faith made men in his unit "think through their own positions." In Ogden's case it would turn him in the direction of Unitarianism after the war.[25]

The question of conversion remained a complicated one. Judaism had traditionally avoided proselytizing in the modern era, and the war only reinforced this inhibition. The Responsa committee/the JWB prohibited chaplains from sanctioning conversions during the war. Yet some Christian denominations had a strong ethos to seek converts. In the case of Southern Baptists, the question of conversion, when deployed abroad, would be a complex one. Under Baptist tradition the baptism of an individual must be sanctioned by a Baptist congregation, and for some chaplains this created a barrier. L. C. Lemons, a naval chaplain serving in the Pacific, solved this problem by forming a "Battalion Baptist Church."[26]

Not all GIs welcomed the ecumenical services they often found themselves attending, and many Protestants found the general Protestant services unfulfilling. In a letter to his aunt, Kenneth Vance appreciated the opportunity, while overseas, to attend a Lutheran service and take communion. In his March 1944 letter, he stated that he had not had an opportunity to attend services in his own denomination since the previous August. After the war ended, while awaiting return to the States, he wrote his sister and brother-in-law of a less than satisfactory experience at a service "with a raving minister." [27]

One of the sources of tensions between Roman Catholic and Protestant chaplains stemmed from efforts to lead members of their flock astray in an underhanded way. A Catholic chaplain serving with the 1112th Engineers Combat Group protested to the military ordinariate about Protestant chaplains in his unit who held services just before the start of movies being shown to troops for recreation. This chaplain protested that men who wanted to get a seat for the film knew to come early, and that added to the injustice visited upon observant Roman Catholics. He was pleased many of his men skipped the motion picture instead of having to "sit in on the services." [28]

There were other challenges as well. Accommodating the dietary restrictions of GIs was even more difficult once they were posted overseas. Jews were not the only GIs confronting the tension between the military's mess practices and the tenets of faith. On one Good Friday in the Philippines in 1945, a Protestant GI, Carl Becker, recalled the dilemma that many of his Catholic friends faced at the unexpected delivery of pork chops from a supply ship. Unfortunately, the pork chops had to be cooked immediately since the unit lacked any refrigeration to store them safely. Becker described the various lines individuals drew in observing the tenets of their faith; many of the Roman Catholics refused to eat the pork chops on this Good Friday, even though many of them had, when staging in Oahu, eaten pork or beef on days it was prohibited, despite church teachings. As Catholics made up half his battery, and they mostly adhered to Church injunctions, that Good Friday became a feast for Protestants. Becker recalled eating nine chops that day and recorded in his memoir that "agape and angry, my Catholic friends saw it all. I praised their church for its loyal communicants. Luther for his break with Rome." [29]

Even with hundreds of Roman Catholic priests in the service, there were significant pockets of troops that were unable to regularly attend Mass. In some cases the military ordinariate enlisted the assistance of Roman Catholic bishops in other parts of the world to tend to the spiritual needs of GIs. In other cases devout

Catholic GIs took on the task of organizing services for the saying of the rosary.

For Jews the absence of rabbis did not preclude holding religious services, although a minyan, a gathering of ten Jewish men, was necessary to say the complete liturgy for a service. But finding Jews capable of leading services could be difficult, especially if they were from a Reform tradition and had only acquired a smattering of Hebrew. Alfred V. Sloan, who served with the Eighth Air Force, remembered the efforts of a rabbi to persuade a group of Jews on his air base to conduct weekly services when he was unavailable. In his oral history, Sloan recounted how a small group rotated, taking turns reciting the prayers for the Friday night service. Concerned the Hebrew he had learned for his bar mitzvah was lost, Sloan described how the rabbi handled these fears and, at one point, told him if he could not say the prayers in Hebrew, say them in English since he was confident that the Lord understands this language. In terms of the minyan, he declared that two men were acceptable. As Sloan reflected, "He was clearly a Reform rabbi."[30]

The war could be a profoundly isolating experience for GIs far from home and residing in a profane world marked by fear, dirt, and death. One Catholic chaplain, Rev. Charles W. Kolek, deployed to Palmyra Island, lamented that, as a Benedictine, the community way of life had "become the Flesh and blood of me." He observed that the nearest fellow priest was beyond seven hundred miles away and he was unlikely to meet him for at least six months. For Kolek the absence of another priest not only generated a lonesome quality but also meant no one could hear his confession or administer the sacrament of last rites if he was gravely ill or wounded. Kolek did feel that he had made a difference at his naval air station. Censors informed him that men writing home often expressed their appreciation of having a chaplain deployed among them. Men told Kolek that his presence helped order the week and made the distinction between Sunday and the rest of the week. He was also told that profanity had decreased over 75 percent since his arrival.[31]

Many chaplains took advantage of the freedom offered by the absence of congregations and church superiors to drink, smoke, and take part in other vices. One young army officer wrote to his wife and described the chaplain who had recently conducted a service for his unit. The chaplain struck him as a "nice fellow" who would "take a drink with [the] boys and smokes quite regularly." Of course, this would change once he left the army. "I told him that he'd have to cut that stuff out when we went back to the States and he said, I wasn't kidding."[32] In his memoir, Albert Engel, a U.S. Army officer during the war, recalled his fondness for the married Baptist minister who served his unit. This retired judge recalled that he and this chaplain would often bike in rural England, frequently stopping at a pub for a refresher. This Baptist minister often ran afoul of his superiors because he "liked his liquor" and was not "immune to good looking women."[33]

This Baptist chaplain represented a pattern of interaction with individuals from different cultures that was typical of most soldier GIs who served overseas. American ground troops fought in the homelands of others and had to interact with allies and enemies. For many GIs their knowledge of the world was fragmentary and largely formed from an occasional article they had read in *National Geographic,* viewing motion pictures set in exotic locations filmed on the back lots of Hollywood, or the stories told by missionaries that might appear in denominational publications and news accounts. To close this gap, the military developed small pamphlets about the various nations that would host American troops. Overall these guides, though sometimes condescending and simplistic, sought to convey to GIs the need to respect local cultures, if for no other reason than to prevent bodily harm. Many guides tried to explain the importance and role of religion in other cultures. One of the lengthier discussions about religion can be found in a pamphlet for troops headed to Iraq. The guide gave an overview of the basic beliefs held by Muslims, noting that Islam centered on the belief in one God, Allah, and that Mohammed was his prophet. GIs were discouraged from visiting mosques in this country since outsiders were unwelcome. The pamphlet also cautioned, out of respect, against watching anyone praying or "preaching." Overall, the guide encouraged GIs to stay away from discussion of religion and politics.[34]

GIs' encounters with other cultures defy easy categorization.

Deployment overseas afforded the opportunity for many Protestants and Roman Catholics to make pilgrimages to the Holy Land. One Catholic chaplain said the nurses in his hospital unit stationed in Palestine "have taken to reading the Bible, especially the New Testament, as they find it the best guide to the Holy Land" and had taken regular tours of the shrines and holy spots.[35] A GI recalled that the priest in his unit, after the liberation of Paris, took a few men from his unit and said Mass at Notre Dame in Paris.[36] After the liberation of Rome thousands of Roman Catholic GIs and chaplains, often joined by their Protestant and Jewish comrades, took advantage of the opportunity to take part in a papal audience. Roman Catholic chaplains often recorded in their correspondence the privilege of meeting with the Holy Father and being able to say Mass in the Vatican. While on occupation duty in Germany with the army, Henry Francis Buinicky gushed, in a letter home to his wife, after learning from his commander that he would be able to make a pilgrimage to Lourdes. Buinicky, who had studied for the priesthood before withdrawing from seminary in order to marry, welcomed the opportunity of several days of prayer and meditation at Lourdes and to visit the grotto there. As he declared to his wife, Priscilla, "Our Mother appeared there and the thousands of miraculous cures wrought at the grotto show Her love."[37]

The effects of these experiences on GIs was mixed. Their experiences abroad could reinforce prejudices and enable them to gain new understanding of other faiths. James Parton, an army staff officer and Protestant, had the opportunity to attend a papal Mass and sent his family the picture of Pius XII distributed to those who attended. The note Parton wrote on the back of the picture reflects a condescending attitude toward the devout and the papacy: "This is what they hand you when you go see the Pope. I went no further than the door for I saw that all were kneeling and I won't genuflect to any mackerel snatcher, even the top one!"[38] While the papal audience had left Parton unimpressed, earlier in the year he had gained a whole new perspective on Islam. In a letter to his aunt, Parton described in detail his visit to the Sofia Mosque in Istanbul. He was stunned by the aesthetic beauty of the mosque, which he found much more striking than any church he had ever visited.

11. Interior of a mosque in North Africa. Roland E. Murphy Collection, Institute on World War II and the Human Experience.

(He noted that, as result of his pagan upbringing, he had visited very few.) He declared that this visit had given him an "enhanced concept of the dignity" of Muslims and their faith.[39]

Americans in Europe encountered cultures that were heavily Christian, often with significant Jewish communities. The universalism of Latin in the Roman Catholic Mass and the use of Hebrew in synagogues served to further bridge the divide. In Great Britain, where over a million Americans were stationed, sometimes for several years, the absence of a language barrier increased interaction between the GIS and the British. Many GIS attended religious services at British churches or synagogues, drank at neighborhood pubs, visited historic sites, and took in local movies. Chaplain Howard M. Wilson was stationed at an air base in England and organized several tours for GIS to visit nearby historic churches and attend services in them. Besides chaperoning men on these tours, he undertook personal sightseeing trips throughout England, which included worshiping in different churches, visiting historic sites and museums, and regularly attending concerts.[40]

The Missionary Impulse

A missionary impulse did exist among some chaplains and GIs stationed abroad. Many serving in the Pacific sought out opportunities to visit missionaries and their congregations. Chaplain Mark Warner wrote his commanding officer seeking to establish a formal relationship with the Episcopal bishop in New Guinea. One WAC described how her attitude toward the indigenous peoples of New Guinea had changed after a visit to a "real native village." Far from "being stupid, dull-witted savages, they are alert, clever, intelligent, peace loving citizens." She noted in a letter to her parents that the "largest and finest building" in their village was the church.[41]

American chaplains and GIs were not the only ones to proselytize. In one case the chief of chaplains summarized with pride, in a circular letter to all chaplains, that the *New York Times* had reported the experiences of seven fliers shot down who managed to make it to an unnamed South Pacific Island. They encountered "natives made Christians by American missionaries." When meeting the aviators, the natives handed them a Bible and hid them from the Japanese for eighty-seven days, until they could escape on a raft. The aviators reported that each night they took turns reading the Bible handed to them and the "natives sang songs which we know." In the words of one aviator, "that and our experiences made us Christians."[42]

In some places, shared religious beliefs served to bridge the cultural and racial divide between white GIs and indigenous populations. On several islands in the Pacific, indigenous peoples collaborated with GIs to build chapels. For instance on Banika, in the Russell Islands, not only did the local population provide labor for the chapel, but they joined U.S. Marines stationed there at the dedication service for Sugana Tareie (House of Worship). During the service the "native choir" performed two anthems, and an observer noted the excellent "training in Christianity from the Anglican Church mission."[43]

There did exist a significant missionary impulse, often mixed with humanitarianism. Chaplains had the authority, and often the inclination, to engage in humanitarian projects that went beyond passing out candy to children. But not all of these efforts were welcome or appreciated. For example, one Catholic chaplain complained bitterly of the missionary work of Protestant chaplains in Italy who sought to lure Italians to their services since they could not get enough GIs to attend them. Equally disturbing to this priest was the American Bible Society using these chaplains to distribute their literature and Bible. Denouncing this "evil work" of spreading "error," he bemoaned the fact that, as he saw it, these Protestants hid behind the "platitude" of "religious freedom."[44]

Not all GIs or chaplains wanted to win converts; for many, deployment abroad entailed grappling with questions of faith and great introspection. One Baptist chaplain, who had initially come into the army by serving as a line officer, recalled his disillusionment with the apathy toward religion of many of the American GIs in his unit while he was stationed in India. He found a visit with one Hindu Royal Air Force pilot highly rewarding and expressed admiration for the pilot's "grasp of the spiritual."[45]

For some the experience of interacting with a foreign culture fostered sentiments that reinforced American patriotism and ethnocentrism. The climate, geography, and absence of the familiar often alienated GIs. The poverty that engulfed other societies staggered many GIs and left them numb. As one Catholic priest serving in New Guinea declared, in a letter to the military ordinariate, these islands were not fit for white men and he found the people and environment entirely alien.[46] The sense of alienation from people from other cultures was not limited to those GIs who found themselves stationed in what would later be termed "Third World countries." While many Catholic chaplains relished the opportunity to visit Rome and take part in papal audiences, and even say Mass at the Vatican, there were critical sentiments toward Italians. In a report to Bishop O'Hara, one chaplain described Naples as a cesspool of venereal disease and said more could be done by the church and military authorities to address this rampant immorality. He was also highly critical of the amount of begging that occurred at Italian churches, noting that this practice discouraged many GIs from attending local services. This priest looked equally askance at the begging by individuals wearing religious habits."[47]

GIs did seek out "the other," especially for companionship and, to the dismay of many chaplains, for sexual relations. GIS were rich in dollars and cigarettes, both of which went a long way toward securing dates or paying for prostitutes. Even further removed from the strictures of home, GIS could be quite blunt in soliciting local women for sex. Frank Dietrich—a soldier serving in the Philippines who had been a social worker before the war—lashed out, in a letter to his wife, at Americans' appalling "disregard and disrespect" for the code of morality and the taboos of the Filipinos, who had recently been liberated from the Japanese. GIS often solicited every girl on the street, asking if she was a "pom pom," and deemed Filipinos to be promiscuous given their "different" or "primitive" culture.[48]

Dietrich became progressively disillusioned with the conduct GIS displayed abroad and this behavior simply reinforced his religious skepticism, which had developed even before the war. While his brother was a religiously motivated conscientious objector, Dietrich questioned both the possibility of a personal God and the value of prayer. In a letter written shortly after V-J Day, Dietrich told his wife that, in his search for a table and bright light for writing, he had gone to the chaplain's office and found himself in the midst of a heated argument by "two religious fanatics." He participated in the argument by dismissing Christianity as a "complete and total failure" and noted after he left the argument "one of the boys is explaining the Presbyterian dogma of Predestination." A few weeks later Dietrich attended a chapel service with a friend and expressed to his spouse his disdain for the message offered by the army chaplain—the "vague and undefined concepts and dogma of the church that have repeatedly frustrated Christianity." However, he did express some hope in the values offered by such liberal religious leaders as "Stipek, Niemoller, Fosdick, Rabbi Freehof, . . . and Dr. Clausen."[49]

The quest for female companionship did not always mean that men automatically turned to prostitutes. Some GIS did fall in love with women they met in foreign countries. Aviators and their ground crews in England, often stationed near English towns and villages, had ample opportunities to seek out companions. Deployment overseas often fostered an increase in marriages, especially when a unit was stationed in one place for an extended period.

Chaplains did more than preside over weddings; they were also often tasked by the commanders with investigating the character of a woman a GI sought to marry.[50]

Many GIs, especially if out of harm's way, found much they enjoyed about their overseas deployment. But even in the best of circumstances, GIs yearned for home, and nostalgia permeated the ranks. Religious services often filled the void. Many chaplains recognized that chapel attendance soared among GIs at Christmas, Passover, and Mother's Day. Mother's Day, an invented tradition started in the early 1900s, would become a major holiday in the liturgical calendar for chapel services. Future army chaplains attending chaplain school were instructed to make a special effort to commemorate the day. Many took this admonition to heart and did so, emphasizing Mother's Day with appropriate hymns, sermons, and prayers. The importance of marking Mother's Day is clear; the army and chaplains wanted to remind GIs of their ties to hearth and home and demarcate gender lines. Men fought to protect the women who had nurtured them: mothers. Mother's Day, along with such civic holidays as Memorial Day, could be emphasized by chaplains of all faiths.

For Christian GIs Christmas was among the most important religious holidays on the liturgical calendar. Most GIs would note the holiday in their memoirs or letters home, whether they were informing parents of services attended or expressing gratitude for presents received. Christmas sparked a yearning for home that would be encapsulated by Irving Berlin's popular score, written during the war, "I'm Dreaming of a White Christmas." The armed services made major efforts to foster continued ties between the home front and those deployed overseas, devoting substantial resources to ensuring GIs received Christmas cards and gift packages. Because of shipping requirements, many civilians had to mail Christmas packages months before the actual holiday. Florence Lillibridge, in August 1943, asked her spouse, serving with the marines in the Pacific, what he would like for Christmas.[51]

Army chaplain Ed Bradley, writing to the military ordinariate shortly after his arrival in New Guinea in late 1944, noted both pathetic and interesting qualities of Christmas. Bradley made clear that he and his men yearned for home and missed the markers of

12. Easter Mass in New Guinea, 1943. Gordon D. McCraw Collection, Institute on World War II and the Human Experience.

the holiday. "There was no snow, no threat of snow, not even the remote possibility of snow. No Christmas trees with their tinsels and lights. Nothing in nature to help. Just a blasting sun in the day and a tropical downpour in the evening." GIs attended the Christmas Eve Mass not under the "vaulted ceiling of their parish" but in a corrugated metal building. What remained of Christmas? Bradley described how important the Christmas Mass was for the GIs since it brought into focus the "Holy Sacrifice" that is the "very soul of Christmas." Attending Mass offered solace and "for a short time the men forgot they were in New Guinea, far from home, and were transported back, through the familiar ritual of Christmas Mass, to home and loved ones."[52]

Letters were the main way those serving overseas stayed in contact with the home front. By the same token families clamored for letters from their kin in uniform. To foster attendance at services, chaplains wrote brief letters to the parents of GIs informing them of their recent presence at services they had conducted. Even though most chaplains relied on form letters, parents often sent gushing letters in reply, expressing how much they appreciated hearing from the chaplains and how pleased they were to learn about the religious life of their sons and daughters. Hazel Peters could not have been more pleased to have received a letter from a Jewish chaplain indicating that her son, with the Second Marine Division, "was in good spirits and good health" and attended his services. This Arizona mother described how Chaplain Samuel Sandmel's letter helped a "sad h[e]art so much. It made me happy to know some one knew and appreciated my son." It did not matter that her family were Protestants. Hazel declared, "We love and appreciate knowing All Good People who are working & helping for the Right[,] we are all Free to worship in our way[,] and we should all love one another and we have tried to teach Everett just that."[53]

For other men, spouses sustained them during the conflict, and many kept up an avid correspondence. George Lucas, a naval officer stationed aboard a smaller vessel, wrote his wife frequently about religion and his admiration for the fervent faith of one seaman. In one letter he declared he had not yet "found my God or faith in the Supreme Being" but recognized the importance of having something to believe in to offer "a good anchorage." In a heartfelt plea, Lucas declared his love for his wife, Gretchen, beseeching her to be "my faith."[54]

The army and navy ran a sophisticated public relations effort to promote the chaplaincy and its efforts to meet the religious needs of GIS. A steady stream of press releases and photographs were disseminated to newspaper and radio outlets. The army chief of chaplains supplemented these efforts with a radio program, "Chaplain Jim," that aired on the NBC Blue Network."[55] The army chief of chaplains even sent around a traveling exhibit to department stores to highlight the work of chaplaincy. The output was prodigious, and many press releases evolved into published articles. For example, the navy's chaplain division sent, between August 1943 and the end of the year, over 1669 press releases and produced 492 stories. Press releases were often crafted for specific audiences. For instance, a press release, "Lutheran Chaplain in Aleutians Commemorates Reformation Sunday," was sent to the *Lutheran, Lutheran Men, Northwestern Lutheran, Lutheran Witness,* and *Lutheran Herald.*[56] The U.S. Navy, in one release, implicitly acknowledged that not all sailors had access to a chaplain. A release titled "Seaman Conducts Religious Services Aboard Freighter" described how "Willard E. Thomas, Seaman First Class regularly organized services for the naval gun crew serving aboard a merchant ship." The release quoted one seaman: "Bill led the hymn, then read some Scripture and gave us a simple explanation of it."[57]

These efforts were supplemented by church organizations, with Roman Catholics earning a reputation for being particularly adept in sending a positive message. The General Commission of Army and Navy Chaplains developed a public relations program, in part to disseminate positive news stories about the role of Protestant chaplains. Even with censorship and systematic efforts to shape public opinion through the military public relations efforts and the civilian Office of War Information, certain unfavorable news still made it to America. After newspaper reports of an American soldier having died upon the gallows in London, for murder, under British law, cases in the press of illegitimate children by American soldiers, and more than a hundred convictions of soldiers participating in the black market on the Continent, one chaplain drafted a release about his AAF station, "Somewhere in England," to offer more positive news. He described how each week about 20 percent of men on this base "worshipped God" and this helped them perform their duties more effectively and "associate with the British people on a normal basis." This press release described how these regular worshipers purchased gifts for more than nine hundred needy and orphaned children.[58]

Information was rationed in other ways as well. GIs had their mail censored, and the same applied to reporters overseas. This censorship served to magnify the role of officially sanctioned images offered by the American military. In writing about the religious lives of World War II GIs, it is important not to be seduced by the often overly positive portrayals offered by the government and religious organizations as part of their public relations efforts. On the surface military and religious leaders stressed the strong ecumenical bonds in the chaplaincy and the tremendous cooperation among Roman Catholics, Protestants and Jews. But private correspondence reflected significant sectarian discord, and both

Protestants and Roman Catholics expressed fears the other religion was being granted undue favoritism.

Censorship encouraged self-censorship, as GIs remained acutely aware that a commander or a designate would read his correspondence. Sometimes chaplains were even assigned the duty of unit censor. One can only wonder how this influenced what GIs said in their letters home. Did self-censorship discourage GIs from saying more about their spiritual lives? Could they have said little about their faith, knowing an officer with low regard for organized religion might mock it? In a society that overwhelmingly affirmed belief in God, could an agnostic or atheist have been uncomfortable revealing his inner beliefs?

If there is one positive aspect of the long deployments overseas and the relative isolation of many GIs, it is the fact that it fostered unit cohesion. Men serving together for months, and even years, in foreign posts were often drawn together by a shared identity and a comradeship that crossed religious, ethnic, and class lines. These ties among GIs would prove to be among their positive memories of wartime. For units sent into combat, the fostering of unit cohesion proved an important ingredient for survival on the battlefield.

FIVE

Religion and the Ethical Conduct of War

T wo years after World War II ended, the journalist turned military historian S. L. A. Marshall claimed, in *Men Against Fire*,
that not more than 15 percent of infantrymen regularly fired
their weapons in battle. He argued that one contributing factor to
this pattern stemmed from societal beliefs that condemned killing as morally wrong.[1] Marshall's assertion has been challenged
by historians, and many infantrymen have bristled at his claims
that men in this branch did not fight in battle.[2] Marshall's statement that religious and cultural inhibitions made American GIs
reluctant killers begs for closer analysis. This chapter presents
substantial evidence that many GIs offered no religious or ethical
objections to killing the enemy.

A naval officer heading overseas on a U.S. troopship for deployment to the Pacific kept a log with examples of the letters he censored, which gives important insights into the state of mind of
many GIs. Ardath W. Burkshad found that most GIs expressed
no "moral or religious scruples about their big 'aim'; to get a Jap."
In one letter, an army officer writing to a friend based stateside
described a conversation he had with a combat-hardened veteran
officer who had fought in Kwajalein. He wrote with satisfaction
that this "Lieutenant from Georgia" had gotten "three of the yellow bastards himself." With implicit approval he implied that this
officer had killed two prisoners in cold blood, noting "he had to
go on about his work so he shot two and turned one over to H.Q."[3]

Before the United States entered the war, President Franklin D.
Roosevelt publicly criticized the Nazis for their attacks on civilians and their destruction of sacred religious sites. Even after the

United States entered the war, FDR continued to assert to Pius XII that the United States remained on a higher moral ground than the Axis powers. But over the course of the war, American forces took actions they had once condemned, including destroying sacred religious sites, even those dear to Christianity, if military necessity required it. Although the army air force engaged in strategic bombing, seeking to destroy factories, military installations, transportation infrastructure, and oil refineries, the United States offered no objection to British area bombing that deliberately targeted civilian homes. Most GIs, including military chaplains, were untroubled by an air campaign that killed enemy civilians. Even among religious leaders at home, only a small minority questioned the slide to killing large numbers of civilians in the aerial campaign that escalated, in 1945, to leveling whole Japanese cities by conventional bombing and, at the end, with atomic weapons.

Despite the escalation of violence, which included targeting civilians in the air campaign, there were times when humanitarian sentiments prevailed. Overall, the United States adhered to the Geneva Convention in its treatment of prisoners of war, although a gray zone existed on the battlefield where GIs refused to take captives, especially in the Pacific. The United States observed the interwar treaty prohibition against the use of poison gas on the battlefield, but the army chief of staff contemplated using it in a projected land invasion of Japan. Although some chaplains wanted to bear arms, the U.S. Army chief of chaplains insisted that clerics abstain from engaging in combat and adhere to long-standing customary and legal prohibitions against bearing arms. Many religious observants, even chaplains, denied the humanity of the enemy, especially if they were of a different race.

The Morality of the Air War

Questions of morality and religion shifted over the course of the war with regard to use of air power. Prior to the attack at Pearl Harbor, the Roosevelt administration had condemned the Japanese bombing of civilians in China as immoral. Soon after Germany invaded Poland, FDR, in declaring neutrality, also called on belligerents to not bomb innocent civilians.[4] In his bill of indictment against the Axis powers offered in 1940 and 1941, Roosevelt stressed the barbaric behavior of the enemy, including their indiscriminate attacks on civilians. After the United States entered the war, the Roosevelt administration and the armed forces declared that America took the high moral ground in waging war against an implacable enemy. When Allied forces invaded Italy in 1943, FDR said, in a letter to Pius XII, "there is no need for me to reaffirm that respect for religious belief and for the free exercise of religious worship is fundamental to our ideas. Churches and religious institutions will, to the extent that it is within our power, be spared the devastations of war during the struggle ahead."[5] In a public statement issued on March 14, 1944, FDR blasted the decision by the Germans to use the "Holy City of Rome" as a military center. For Roosevelt this was part and parcel of the well-known "Nazi record on religion." He said, "Both at home and abroad, Hitler and his followers have waged a ruthless war against the churches of all faiths." The American president also said, "We on our side have made freedom of religion one of the principles for which we are fighting this war. We have tried scrupulously—often at considerable sacrifice to spare religious and cultural monuments, and we shall continue to do so."[6]

FDR's claims were not empty rhetoric; during the Italian campaign, the Allied forces took care to avoid bombing Vatican City and other sites under the control of the Holy See. The United States armed forces consulted with the American Council of Learned Societies and distributed maps of Italy indicating sites of religious and cultural importance that should be spared if at all possible.[7] In December 1943 Gen. Dwight Eisenhower, commander of the North African theater, issued a directive that stressed the importance of safeguarding sites of religious and cultural importance. Eisenhower mandated that saving the lives of American GIs would take precedence over the preservation of buildings of religious and cultural significance, but he encouraged his subordinates to seek alternatives and avoid reckless actions that would destroy the patrimony of Western Civilization.[8] The Roosevelt administration was quite sensitive to the diplomatic pressure from Pius XII to spare Rome, especially the independent city-state of Vatican City. Roosevelt closely followed any military decisions regarding the bombing of Rome, and his top-secret map room files bulged with messages that indicated a reluctance by him and senior commanders to bomb the holy city.[9]

Despite these inhibitions Roosevelt and Allied leaders refused to declare Rome an open city and conducted several raids against it. Commanders were aware of the opposition of Pius XII to bombing, and American aircrews were given detailed instructions to avoid hitting the Vatican and other sites of religious and cultural importance. Gen. James Doolittle offered Roman Catholic aviators the opportunity to avoid taking part in the raid, but none asked to be excused on religious grounds. Nor did Roman Catholic chaplains under Doolittle's command openly object.[10] Although Vatican City did not suffer major damage in these raids, papal territories in other parts of Italy were damaged, and refugees taking shelter at the summer palace were killed.[11] Given the state of aviation and targeting technology during World War II, Allied officials accepted collateral damage as an inevitable part of modern war.

In February 1944 military necessity overrode inhibitions about bombing the abbey of Monte Cassino, Italy, a site of unquestioned religious and cultural significance. Historians differ as to whether the bombing of Monte Cassino was even militarily necessary and point to the fact that Germans actually did not occupy the grounds until Allied bombers destroyed it. But the senior Allied leaders in Italy perceived that they had no other choice, and the evidence available at the time pointed to German use of the structure, which sat on a mountaintop looming over Allied lines. Here again religious objections did not prevent Roman Catholic pilots and aircrews from taking part in the raid that destroyed the abbey. For soldiers facing artillery fire coming off the mountain on which Monte Cassino sat, the destruction of this centuries-old abbey was welcome as being necessary to save their lives.[12] Even several Catholic chaplains, attached to army units seeking to breach the Gothic Line, accepted the demands of military necessity and voiced no objections to the decision to destroy this sacred site.[13]

The decisions to bomb Rome and Monte Cassino were not taken lightly. In contrast, in the struggle against Japan, Americans were more willing to consider targeting non-Christian religious structures. Even Reverend Robert Spencer Steward, a former missionary born in Japan and the son of Methodist missionaries, endorsed bombing Japanese religious sites. Prior to Pearl Harbor, Steward had held several positions with the Methodist Church of Japan before returning to the United States, where he rose to the rank of colonel as an intelligence officer. In this role Steward penned a memorandum, in early 1942, proposing an aerial attack on the Ise Grand Shrine, dedicated to the sun goddess. In Shinto belief this shrine protected Japan from foreign invasion. Stewart believed a successful attack on this religious site would undermine Japanese support for the war effort. Stewart argued for restrictions in the bombing campaign, not for moral reasons but for pragmatic reasons. Even while advocating destroying this religious structure, Steward cautioned against bombing the Imperial Palace or trying to kill the emperor. In his view, rather than demoralizing the Japanese public, it would enflame them in much the same way as the attack on Pearl Harbor had united Americans.[14]

There were religious leaders at home who publicly called for the destruction, by American air power, of state Shinto shrines in Japan to bring a speedy end to the war. In September 1943 the fundamentalist American Council of Christian Churches, led by Carl McIntire, sent a telegram to FDR urging him to order the bombing of the Yasukuni Shrine, the "supposed dwelling of the spirits of the deified war dead," and the Shrine at Ise, where the "Sun Goddess who has commissioned Japan to conquer the world" dwells. This fundamentalist group argued that destroying these sites would dispel the notion, among the Japanese, of "the protective power of the divine emperor and his ancestors."[15]

The willingness of a former missionary and some religious leaders to bomb shrines denied the protections accorded to religious sites, under international law, to non-Western religious sites. It represented rejection of religious pluralism by denying legitimacy to non-Christian faiths. Not all American leaders were as cavalier about Japanese religion and culture. In 1945 Secretary of War Henry L. Stimson ensured that Kyoto was taken off the target list for the atomic bombs because of the cultural importance of this city, which contained hundreds of Buddhist temples.

Given the postwar controversies surrounding the decision to engage in strategic bombing campaigns that caused significant casualties and the even greater death toll from British area bombing, remarkably few dissented publicly during the war. Some Roman Catholics, those who embraced the "just war" tradition and the righteousness of America's entry into World War II, condemned the killing of civilians. A prominent group of pacifists voiced their objections and managed to garner a brief flurry of public attention. In 1944 the Fellowship of Reconciliation issued an American edition of Vera Britain's "Massacre by Bombing" pamphlet, which offered a searing attack of the British and American aerial campaigns. Twenty-seven American Protestant leaders, including such pacifist stalwarts as Henry Fosdick, John Haynes Holmes, and Oswald Villard, signed a preface endorsing Britain's indictment of Allied bombing.[16] Yet when the *New York Times* reported the publication of this pamphlet in a front-page story, on March 6, 1944, it produced a firestorm of criticism. Scores of letters poured in, and most defended the deliberate targeting of German civilians as proper punishment for their actions. As one rabbi wrote in a letter to the editor, "The Germans must reap the fruits of their own wicked deeds." In the view of fundamentalist and evangelical leaders, military leaders had a moral right to use any weapon at their disposal to win the war. Carl McIntire lambasted liberal Protestants for their lack of patriotism and expressed no misgivings about the bombing campaign. McIntire bluntly declared, "God has given us the weapons, let us use them."[17]

Inhibitions about bombing civilians eroded over the course of the war. Privately, FDR and his senior air force leaders did not completely rule out targeting civilians, and they offered broad discretion to air force commanders in Europe and the Pacific on how to execute the air war. During the interwar years, the army air force had developed the doctrine of strategic bombing. It now did so throughout much of the air campaign in Europe but largely confined itself to bombing submarine pens, defense factories, oil facilities, and transportation networks. But while the army air force focused on strategic targets and avoided the area bombing of cities, they raised no objections to the British waging an area campaign that ultimately resulted in high civilian casualties. Flying at night the Royal Air Force Bomber Command used fire raids to destroy whole German cities with the aim of crushing enemy morale. Although scholars disagree about the intentions of army air force leadership in World War II, it is clear that even when they adhered to strategic bombing, they were willing to accept a high degree of collateral damage. This resulted in the deaths of a substantial number of civilians in occupied Europe.[18] In the final year of the war, Curtis Lemay, as commander of the Far East army air force, deliberately abandoned strategic bombing in favor of area bombing of Japanese cities, resulting in massive civilian casualties, with over 100,000 Japanese people dying in two days of fire raids against Tokyo. Publicly, U.S. Army Air Force officials insisted it had targeted enemy forces and installations, ignoring civilian casualties.[19]

Not all historians argue the shift to area bombing, inaugurated in early 1945, was inevitable. In fact, before Lemay took charge of the bomber command against Japan, his predecessor, Haywood Hansell, launched strategic bombing raids that caused high casualties and had only sporadic success in destroying selected targets. Moreover, the U.S. Army Air Force did spare some important cultural and religious structures, most notably the Imperial Palace in Tokyo, the Grand Shrine of Yamada, and much of Kyoto. In fact the importance of Kyoto to Japanese history and cultural life was recognized at the highest level. Secretary of War Henry L. Stimson insisted that this former imperial city should be taken off the list of potential targets for the atomic bomb.[20]

Some GIs did develop moral qualms about the air war. One aviator, from a very religious midwestern family, rose to the rank of sergeant in the army air force and served as a gunner on a larger bomber. Despite the fear and danger he regularly encountered, including one mission where the plane he was flying on lost three engines and another where the pilot was killed, this sergeant completed the required twenty-five missions. But after returning from a furlough, the aviator completely broke down over the "heinous crimes for which his family, his community, and his God must always condemn him." He confided to an army physician, during his hospitalization, that his participation in a raid on Christmas Eve particularly distressed him and he felt great remorse for shooting down a man.[21]

The slide to attacking civilians stemmed from the ambiguity of international law prior to the Second World War regarding the use of air power. Although the Hague Convention of 1907 had banned aerial bombardment, the interwar years had not seen a major effort to emphatically prohibit the destruction of civilian targets.[22] The lack of more explicit restrictions is unfortunate, for international law prevented the escalation of violence with regard to the use of poison gas before the Second World War broke out. During the interwar years international law explicitly prohibited the use of poison gas on the battlefield and, with a few notable exceptions, this ban was observed by nearly all combatants during the Second World War.[23]

The destruction of religious sites came not only from the air but also from ground combat. In a postwar army-sponsored report seeking to assess the religious life and the chaplaincy in the European theater, a board of senior officers offered no discussion of the ethical issues entailed by the level of violence civilians had endured during the war. But the report was quite critical of the degree to which American GIs violated the clear laws of land warfare by looting religious objects from churches. The number of these incidents was shockingly high, and the report noted that 50 percent of combat chaplains interviewed knew of incidents involving looting of churches. In one division a commander took vigorous action, including ordering that parcels sent home be opened and inspected. But in other cases, while investigations were sometimes initiated, often little came of them.

The report maintained that "intentional irreverence appears to have been a minor motive" in the theft of religious objects. Instead, the report viewed these thefts mainly as the result of "the average American soldier's incurable penchant for souvenir-hunting." The bulk of this looting involved Roman Catholic churches in France and Germany. The fact that GIs felt empowered to loot German churches during active combat and during the postwar occupation is not entirely surprising. But the looting of French churches suggests the degree to which GIs acted with impunity even in a country they were liberating. The report surmised that the high incidence of Roman Catholic churches being looted reflected the fact that there were few Protestant houses of worship where American GIs fought in France and Germany. It is regrettable that the report did not delve more into the sectarian dimension of the looting and whether most looters were Protestants. The degree to which churches were looted certainly reflected the degree to which GIs failed to follow the established laws of war and violated the precepts of all the tri-faith religions regarding theft.[24]

Praise the Lord and Pass the Ammunition: Chaplains Bearing Arms

International law had a major impact on the place of the American chaplain on the battlefield: the laws of war specifically prohibited him from being armed. Throughout the war, the War Department insisted that chaplains adhere to the Geneva Convention, which classified chaplains as noncombatants, and admonished them to refrain from bearing arms against the enemy. In 1942 the army chief of chaplains cautioned chaplains against carrying side arms, even though they held officer commissions.[25] Some field commanders were quite rigorous in making sure their chaplains adhered to the letter and spirit of the Geneva Convention. One chaplain in Italy was dressed down by his commander for carrying a Boy Scout sheath knife; he was ordered to get rid of it. With a stern warning the commander cautioned the chaplain that carrying such a knife would cause trouble if the Germans captured him.[26]

Not all chaplains agreed with these prohibitions against bearing arms. While recounting his experience at the Battle for Attu, army chaplain Francis W. Read suggested to his command chaplain that chaplains receive training in all types of arms, since the "Japanese do not respect the Geneva Convention, and to send a Chaplain to the front is folly if he is unarmed." As he recalled, "One chaplain was killed in the Clearing Station while ministering to the wounded."[27] In his after-action report following Attu, Chaplain Frederick A. Barnhill reported that he carried no arms during the first ten days of the battle; but after an experience in the midst of a major Japanese counterattack that proved fatal to several GIs in a nearby foxhole, he decided to carry a weapon for the duration of the battle, though he never fired it.[28]

While pleas arose in some chaplains' quarters over their right to carry arms, the army chief of chaplains reaffirmed the official policy in a circular letter that stressed that chaplains should not carry arms; doing so would violate international law. The letter stressed that chaplains could be subject to punishment—including the death penalty—if captured by the enemy, since carrying arms violated the laws of war. The military bishop for Catholic chaplains admonished all priests in the American armed forces not to carry arms because it violated international conventions.[29]

Despite official policies that mandated chaplains (and also medical personnel) remain unarmed, a significant number did carry weapons in the Pacific. One navy chaplain, landing at Iwo Jima, described how each night of battle he loaded a single bullet in the chamber of his pistol. In his diary he described the grim ritual of loading his pistol every night with the single bullet and emptying it at the morning light. Why only one bullet? Was it simply to alert nearby marines of enemy infiltration of the lines? Or was it intended to allow him the option of committing suicide rather than being taken captive?[30]

Some chaplains embraced a wider view of what roles they could undertake without jeopardizing their status as noncombatants or going against the injunction, which many religious faiths applied, that clergy should not engage in violence. Chaplain Alfred C. Oliver, during the defense of Bataan, reported distributing fifty-five thousand cigarettes to American and Filipino troops on the line. He also wrote a marching song for American and Filipino troops, and one for the Chinese army. Despite leading services (including sixteen at hospitals), Oliver still found time to devise a "game to teach Chinese Soldiers cooperation and minor tactics," which he gave to the Chinese army liaison, who dispatched them to China.[31]

Prior to the invasion of the Marshall and Gilbert Islands, Chaplain Edwin L. Kirtley volunteered to assist his division intelligence officer by procuring information from former missionaries who had been based there. Kirtley interviewed a couple that had resided on the Marshall Islands in the late 1920s and early 1930s. He also took it upon himself to learn the language of the Marshall Islands, even developing, from varied sources, a six-hundred-word lexicon for use by military intelligence. As a result of his efforts, five thousand cards were distributed throughout the division with such useful phrases as:

Have no fear!	Jahb mee-joke!
We are friends!	Jay-rarh weej!
We come to help you!	Jayj e-toke een jee-bong kom!

During the invasion Kirtley interviewed Marshall Islanders who crossed American lines. As the campaign progressed Kirtley joined a multi-island patrol in search of Marshall Islanders to provide them much-needed food and medical assistance but also to obtain intelligence regarding Japanese actions. Not only did Kirtley make contact with islanders; he came under fire from a Japanese position and aided in the evacuation of a wounded medical officer who had gone in search of souvenirs and had been caught in the crossfire. Kirtley's group killed all the attackers, except for one Japanese soldier who survived the attack but was severely wounded. Kirtley rendered first aid to this soldier while directing that the Japanese interpreter accompanying the group interrogate him.[32]

The ambiguity of the chaplain's role in battle was reflected in one of the first successful wartime hits. Shortly after the Japanese attack on Pearl Harbor, the popular music composer Frank Loesser penned a song that joined the spiritual with the weapons of war. "Praise the Lord and Pass the Ammunition" tells the story of a "sky pilot" that offered praise to the divine while urging those around him to fight back so we may all remain free. In one early version of the song, recorded by The Merry Macs, the chaplain offered more than spiritual guidance. After the gunner and the gunner's mate went down, this unnamed chaplain "manned the gun himself as he laid aside 'The Book' shouting, 'Praise the Lord and Pass the Ammunition.'" In the version performed by Kay Kyser and His Orchestra, the chaplain's combat role became more oblique, offering this account instead:

Yes, the sky pilot said
You've got to give him credit
For a son-of-a-gunner was he

The Office of War Information (owi) and the wider public embraced Loesser's song. Sheet music sales remained brisk in 1942, and Kyser's version of "Praise the Lord and Pass the Ammunition" reached the top of the Billboard charts. So popular was the song that Columbia Records struggled to meet the demand and the OWI, charged with coordinating propaganda efforts for the federal government, wanted radio stations to restrict the playing of the song so this tune would not be overexposed.[33]

"Praise the Lord and Pass the Ammunition" highlighted the spiritual implications of the attack on Pearl Harbor. The Japanese had attacked Pearl Harbor before transmitting a declaration of war, and they had also struck on the Christian Sabbath. Franklin D. Roosevelt would wait until Monday to address Congress and the nation. It was the first lady who spoke, during her regularly scheduled Sunday night program, about the events that had transpired in Hawaii. Eleanor Roosevelt's program centered on the state of morale in the U.S. Army, in a script composed prior to the attack, with last-minute additions that took into account the outbreak of war.[34]

On the eve of the attack on Pearl Harbor, chaplains on the many warships docked in the harbor were preparing to lead chapel services for their crews. Chaplains aboard these vessels came under fire, and two lost their lives: Thomas Kirkpatrick of the *Arizona* and Aloysius Schmitt of the battleship *Oklahoma*. Kirkpatrick, like most of the crew of the *Arizona*, died instantly as flames engulfed the battleship. Schmitt, a Roman Catholic priest who had attended theological school in Rome, was on the deck of the *Oklahoma* when a torpedo struck his vessel. Racing below with a group of sailors, Schmitt rescued dozens of trapped men. In the end Schmitt was unable to escape and drowned as the *Oklahoma* slipped into the water.[35]

Did a chaplain actually utter the words "Praise the Lord and Pass the Ammunition"? Did a chaplain violate international law and bear arms against the enemy? Initially, Chaplain Thomas McGuire, a Roman Catholic priest, was hailed by the public as the man who had uttered these lines, and for nearly a year he failed to definitively clarify his role during the battle. During a publicity tour of the states, McGuire even appeared on Kay Kyser's radio program and did not effectively correct these assertions about his role on December 7, 1941. Only ten months later, in October 1942, did McGuire put to rest the legend that surrounded him. In a press conference held with Bishop O'Hara, McGuire announced he had not taken part in combat nor pronounced the slogan attributed to him. In this press conference and later, in a memoir that appeared in 1943, McGuire recounted the experience of being on deck in the midst of the action when a young gunner asked him for absolution. McGuire recalled that, lacking a helmet, he admonished the young sailor to make it quick.[36]

In 1944 a Protestant chaplain came forward and claimed to be the one who had uttered the phrase. In his memoir "*. . . And Pass the Ammunition*" Chaplain Howell M. Forgy described the scene aboard the *New Orleans* during the fateful hours of the attack. He depicted a desperate struggle by the multiethnic crew, which included a Jewish sailor and a Filipino mess boy, to get ammunition to the gun crew. As a chaplain Forgy could neither fire a gun nor offer material aid in repelling the onslaught. But he sought to bolster the morale of those who were fighting and recalled slapping sweating men on the back declaring, "Praise the Lord and Pass the Ammunition."[37]

"Praise the Lord and Pass the Ammunition" proved distinctive on several counts. Most tunes favored by wartime Americans, especially GIs, during the Second World War lacked the militaristic tone of "Praise the Lord." Musically, GIs favored sentimental tunes such as Irving Berlin's "White Christmas." Even songs that alluded to combat remained far from bellicose in overall tone, such as "Comin' in on a Wing and a Prayer," which described the quest of the pilot of a damaged warplane to return safely to base. Others expressed longing for home, mixed with a concern that those left behind remain faithful, as exemplified by the Andrews Sisters' "Don't Sit Under the Apple Tree." Social commentators, in observing the differences between those in the service and those remaining at home, noted profoundly different musical tastes, with civilians more likely to sing militaristic tunes such as "Praise the Lord."[38]

Works like "Praise the Lord" fed into the public perception of what roles chaplains should play in battle. In their memoirs both McGuire and Forgy emphasized the importance of serving men spiritually, even in the midst of combat. The attack on Pearl Harbor underscored the greater danger a chaplain faced aboard a naval vessel, in combat, compared with those who were based on land. Although navy regulations called on chaplains to station themselves below deck or in the sick bay, this offered only a modicum of safety, especially if a naval vessel sank or suffered severe damage.

Despite the bellicosity of "Praise the Lord and Pass the Ammunition," most chaplains followed the norms that called upon them not to bear arms. In fact, there existed a sentiment that GIs and chaplains should reach across the battle lines and recognize the humanity of their enemy. Christianity stressed the brotherhood of all believers, which meant that many chaplains and GIs saw some of the Germans and Italians as fellow Christians, albeit Christians fighting for a misguided cause. Frank Kneller's first experience in combat was as a replacement in the 82nd Airborne, and he hoped life would imitate art. While on the line, this New Jersey native remembered growing up watching Nelson Eddy in the movie *Balalaika* singing Christmas carols to the Germans in World War I and the Germans singing back. A naïve Kneller started singing on Christmas Eve 1944, while on the line at Bastogne, but the Germans had little interest in any display of Christian brotherhood. They started firing at him. This gesture almost got Kneller and his fellow GIs killed, and he quickly abandoned the effort.[39]

There was, however, a more organized and more successful effort to reach out across the battle lines earlier that year on the Italian front. The regimental commander and chaplains of the infantry regiment fighting on the Cassino Line in April of 1944 sought to share the Easter message with American and German troops. Roman Catholic and Protestant chaplains built a temporary altar within sight of enemy lines, and they broadcast their service on loudspeaker so that troops on both sides of the line could hear it. Chaplain Oscar Reinboth, a Lutheran–Missouri Synod pastor, issued the following prelude before Protestant and Catholic services: "Happy Easter. As an American chaplain I greet Protestants and Catholics of the German Army." He further declared, "Should not all Christendom be jubilant on this day? Should not all people rejoice—-now that Christ died and rose again from the dead for all men—for Germans and Americans alike—therefore I wish you also today in the name of my soldiers a happy Easter." For two hours the fighting stopped on a small part of the line, and this service would be widely reported in the American press.[40] This incident is striking because it came several weeks after the bombing of Monte Cassino. Did this effort seek to reassure Americans in uniform and those who read press reports at home of their inherent goodness, in an effort to preserve Christian values despite the pressures of total war?

Hate and the Enemy

While many Christian leaders and chaplains accepted the necessity of taking human life in a just war, they still urged GIs to forgo sentiments of hate in fighting against the enemy. This view was even voiced in the army chief of chaplains' circular letter on March 1, 1944, under the headline "War without Hate," quoting from a recent article in the *Christian Advocate* by Dean W. A. Smart. The article discussed the religious devotion of the "great modern Christian, Generalissimo Chiang Kai-shek" who had "not sunk to the animal level of hate." In his evening devotions, Smart reported that in "his family devotions he pray[ed] for the Japanese, that the once great nation might not lose its soul in the bitterness of aggressive war." Smart acknowledged that bearing the proper Christian attitude was difficult, but avoiding anger was essential to creating a "lasting peace."[41]

Some found that hate would be a difficult thing to sustain, even for those who wanted to harden their hearts. In a letter from "Somewhere in France" on July 31, 1944, one Jewish chaplain disagreed with the premise of a friend and fellow rabbi—a chaplain at Fort Ord—who had stressed in an article that "We Can't Win the Peace with Hate." Chaplain Herman Dicker expressed real hatred of the enemy, given the suffering of French "Children and Women Victims" caused by the Germans, who were destroying cities, were launching robot bombs at London in the "middle of the night," and had "exterminated" three million "of their own group." While Dicker insisted hatred remained necessary in war, he also found it difficult to sustain this enmity when he "saw German prisoners working in our hospitals or interned in the Prison Camps." He reflected, "I didn't see any trace of hatred in my conversation" with German POWs, and his dominant emotion was replaced with pity.[42]

While some GIs were reluctant to kill, many accepted the necessity of taking another's life out of simple self-preservation. There were GIS whose inhibitions diminished to such an extent that they were willing to kill unarmed prisoners, even in the presence of a chaplain. During the assault on St. Lo, Roman Catholic chaplain John Bradstreet watched in horror as GIS shot unarmed Germans who were attempting to surrender. In one incident three German prisoners being marched to the rear never made it because men from another unit killed them.[43]

Compared with other issues, especially sexual immorality, religious and ethical qualms about killing did not dominate the conversations among chaplains or most GIS. Few sermons offered by chaplains said much about the question of morality and killing. Ben Rose, who served as chaplain for an infantry unit in Europe, compiled an anthology of his wartime sermons, and none directly touch on the morality of killing.[44] *The Link*, a publication aimed at Protestant GIS, barely touched the topic either. A rare exception, "Killing in Battle: Is It Murder," which appeared in the June 1943 issue, was a reprint of an article written by the late Samuel Logan Brengle for the generation that went off to the First World War.[45] In another article, appearing in December 1945, an army chaplain focused on a narrow question: does the sixth commandment condemn all killing? He argued no, asserting that views to the contrary relied on an inaccurate translation. In short this chaplain argued that a proper reading of the sixth commandment is "Thou shalt not murder," not the King James rendering, "Thou shalt not kill."[46]

Why so little discussion about the ethics of shedding blood in wartime? Does it indicate that citizen soldiers could easily make the transition to trained killers? Not necessarily, but the relatively few instances of GIS expressing angst about the morality of their actions may suggest that the relatively permissive policies regarding conscientious objectors managed to screen out those who might have been troubled by the ethical dilemmas of killing in wartime. Although GIS seeking conscientious objector status had to surmount significant bureaucratic hurdles, clergy with objections to war could easily avoid military service.

From those writing recommendations on behalf of Protestant ministers seeking chaplaincy positions, the General Commission of Army and Navy Chaplains sought information about each prospective candidate's "attitude" toward "pacifism and militarism."

Those written recommendations volunteered such statements as that offered on behalf of Rev. Russell George Honeywell of Ames, Iowa: "He sees the need of protecting our way of life at any cost."[47] Similarly, a seminary professor sympathetically characterized his former student's attitude toward pacifism and militarism: "Like the rest of us he does not like war, but is sympathetic toward the nation's efforts in this war."[48] A dean at Emory University vouched that Rev. Joseph Pryor McCluskey Jr. of Knoxville, Tennessee, was "not pacifist."[49]

In fighting Japan the United States confronted a non-Christian country, where most citizens adhered to Buddhism and state-sponsored Shintoism.[50] The perception of Japan as a religious "other" certainly reinforced the fact that most GIs had few inhibitions about killing in battle, and it even contributed to the escalation of violence.[51] Many GIs and even some chaplains refused to recognize the essential humanity of the Japanese who fought against them. Even in the writings of chaplains, the Japanese were referred to as "Japs." Most Japanese people were viewed as members of a race that was irredeemable, and many chaplains expressed little concern about their spirituality, even when Japanese soldiers were held as captives. When Mark Warner, a Protestant chaplain, was based in New Guinea, he blamed the Japanese refusal to surrender on their "pagan" religions. When Japanese soldiers did surrender, they expressed a strong death wish. Warner described a group of hospitalized prisoners engaging in a hunger strike as declaring their desire to die. In another case, a group of Japanese prisoners committed mass suicide in an army stockade by hanging themselves with tent ropes. Later in the war Warner had the opportunity to join an interrogation of Japanese prisoners, who described their strong fear of reprisal if they ever returned to Japan.[52]

The army journalist Mack Morriss expressed dismay, in his diary, over one Catholic chaplain's bloodlust over the actions of "one of [his] boys" in combat on Guadalcanal who had returned to headquarters loaded down with souvenirs. Morriss described writing up the story, ultimately never published in the army-sponsored *Yank* magazine, about a young GI who had once studied for the priesthood and who killed, at close range, two wounded Japanese soldiers. This "boy," while carrying grenades to the front, beheaded a wounded Japanese private he encountered. Then a nearby Japanese officer groaned and grabbed onto the young GI, "either in the desperation of a dying man, or at the end of the usual possum act." This "kid" went berserk and stabbed the Japanese officer in the "gut, chest, back, cut off the left cheek of his ass" before finally decapitating him. While the actions of this "kid" could be considered one of the many things that happen in war—"C'est la guerre"—Morriss was disturbed at the attitude of the Catholic chaplain toward what the young GI had done. As his colleague took a picture of the "kid," Morriss recounted the priest "needling me" with these statements: "'My, isn't he blood-thirsty. Nothing the American boy won't do if you get him mad'—then to the kid: 'Stand steady there for your picture, boy, or I'll whip you good'—to me, punching—'He knows I'll do it, too.'"

The chaplain's attitude so disgusted Morriss that, in his diary, he described wanting to "push the fat bastard" off the cliff. He bluntly stated, "It's not my conception of a chaplain that he should glory in blood and sort of buzz around like a school kid in the dubious fame of a guy who killed a couple of Japs—wounded or not."[53]

The Texas-born John Gaitha Browning, who became a major artist in the genre of Southwestern painting, kept a brutally honest journal of his experiences with an army amphibian unit deployed to the Southwest Pacific. His journal is unflinching in describing the brutality carried out by both sides on the battlefield, including acts committed by American and Australian troops. He recounted the mutilation of the enemy dead by GIs, the collection of gold teeth from corpses, an American marine beheading a Japanese prisoner for refusing to answer questions during an interrogation, and the capture of a Japanese hospital by an Australian unit that machine gunned or bayonetted patients in their beds. Browning describes the constant sexual banter among many of his fellow soldiers, the incompetence of many officers, and soldiers getting drunk or going AWOL while on leave.[54]

The truism that the experience of war amounts to days of boredom interspersed with moments marked by pure terror fit Browning's experiences. He often reflected and conversed with like-minded comrades, but he noted that one soldier from the hills of Kentucky rarely engaged in either and spent all his time reading the Bible. Religious holidays were observed to varying degrees, Browning reported, noting that Roman Catholics tended to attend Good Friday services while attendance among Protestants was lackluster. As an intellectually curious and perceptive observer of his environment, Browning—during his first Easter abroad in Australia—wrote that he longed to return to his beloved Southwest to spend an Easter at the Shrine of the Ages at the Grand Canyon. In his journal, he included a poem that made it clear that wartime had influenced his faith and encouraged him to make it more eclectic. The poem reads in part:

> Easter Day, sound of morning born anew.
> Far away my Canyon echoes too,
> Not from bomb or gun or place
> But age-old anthems sung again
> As the Canyon's blue is shattered
> By sunlight jewels scattered—
> Brahman, Buddha, Zion, one by one
> Their crests flash crimson in the sun
> Like sacred candles lighted for the day.
> Shrine of the Ages that points the upward way
> And knows with wisdom, old as time, all men's creeds
> Love each one: and then proceeds
> On Easter morning to give an hour of serenity
> And steal their hearts for all eternity[55]

Browning did not keep his religious eclecticism to himself; while he was deployed in New Guinea, his senior officers took a religious census of everyone in the unit so dog tags could be updated. Annoyed because he had been asked this question before, when filling out countless forms, and also because he believed it was "none of their damned business," Browning decided that he wanted to be classified as Mohammedan. The regiment sent back his paper, wondering if this religious classification was correct. "I stood my ground and was very indignant that anyone should question my religion and signed the sheet as proof of my determination," he said. He was pleased that "there was something in the army that I could demand being done for me." Within a few days, Browning received his new dog tags stamped with the *M* for Mohammedan, and he expressed a certain resignation about death and faith: "It would make little difference as to religion once you were a casualty in battle, and I doubt if any chaplain we have had would know what the 'M' was for."[56]

The pattern of demonizing the enemy was not universal. Other chaplains and GIs recognized and emphasized the humanity of the Japanese. Before becoming a navy chaplain serving the marine corps, Samuel Franklin had been a missionary to Japan, and in uniform he sought to instill in the marines he encountered an appreciation and understanding of Japanese culture and the precepts of the Buddhist faith. In a letter to his wife, Franklin recounted instances where GIs showed humanity toward enemy civilians. He recounted a story about marines who encountered orphaned Japanese babies on an island and cut up their own trousers to make diapers for them.[57]

One Catholic chaplain in New Guinea asked the military bishop about his responsibility toward the diverse prisoners of war he encountered in the military hospital. They included not just those of Japanese descent, but also those from Formosa, Korea, and China. He said, given the language barrier, "it is impossible to instruct them even should they desire it," and he asked whether "justice or charity" should lead him to "administer conditional baptism" for those destined to die or if he should "commend them to God's mercy."[58] Another Catholic chaplain, who took part in the invasion of Kwajalein, reported to the military ordinariate: "Our boys are on the lookout for Catholics among the enemy." An aid man comforted a "wounded Japanese boy" whose scapular medal had been taken from him prior to his operation. The Catholic aid men recognized the cause of his distress and gave this enemy soldier his rosary. The Japanese boy blessed himself and began the rosary prayers.[59]

R. A. W. Farrell, a Catholic chaplain serving aboard the USS Yorktown, wrote to his superior expressing dismay at the hatred he witnessed in many GIs aboard his ship. They often had no problem with the idea of exterminating the Japanese and with killing enemy soldiers who were trying to surrender, strafing pilots bailing out of planes, and gunning down men left in the water from sunken ships. In justifying these actions, GIs told him it was just retribution for what the enemy had done to us; after all, they claimed, "The Japs aren't human." They insisted the greater good called for it, since upon "exterminating [the] Japs and Germans, international crime will be wiped from the face of the earth, and we'll be happy and at peace forever after."

This frame of mind stemmed from experiences beyond combat, and the propaganda they had been fed allowed for such callousness that GIS sometimes disregarded the "humanity of some men." Farrell described his efforts to challenge such troubling attitudes. Many GIS, when confronted, saw the "absurdity of their position"—"even if they are back at the old position [later] they are never so loudly sure of themselves," and fewer make a "point of a necessary difference between Christian and a pagan nation."[60]

Chaplain John David Zimmerman, who joined the regular navy after 1945, recalled that compared with his experiences during the Korean and Vietnam Wars, few officers or enlisted men expressed ethical doubts during the Second World War. In an oral history conducted at his retirement from the navy in the early 1980s, Zimmerman remembered an incident in which several enlisted sailors came to talk to him about an order issued to his vessel by Admiral William Halsey, calling on them to kill Japanese sailors who had escaped from a torpedoed warship. In issuing the order, Halsey had declared that the only "good Jap is a dead Jap," a sentiment that not all enlisted men accepted as morally justifiable. In fact, Zimmerman raised the issue of shooting helpless enemy sailors with his vessels commander, but his concerns went unaddressed. Fortunately for those with moral qualms about shooting helpless survivors in the water, Zimmerman's warship never came into contact with any Japanese sailors.[61]

Although many GIS recognized that Japanese Christians existed, racism and hatred of the enemy, born from experience and the impact of propaganda, would be difficult to overcome. Chaplain Reuben E. Curtis, in his after-action report on the battle of Attu, recalled signs that some of the enemy dead were Christians. One Japanese officer carried a New Testament given to him by his father with the call to follow the "teaching of Christ." Another had written in his diary that he was "dying for the Emperor and for Christ." Curtis could not accept the fact that Japanese Christians could be both patriots and true followers of the tenets of his own faith. Instead, he saw the "Japanese line of thought" as having a muddling effect and felt that their approach to Christianity reflected that fact: "They have so recently embraced our Western Civilization and tried to mix it with their own ancient philosophies that they seem to be confused."[62]

SIX

Fear, Faith, and the Will to Fight

The veneration of the "Greatest Generation" has obscured a long-standing debate among historians regarding the combat effectiveness of the American GI. Although historians have differed in their assessments of battlefield performance, even the official history on manpower procurement documented how the U.S. Army, in the early years of the war, made the infantry a dumping ground for many of the least capable recruits.[1] Critics have argued infantrymen were often given inadequate training and led by lackluster junior officers.[2] They assert that the American army never reached the capability of their German counterparts, and victory came only as a result of superior firepower and numbers. Not all historians accept this indictment, but even defenders of the combat performance of the American GI have portrayed the U.S. Army as having endured several brutal defeats before emerging as an effective fighting force.[3]

The evidence of whether religious beliefs, values, and rituals made any difference to combat effectiveness is at best contradictory, and this chapter will underscore the varied responses of GIs to combat. Many GIs on the battlefield turned to religion and sought comfort from prayer or sought out chaplains. Battlefield conversions occurred, and individuals prayed for divine intervention to aid them in their struggle for survival. When going into battle, many GIs found it inspiring to attend services led by a chaplain. GIs often strayed from the orthodoxy of their faiths, and many embraced a battlefield ecumenicalism that surprised many chaplains and outside observers. This sentiment prompted Protestant and Jewish GIs to take Holy Communion from Roman Catholic

13. Catholic chaplain serves Holy Communion while holding Mass on the quarterdeck, during the Okinawa operation, April 1, 1945. Still Picture Branch, U.S. National Archives (80-G-325209).

priests and Roman Catholics to attend services led by Protestant or Jewish chaplains.

Another sign of GIs, especially aviators, straying from the orthodoxies of their respective faiths was their embrace of magic to protect them from the randomness of death and their inability to fully control their fates in combat. Going into battle, men wore lucky items of clothing, carried a variety of stuffed animals and other objects, and wanted to avoid anything incorporating the number thirteen. The sight of a black cat prior to battle led to panic among aircrews.[4] We are thus left with the task of identifying the boundaries between magic and religion, and it is difficult to determine. But it is clear many GIs carried scriptures—Hebrew Bibles and New Testaments—that were viewed by some as offering supernatural protection against harm.

Considering the prevalence of superstitious beliefs, it is important to be cautious about portraying the rise of modern technology and science as something that swept away religion or magic. The prevalence of magic among aviators is even more striking given the association of aviation with modernity in the first part of the twentieth century. In the view of advocates, aviation represented a decisive break with the past and aviators a new vanguard. Furthermore, U.S. Army personnel policies sent the best and brightest, often college educated, to the army air force.

Modern technology on the land, sea, and air had made the battlefield more lethal, especially as warring armies mastered combined arms warfare, which efficiently coordinated the use of tactical air power, artillery, armored vehicles, and the infantry. The killing zone stretched for miles, and GIS who fought on the battlefield sought safety in scattered foxholes, where groups of men endured grim conditions, living in the dirt. Throughout the war the U.S. Army grappled with how to motivate and sustain soldiers on the battlefield. Not only would staggering numbers of men be killed or physically wounded, but scores also broke down mentally. Even worse some GIS, especially in Europe, escaped the battlefield by taking unauthorized leaves of absence or deserting outright.[5] For the navy, battlefield desertion was generally not an issue. Fear might have paralyzed some members of a ship's crew, keeping them from performing their duties, but on the high seas a sailor had no easy escape from harm.[6]

For those on the front lines of ground forces, the terror of combat was mixed with unpleasant living conditions. Ready-to-eat meals were often the norm and hot meals a luxury. Infantrymen and marines literally lived in the dirt and frequently endured extreme cold in the winter and heat in the summer. Life revolved around such basic acts as eating, sleeping, and the struggle to stay alive. Men went weeks, even months, without showers or access to laundry facilities.

If there were any advantages to frontline service, it was the grim satisfaction and sense of achievement experienced by those who had managed to survive an unforgiving environment. Greater informality ruled and the spit and polish of garrison life was difficult to maintain, especially for those forced to live for weeks in foxholes. To increase their chances of survival, officers usually removed their insignias so as to not attract sniper fire, and enlisted personnel did not salute them for the same reason. Survival depended on unit cohesion, individual abilities, and a series of imponderable factors that might be deemed luck or divine intervention.[7]

The God of Battle

There were generals who believed that religious faith could make soldiers brave and tenacious. In his address to a training conference held for chaplains under his command, Maj. Gen. Walter K. Wilson, in June 1941, discussed how the nature of modern warfare had changed from the "old days when soldiers entered the battlefield shoulder to shoulder." This meant that a soldier in battle "finds himself at considerable distance from any other human beings, and to carry out his mission in combat he must be able to think clearly." In his view the ideal soldier was not one who had no fear, since such men "expose themselves uselessly" to harm; even more importantly, they could endanger their comrades. Instead, the "ideal soldier" had not only a healthy sense of physical fear but also "moral courage that will enable him to do his duty nor matter how difficult or dangerous." Not only did religion boost morale and foster more disciplined troops; a "strong faith in God" sustained the soldier in his "hour of danger."[8] Wilson's observations about the importance of faith would be partially confirmed by social scientists employed by the U.S. Army to study combat motivations.

When asked by social scientists, in surveys, about what sustained them in battle, a majority of enlisted men said that prayer ranked highest, even above comradeship.[9] How did GIs pray and what did GIs seek from their prayers? A great many prayers were silent missives, but others were said aloud and even collectively, often born out of desperation. Lt. Col. Warren J. Clear, an army staff officer who had been stationed briefly in the Philippines after the attack on Pearl Harbor, offered the following anecdote, on the Army Hour Broadcast, regarding the prevalence of prayer in battle. He recalled jumping into a foxhole when bombs started falling. He was not surprised to find himself praying out loud.[10]

Did the promise of eternal life and resurrection of the dead, central to the Christian faith, comfort men in battle? Did reciting the lines from the Amidah—one of the central prayers of the Jewish liturgy, which promised that God will keep faith with those who sleep in the dust—offer any reassurance? In his philosophical treatise on men in battle, J. Glenn Gray maintains that religious beliefs influence combat performance. Gray, a philosopher who received his draft notice to report to the army on the same day he received his diploma for his doctorate in the mail, asserts that there are those in battle with a religious worldview that accepts "physical death" as "a portal for him to a greater and immeasurably happier life beyond." In Gray's view, these GIs face less fear and foreboding in battle.[11] How much these precepts influenced most GIs in World War II is difficult to ascertain. Certainly the fear of death undergirded the high number of mental breakdowns on the battlefield, which troubled army leaders and psychiatrists. This will be further considered in the chapter examining the medical care system for GIs.

The questions chaplains often pondered were how best to meet the spiritual needs of men heading into battle and whether they should accompany them. Those serving on naval vessels had no choice but to remain on board when their ship engaged in action. U.S. Army Air Force regulations prohibited chaplains from taking part in combat missions, and to show their support of aviators going off to battle, chaplains often stood on the flight line. Army regulations advised them to station themselves at battalion headquarters or medical clearing stations. But even though army regulations did not mandate it, many chaplains embraced frontline roles. Some chaplains took part in amphibious assaults, and others—assigned to airborne units—jumped into battle. The fluid nature of battle often meant that chaplains who sought to serve GIs as close to the front as possible found themselves in the midst of an artillery barrage or frontal assault if events moved more quickly than anticipated, such as during the Battle of the Bulge. Propaganda issued by the chaplains corps of both services heralded the actions of chaplains who died at the hand of the enemy or were decorated for battlefield bravery.

Army chaplains who stayed close to the front often acclimated to the conditions found on the line. They organized religious services in any available space, often holding them outdoors. Chaplains turned Jeep hoods into altars, abridged liturgies, and offered succinct sermons to men pressed for time. If enough men could not leave the line, chaplains tried to gather small groups for prayer services or simply went to individual foxholes to offer a few words of encouragement. During the defense of Bataan, in February 1942, Chaplain Alfred C. Oliver reported to his superiors that he had led twenty-seven Sunday services and twelve weekday services with a total attendance of over 2400.[12] In the heat of battle, chaplains often centered their actions on tending the wounded, ministering to the dying, and caring for the war dead.

Fear and Courage in War

In contrast to Civil War soldiers, imbued with Victorian sensibilities that suppressed fear allowing them to, at best, talk about it euphemistically, GIS in the Second World War were often allowed to acknowledge their fears.[13] In fact, U.S. Army manuals issued during the war openly discussed fear and maintained that it was an inherent part of modern warfare. A pamphlet issued to all trainees in 1944 offered the following discussion of the prevalence of fear: "You'll Be Scared. Sure you'll be scared. Before you go into battle, you'll be frightened at the uncertainty, at the thought of being killed. Will it hurt? Will you know what to do? If you say you're not scared, you'll be a cocky fool. Don't let anyone tell you you're a coward if you admit being scared. Fear before you're actually in the battle is a normal emotional reaction."[14] Many GIS recognized the prevalence of fear, often induced by artillery and aerial attacks. Abraham Felber, a marine sergeant with an artillery battery on Guadalcanal, described, with little condemnation, the fear that gripped men when the air raid alarm sounded: "They plunge into the shelters and remain there wide-eyed with fright until it is over. Nearly every raid produces some men who have suffered bruises in diving into the shelters in a panic: and Reick has had two front teeth knocked out thus. I hardly blame them, for it is a disconcerting experience to have 500-pound bombs exploding about one."[15] Fear increased the risk of friendly-fire casualties. As Felber recorded in his diary, the first death in his unit resulted when a marine, described as "confused and scared," thought "some Japs had sneaked through; so when he saw the dark form of . . . [someone] moving about, he thought it was somebody who had come out of the woods, and he instinctively grabbed his rifle, aimed it at the shape, and fired," resulting in the death of a fellow marine.[16]

Fear did lead to panic, especially among green troops. Even a chaplain could do little to control these troops. In the closing weeks of the Guadalcanal campaign, a group of sailors working at the Lunga Point beach came under aerial attack. An army journalist recalled in his diary how an officer urged the sailors to take cover, apparently misjudging the Japanese's intentions and setting off a panicked flight for perceived safer ground. One sailor was so panicked that he ran a considerable distance, completely naked, to the airport; others went even farther. Efforts by the Catholic chaplain to calm the men proved useless, and he was physically pushed aside in the chaos. This incident suggests the limits of moral suasion and its limited effectiveness in quelling fear.[17]

In some instances fear drove men to kill their commanders. Felber recorded an incident when a member of the Raider Battalion not only refused to move into the battle line but shot the marine who gave the order.[18] Scores of soldiers deserted when afforded the opportunity. During the land campaign for France and Germany, so many GIs and British Tommies left the ranks that some formed marauding gangs in Paris; they stole supplies and motor vehicles and even held up civilian banks. These actions, while not the norm, nonetheless point to a failure by armed forces, including chaplains, to fully inspire all men to fight.[19]

In battle there were Jews who went to great lengths to show their courage. In an oral history Herbert Gross, who served in the U.S. Marines, described how his fellow officer, also Jewish, was often the first to volunteer for dangerous missions. This officer's propensity to accept dangerous missions led some men, seeking to join him, to request transfers to his unit; those wanting more cautious commanders, of course, sought transfers out. A Jewish "coward" might earn not only the disdain of anti-Semites, confirming their prejudices, but also the ire of fellow Jews.

In a letter to his parents, Leon Uris described the comradeship he experienced at Guadalcanal and Tarawa. This letter, published as part of the wartime anthology *Jewish Youth at War*, described how the value placed on courage caused Uris and his fellow marines to categorize a man not by his religious affiliation but by how that individual performed in battle. Being a "good man" and a "regular fellow" helped Uris get along with the "Catholics, Protestants, and Mormons, Indians, Irish, Italians, [and] Poles." Uris described how he joined his Christian comrades in hating the "Jewish boy in [his] platoon," not because of his religion but because he was a "coward" and a "rat." By contrast, one heroic Jew, marine captain Bill Scherewin, was beloved by Uris and the rest of the men in his unit, who said they would be willing to "follow him to hell."[20]

Chaplains were not immune to fear. Eichhorn, serving an entire army sector in Europe in 1944, made it a point to travel hundreds of miles in a week to conduct services for frontline units. In his diary he wrote derisively of the chaplains whose polished boots and neatly pressed uniforms contrasted with his muddy boots, implying they stayed in the relative safety of rear headquarters. Eichhorn had been quite close to the front line on more than one occasion. Obeying direct orders from his army commander, he led High Holiday services in a French town that had only recently been liberated and was not yet fully secured. After the services were over and he was leaving the town, an army intelligence officer reported that they were not sure the synagogue he had used had been out of German artillery range when the GIs had gathered in it for Eichhorn's service. The fact that it had not been shelled meant the Germans had moved their artillery.[21]

There were also chaplains who shirked their duties in the eyes of their superiors. One army chaplain, an Episcopalian priest, was court martialed and convicted for refusing to follow his commanding officer's order to man a battalion first aid station. Although the commander did not expect the chaplain to serve as a straggler officer, he did expect this cleric to counsel uninjured men who found their way to the rear, helping boost their "morale and effectiveness" and encouraging them to return to their stations "before they got into service difficulties." Instead, the priest retreated to a collecting station ten miles to the rear and went AWOL for over twenty-four hours.[22]

Interreligious tension developed among chaplains regarding the question of bravery. One Catholic chaplain relayed to the military ordinariate that he had, as supervisory chaplain, the opportunity to deploy another Catholic chaplain to Espiritu Santo, in late 1942, as replacement for a Protestant chaplain who had "gone over the hill." He noted that the commanding officer had specifically requested a Catholic. From his perspective Catholics were eager for the front line, while certain Protestant chaplains remained in the rear and refused to move out with the units.[23]

But not all Catholic chaplains were fearless. Another Catholic chaplain informed his religious superiors that, while the numbers were relatively small, there were "too many priests succumbing to nervousness under fire." These priests had to be released from service, which not only embarrassed the priests but also created a bad impression of the entire chaplaincy, even "when there is a hundred officers in the same condition of nervousness." There were important religious implications of a priest's inability to cope with combat, because it indicated that he was afraid of death. This fear of death was an embarrassing thing to acknowledge, and it caused considerable comment among officers and men.[24]

There were brave and fearless chaplains in much larger proportions than the shirkers. No doubt many inspired the men they ministered to in combat. One Catholic chaplain, Edward Connolly, recalled several brushes with death on the front. In one instance an enemy sniper spotted him in the early morning while he was giving absolution to a group of men, but fortunately he and everyone in this group escaped harm.[25] In explaining to the military bishop why he was shot in the back, Chaplain Emmett T. Michaels recounted that he had just anointed five marines and had consoled an officer who was experiencing a case of "combat fatigue." After receiving a bullet wound, this chaplain yelled at the officer to "scram" as he crawled onto a stretcher. The sight of the chaplain hit by gunfire forced the officer to snap "out of it very quickly" and resume his duties.[26] Other chaplains paid an even higher price. During the Solomon Islands campaign in July 1943, the senior chaplain, Mark T. Warner, had to arrange for the funeral of a "young Catholic chaplain" killed by a shell fragment at Munda.[27]

Chaplains varied in how close to enemy fire they were. Chaplain John B. Young, with the 162nd Infantry Regiment, described how in the New Guinea campaign he and his colleague, a Roman Catholic chaplain, Frank Haley, landed with the combat force during their assault on Nassau Bay. Joining the second wave of the assault, Young knew reinforcements would not follow until the next day. Losses in the two waves that made it ashore were high, and after the first thirty-six hours, Young and Haley had "buried all but five of the men who were in our particular boat." He attributed his survival to divine intervention, remarking that the "Lord spared us for the work that lay ahead."[28]

Frequent and unpredictable artillery barrages, especially during the daylight hours, on the Anzio beachhead in 1944 put everyone, including chaplains, in harm's way. Battlefield conditions often encouraged chaplains to meet the spiritual needs of others in ways that would have been unlikely in civilian life. Chaplains under these conditions often felt it necessary to take a more ecumenical outlook. One Reform rabbi recalled in a memoir, published immediately after the war, watching an Orthodox rabbi from Flatbush, "who had been confined within the four walls of Brooklyn Jewry," now regularly conducting bedside visits to comfort sick Catholic and Protestant GIs at the Anzio beachhead. The senior chaplain at the beachhead, a Roman Catholic priest, attended Passover seders, begged to be counted in the minyan for kaddish prayers, and often preached at Jewish services when no rabbi could be present.[29]

Bert Manhoff, fighting with an armored unit through France and Germany, recalled never having a chance to attend Jewish services while in combat. The closest thing to a formal service was a chance encounter in Normandy, France, with Chaplain Goldberg, a Jewish convert to Roman Catholicism who had become a Roman Catholic priest. Manhoff asked Chaplain Goldberg if he would say the Sh'ma Israel prayer with him. Goldberg was more than happy to oblige, and they prayed, "Hear, O' Israel, the Lord Our God, the Lord is One."[30]

For many GIs the chance to attend religious services offered inspiration to continue to fight and build a sense of common purpose. In a letter to the JWB, Chaplain Eichhorn described the remarkable Yom Kippur service he had held in a recently liberated synagogue in Luneville, France, in 1944. As Eichhorn struggled to clean up the desecrated synagogue, "350 battle-grimed Jewish fighters came to the synagogue for Kol Nidre." The sight of these men and the solemnity of the holiday, which required Jews to repent for sins committed against God, brought Eichhorn to tears for the first time since he had arrived in France. Even before the service concluded, soldiers had to leave to take part in a nearby battle.

A lost member of the tribe made it to that service as well. Without mentioning his name, in a report to his colleagues at the JWB, Eichhorn described how a senior officer who had "tried to conceal his Jewishness," and had also compiled a poor combat record, came to speak to him following the service. Despite his high rank he told Eichhorn, a "lowly captain," that the service had inspired him to be a "faithful Jew and a good soldier." For this officer the chance to make "his open profession of Judaism" by attending the service and to admit his "guilt before God" had taken "a great load off his mind and heart."[31]

Sacred Time in Battle and the Blurring of Sectarian Lines

Maintaining sacred time—observing religious holidays—under combat conditions blurred efforts to demarcate the sacred and secular. Fighting occurred every day of the week, and there were no formal truces with enemy forces to mark Christmas, Easter, or other major days in the religious calendar. In turn the United States did not suspend operations on these holidays, even launching the last major offense campaign of the war, the assault on Okinawa, on Easter Sunday.

Keeping the Sabbath led to disagreements with allies. During the struggle for Guadalcanal, U.S. Marines vigorously objected when the crew of an English ship in the harbor wanted to honor the Sunday Sabbath and delay unloading for a day. In the end, the marines won the argument and the Christian Sabbath was profaned.[32] Army sergeant Mack Morriss, serving as a correspondent for *Yank* magazine in the Pacific, observed that, while based at headquarters, it was still possible to "sense the feeling of Sunday." But on the line, it was no different from any other day. A Japanese soldier interrogated after capture confirmed the sentiment Morriss recorded in his diary, expressing his surprise and disillusionment upon discovering "that Marines fight just as hard on Sunday as any other time, which was contrary to the information apparently given out by Jap officers."[33]

Camaraderie could, at times, encourage all men from a unit to attend the same service, irrespective of the affiliation of the chap-

14. *S/Sgt. John F. O'Brien of Pittsburgh, Pennsylvania, while in a foxhole decorates a Christmas tree with* C *ration can and tinsel dropped from U.S. planes (1944).* Still Picture Branch, U.S. National Archives (111-SC-198234).

lain. There were instances when Jews and Protestants took Holy Communion from a Roman Catholic priest who did not inquire too closely into the faiths of the communicants. In turn, many Roman Catholic GIS, when unable to access a priest, attended—to the consternation of their church's hierarchy—services led by a Protestant chaplain. In other instances, only a Jewish chaplain could be present. One Jewish chaplain found himself the only cleric aboard his naval vessel with hundreds of men ready to take part in an amphibious assault. This rabbi felt comfortable in overseeing all three services, beginning with one for Roman Catholics. Although this rabbi could not say Mass, he deputized a Catholic officer to say the rosary. Most of those ready to embark on the invasion stayed for all three of the services, including the one he led for Jewish GIS.[34]

Chaplains in the combat zone grappled with their faiths' theological precepts and the need to succor men who were gravely imperiled. Chaplain Roger Barney expressed admiration of the spiritual sustenance that Chaplain Hammond offered Catholic marines at the battle for Iwo Jima. Going into battle and placing himself at great risk, Hammond carried significant quantities of reserve sacraments to distribute to men under fire. Much to Barney's surprise, Protestants clamored to receive Holy Communion, something he had never expected from Baptists, Methodists, and other Protestants. He expressed regret at his "callow ineptness" and for not expecting this demand; despite "their training," he noted, these men "expect from their chaplain nothing less than the Body and Blood of Christ."[35]

Barney was not the only chaplain who recognized the need for broadening the group of people who should partake in the sacraments of the Episcopal Church. In his postwar memoir, George Wickersham described a letter from a fellow Episcopalian chaplain who had been at Iwo Jima. This chaplain expressed his angst over giving Communion to those who had not been confirmed into the Episcopal church, violating the precepts of the prayer book rubric. Wickersham expressed his dismay with those who had narrow views of Holy Communion and other sacraments. Wickersham maintained that it was "blasphemous so to inhibit the Almighty." After all, in the Apostle's Creed, Episcopalians pledged a belief not in the "Holy Episcopal Church" but in the "Holy Catholic Church."[36]

Sectarian differences were not always forgotten, even in moments of sheer terror. Chaplain Francis Sampson was a Roman Catholic priest who jumped with his unit on D-Day, on June 6, 1944, and was briefly held as a prisoner of war in the battle for Normandy. He would later have the misfortune to be captured again at the Battle of the Bulge. In his memoir Sampson described how his German captors and the group of wounded American POWs he had shepherded were held in a farmhouse that came under heavy bombardment. Prayer calmed nervous soldiers, and Sampson had the men take turns reciting the Lord's Prayer. But soon an argument developed between Protestants and Roman Catholics over the proper text for this prayer. "Of all times and places for a religious argument! When one of the boys finished with '. . . for Thine is the Kingdom, and the Power, and the glory forever and ever,' one of the Catholic men said that it didn't belong there. The Protestant men insisted that it did. The other Catholic men joined in to insist it didn't belong. I told them each to say it in whatever way he had learned it. Scared as I was, this argument struck me [as] so funny at the time that I almost became hysterical."[37]

Roman Catholic chaplains stressed the importance of their men availing themselves of the sacraments before entering combat. Ideally, a good Catholic should be able to make a personal confession before a priest followed by a Mass, where he could receive the sacrament of Holy Communion. Under canon law then in force, Roman Catholics availing themselves of sacraments at a morning Mass should have fasted at least since midnight. In response to the extreme conditions GIs faced, the military ordinariate received a papal dispensation relaxing the requirements for fasting and looked favorably on priests offering general absolution.

Catholic chaplains often wrote in glowing terms about the piety of men ready to enter combat. Many sought to attend Mass when available and to make confession and receive absolution even in the midst of battle. One naval chaplain, Raymond O'Connor, described how impressed he was by the devotion of the Catholic men and officers aboard the USS Monterey. Not only did many attend a daily Mass, but on some Sundays approximately 90 percent of Catholic GIs could be found at Mass. O'Connor praised the devotion of the ship's captain after one harrowing attack by enemy torpedo planes, which led the captain to ask the next morning that the Mass of Thanksgiving be celebrated, "for the unquestionably Divine protection the ship had."[38] During the assault on Salerno, another chaplain described how the night before D-Day over 1,200 out of 2,000 GIs aboard ship received communion. Chaplain Francis Keenan recounted to Bishop O'Hara how, in the initial hours of the invasion, twenty wounded men were brought back to his warship, where he anointed them and gave them Communion.[39]

But not all Roman Catholic chaplains agreed with this assessment of the piety of their flocks. One chaplain at the Anzio beachhead bemoaned how, even after seeing battle, many Catholics remained lax in following the precepts of their faith. In his view this abundance of lackluster Catholics called into question what "we were doing back home [as] parish priests."[40] Another chaplain, in the Solomon Islands, expressed dismay at the attitude of so many Catholic GIs, who decided that attending a beer party was more important than preparing themselves spiritually for the Mass. When he greeted the returning GIs, this chaplain informed the group that the men who had imbibed food and liquids could still receive Holy Communion, but this would not apply to those who had drunk any alcohol. While willing to bend the rules regarding the fast required before receiving communion, he could not accept indulging in alcohol. There were some who had remained faithful to the tenants of their faith, and these men regularly attended Mass and received Holy Communion. For these more devout men, the chaplain gave up his supper to hear their confessions. His naval superiors were not pleased, and an unnamed officer asked for his name and threatened to report this chaplain to his religious superiors for refusing to be more lenient in allowing sailors to take communion on the eve of battle.[41]

The attitude of commanders toward religion could be complex, especially in war zones. Many chaplains reported to their religious superiors the considerable support they received from their commanders in fulfilling their mission to meet the religious needs of GIs.[42] There were officers who embraced religion and offered outward displays of piety. The correspondent Stanley Mitchell Swinton, in a letter to his family, recalled attending an Easter Sunrise Service, along with hundreds of soldiers, where they heard the commander of the 5th Army, General Lucian Truscott Jr., read from the Bible.[43] But there were also commanders who had little use for chaplains and religion. Chaplain Francis J. McGarry complained to the military ordinariate that when the executive officer of the USS Sampson wanted fewer shipboard announcements made over the public address system, to avoid disruptions, the first one dropped was for daily Mass.[44] One Catholic chaplain stationed in India fumed at the attitude of his colonel, who bluntly declared to him and his Protestant counterpart that he had no interest in their religious activities or recommendations.[45]

The Comforts of Prayer

Before entering battle GIs received significant guidance on how to pray. Religious tracts by a variety of Christian denominations included a range of prayers for many purposes. The JWB widely distributed a pocket-size prayer book. Commercial publishers issued compendia of soldiers' prayers. Even commanders drafted prayers for their men, to gird them for battle. On the eve of the battle of Guadalcanal, Capt. Harry D. Power USN, decided that gathering the crew in one place to pray in unison would be too dangerous. Instead he wrote and mimeographed a prayer to be recited by his crew that called on the: "Lord God, the Lord of Hosts" who "sittest [sic] in the throne judging right, and therefore we make our address and to Thy Divine Majesty in this our necessity, that Thou woldst take the cause into Thine own hand, and judge between us and our enemies." Invoking God's assistance while also imploring God not to "let our sins now cry out against us for vengeance," the prayer contained sectarian pleas to "our Savior and Mighty Deliverer, through Jesus Christ our Lord."[46]

Were their prayers answered? Did God actively intervene in the fates of men and women facing danger? There were chaplains and GIs who answered this question affirmatively. One Christian Science army air force chaplain in the China-Burma-India theater flew across the Himalayas in such a fierce storm that it knocked out the radio and so badly iced the ship's wing that the pilot told the crew to don parachutes and be ready to jump. The chaplain persuaded the pilots to continue flying and to place their "complete trust in God." In the words of one biography written after the war, this chaplain "worked harder than ever" and they arrived at their field with only five minutes' worth of gas left in the tank.[47]

Sometimes the prayers sought God's intervention in the ordering of the world and in international affairs. Perhaps the most prominent individual in the U.S. Army to seek divine intervention was Gen. George Patton, who requested that his chief chaplain write a prayer, to be circulated among the rank and file, that asked God to bring better weather in order to ensure victory against the Germans in December 1944.[48] Other generals were humbler in their relationships with the Divine. Gen. Alexander Patch chastised his command staff during the Battle of the Bulge for participating in a Christmas Eve party "when our comrades are fighting and dying less than twenty miles from where we are." Patch, who had just lost a son in combat, declared to his staff that he would celebrate the Christmas Eve holiday in prayer in his room.[49]

Prayer could comfort and sustain, but it could also distract. Not all embraced it. One pilot commanding a B-17 chastised his gunner for praying when he should have been focusing on incoming aircraft, threatening to relieve him of duty.[50] Others doubted the value of intercessory prayer. One pilot observed in his memoir that he thought God had no part in war.[51] On one base the ritual of the chaplain praying with the men going on a bomber run had become so fixed that his absence provoked a roomful of aviators to refuse to depart unless he could be located to fulfill his obligation.[52] In Protestant theology, the prayers offered by someone other than an ordained minister would have sufficed in the eyes of God. Thus this incident raises questions regarding the line between ritual that has magical implications and the power of prayer.

Sacred Objects and the Thin Line Between Religion and Magic

Soldiers prayed, but they also placed great value on a variety of objects imbued with spiritual qualities. This pattern is hardly unique to the Second World War. Some talismans had the blessing of religious authorities; Roman Catholics often wore religious medals and prayed using rosary beads. Other objects, such as New Testaments, were distributed by the armed forces or religious institutions and were not intended to operate as talismans. But many GIs placed these books in their breast pockets with the hope that they would stop a bullet. One naval chaplain reported to his church superiors that a New Testament had saved the life of a Catholic soldier in the amphibious assault at Salerno, Italy. Without overtly declaring a miracle had happened, Chaplain Keenan described how the bullet had hit the book and "grazed to one side" without piercing it. If this bullet had pierced the missal, it would have killed this soldier. Keenan ended his letter to Bishop O'Hara by asking for more of the medals, beads, and prayer books which were eagerly sought by soldiers.[53]

The lines between religion, magic, and superstition were difficult to delineate. Certainly some clergy, especially from Protestant traditions, denounced talismans as theologically suspect. One recently ordained Methodist chaplain applauded his father, also a Methodist cleric, for clearly differentiating between religion and magic in an editorial.[54] And chaplains were not alone in rejecting the talismans. One sailor bluntly rejected efforts by his folks to purchase a "mezuze" for him, and he adamantly declared, "I don't believe in 'good-luck.'" Abraham Shafer said it would be a waste of "a lot of valuable money" to buy something he would never wear around his neck.[55]

Aviators, like their counterparts on the ground, wore talismans like St. Christopher medals in abundance. They also carried a vast variety of secular objects deemed to give them luck, including silver dollars, rabbits' feet, charms, baby booties from their children, and dice. These were among the objects they carried often. Aviators wore lucky hats, uniforms, and jackets, in some instances refusing to wash them until they completed their tour of duty. Fear of certain numbers, especially thirteen, evoked concern, especially if a mission or aircraft was designated with the number thirteen.[56]

Some nose art painted on planes by aircrews had distinctive religious themes. A crew in the 379th Bomb Group named their ship the Ava Marie and featured the image of a modestly attired woman. But religious themes were not dominant in the nose art created by and for aviators. Images of female sexuality, often of the most misogynistic type, remained dominant. Sometimes the allusions to things spiritual were irreverent, even sacrilegious. One crew portrayed a "diabolical angel" on their plane, featuring a scantily clad woman, with the outlines of her breasts clearly visible, sitting on a cloud with bombs beneath it. "Satan's Baby" was even more graphic, displaying an image of the devil, complete with horns, staring down at a fully nude woman standing with her legs spread apart.[57]

No doubt some aviators embraced pornographic nose art and saw no contradiction in going to chapel and praying with the rosary. But there were chaplains who bridled at the pornographic nature of nose art and announced their displeasure in sermons. Joseph W. Rutter described how his unit chaplain, a Roman Catholic priest, expressed his dismay over the salacious artwork adorning planes

15. An example of the type of nose art that raised the ire of some chaplains. "Ruff 'n Reddy" was painted on a bomber of the 720th Bomb Squadron based in Europe Theater. Gordon P. Brown Collection, Institute on World War II and the Human Experience.

and openly expressed a fear that some would go to their deaths with these "obscene paintings and worse slogans as our epitaph." Even more disconcerting, from the chaplain's perspective, was that the "heathen enemy" did not decorate his planes with such images. This zealous chaplain even singled out one plane's nose art—titled "Hot Box"—in his periodic newsletter: Chaplain's Chatter. To the chaplain's remorse, this plane was eventually reported missing and the crew lost.[58]

Some men did undergo religious conversions in combat and in moments of extreme peril. Foxhole religion was recognized by chaplains and provoked considerable discussion overseas and at home. Chaplain Ben Rose, a Presbyterian minister, dealt directly with the question in a sermon he preached to his infantry unit shortly before their deployment to fight in France in late June 1944. In his sermon Rose said he expected that men in distress would call on God in their hour of need and accepted the claim that there were "no atheists in foxholes." No doubt there would be many "miraculous" deliverances, but Rose feared that when the danger passed, many "will forget him."[59]

In two wide-ranging letters to the home front in early 1945, Chaplain Harry W. Webster described in detail the conversions to Christ that had taken place. He recounted conversions that "followed two days and five days of preaching," and yielded "thirty-one souls." During the baptismal service held on Christmas Eve 1944 at Aitape, New Guinea, a group of GIs watched Webster's immersion of twenty GIs and four Australian soldiers. Webster reflected at length on the temperaments of Victor and Tom, describing the former as a "Syrian boy, a quiet, introspective fellow, slightly mystical in temperament." Only Tom and Victor had their photographs taken for this occasion. At the time Webster had little way of knowing that they would "join each other at Jesus' feet in a very few weeks," and that these photographs would offer some solace to their grieving parents.[60]

Webster, who tried to stay close to the line, also expressed skepticism about whether men in battle were even capable of conversion, "in spite of a few well-publicized cases of men turning to the Lord at the last minute while staring death in the face." Webster defined the problem in a letter to those at home: "In battle a soldier is more of a fighting machine than a man—his heart is so filled with fear, bitterness, and anger, that he is more apt to give expression to his feelings in curses and profanity than in prayer." What did GIs also do in the midst of combat? Webster described their "cursing and raging," usually directed against "the sly enemy, calling them every foul name they could think of."[61]

Some GIs entered the war with strong religious practices, and their experiences in combat only strengthened their faith. In writing to his minister in Meridian, Mississippi, Corporal William O. Moss described how the protection offered by his "Lord and Savior Jesus Christ" and his experiences over the past eight months were proof that "he is watching over me and will carry me back to safety." Moss found spiritual fellowship in a Bible study class that met on Tuesday and Thursday evenings.[62]

There were other sources for religious inspiration, and some GIs found it in Hollywood fare. Even GIs in combat zones frequently had access to motion pictures, especially when pulled off the line. As a pilot with an army air force photographic reconnaissance unit based in the Mediterranean, Bob Earhart regularly commented on the quality of the Hollywood movies he had an opportunity to view. In Earhart's letters to his wife, he often expressed religious sentiments and, instead of quoting scripture for solace, reflected on one film in particular that had touched him deeply: *A Guy Named Joe*. In this film a guardian angel takes an active role in protecting a pilot, and Earhart genuinely reported his confidence that such divine protection was being offered to him. Several weeks later Earhart was killed in battle.[63]

In seeking to understand the religiosity of men under enemy fire, it is possible to overestimate—as well as understate—the piety that existed. Elisha Atkins, a member of the Harvard College Class of 1942 and a U.S. Marine who was wounded in the battle for Cape Gloucester, grants that men in combat offered prayers. In an essay contributed to the anthology *Religion of Soldiers and Sailors*, compiled by Willard L. Sperry and published in 1945, Atkins stresses that these prayers stem from a basic human instinct of survival and avoidance of death. According to Atkins, men do not pray for eternal life or forgiveness of sins, only to live another day. For many, prayer represents a "last-minute everlasting life insurance which can be bought with low premiums and pay big dividends." Once the heat of battle passes, the sense of religiosity likewise fades.[64]

Atkins stresses the religious pluralism that existed among World War II GIs; every shade of opinion was represented, from "belief in its highest form to an active and vociferous atheism."[65] The truly devout were few in number. Atkins speaks of the quality of the comradeship that emerged, born of the sacrifice and suffering of combat. Men sacrificed themselves so that others could live, and this, in Atkins's view, serves as an "affirmation of that basic truth of Christianity: that only he who loses his life shall save it." But Atkins again makes it clear that religiosity does not necessarily inspire all courageous acts; in fact, "many of the most courageous men I have ever known have been either nonreligious or actually antireligious in nature."[66]

Those who experienced combat found it difficult to reflect on their experiences with spouses and other loved ones on the home front. Despite this chasm GIs sought to maintain ties to their homes, especially with loved ones. Mail, for those in foxholes or at forward air bases, took on added significance. Many implored spouses, girlfriends, siblings, and others to write frequently. Those on the home front did write to GIs, telling them of the many prayers offered on their behalf. At Our Lady of Lourdes Church in Cleveland, the 11:00 Sunday Masses were dedicated to the soldiers, and other churches and synagogues frequently held special services for those abroad. On the first Sunday of the month, the congregation in Cleveland placed flowers and lighted vigil candles along a dedicated "Victory Altar." The church also maintained a Military Affairs Committee, which sought to remain in touch with GIs in the field.[67]

Some wartime correspondence, like that of Donald and Florence Julie Lillibridge, divulged intimate thoughts about religion. Florence had planned to join the Women Accepted for Volunteer Emergency Service (WAVES) but fell in love and married in 1943. While based in Quantico, Virginia, they shared a home, but after she became pregnant and he was deployed overseas, she returned to live with her mother in South Dakota. Florence prayed often for her husband's safe return and wrote to him that she had started a novena "with a joint petition to bring my husband home safely, and to bring a normal baby into the world." She also promised Donald that she would say the rosary every day until he came home. In her letter she recognized that Donald's faith did not match her own. "I can see you smiling your tolerant smile about me and my prayers, but Don, even though God is too busy to listen, it is a help to me, and sometimes I feel so futile and helpless that it seems the only way I can gain relief."[68] Although Donald was often open about his fears and shortcomings, there were limits to what he disclosed. The Battle of Tarawa was his initiation into combat, and all he initially confided about that event stuck to the official line: "It was a hard and bitter fight." Even without official censorship, this was something Donald would not discuss with his wife.[69] In a letter a few days later, he confided to Florence that he felt down because he had done a "lousy job" as a leader. It hurt, he wrote, that he "lost more men than any other platoon in the battalion."[70]

The Lillibridge exchanges were emblematic of the chasm between those on the home front and those deployed overseas. New Yorkers never endured the Blitz as London did, and unlike Leningrad, Chicago never faced an enemy siege. A full employment economy led to soaring wages for workers on the home front, and American productive capacity allowed the United States to not only become the Arsenal of Democracy but to produce a cornucopia of consumer goods. New housing remained in short supply, and several essential products were rationed but, overall, Americans consumed more in 1944 than they did in 1940. GIs lived in a world of violence and witnessed the scourge of war, which took a heavy toll on Allied and enemy civilians alike. Willie and Joe, the cartoon characters created to represent the archetypal GIs, remained perpetually grimy, in desperate need of a bath, a shave, and a clean uniform.[71]

Religion, for many GIs, remained an important link to identity and fortified them in the struggle to survive on the battlefield. Many found solace in prayer, worship services, and scriptures. Despite the grumbling that occurred in many quarters, chaplains of all faiths lived up to the expectations of army leaders for meeting the spiritual needs of GIs even in the most stressful situations. But for many GIs faith proved a slender reed that was simply not enough to sustain them. Many suffered mental breakdowns even with religious support. Before considering the wounded, we will first consider the distinctive religious experiences of African Americans, Asian Americans, and Native Americans, which were heavily shaped by pervasive institutional racism.

SEVEN

The Question of Race and Religion

Military conscription and total mobilization resulted in the United States armed forces evolving into one of the most diverse institutions within American society in the 1940s. Conscription increased the number of African Americans, Japanese Americans, American Indians, and Chinese Americans in the armed forces exponentially.[1] Barriers fell as the U.S. Navy reluctantly ended the policy of making stewards (dining room attendants) of all Black sailors and started placing these individuals in other specialties. The war years even resulted in the commissioning of the first group of Black officers in the navy's history.[2] Under pressure from civil rights organizations and First Lady Eleanor Roosevelt, opening aviation to African Americans led to the formation of the storied Tuskegee airmen.[3] The U.S. Marine Corps, with great reluctance, incorporated African Americans into the ranks of this previously "lily white" branch of the armed services.[4] Doors also opened to Japanese Americans. In the immediate aftermath of the attack at Pearl Harbor, they were excluded from the armed forces, but by 1943 several segregated army combat regiments of Japanese Americans had been formed and deployed to the European theater.[5] American Indians were never formally segregated, and the U.S. Marines embraced their linguistic diversity when they created a special unit of Navajo code talkers to transmit messages in their indigenous languages.[6] Once America entered the war, with China as a major ally, Chinese Americans were further integrated into the ranks. In addition the army air force created two all–Chinese American units and deployed them to China.

Despite the universalism of Christianity, the chaplain corps of both the army and navy mirrored the institutional racism that permeated American society. Even when Black GIS worshiped God, segregation remained the norm. When assessing the question of race, the failure of the Rooseveltian ideals regarding the free exercise of religion is most pronounced. The U.S. Army and Navy offered scant recognition to non-Western traditions, which fell outside of the tri-faith paradigm, despite the large number of Chinese Americans and Native Americans who embraced them.

Racialized categorization extended beyond the Black-and-white binary. For instance, the U.S. Army drew racial distinctions in how it met the religious needs of Asian Americans and American Indians. On the one hand, the army did commission a Japanese American Protestant chaplain to serve the segregated Nisei units that fought in Europe. The army chief of chaplains balked at commissioning either an American Indian or Chinese American chaplain, insisting that clergy from these racial groups could not meet the religious needs of white GIS.

A few months after the Pearl Harbor attack, the OWI issued a pamphlet celebrating the achievements of African Americans and making a case for the African American community's support of the war. Heralding the collective achievements of prominent Black leaders and the wider African American community, *The Negroes and the War* emphasized the size, stature, and resources of the Black church. It stressed the militant nature of the church under slavery and described this institution as the bedrock of the Black community. Skirting such sensitive issues as Jim Crow, lynching, and higher levels of poverty among African Americans, the pamphlet stressed the threat of the Axis powers to Black Americans. Italy had made Ethiopians one of the first victims of Axis aggression, and a Nazi victory would pose a major threat to the Black church along with all other religions.[7]

Many films the armed forces produced either ignored or minimized the African American presence, but there were important exceptions. The army's *The Negro Soldier* (1944) was produced in part as a result of pressure from civil rights activists for a positive representation of Black soldiers. With a script written by a civilian African American playwright, Carlton Moss, this film embraces

16. *Easter morning, T/5 William E. Thomas . . . and Pfc. Joseph Jackson . . . will roll specially prepared eggs on Hitler's lawn.* Still Picture Branch, U.S. National Archives (111-SC-202330).

the Rooseveltian vision of religion as a bedrock of American society. This documentary uses as a backdrop a Black church with an African American minister narrating the story of Black military service from the American Revolution to the righteous struggle against fascism. Through a letter read aloud by a mother in the congregation, recounting her son's experiences in the army and his impending acceptance into officer candidate school, the film provides scenes of African Americans going through induction at an integrated induction center followed by stock film of Black soldiers performing their duties in the various branches in which they served. Chaplains appeared in important cameo roles with a white chaplain at the induction center encouraging a biracial group of soldiers to take their troubles to the chaplain. In another scene a Black chaplain addresses a segregated unit, extolling the achievements of Black troops. Hymns bookend the documentary, with the choir in the opening scene offering the final lines in "Since Jesus Came into My Heart," and the film concludes with "Onward Christian Soldiers" and "Joshua Fit the Battle of Jericho."[8]

The Negro Soldier underscores the liminal position of African Americans, who were buffeted by institutional racism but also afforded opportunities denied to them in the United States. For African Americans coming from the segregated South, deployment overseas exposed them to societies that did not establish a color bar in accommodations or entertainment. Paradoxically, Chinese Americans and Japanese Americans deployed to the Southern United States found themselves treated as honorary whites in terms of public accommodations. The wife of one Nisei soldier remembered that when she and her husband boarded a bus in the Southern United States, she was directed by the driver to the front of the bus, where white passengers sat. No doubt this spouse, part of the first generation of Japanese Americans, was stunned given the widespread segregation and discrimination she had faced living on the West Coast.[9]

The Racial Divide and Chaplains

The army and navy policies on race played an important role in structuring the religious lives of soldiers and sailors. Racial discrimination remained rife in the army, but it was counterbalanced by a long tradition of African American military participation in this branch of the armed services, albeit in segregated units. While few in number, Black line officers and chaplains had been commissioned by the army as far back as the Civil War.[10] On the eve of America's entry into the Second World War, a Black officer, Benjamin O. Davis Sr., rose to the rank of brigadier general.[11] In 1941 three Black chaplains served in the regular army, and seventeen were in the reserves. Chief of chaplains William R. Arnold and his office genuinely wanted to secure more African Americans, and army press releases were regularly distributed to outlets, publicizing the achievements of Black chaplains.[12]

The advent of the modern fleet in the late nineteenth century had led to a deliberate policy of excluding African Americans from the enlisted ranks, consigning them to serve as stewards. Steward mates wore a distinctive uniform that visually established their primary function on naval vessels as waiters and personal servants for officers.[13] The depth of institutional racism is exemplified by the experience of Doris "Dorrie" Miller. On December 7, 1941, Miller—a ship's steward—single-handedly shot down a Japanese plane during the attack on Pearl Harbor. Decorated for gallantry, Miller was prominently featured in a publicity campaign to increase war bond sales. Despite his heroism Miller remained a ship's steward until he was killed in action when the Japanese sank the ship he served on in the Gilbert Island campaign. Thus for Black soldiers and sailors, heroism counted for only so much.[14]

Furthermore, the army and navy took different paths in meeting the spiritual needs of Black GIs. The army believed Black chaplains were crucial to meet the needs of Black soldiers. Arnold aggressively sought qualified African American chaplains and managed to recruit several hundred. They carried out an extensive campaign with historically Black churches, urging them to nominate qualified candidates. Public appeals were sent out through the media, aiming to convince Black clerics to enlist. Denominational leaders of both historically Black churches and predominantly white denominations aided these recruitment efforts. Some of these appeals received favorable responses. T. W. Medearis, general superintendent for the Missouri Baptist General Association, affiliated with the Southern Baptist Convention, recommended Rev. William Edward Hall, a Black minister, for chaplaincy and expressed a willingness to provide him an ecclesiastical endorsement.[15]

Why did the navy have such a difficult time recruiting Black ministers and priests as chaplains? Official histories of the naval chaplaincy in the Second World War blame it on the inability to find suitable candidates. This claim is self-serving, given the navy's willingness to take candidates for the chaplaincy directly out of theological school, while the army required prospective chaplains to have several years of experience as civilian clerics. If the navy had been committed to increasing the number of African American chaplains, it could have initiated a V-12 program at a historically Black theological school to increase the number of Black ministers.[16]

When comparing the navy's pathetic efforts to recruit Black chaplains with the more successful efforts of the army, it is tempting to categorize it as one of the small advances African Americans made in the long struggle for equality and dignity. But the quest for Black chaplains also represented a deeply embedded view that clergy should only meet the spiritual needs of their own racial groups. Even more stark was the policy, implemented by Arnold, which mandated that nonwhite clerics could not minister to white soldiers. For instance, the first Black Roman Catholic priest appointed as a chaplain during World War II was assigned to the segregated 93rd Division, even though this unit was overwhelmingly Protestant, instead of to a white unit with a higher proportion of Roman Catholics.[17] Moreover, assigning this Black priest to an all-Black unit came at a time when church leaders and many GIs complained about the dearth of Roman Catholic chaplains capable of administering the sacraments. In this case segregation simply trumped these complaints.

Segregation generally made it difficult for the small number of Black Roman Catholics to gain access to a priest. In 1943 1st Sgt. Walter J. Pierre implored Cardinal Francis J. Spellman to send more priests to the faithful. Pierre observed that when his unit was stationed in Fort Benning, he and fellow Catholics were able to attend Mass celebrated by "Good Father Waterstratt of Rochester." When Pierre's quartermaster battalion was deployed to Africa, they had access to a French priest, but many other units lacked regular contact with a priest because they were "far [from] the Colored bivouce [sic] areas." He informed the cardinal of his desire to become a missionary brother in the church after leaving the service. While stationed abroad, this pious sergeant strived to better understand "native customs" for the day he would become a missionary, asserting, "If the Catholic young men and women back home could see these poor Arab [children] and adults they would forsake every thing like the Apostles of old to help open the gates of heaven for them."[18]

Other racial groups faced similar problems. When the Congregational Church put forth one of their Chinese American ministers, Reverend Wong of California, as a prospective chaplain, senior army chaplaincy officials rejected his application. In the view of the chaplaincy corps leadership, a Chinese minister, even one ordained by a predominantly white Protestant denomination, could not serve as an army chaplain given the absence of segregated units. (Later the army air force created two all–Chinese American service units, to serve in China, that went without chaplains.) In rejecting his application, the chaplain corps implied there was no possibility of Reverend Wong deploying with white troops.[19]

A similar pattern of exclusion almost prevented Rev. James Ottipoby, a Comanche and Reformed Church minister, from becoming an army chaplain. Characterized by his church group as "cultured, well educated and gifted in his ability to deal with men," Ottipoby's candidacy for chaplain was justified by his marriage to "a college woman of full Caucasian blood."[20] When presented with Ottipoby's application, the military made inquiries to see if there were sufficient numbers of American Indians in the ranks of the army to warrant his appointment. Queries to two units believed to have high percentages of American Indian troops showed quite the opposite. Claims that half the men with the 79th Coast Artillery Regiment were Native Americans proved inaccurate; the commanding officer reported that only seven American Indians served with the unit.[21] The commanding officer conveyed that a significant number of Mexican Americans were with the regiment and that they were quite pleased with the Roman Catholic chaplains assigned to the unit.[22] Ottipoby was initially rejected because of the lack of a "sufficient number of communicants of your ancestry at this time to warrant appointment." Pressure from church officials led the army to relent, and they eventually commissioned Ottipoby as a chaplain.

This discrimination directed at American Indian and Chinese American ministers as chaplains is striking because neither the army nor the navy had formal policies mandating the segregation of GIs with these ancestries. Paradoxically, diffusing American Indians and Chinese Americans throughout the army and navy led both branches to ignore their distinctive religious needs. In the case of Japanese Americans, segregation prompted the army to consider ways to meet those needs, specifically for the Buddhists in the ranks of Nisei units. Besides commissioning Japanese American Protestant ministers to serve Japanese American troops, the army chief of chaplains tried to locate a suitable Buddhist cleric for appointment as an army chaplain. Ultimately, the army demurred at commissioning a Buddhist chaplain, asserting a qualified candidate could not be secured.[23]

Embracing an AME Bishop and Spurning Fundamentalist Leaders

Racial and theological hierarchies were not a simple binary. While the army placed African Americans lower in the hierarchy than it did mainline Protestants, Roman Catholics, and Jews, the status of the Black church rated more highly than the fundamentalists associated with the National Association of Evangelicals in the eyes of the War Department. An African American bishop of the AME church would be granted the same opportunities as representatives of the Federal Council of Churches, Roman Catholic Church, and JWB to take official overseas tours to visit American troops. In sharp contrast the War Department ignored pleas from fundamentalist leaders for the opportunity for similar tours. In a letter the Rev. Harold J. Ockenga sent to the U.S. Army chief of staff, Gen. George Marshall, the day after Christmas 1944, he expressed the dismay of white fundamentalist leaders at this snub. The prominent evangelical leader asked for the military to let them send preachers and musicians overseas to promote an aggressive ministry among American soldiers stationed abroad.[24] Protesting that this privilege had been extended to Roman Catholic cardinal Francis John Spellman and a churchman from the Federal Council of Churches, Ockenga wondered when the evangelicals' turn would come. Marshall replied to this missive in the new year, refusing to grant this request and declaring that if special privileges were extended to evangelicals, they would have to be applied universally.[25]

Ockenga had legitimate grounds for his complaint; the army had favored representatives of the mainline Protestant establishment and the Roman Catholic hierarchy in sending them abroad for world tours that drew substantial publicity and required significant military resources. The army had also accorded this privilege to a senior official from the JWB and to a representative of the Fraternal Council of Negro Churches, Bishop J. A. Gregg of the AME Church. Despite the pervasiveness of institutional racism within the military and American society, the Roosevelt administration and the army had privileged a Black bishop over a white evangelical minister who led a prominent church in Boston's Beacon Hill.

This snubbing of Ockenga underscores the conflict between army leaders and fundamentalists. The religious hierarchies favored by civilian and military leaders during the Second World War included mainstream Protestants, the Roman Catholic church, the JWB, and African American churches.

The decision to send a Black religious leader on an overseas tour was initiated in April 1943 by Rev. R. R. Wright, the executive secretary of the Fraternal Council of Negro Churches, who contacted the White House to inquire whether the Roosevelt administration would sponsor a world tour of overseas bases by a prominent Black leader. Marvin H. McIntyre, Roosevelt's presidential secretary, wrote the War Department supporting the idea and noting that "the Catholic churches, Protestant churches, and those of the Jewish faith have all been given an opportunity for a representative of each of them to visit the fronts, a representative of all the colored churches should be given the same privileges."[26] Chief of Chaplains Arnold quickly endorsed this idea, remarking that this trip would be interpreted as a further endorsement of institutional segregation. He said it "would conform to the War Department policy of formation of separate units of Negro troops" and would be "helpful for the procurement of Negro chaplains needed for Negro units." Arnold suggested such a visit would further bolster morale among both "Negro" troops and the Black civilian population at home.[27]

Wright's group nominated Bishop J.A. Gregg as its representative for the tour, and the White House and the War Department quickly concurred with the choice of a leader with a strong military background. Gregg, who had fought as an enlisted man in the Spanish American War and had been a chaplain in the First World War, embarked on a worldwide tour that took several months to complete. Accompanied by J. A. DeVeaux, the highest-ranking Black chaplain in the regular army, Gregg traveled to Asia, Australia, the Southwest Pacific, Europe, and Africa. Garnering substantial publicity in both the white and Black press, Gregg even had the opportunity to visit Palestine and return to the Republic of South Africa, where he had lived as a missionary earlier in his career.

Gregg's world tour operated on several levels. For the army it provided a means to promote a positive public image of African American troops. Unsurprisingly, the Black press offered extensive coverage of Gregg's journey. For Gregg this tour bolstered his authority and status within his denomination and the broader Black community. It also allowed him to meet the spiritual needs of Black troops by serving as their advocate and bringing attention to them. Gregg wrote a memoir of his tour, and this text suggests the tightrope he walked and, by inference, many Black chaplains walked. A frontal assault on Jim Crow would have likely led to a cancelation of the tour. Nonetheless, the tour afforded an opportunity to pose nuanced challenges to the institutional racism pervasive in the army.

Gregg's memoir is upbeat, emphasizing the positive and stressing that the purpose of his trip was neither to investigate nor sermonize but to offer a measure of comfort to Black troops stationed in all parts of the world. He recorded the isolation and homesickness many Black GIs experienced, especially those in the Pacific. Throughout his memoir Gregg stressed the contribution Black GIs made to the war effort and only obliquely referred to the institutional racism that consigned most Black troops to support roles. He observed that in New Guinea African Americans had no difficulty manning bulldozers or other construction vehicles, despite the objections voiced at home, by union officials, that these vehicles were too complex for Blacks to operate.

Gregg's travel narrative, published in 1945, offered subtle challenges to the army's racial policies. For instance, if Gregg personally received unequal accommodations, he made no mention of it. Instead he described the hospitality he received from white army and navy commanders and civilian leaders in other countries, such as being hosted in the Government House in Papua New Guinea by Gen. Douglas MacArthur. Although Gregg primarily interacted with Black troops and often led religious services for them, on more than one occasion he spoke to white GIs and even participated in their worship services. In recounting his time spent visiting the sick and wounded, he stressed how well these integrated facilities met the needs of men of all races. He wrote approvingly of an interracial marriage between a Black GI and an Indian woman, during his journey in South Asia, and openly criticized the British for not doing more to ameliorate the famine gripping parts of India.

Gregg called on America to live up to the ideals set forth in the Four Freedoms and the Atlantic Charter. This is not an isolated plea. It reflects a trope frequently used by Black leaders to achieve a double victory in the war against the Axis powers abroad and racism at home. One air force private, writing to FDR, expressed his approval of the president's "affirmation of our war aims": "Your use of the word for freedom, equality, and justice for our Negro Americans, no less than for our white Americans, or our Jewish, Protestant, and Catholic Americans, or for the subjugated peoples in Europe and China and all other lands." While praising FDR for Executive Order 8802 and other actions in support of civil rights, he also described at length the undemocratic nature of the armed forces engaged in a fight for world democracy.[28]

The Burdens of Segregation and Finding Solace

Despite widespread prejudice Black chaplains, especially if endorsed by predominantly white churches, had allies. Some denominations were quite assertive in supporting their African American chaplains and members. The Congregational Christian Churches were proud of African American ministers from their denomination commissioned as chaplains with the U.S. Army. They were also appalled at the discrimination some of them endured. In a letter to a hotel manager, forwarded to the army chief of chaplains, Rev. Frederick L. Fagley—a senior official with the church—lambasted the Charlotte Hotel in North Carolina and was aghast at the way they treated "a Captain in the Army, and a highly respected negro clergyman" who was his guest at a lunch and conference held for Congregational chaplains. In his letter Fagley recounted how Chaplain Harvey E. Johnson, after leaving the event, was "compelled to ride the freight elevator, while the white chaplains used the main elevator." Fagley viewed this treatment as an "insult to the Army and also contrary to the standards accepted among Christian gentlemen."[29]

There remained a keen awareness within the senior leadership of the chaplain corps of the need to walk a tightrope between unrepentant bigots and growing pressure by civil rights organizations

17. *African American Chaplain standing at the podium conducting religious service on the deck of a U.S. Coast Guard Vessel, South Pacific.* Schomburg Center for Research in Black Culture, Photographs and Print Division, New York Public Library.

and some churches for the army to offer greater opportunity to African Americans. One detailed memorandum on how to complete a chaplain's report advised that reporting of services should not be "separated as to races," even though it reflected an effort by many chaplains to indicate that "*all* races are being served." It cautioned that "should such a report fall into unfriendly hands it may appear to them in another light."[30]

There were limits to what the army chief of chaplains would do to accommodate African American chaplains and troops. For instance, while Protestant, Roman Catholic, and Jewish chaplains held senior leadership positions in the chaplain corps, Arnold rejected calls made by Arthur Devan of the General Commission to appoint an African American chaplain to a senior position in his headquarters.[31] Relatedly, in June 1945 the *Chicago Defender* ran a story seeking to explain the lack of Black chaplains. The article blamed this shortfall on the bigoted attitudes of white officers and their frequent censorship of sermons, combined with low pay, which contributed to discouraging ministers from volunteering.[32] Although the army, in July 1943, had 246 Black chaplains, this number fell short of the quota allotted to historically Black denominations by several hundred.[33]

The army's educational requirement excluded a number of Black ministers, as many had never attended either college or seminary. But the mandate that army chaplains must have prior pastoral experience meant that Private First Class Jubie B. Bragg Jr. could not hope for chaplaincy, although he held a degree from Florida A&M University and a master's from the University of Michigan in public health and was deemed a "licensed minister" by his denomination, merely awaiting ordination in the "near future."[34] A. E. McWilliams, who held a divinity degree from Yale University and was endorsed by the Presbyterian Church for the army chaplaincy, expressed his disappointment and "hurt" because he had been disqualified on a rather "shallow pretext" of being overweight. He requested that church officials look into the matter since he wanted an appointment, particularly emphasizing that the army needed Black chaplains.[35]

African American chaplains, like their white counterparts, benefited from their status as officers. In many Black units, they were the only African American officers, and their status gave them unique access to the chain of command. Moreover, chaplains—as a result of their formal education and prior pastoral experience— could prove crucial to many illiterate and poorly educated Black GIs in navigating the complexities of army regulations. Many Black chaplains embraced the responsibility of providing social and recreational opportunities for their men to ameliorate their being barred from many nearby towns and cities when stationed in the United States. For instance, Chaplain Edward Carroll, assigned to Black GIs building the Alcan Highway, traveled a weeklong circuit in a half-ton pickup truck with both religious and recreational equipment. He regularly pitched a recreational tent, allowing men access to games, records, books and shortwave radio broadcasts. To both enhance chapel services and provide another outlet for recreation, he organized a band and an accompanying glee club.[36]

Some chaplains who overtly challenged the system often ran into trouble. In his inspection report of the 2nd Cavalry Division at Fort Clark, Texas, the army's only African American general, Benjamin O. Davis, reported that "the colored chaplains are not very much assistance in helping the unit commanders in matters of racial adjustment." Part of the problem reflected tensions between the division chaplain and the individual unit chaplains. The problem, Davis claimed, stemmed in part from the belief that "any expressions setting forth complaints of enlisted men regarding alleged discrimination would bring about their immediate transfer." The chaplains reported their strong belief that two recent transfers of Black chaplains stemmed from their willingness to intercede on behalf of enlisted men.[37] "A Negro Soldier" complained, in a letter to the *Atlanta Daily World*, that the chaplain at Fort Clark, Texas, had been run off his post by the commanding general when he "protested to him against using the word *n*—when referring to colored troops."[38] In the case of Chaplain Luther M. Fuller, it led to court martial and dismissal from the service. Fuller, from the pulpit and other outlets, publicly criticized the treatment Black GIs endured on transport ships in the South Pacific. While he was in New Guinea, white GIs threatened to attack him; it was only through the intercession of Black troops that physical harm to his person was prevented. Court martialed and discharged from the service, his case was reported in the Black press, and protests were sent to Washington DC, urging authorities to charge the military with a miscarriage of justice.[39]

Other chaplains would not directly confront institutional discrimination but still strived to ameliorate its impact on Black GIs. With the support of the Supreme Headquarters of the Allied Expeditionary Force (SHAEF) chaplain, Beverly Ward joined several other Black chaplains in a campaign of moral suasion aimed at preventing Black soldiers from committing rape. In December 1944 Ward toured the Brittany base section and participated in twenty-two "Crime Prevention Programs" that reached 7,894 GIs. He also authored a widely distributed pamphlet, "Let's Look at Rape," which is striking for the punitive nature of the appeal, insisting that rape had been deemed the "vilest crime that a man can commit." To emphasize the point, the pamphlet included the image of the hangman's noose. The widely distributed pamphlet underscored a truism: army authorities disproportionately investigated, convicted, and executed African American GIs for the crime of rape. In many ways the pamphlet is a subversive document, for it was probably read by some Black GIs as confirmation of the institutional racism inherent in army life.[40]

This pamphlet relied on several tropes common to sexual morality lectures. Besides underscoring the risk to life and limb, it reminded Black GIs of the harm that a rapist would cause not only to his family but also to his race. Wartime service had advanced the cause of African Americans, the author insisted, but the distressing statistics regarding rape committed by Black troops would lead enemies to brand all Blacks as rapists. It underscored the dangers posed by loose women and the consequences of alcohol in dimming moral judgment. Beverly did not take credit for his authorship of the pamphlet; instead, SHAEF distributed this "restricted" document under the signature of a "Negro Chaplain."

Captain Henry C. Bryant, serving with the medical corps, found this pamphlet appalling and wrote a letter of protest to the SHAEF commander, Dwight Eisenhower. This pamphlet, in Bryant's view, smacked of the "same bit of propaganda Dr. Goebbels has disseminated about colored troops to the people of Europe." He expected the pamphlet would "create more racial antagonism among white troops," and among Black troops it would only fuel further resentment. Bryant also blasted the pamphlet as factually incorrect in places and poorly edited, noting that throughout the publication the word "Negro" was rendered with a lowercase n.[41] Eisenhower did not defend the content but maintained that the person who wrote it was acting in the "best interests of all concerned."[42] His headquarters passed on the letter to General Davis, who offered a defense of Ward. Initially, the pamphlet was such a success with men in Ward's unit that Davis, along with the theater commander, decided on a wider distribution. Davis maintained that Bryant's letter of protest was the first "unfavorable reaction which has come to our attention."[43]

Several interpretations of Ward's actions can be offered. Like his white counterparts in the chaplaincy, he viewed issues of sexual morality as a paramount concern that warranted every possible use of moral suasion. Ward and other Black chaplains' efforts to discourage rape certainly had the approval of the senior leadership and of the U.S. Army in Europe; otherwise a tour of the bases would not have been possible. The support given to the distribution of this pamphlet reflected the difficult tightrope the American high command traversed in 1944 and 1945. Rape did represent a problem, on several counts, for American forces, beginning with a significant number perpetrated by American troops on French women. When carrying out the death penalty in France for rape and murder, the army often erected the gallows close to the site of the crime to assure the local population that perpetrators were actually punished. In occupied Germany the army was less solicitous of the civilian population, and neither white nor Black troops faced the death penalty for the crime of rape. SHAEF did face pressure from the NAACP and other civil rights organizations, who were quite critical of the army's inequitable court martial system, which often imposed far harsher punishments on Black GIs than on their white counterparts. The pamphlet confirmed what civil rights leaders protested: African Americans were hanged in greater numbers than white GIs for the crime of rape.[44]

The shortage of Black chaplains in the army meant white chaplains frequently met the religious needs of Black units, often on an itinerate basis. The racial bar that prevented Black and Asian American chaplains from ministering to white troops did not apply to white chaplains serving Black troops and other racial minorities. A significant number of white chaplains were ill-suited for this task. One chaplain's assistant recounted how a Roman Catholic priest he worked under "was so bigoted he became physically ill when he encountered black troops." Another priest and chaplain, named Father Daniel, was stunned that a man with these beliefs could become a Catholic priest.[45] The attitudes of white chaplains assigned to Black units in the army could be condescending and oblivious to the discrimination endured by Black troops. One Universalist minister, Chaplain Phillips L. Thayer, wrote to a senior church official about his "enjoyable" experiences spending a month with a Black unit, the 828th Tank Destroyer Battalion, while in training at Camp Claiborne, Louisiana, He praised the "fine singing of the spirituals" because the Black GIs had their "heart[s] in it." The absence of Black officers from the battalion was not only acceptable; Thayer claimed that "most of the boys prefer it that way," since these white officers understood them better and trusted them more than "colored officers." Thayer acknowledged that there were a few misguided malcontents who did not know any better, but these were men who "had never served under colored officers and seemed to think they were being mistreated."[46]

Thayer's experience serving Black troops may have been favorable, but the Christian Commission for Camp and Defense Communities of the Federal Council of Churches offered a less sanguine view. In their monthly newsletter issued for December 1942, they reported the observations of a field representative who visited northern army bases to collect information on Black soldiers. The report observed that in places with substantial numbers of Black troops and no African American chaplains, such as Aberdeen Proving Ground and Indiantown Gap, attendance at chapel faltered.[47]

In 1942 U.S. Army chaplain Edwin R. Carter Jr., a white Episcopal priest, investigated—at the behest of senior leaders—racial tensions between white and Black troops in a small borough in England. The conflict centered upon invitations to Black and white troops from the British to attend dances and other social functions. Carter argued that it remained imperative to maintain segregation while seeking to improve the recreational outlets for GIs. His final report on the "Racial Problem in Britain" ended up in the files of Gen. Benjamin O. Davis. Carter criticized the fact that "leadership often comes from the more radical group or semi-educated negroes, who seek as a goal social equality with the white race, which equality is interpreted to mean amalgamation."[48]

There were, however, white chaplains who were dismayed and appalled by the racial discrimination they witnessed. Even by the standards of wartime chaplaincy, Rabbi Morris Gordon had a unique experience in Burma, ministering to those who were building the Burma Road. In his memoir, Morris recalls how he deliberately picked a Black Catholic sergeant who had graduated from Oberlin College as his chaplain's assistant. The two of them traveled to what was becoming the Burma Road to China, conducting services for groups of soldiers working in construction units, which were often Black units. In a segregated army they were a unique pair, with "Eddie playing his harmonica, or a flute" and him preaching a "good old Jewish sermon, laced with stories of Jacob and Moses." They were sure to catch the attention of soldiers who witnessed their services. A perceptive chaplain, Morris painfully observed that at the dedication ceremony opening the Burma Road there was not a Black face in sight. The war had brought him personal tragedy; he had lost Eddie, his right-hand man, when a bomb hit his Jeep. To mourn his passing, Morris arranged for a well-attended Catholic service at his base camp and also presided over an impromptu traditional kaddish service.[49]

Moreover, not all white GIs accepted the existing racial order. Mary Robinson, a white WAC, described the searing racism at Camp Robinson, Arkansas, that almost led to the murder of a Black GI. She also recalled berating the chaplain who led the WAC service for being so fastidious about enforcing the color line in chapel services.[50] Hyman Samuelson, a Jew from New Orleans, found himself serving as a captain with a Black engineer unit in New Guinea. He too came close to despair over the systematic mistreatment of his men by the army and his commander. The chain of command limited how much he could do for his men, but his diary and his letters bristled with a stream of complaints about his superior officers and their many actions inimical to his men's well-being. His diary offers keen insights into efforts by a commander to subvert religious autonomy in his ranks. In one entry Samuelson noted that his commander wanted his men to sing martial songs and not the spirituals favored by his chaplains. Samuelson developed a close friendship with the first chaplain assigned to the 96th Engineers (Colored) and found his services inspirational. Samuelson sought to ameliorate the discrimination they faced and used his authority as a company commander to make sure his men received most Sundays off.[51]

Samuelson wrote at length about the depth of spirituality expressed by the men when they sang at services. These songs, along with his colleague's sermons, offered him comfort as he battled the isolation and homesickness of being far from his wife, who had just given birth. Is it music that made the religious life of the African American GI distinctive? Samuelson was not the only one to express this sentiment, which was reflected in many private and public observations by white officers and enlisted men, as well as journalists.

When Chaplain Charles Fisher, attached to the 366th Infantry, was asked by Frederick Fagley of the General Council of the Congregational Christian Churches what music was suitable for Black troops, he was surprised to learn that such classic hymns as "Abide with Me," "All Hail the Power of Jesus' Name," "Am I a Soldier of the Cross," and a host of others were considered "unsuitable for Negro troops." All of the hymns deemed unsuitable were in the official army and navy hymnal, and several of the songs were even listed as spirituals. Fisher argued for using the simple hymns of the church, because they were better at conveying the proper message. He also thought, "Colored troops as a whole shrink up when Chaplains ask for spirituals because they believe that the Chaplain is just trying to place them in the category of the 'Big me' and the 'Little you' in other words because of the many hardships suffered by the Negro troops. They believe this is just another medium of being reminded that 'Never the Twain Shall Meet.'"[52]

For many Black GIs religion offered a refuge and a place of cultural identity. Although silent about his religious beliefs and practices, one Black future paratrooper noted that the chapel on his base served as a place of equality among all men. In his memoir this New Jersey native recounted how he faced court martial for directly disobeying the orders of a senior officer. He met with the army's senior Black officer, Gen. Benjamin O. Davis, in the chapel to discuss his situation.[53]

The absence of African American chaplains in the U.S. Navy constrained the religious lives of African American GIs. On many smaller naval vessels, African American sailors, like their white counterparts, seldom had access to a shipboard chaplain. Some stewards found themselves as the sole Black sailor on the crew. One white naval officer recounted the tragic experience of a steward's mate on a small tank landing ship who was better educated than most of the white Southern sailors aboard his vessel. The antipathy directed toward this lone Black sailor was unrelenting, and in one incident his white shipmates almost let him drown. One day this Black steward had enough; he disobeyed a simple request from the vessel commander for an extra portion of ice cream, walked away, and started screaming obscenities. One can only imagine how circumscribed this sailor's religious life was on such a vessel.[54] When the war ended, one former navy chaplain publicly criticized the racial hatred directed against Black and Jewish sailors aboard his vessel. Lt. Commander Harvey Swanson recalled that intolerance was so great that "Negro sailors were jim-crowed in practically every phase of sea life and seamen of the Jewish faith concealed the fact to escape like treatment."[55]

On bigger ships with chaplains, Black messmates would come into contact with chaplains even if they did not attend shipboard services. Black sailors encountered chaplains and commissioned officers when they served them their meals, made their beds, and cleaned their quarters. Because of these daily encounters, relationships formed between Black messmates and chaplains. While aboard the USS *Miami*, Chaplain John David Zimmerman taught several mess attendants to read, and one mess attendant gained the ability to write letters to his wife as well as read the Bible.[56]

Chaplain Daniel F. Meehan, assigned to a Seabees unit, wrote an editorial for his unit's newspaper welcoming the arrival of a Black battalion to start their training at the Norfolk Naval Station in 1942. Welcoming these "Brothers-in-Arms" to the "titanic struggle to defend the spiritual and material welfare of the great republic," Meehan declared that every "Seabee takes pride in this demonstration by the colored race of its loyalty and fidelity to the high principles of American democracy." This chaplain declared that the arrival of the 34th Battalion represented a "telling answer to the slave nations of the Axis that democracy not only exists, but works, in the free United States."[57]

Even chaplains solicitous of the religious life of Black sailors could reinforce the racial hierarchy dominant within the U.S. Navy and the broader society. When sent to the Naval Air Station in San Diego, California, Chaplain Donald Mackay, a Methodist minister fresh out of Duke University seminary, made a special effort to reach out to Black stewards at the base by organizing segregated services for them. His first effort proved a disappointment; only thirty Black stewards attended. In a letter home to his mother, he reflected on the service. While the "singing was not as good as I hope it will become, it was nevertheless characterized by [the] rhythm and spirit I had expected." For this special service he preached a sermon on "brotherhood" to mark National Brotherhood Week. By contrast, the white chapel service attracted a standing room only crowd of over 320 sailors and marines.[58] Two months later Mackay reported to his parents that 146 stewards had attended his recent Sunday service, and one of the chief petty officers had brought his family to attend. The music had also improved, as a "special quartet of newly arrived stewards furnished some typical Negro spirituals along the lines of the four Mills brothers."[59] Not only were the services segregated, but Mackay held the worship services for Black sailors in the recreational hall at 0900 while white personnel took part in Protestant services at 1000 in the chapel.[60] Unfortunately, no known accounts exist from the Black sailors who Mackay led in worship about the degree to which they either welcomed his paternalism or resented it.

How should a chaplain respond to the cry for justice and opportunity? Naval chaplain Jacob K. Shankman, a Reform rabbi, recounted that one day "a group of colored boys almost stampeded me"; they were seeking a reprieve from "cleaning and washing and waiting on table[s]" and instead sought "glamour, excitement, and fighting." As one sailor bluntly declared, "I don't want to work in a B.O.Q. (Bachelor Officers' Quarters). I want a gun. I want to fight. This is no war!" Shankman's recounting of the advice he offered these men suggests the degree to which institutional racism was embedded and the degree to which many chaplains reinforced it. He said, "One had to talk to them patiently, persuade them that 'they also serve who only stand and wait,'" with the vague promise "that their turn would come."[61]

The absence of chaplains on many vessels often encouraged African Americans to organize worship services, Bible studies, and other religious activities on their own initiative. Before the navy commissioned the first Black chaplain in 1944, the uss *Mason*, a destroyer escort, sailed with a predominantly African American crew and a complement of white officers. Like many ships of a similar class, this vessel went without a chaplain, and regular worship services were not held. But a group of Black crewmen took it upon themselves to organize regular Bible studies on their maiden voyage across the Atlantic.[62]

18. *However pressing his duties* STM2/c *James Lee Frazer always finds time to read a few chapters from his Bible each day. In this study he is especially intense about his devotional routine . . . it was the night before the opening strike of a raid on Manila Bay* [January 9, 1945]. Still Picture Branch, U.S. National Archives (80-G-30524).

Were African American GIS more observant than white GIS? One of the tropes common in American propaganda and in the role staked out for chaplains is that Black Americans were more religious and that this could be used as a mechanism of social control. But when on leave or on a pass, Black GIS did not always seek out religious services. The Booker T. Washington Service Club in Staten Island discussed how to meet the religious needs of Black GIS and advised against holding Vesper Services.[63] They noted that Sunday services, piped throughout the club, drew only minimal interest on the part of club patrons.

The Limits of Pluralism and Asian Americans

African Americans and white Americans were firmly in the Judeo-Christian tradition. While the religiosity of African Americans remained a trope in many Hollywood depictions of them, other racial groups could not be so easily categorized. In fact, among Japanese Americans and Chinese Americans, there were significant numbers of adherents to non-Western religions, and this had been a central argument put forth by nativists for banning their immigration to the United States. In 1882 Congress had banned immigration from China, and by early 1921 this had been applied to all migrants from Asia.

After December 7, 1941 fear led to the internment of Japanese Americans living on the West Coast in camps maintained by the U.S. Army and administered by a civilian agency. The U.S. Army struggled with what to do about the Japanese Americans who were already members of the military. In the end many were discharged and transferred to reserves, and still others continued to carry out their duties. One Japanese American officer with a National Guard artillery unit took part in the ill-fated defense of the Dutch East Indies and found himself spending the rest of World War II as a prisoner of war. Japanese Americans not in uniform were initially turned away by army recruiters and by draft boards. But in late 1942 first- and second- generation Japanese American citizens were permitted to volunteer within the U.S. Army, and eventually all draft-age Japanese Americans were subject to conscription.

The decision by FDR and the War Department to form a regimental combat team made up of volunteers from the Japanese American community required the army to consider how to meet the religious needs of this unit, which included not only Christians but also Buddhists. The army chaplaincy made a half-hearted effort to find a Buddhist cleric who could be commissioned as a chaplain. But the one candidate put forth by Buddhist leaders failed his physical examination, and efforts to locate an alternative Buddhist cleric faltered. This meant only Christian chaplains were posted to the 442nd and other Nisei units.

The army was more successful in securing Japanese American Protestant ministers for the Nisei troops. Hiro Higuchi, who grew up in Hawaii and graduated from Oberlin College prior to the war, served a Japanese American congregation in the continental United States. Joining the 442nd while in training at Camp Shelby, Mississippi, Higuchi noted the divide that existed between Japanese Americans from Hawaii and those from the continental United States. While his unit trained in Camp Shelby, he counseled men from the latter on a range of issues surrounding the internment of their families in concentration camps, something the men from Hawaii did not have to endure in such wide numbers. At the same time he described efforts by the head of the local USO in Mississippi to make his men feel welcome by featuring a Hawaiian motif to remind men from the island of home. The emphasis on the Hawaiian origins of many of the men would provide a bridge to the skeptical and even hostile white community outside the base. Hawaii, for many Americans, conjured associations of an exotic and alluring island paradise.[64]

In correspondence with his wife, Higuchi described the small, close-knit Japanese American community. He often asked his wife to send messages to families with the latest news of their sons. When performing a marriage ceremony for one member of his unit, he recalled that this man had attended his church in the States. Although Higuchi did not dwell on the racism he and his men endured, he used the pulpit to indirectly attack the racist structure of American society. In one letter home, Higuchi recounted preaching a sermon at the post chapel, one Sunday morning, focusing on the theme of the brotherhood that should exist among all Christians. The senior chaplain of the post, a white Southerner, did not comment favorably on the sermon, which delivered a subtle but direct challenge to the segregation practiced by Southern churches.[65]

Higuchi's correspondence with his wife and children was remarkably forthright, especially in discussing the question of fear in a unit that was praised for its valor and bravery. In writing about his first experience in combat, Higuchi described his baptism by fire in a low-key manner, even though he had crouched in a culvert for five hours and experienced an overwhelming sense of fear. Higuchi assured his wife that he would be careful and dig trenches a few inches deeper whenever near the battle line, for the sake of his son and daughter.[66] After six months of combat, with no end to the war in sight, Higuchi's mood darkened considerably. He remained remarkably open about his fears, writing, "Lately I have been very shaky and nervous and scared" and sharing his fear that a major barrage like the ones he had experienced earlier would lead him to quit serving in the war. In one letter, Higuchi's assessment of his chances of surviving the war did not mention the working of the Divine as playing a direct role in his survival. Instead, Higuchi dwelled on the question of luck and fate. He could not worry about his chances of being killed and had accepted the fact that there was nothing he could do if his number was up.[67]

Minora Musada, a medic with the 442nd, spoke highly of Higuchi's abilities. Musada, a native of Seattle, Washington, praised the chaplain's ability to integrate into the unit as "one of the boys" and said he stayed near the medics practically all the time. On one occasion Musada opted not to attend services in order to write to his wife, expressing the sentiment that this would be a more profitable use of his time and "besides, religion is all in the heart and mind anyway." But over the course of the war, Musada expressed that attending Higuchi's services helped to sustain him. He assured his wife that it was "God's truth" that "there are no atheists in foxholes."[68]

The army's emphasis on meeting the needs of Protestants, Roman Catholics, and Jews left Buddhists out in other crucial ways, especially with regard to honoring the war dead. Officially, Buddhists could not have *B* engraved on their dog tags as a signifier of their faith. This was a point of contention for many Buddhists, especially after press accounts identified them incorrectly as atheists. Israel Yost, a devout Lutheran pastor assigned to the 442nd, counseled one GI, who protested this lack of recognition, in a way that underscored Yost's ambivalence about promoting Buddhist observances. When Sgt. Jimmie Shiramizu described his dismay about not having his religion recognized by the army, Yost's immediate reaction was to express surprise that this GI was a Buddhist: "Jimmie, I had no idea you were not a Christian. You always attend my services, and you conduct yourself like I think a Christian would." Shiramizu saw no contradiction in attending Yost's services while adhering to Buddhism. While Yost told the sergeant, "You should be allowed to believe what you want," he also expressed dismay in his diary about his failure to proselytize Shiramizu due to his incorrect assumption that he was already a Christian.[69]

How did individual soldiers identify themselves along religious, racial, and ethnic lines? Sometimes these lines could be permeable despite societal norms and army regulations. Frank "Foo" Fujita, the son of a white mother from Oklahoma and a Japanese immigrant father, had come of age without any knowledge of the Japanese language. His father had deliberately raised him to embrace all things American, including the English language, Boy Scouts, and American food and cultural traditions. In his youth Foo joined his mother in attending the Church of the Nazarene.[70]

Most Texas National Guard units fought in Italy, but Foo's artillery unit was sent to the Pacific theater to reinforce the Dutch East Indies. After Pearl Harbor Foo and his unit had found themselves in Java, and they had been pressed into the hastily organized Australian, British, and Dutch forces formed to repel the attack on the Dutch East Indies. Despite his ancestry Foo expressed little difficulty in killing the enemy during the doomed battle to defend Java in 1942. But combat did lead to a crisis of faith as he remembered how his childhood church, the Church of the Nazarene, had sent missionaries to Japan. They had, no doubt, made converts, Foo thought, and while killing Japanese soldiers did not make Foo uneasy, killing fellow Christians prompted angst.

Yet the experiences of Chinese Americans diverged significantly from those of Japanese Americans. Chinese Americans benefited from America's alliance with China, and their status within American society improved. The U.S. Army welcomed the service of Chinese American citizens. This even extended to Chinese immigrants who had entered the country illegally, and in several instances the military arranged for these soldiers to travel to Canada so they could reenter the United States and have their status legalized.

In contrast to both African Americans and Japanese Americans, Chinese Americans were not uniformly placed in segregated units. The U.S. Navy made no provisions for segregating Chinese American sailors and, during the war, a Chinese American even rose to the rank of rear admiral. Many Chinese American army officers who had received peacetime training through ROTC sought assignments to white army and army air force units. The army air force created two predominantly Chinese American units and eventually deployed them to China. These units embodied the sharp distinctions within the Chinese community regarding class, language, and identity. In the enlisted ranks, many GIS had lived their entire lives in Chinatowns, in different parts of the United States, and possessed only limited fluency in English. In contrast, many Chinese American officers possessed degrees from American universities and had a history of substantial interactions with the dominant white community.[71]

No chaplain was assigned to the 407th Air Service Squadron, and surviving issues of the unit's newsletter, *Gung Ho*, make only sporadic mention of religion. While this unit was training at Dayton, one news feature noted the confirmation of several of its members into the Roman Catholic Church.[72] On Christmas Eve the entire unit participated in a festive banquet at an area Chinese restaurant that featured seasonal carols. On New Year's Eve, the Lorretta Club, a Catholic Women's group based in Dayton, threw a party for the unit that included participants from the Catholic community, GIS from other units, and members of British Commonwealth forces.[73] *Gung Ho* dedicated greater space to promoting Chinese culture and language, with a portion of each issue published in Chinese. For instance, the unit newsletter devoted much more coverage to unit members' celebrations marking the Chinese New Year than to Christmas.

Perhaps the most significant discussion of religious beliefs in *Gung Ho* is the short story "A Matter of Time," which told of a Chinese American and a white American commemorating Memorial Day in California. The story begins by describing the "Chinese old-timer," who provides an offering before the "departed one's grave," including "a large slice of roast pig, boiled chicken and fish, and a dish of native vermicelli," along with "incense sticks and sacrificial paper money." A white American, visiting the cemetery to lay a "bouquet of flowers" before a grave, decides to have "a little fun" and asks the unnamed Chinese old-timer, "How soon do you think your friend will come from below to eat all this food you've got spread out here?" "Just as soon as your friend comes up to smell the flowers" is the humorous reply of the Chinese mourner. This story implicitly sets forth a pluralistic view of cultural and religious rites, challenging those who sought to deem them as primitive.[74]

The memoir of Eddie Fung highlights how difficult it is to parse out religion and ethnicity. Fung, who grew up in San Francisco's Chinatown, described the blend of traditional Chinese rituals and beliefs that ordered his youth even though his father had embraced Christianity. As a teenager Fung ran away from home and eventually found work as a cowboy on several ranches before joining the Texas National Guard. Despite his outsider status, Fung recalled the acceptance he gained while working on several ranches and being assigned to the same artillery battalion of the Texas National Guard as Frank "Foo" Fujita. Like Fujita, Fung endured several years of Japanese captivity, but he made few overt comments about his personal religious beliefs. He did observe that the Thanksgiving and Christmas holidays did not hold the same importance for him as they did for his comrades and failed to produce the same feeling of depression. In the final weeks of the war, Fung's captors halted religious services within the POW camp, and he attributed this halt to the Japanese fear that the prisoners' prayers were working. In reflecting on his postwar life and grappling with post-traumatic stress, he also described the religious views that he shared with his second wife. Neither embraced Christianity. "We both thought of God as female, as Mother Nature, as a gentler force than the vindictive God who burned down Sodom and Gomorrah for some infraction or another."[75]

Native Americans and Religious Invisibility

With the exception of an elite unit of code talkers formed by the U.S. Marines and U.S. Army, Native Americans across tribal nations were not segregated within the armed forces. Despite their relatively small numbers, Native American GIs received favorable press accounts that highlighted their loyalty and display of traditional martial virtues. In spite of generations of racial antipathy toward Native Americans, most white GIs embraced their American Indian comrades, even if they attached to them such stereotypical terms as "Chief'" or "Geronimo."

From the perspective of the armed forces, the integration of Native Americans into regular units meant no special religious provisions were needed for this group. The army chief of chaplains never considered offering any official recognition to Native American religions or commissioning "clergy" from these traditions. This decision or, more accurately, this implicit assumption reflected the long-standing efforts by the federal government to suppress Native American rituals and beliefs, deeming them superstitious and barriers to their assimilation into broader white society. Moreover, there is historical precedent for this bent, given the determined efforts of the federal government, since the 1870s, to support missionary efforts by Protestant and Roman Catholic churches within Native American communities. Until the 1930s the Bureau of Indian Affairs saw the abandonment of traditional Native American religious practices and the embrace of Christianity as essential to the assimilation and survival of American Indians. In the 1920s the Bureau adopted regulations that prohibited ceremonial dancing; these restrictions would, however, be successfully challenged in the federal courts by the Pueblo Indians on freedom of religion grounds.[76]

A substantial number of Native American GIs had embraced Christianity prior to entering the service. Serving in all-white units and attending chapel services with comrades did produce Native American converts to Christianity. At the same time, substantial numbers of Native Americans continued to hold tribal traditions and cultural rites with a spiritual dimension. When the Comanche code talkers received a furlough after basic training, many attended Native American Church prayer meetings organized for them and received peyote buttons that many carried with them throughout the war.[77]

There were some significant shifts in how these rites were viewed by the popular press and by the Bureau of Indian Affairs. These changes are best reflected in the Bureau of Indian Affairs' pamphlet issued in 1945, which outlined the participation of Native Americans in the war effort. This short pamphlet offered a statistical overview of Native American service, highlighting the unique role of the code talkers and the American Indian women who volunteered. It also included a list of all Native Americans who had received major awards for valor. This pamphlet included a reprint of one of the last news columns filed by the famed journalist Ernie Pyle before his death by enemy fire, on April 12, 1945, which offered a stirring account of Navajo code talkers, who had organized a special dance on the eve of the invasion of Okinawa.[78]

Pyle's trademark was centering the narrative on the individual GIs he encountered; in this case, it was a story of two brothers in the same unit. He noted that the Indian school attended by Private First Class Joe Gatewood was just down the street from Pyle's home in Albuquerque, New Mexico. Hinting at their role as code talkers, conveying secret messages in Navajo, Pyle described how this group of Indians organized a ceremonial dance. To recreate the necessary customs, they received red cloth from the Red Cross and incorporated such varied items as "chicken feathers, sea shells, coconuts, empty rations cans, and rifle cartridges." Several thousand marines watched this group of Navajo as they conducted traditional chants and dances that, among other things, "asked the great gods in the sky to sap the Japanese of their strength." As part of the ritual, Pyle said, they "put the finger of weakness on the Japs" before ending the ceremony by singing the Marine Corps song in Navajo."

Exploring the life and service of one code talker, Samuel Holiday, offers insights into the worldview of many from his tribe in the armed forces. Holiday's first language as a child was Navajo, and he lived a hardscrabble life on a reservation in southern Utah, growing up in a home without running water or electricity and far from paved roads. He spent his early childhood raising sheep and assisting his mother in eking out a subsistence living. In his youth his mother described the suffering experienced by the Navajo during the war waged against them by the army and white settlers. She expected him to run out into the open at a moment's notice, ready to defend himself against a surprise attack. To further toughen him, he regularly bathed outside, even in winter. Navajo beliefs and rituals governed his early life.[79]

Holiday recalled his time in boarding school with more trepidation than his time in the service. Regularly bullied by older and even younger boys, forced to speak English, and far from his mother and family, Holiday's experiences mirrored those of many

Native Americans attending federally sponsored Indian schools. However, the roughness of boarding school prepared Holiday and many others for the rigors of the military. One member of the Comanche tribe remembered the drill sergeant's surprise at their ability to perform close-order drills and make their beds according to army regulations.

Navajo spiritual practices certainly helped sustain Holiday during the Pacific campaigns. Before departing he received special blessings and prayers offered by his father and other medicine men to spiritually offer protection against the enemy. During the ceremony Holiday received a medicine pouch and an eagle feather to protect him. Throughout the war Holiday carried this sacred pouch, containing cornmeal and his eagle feather, which he hoped would protect him, along with his prayers and those of his mother. While recalling his wartime service in a postwar oral history that includes his participation in the Battle for Iwo Jima, Holiday stressed the importance of prayer. Holiday credited his power to use a weapon to prayer, which was a highly personal act; he did not join in collective prayers with other Navajo. He also interpreted much of what happened in terms of his traditional beliefs and did not see the world as neatly divided between the secular and the spiritual.[80]

Even though the armed forces did not officially recognize it, religion remained a crucial part of Holiday's identity. Institutional racism compromised and limited the free exercise of religion for Native Americans, Asian Americans, and African Americans. Despite these barriers religion proved a source of comfort and identity for these marginalized groups in their efforts to fight for victory against enemies both foreign and domestic.

EIGHT

Patriarchy and the Religious Life of Military Women

I n June 1943 Barnett R. Brickner of the JWB, Msgr. Michael J. Ready of the National Catholic Welfare Conference, and S. Arthur Devan of the Commission of Army-Navy Chaplains, joined by denominational leaders for the Disciples of Christ, Episcopalians, Methodists, Presbyterians, and North Baptists, traveled to the Women's Army Auxiliary Corps (WAAC) training camps in Fort Oglethorpe, Georgia, and Fort Des Moines, Iowa. Led by Oveta Culp Hobby, leader of the WAAC, this delegation had been formed to bolster public support for allowing women to volunteer to serve in uniform. Garnering significant press attention, members of this august group praised the WAAC program, declaring: "We feel that parents concerned about the moral and spiritual welfare of their daughters can be reassured. A hopeful harbinger of the new world is evidenced by the sacrificial contribution which American women are making through the WAAC. [It] will strengthen their character."[1]

On one level the need for this trip mirrored public concerns, which had been raised during the pre–Pearl Harbor attack mobilization, about the impact of army life on young men drafted into the senior service under the peacetime draft of 1940. In response to these concerns, the army expanded the chaplaincy, built chapels, and established the USO to promote morality among GIs. In many ways public fears over the corrupting influence of military life had even greater consequences for permitting women to serve in the armed forces. In fact, public antipathy toward the idea of military women almost derailed efforts to include them in the service. In contrast to the mobilization of men into the military which, after December 7, 1941, was widely accepted as necessary, debates smoldered throughout the war over the wisdom of using women in the armed services. In May 1941, when Congresswoman Edith Nourse Rogers proposed creating a women's auxiliary for the army, she faced opposition from her male colleagues, the War Department, and a significant portion of the public. Only a year later would the barriers fall and the WAAC be established, but controversies dogged this organization as well as the WAC, which replaced it in 1943.

Male soldiers filling noncombatant billets were less than enthusiastic about their positions being taken over by women. Some men responded by spreading rumors. Rumors spread most effectively through the idle gossip of scores of GIs who claimed to family, friends, and acquaintances that military women were sexually promiscuous. These aspersions cast doubt in the minds of many recruits and parents. Tilly Spetgang recalled how her father quashed her efforts to join the WAC during the war by declaring, "Only prostitutes become WACs." Tilly insisted she was not a prostitute, but her father refused to relent. In the end Tilly bowed to parental pressure and never joined.[2]

In structuring the religious life of women GIs, the armed forces recognized they needed to reassure potential recruits, parents, and the wider public that the virtue of military women would be preserved. Recruiting literature made note of the access the military had to chaplains and the opportunity to attend chapel services. Chaplains, in ministering to women GIs, reinforced the message that called on women to remain virtuous. As with male GIs there were women who refused to adhere to the moral suasion of chaplains. By the same token many women, like their male counterparts, took the opportunity to attend chapel and turned to chaplains for counsel.

Religion and Female Purity: The Double Standard Reigned Supreme

In understanding the religious lives of the women GIs, the importance that broad swaths of the public attached to female sexual purity cannot be overstated. Chaplains, in their sermons and counseling sessions with women GIs, underscored the need for uniformed women to avoid sexual relations outside of marriage. Many females internalized these values and denigrated those women who engaged in premarital sex, labeling them with such pejorative terms as "tramp." The double standard that permitted men broad discretion in engaging in sex outside of marriage was reflected in the official policy on contraceptives. Male soldiers endured sexual morality lectures but received condoms when going on leave. Unmarried women not only faced moral suasion from chaplains but were prohibited by the armed services from receiving condoms or other birth control devices.

The army's reaction to charges of sexual immorality within the ranks led the WAAC, and later the WAC, leadership to double down on policies limiting access to contraceptives. Eager to stifle rumors that lesbianism was rife in the ranks, WAC leaders aggressively investigated allegations of homosexual activity. Although male homosexuals also faced investigation and disciplinary action, the percentage of cases dealing with allegations of lesbianism was significantly higher.[3]

On the flip side, for policies regarding sexuality, army leaders said little about sexual violence and rape against WACs. Training manuals and brochures offered to WACs were silent about this issue. WAC and army leaders took no action to protect women against sexual violence; instead, they simply restricted the freedom of female GIs. For instance, on one base in New Guinea, women were held as virtual prisoners in their barracks and work areas to avoid their being attacked by the hundreds of men at the base.[4]

Despite their vulnerability women were seen as a threat even to the leadership of the army chaplain corps. The latent fear of women as seductresses led the U.S. Army chief of chaplains, William R. Arnold, to initially prohibit women GIs from serving as chaplain's assistants. Arnold feared working in such close proximity with WACs would potentially compromise male chaplains. Another concern centered on ensuring average GIs would be comfortable coming into a chaplain's office for counseling. Would a GI share intimate and confidential matters with a chaplain if his conversation might be overheard by a woman? Over time, chaplains in the field chipped away at this prohibition and asked commanders to assign women to serve as their assistants. In sharp contrast the navy was far more accommodating of women as chaplain's assistants. By the end of the war, women became an ubiquitous presence as chaplain's assistants at stateside army, navy, army air force, and marine bases.[5]

Gender fears held by some had a strongly irrational quality. Some aviators held fast to the superstitious belief that having a woman set foot on a military aircraft engendered bad luck. Other aviators, especially those based in England, sought out female companionship, but they also viewed certain women as bad luck and to be avoided. On an airbase in East Anglia, one navigator described how several members of his crew tried to talk the copilot, Curt Mosier, out of dating a woman named Kaye, because six aviators who had been involved with this woman had been shot down. The pilot failed to heed this warning from his comrades, and only two days later he was killed by flak during a bombing mission.[6]

The more widely held fear, especially among army soldiers, was that they might find themselves transferred from safe billets into frontline positions. Senior army leaders encouraged women to join the WAACs, and later WACs, to free men up for combat, but many male GIs serving in support functions did not want to join the ranks of the infantry or other combat arms. This fear remained at the heart of the slanderous rumors GIs circulated about WACs. The details varied, but essentially they alleged that women GIs had loose morals. In more salacious stories, the army used WACs as prostitutes for officers or subjected them to other deviant activities.[7] One unfounded rumor, generated by a mentally disturbed army nurse and widely publicized by an Arkansas fundamentalist preacher with a radio show, was that physicians allowed women volunteers no modesty during their induction physicals and showed them nude pictures of men. At the other end of the spectrum, the WAC was charged with being filled with lesbians who morally corrupted young women.

The Ambiguous Position of Women in the Military

Though public support for keeping women in uniform was tepid, army and navy leaders embraced them. Even the U.S. Marine Corps, which institutionally had offered the most resistance to uniformed women, came to see the value of their contributions.[8]

One of the victories for those advocating for increased participation of women in the U.S. Army was the establishment of the
WAC to replace the WAAC in 1943. Although many of the limitations on combat and rank continued, the WAC structure allowed
greater integration of women into a broader range of military specialties. The smaller armed services, the U.S. Navy, U.S. Marine
Corps, and U.S. Coast Guard, granted women in these branches
reserve status.[9]

Senior generals came to appreciate WAAC/WAC for bringing
qualified personnel into a variety of support units, but the continued antipathy toward the service of women in other quarters
remained strong throughout the war. Men's desire to retain safe
billets led to an insurmountable barrier to giving military status
to female civilian pilots with the Women Airforce Service Pilots
(WASPS). Several hundred women in the WASPS overcame significant prejudice and gained the respect of many stateside army air
force personnel for their role in ferrying planes within the continental United States and performing a variety of other noncom-
bat missions. Despite the support of Gen. Hap Arnold, Congress
refused to militarize the WASPS, and even before the war ended,
decided to disband the organization.[10]

The antipathy and fears expressed regarding the employment
of women in the armed forces reflected the fortunate position of
the United States in the Second World War. The United States was
never as desperate as other nations for the mobilization of the entire
society. Although women were encouraged to volunteer for traditional male jobs to boost war production, the country never compelled women into national service. In the Soviet Union women
were conscripted into the armed services and allowed to volunteer to serve in a number of combat arms, including aviation and
armor. Throughout Europe and Asia, the boundaries between the
battlefront and home front conflated as air power made civilians a
target. Americans continued to sustain the vision that women and
children were protected from the enemy by male warriors. The continental United States never faced a sustained air raid from enemy
forces; whereas scores of women and children in most countries—
Axis and Allied—died in bombing offensives.[11]

The United States had the luxury of erecting strict gender barriers differentiating the role of women in the armed forces. In establishing WAC and allowing women to serve in the U.S. Navy, Marines, and Coast Guard as reservists, Congress set strict limits on how they could be deployed. Only men could be assigned to the combat arms and, even after the replacement of the WAAC with the WAC, the status of women soldiers remained subservient to men. Under law, no woman could hold the rank of general or serve as a commander of a male unit. Women serving in the WACs, the WAVES, and the coast guard's SPARS ("Semper paratus"— "Always Ready") became drivers, gunnery instructors, cryptologists, and mechanics, but most were assigned to duties mirroring the roles of women in the civilian work force, with most serving as secretaries, cooks, and housekeepers.

Reflecting how they were treated in general, accommodating the religious needs of women was an afterthought for the U.S. Army and Navy. Although over 350,000 women were in uniform, they remained only a small percentage of those in the armed forces. The legislation for creating the WAAC did not explicitly prohibit women from serving as chaplains, but the army chief of chaplains refused to even consider the appointment of ordained women from recognized denominations.[12] The pleas of women clerics to be allowed to meet the religious needs of women in uniform fell on deaf ears. As a result only male chaplains served the spiritual needs of women, although in at least one instance a civilian female Protestant minister was invited to lead a worship service for WACs stationed at a continental U.S. base as a result of the absence of a Protestant chaplain.[13] Enforcing this ban on women chaplains represented one of the most significant instances of government establishment of religion having important theological and practical impact. In structuring religious life for military women, chaplains placed great emphasis on maintaining widely held gender roles, especially in stressing the importance of women remaining more "virtuous" than men.

The clash between Lt. Col. Charity Adams Earley, who commanded the only African American WAC unit deployed to Europe, and the chaplain assigned to her unit highlighted the efforts of chaplains to uphold a rigid patriarchal view of female conduct.[14] This conflict also reflected a clear challenge by a chaplain, who was a staff officer, to a commander. In her postwar memoir Earley recalled that after her unit's arrival in England, in 1944, she organized weekly Sunday services and a choir, and the unit relied on an occasional visiting minister or lay leadership to conduct the services. Earley recognized the importance of regular services to promote good morale, but she also encouraged weekly dances and tolerated such leisure activities as card playing and shooting pool. The new chaplain, the only male member of the unit, immediately interfered with the smooth running of the unit by excusing enlisted personnel from their duties so he could counsel them. He further challenged her authority when he railed against the dances and most other recreational activities as "sinful." Tensions came to a head when the chaplain, dismayed over the unit's failure to replace a burned-out light bulb over his makeshift pulpit, in the site where, the night before, a dance had been held, openly prayed:

> Guide our commanding officer because she needs it. Keep us safe in these times of war and especially keep our commanding officer because she needs your help. Help us to perform our duties and especially help our commanding officer because she needs help. Lord, she made sure all the lights were burning for the dance last night and for the card party the night before. For all these sinful things our commanding officer made sure the lights were burning. But for Your service this morning Lord there is one bulb burnt out and she did not care. [15]

This direct challenge to her authority was too much for Earley, although she contained her anger until after the sermon finished because the unit's chapel choir sang her favorite hymn, "Be Still, My Soul, the Lord Is on Thy Side." After the service concluded, Earley had the chaplain summoned to her office and ordered him to pack his bags immediately for London; she had arranged for his transfer out of the unit.

The slander campaign waged against WACs impacted how the armed forces campaigned to encourage them to volunteer. They called military women to undertake new roles and occupations while assuring them their femininity would be preserved. All branches designed women's dress uniforms to adhere to widely held perceptions of women's femininity, mandating skirts over

19. Fireplace decorated for Christmas. Charlotte D. Mansfield Collection, Institute on World War II and the Human Experience.

pants. The navy took this emphasis even further by enlisting top-flight designers to craft fashionable uniforms for women in the WAVES. Recruiting posters and brochures offered a mix of appeals that stressed the opportunity for women to aid their country, perform useful jobs with the possibility of advancement, enjoy the companionship of peers, meet young men, and receive generous pay and benefits. The recruiting brochure "Facts You Want to Know About the WAC" included in the section "The WACS . . . questions often asked" a paragraph-long discourse that asserted that while attendance at religious services in the army was optional, "WACS find they go to church more often than they did as civilians." WACS were promised that at "every post . . . there are separate services for all denominations."[16]

Whether WACS regularly attended chapel or other religious services is debatable. For instance, Chaplain Frederick G. Lamb, stationed in Italy, wrote in his October 1944 monthly report to the military ordinariate about his disappointment with the attendance of WACS at Mass. He had found that women soldiers were more interested in dating and "cooing" than gaining spiritual insight. Lamb noted his appreciation of the "character, work, and sacrifices of the many splendid women in the WACS," but he expressed his regret that their attention to "religious duties is seemingly the exception rather than the rule."[17]

Even with parental misgivings, societal ambivalence about seeing women in uniform, and an ongoing slander campaign, women volunteered for the military in significant numbers. Patriotism played a role in encouraging many women to join the armed services. As a youth Nona Baldwin Brown had taken an active role in the Quaker meeting in her hometown of Montclair, New Jersey, and as a student at Vassar College, she had even spent a summer at the American Friends Service Committee camp. While working as a reporter for the *New York Times*, Brown was dispatched to Washington DC after the assault at Pearl Harbor and, in a letter, she maintained that Americans "don't like to fight," calling the recent events a "tremendous psychological about face to put us in a fighting mood." She described her generation as having been brought up on the creed of internationalist pacifism, but America's entrance into the conflict changed that and they altered their life plans to "don a uniform and learn to use a gun in the most effective way."[18] In an oral history recorded in 1987, Brown described how she responded favorably when senior leaders of the recently formed WAVES asked her to leave her position as a *New York Times* reporter to become a public relations officer for the new organization. Brown's parents understood her decision and her "feeling that just because I wore a skirt, I had no right to say 'No.'"[19]

The desire to escape hometowns in search of greater opportunity certainly motivated some women. Hazel Hitson Weidman wrote an autobiography for a graduate class in anthropology at Northwestern University in 1951, recalling that serving her nation in its time of need had been her primary reason for joining the U.S. Navy. But the underlying motivation for her entrance into the service was to escape the confines of her hometown in the desert of California. Lacking a college degree and the financial means to obtain one and stuck in low-paying jobs, Weidman rationalized her decision as being motivated by patriotism.[20]

Weidman's autobiography highlights the complex role religion played in the lives of individual women. Her parents, while embracing a belief in God, never joined a church during her childhood. In the late 1930s, when Weidman was a teenager, she attended Baptist, Methodist, Presbyterian, and Christian Scientist Sunday schools and services to gain acceptance and win popularity. She even joined a Christian social group for young women, Job's Daughters. But Weidman found her involvement with organized religion unfulfilling, in part because "all of them asked me to believe nonsense that I simply could *not*, and so, I rejected God and Churches and religion, per se, and railed bitterly against them, little realizing that much of my vehemence stemmed from their failure to fulfill my needs for security."[21]

Weidman's account suggests the varied reasons women attended church and chapel in the service. Carol Levin recalled, in an oral history, that her family regularly attended Shabbat services when she was growing up in the Jamaica neighborhood of Queens, New York, and she continued this pattern after she joined the WAC. Although she could not adhere strictly to kosher law, a British family obtained matzo for her for the Passover holiday when she was deployed to the United Kingdom.[22] In her postwar memoir and letters home, Katherine Keene frequently discussed the role of religion. During training her base chaplain decided to create a Sunday afternoon Bible study, calling on the WACs and enlisted men to take part. Most of the men fled, except for the prisoners from the stockade, who had no choice but to attend. Keene found herself enjoying the study of the second chapter of 1 Peter; the themes reminded her of the early Platonic dialogues and the Stoic philosophers. The chaplain eventually deputized her as the discussion leader for Bible studies, and she enjoyed the role.

A church member before entering the service, Keene also had her dog tags stamped "Protestant." At the same time, Keene had little patience for hell-and-brimstone services. At Camp Kilmer, New Jersey, awaiting deployment overseas, she tried to allay her boredom by watching army films on field latrines and venereal diseases. She joined a friend in attending church to listen to an inflammatory sermon, which she "considered a diatribe in very poor taste on repenting our sins since we might not survive. The preacher had apparently been to Hell."[23]

Religion remained a frequent topic of conversation with Keene's roommates when she was stationed in London. Although she flirted with agnosticism, she left no argument against Protestantism unchallenged when made by her three Catholic roommates. As she observed to her parents, she refused to concede to her Catholic roommates, who claimed that "they are nearer the proper religion than Presbyterians." Seeking more authoritative information, Keene approached the Catholic chaplain, who "had a real gleam in his eye" that would soon be overshadowed when they disagreed over the nature of free will. Reading the Catholic catechism, she was "fascinated" to learn that "the Catholic is to give obedience to Church before State, that the Pope is infallible . . . and by the bland way which, throughout the Catechism, Christian referred to Catholics."[24]

Ann Kapolwitz Goldberg remembered the strong element of sociability at chapel services mixed with an ecumenical flavor. As a WAC stationed in Asheville, North Carolina, Goldberg and her friends regularly went to different services over the weekend. Her fellow WACs enjoyed going with her to Friday night Shabbat service at a local synagogue, in part because of the chance to eat good food that included "bagels, cream cheese, lox, [and] cookies." Attending Mass celebrated by an army chaplain proved disconcerting to Goldberg, in part because of her unfamiliarity with kneeling during worship. She also found the chaplain's attack on ecumenicalism disconcerting. He declared not only that Roman Catholics should avoid attending the services of other religions, but that "nobody should be there [at Mass] that's not of the faith."[25]

Goldberg recalled encountering anti-Semitism while a WAC. When she first reported for training in Des Moines, Iowa, she overheard another WAC inductee in her barracks declaring to another that she would not room with a Jew. Her fellow WACs took charge of the matter and made it clear to this anti-Semite that her prejudice would not be tolerated, and they gave her the silent treatment during their time at Des Moines. Later in the war, Goldberg experienced an injury that landed her in the hospital. When a male orderly learned she was a Jew, he got down on his knees beside her bed and prayed for her conversion.

Chaplains were not always subtle in imparting a message of moral probity regarding sexual morality. In her unpublished memoir, "When WAC was a Dirty Word," Bertha Marcia Clark remembered well Father Murphy, the Roman Catholic chaplain who was stationed at Stout Field in Indianapolis. During Clark's orientation Father Murphy avoided all subtlety and bluntly told the women who reported to the base that they could either be Madonna or be kicked into the gutter. There existed no middle ground; the line between "Heaven and Hell" remained sharply defined. Their choice was whether male GIs would "put you on a pedestal or kick you in the gutter!" He declared that giving in to human fragility by dispensing sexual favors would ultimately lead to a WAC being treated like a tramp.[26]

Of course not all women were tramps or saints, as both Clark and Chaplain Murphy learned. In her memoir Clark recounted that she tried to help a fellow WAC, also named Murphy, who was absent from duty and engaged in a hunger strike for several days. When Clark found Murphy, her fellow WACs had hidden her in plain sight in the cadre room, which the officers never inspected. When Clark asked Murphy about her troubles, Murphy lashed out at the patriarchal oppression that engulfed her life:

I hate the GIs. I hate my father. He is a drunkard and abuses my mother. I thought that when I got away from home things would be different but they are worse. I despise these GIs. I can't stand them to come near me anymore. Do they ever look at a girl with anything but an unclean thought in their heads? No! Is life just having me use you? Or abusing you like my father abuses my mother?

I keep worrying about her and think of her trying to make ends meet while my father's spends it all on booze.

Clark brought the chaplain to the barracks to counsel this distraught WAC in part because, as chaplain, anything said to him by a soldier had to be held in the strictest of confidence. Unfortunately, this effort to have the chaplain intervene failed miserably when he sat on the WAC's bed, for lack of a chair to sit on, and "Murphy screeched like she had been stabbed. 'Get off this bed! Get Out! Help!'" He told her he was a priest and was there to help her. "Who wants you, anyway? Get the hell off my bed! Help!" Unable to calm Murphy, the chaplain summoned medical help. There were repercussions the next day. The first sergeant asked, "Will the person who went to the chaplain yesterday please step out?" Clark did not own up to summoning the chaplain, because "I thought the only recourse to justice that we had was the chaplain. Anyone could tell him anything. Even the commanding general on our base couldn't change that." Murphy eventually received a transfer to a general hospital, and Clark suspected that she also received a Section VIII discharge.

Irrespective of the official warnings about remaining chaste, some women took pride in their moral probity and were dismayed over the conduct of other WACS. Dorothy Jordan, a WAC serving at Fort Oglethorpe, was disturbed by the attitudes of some of her fellow WACS, who thought "nothing of picking up a guy and going to bed with him." The behavior and attitude of one friend, who was a "tramp," troubled her because she regularly attended Mass and even prayed the rosary. In fact, her friend prodded her to go to Mass even though Jordan's first inclination was to continue to sleep, having been on duty much of the night. One Roman Catholic chaplain sensed Jordan's angst and encouraged her to see him for confession. He also counseled her on how to respond to what she perceived as her friend's immorality and hypocrisy. The priest encouraged her to recognize there were limits to what she could do. "You can't save anybody else's soul but your own."[27]

The chaplains' admonishments to women about premarital sex were supported by the official policies regarding women's sexuality. In contrast to male GIS, women in uniform were not issued prophylactics to prevent venereal disease or unwanted pregnancies. A pregnancy for either a married or unmarried woman serving in the armed services led to an automatic discharge. Francis I. Holway of Alexandria, Virginia—in a letter to Chief of Chaplains Arnold in 1943—protested the sexual double standard. She wrote, "Males are *expected* to use contraceptives in normal relations, WAACS are not supposed to have any available even when endangered by rape from the enemy." Chief of Chaplains Arnold did not deem this letter worthy of a response and noted callously : "When there is a rape on, there isn't much time to monkey with contraceptives."[28]

One WAC wondered at whether chastity—or the lack thereof—fostered more virtuous conduct in other ways. Katherine Keene reflected, in her memoir, on one WAC who came to her aid when she fell ill during training at Des Moines, Iowa. It was not the WAC who read the Bible every night, but instead a woman whose "every other word was one my mother used to threaten to wash out my mouth with soap if I used it." Keene recalls that this woman, whose "background was some sleazy district in Chicago," was the same person who said, "For God's sake lie down. I'll do the floor—you can help me some time."[29]

The regulation of women's sexuality extended beyond efforts to discourage premarital sexual relations. The response of two Jewish chaplains to a WAVE, stationed at the Great Lakes Naval Station, being impregnated by her boyfriend, who was serving with the army air force, suggests the degree to which both chaplains sought an outcome that reinforced patriarchal marriage. Chaplain Selwyn D. Ruslander, at Great Lakes Naval Station, wanted to persuade the GI who had impregnated the WAVE to marry the woman so "that no stigma of illegitimacy might be attached to the child." Ruslander firmly opposed the option of abortion, expressing his "personal objections to such a procedure at any time." He expressed his dismay over the third option of the WAVE having the "child without benefit of wedlock." While the navy would deliver the baby, this "would not solve the problem of her personal reputation or the tremendous shock which her family would suffer under the circumstances."[30]

Ruslander believed this WAVE wanted to marry her boyfriend.

He was corresponding with Chaplain Isador Signor at Chanute Field, where the young man was stationed. In writing to Ruslander, Signor enclosed a copy of a letter the WAVE had sent to her boyfriend disclaiming any interest in marriage and deciding the best option was to obtain an abortion. In the letter the WAVE noted that she had found a physician willing to perform the operation and made an oblique request for help in defraying the cost of the procedure; otherwise she would be starving for several months.

Despite the willingness of the WAVE to deal with the problem, Chaplain Signer recalled that this airman claimed his monthly salary of $23 prevented him from offering any assistance. Furthermore, the airman cast aspersions on her morality, claiming "hints dropped by J–– as well as from a letter from a mutual friend who knows J–– well [indicate] that the latter has been promiscuous in her sexual relationships and that he is not chargeable with paternity. Again he asserts that in each instance of intercourse he was careful to use a condum [*sic*] and therefore cannot be responsible for her present plight." No further correspondence exists on whether Chaplain Ruslander was able to "adjust this matter equitably." While it is uncertain whether this WAVE went ahead with the abortion, this incident highlights the onus on women to adhere to sexual rectitude or suffer the consequences.[31]

Although women serving in the armed forces were given separate housing accommodations, being placed in "single sex units," most—in terms of military occupations—were integrated into predominantly male units. The presence of women on a military or naval base offered the opportunity for a chaplain to recreate congregational life along the same lines as that found in a civilian house of worship. For instance, African American sailors worshiped in the cafeteria of the Naval Air Station in San Diego under naval chaplain Donald M. Mackay, and white WAVEs worshiped in the main chapel with white sailors and officers and even sang in the choir.[32] Mackay found himself counseling not just male naval personnel but also WAVEs. He wrote his parents, describing how one WAVE came to him after the service and—in what Mackay considered a failure of his counseling efforts—he asked her to postpone a mixed-religion marriage with a marine overseas. This WAVE, a Protestant, had known the marine, a Catholic, for just five days.

Despite his words of caution, after one Sunday chapel this WAVE revealed to MacKay that she was now a Mrs.[33]

Classified as noncombatants, women were—nonetheless—often in harm's way. For instance, piloting aircraft was an inherently dangerous specialty in the Second World War, and the WASPs lost thirty-eight members as a result of aviation accidents. Those deployed overseas frequently came under enemy fire, especially from submarine or aerial attacks. Mary Robinson, a WAC serving with Douglas MacArthur's headquarters staff, recalled ruefully how the Japanese greeted her arrival in the Philippines with an air raid.[34]

Like men, women under enemy attack varied in how they reacted. Katherine Keene recalled this variety when she and her comrades came under German aerial attack at their headquarters in London. Keene wanted to watch what was happening and sought a better view to take in the spectacle. One WAC resorted to prayer for comfort, while another WAC rearranged furniture, obsessively putting things in order. Her sergeant refused to use the latrine during an attack out of fear that she would be killed sitting on the toilet; she did not want an obituary announcing such an unfortunate incident in her church newsletter at home.[35]

In structuring religious life, the military reinforced patriarchal values that emphasized sexual chastity and limited occupational roles for women. Despite the limitations placed on the opportunities accorded to military women, World War II represented a watershed, and their presence became a permanent one in the postwar armed forces. But it would not be until the 1970s that female clergy would finally be permitted to serve as chaplains. This barrier could have been broken if the armed forces had been bolder and lived up to the ideals regarding religious pluralism espoused by Roosevelt. Several Protestant denominations, in 1942, were ordaining women, and denying them chaplaincy commissions was one of the most egregious cases of the government limiting the free exercise of religion.

NINE

The Wounded

W hile a chaplain could be avoided and religious services skipped, it was almost impossible for the average GI to avoid having some contact with the army or navy medical establishment. One of the first experiences a GI had, with any branch of the armed services, was the preinduction physical examination. Many stood in long lines, usually in the nude, while physicians probed and prodded with little respect for individual privacy. Every recruit received at least a perfunctory psychiatric examination that often centered on a single question: Do you like girls?[1] A negative response would effectively end one's military career even before it started.

Encounters with military medicine continued when GIs made it to training camps, where they received a batch of inoculations. Even before leaving the states, enlisted men would frequently be subject to "short arm" inspections, where they would be forced to drop their pants and have their genitals inspected for signs of venereal disease. For the fortunate GIs, these encounters would be their only contact with military medicine.

Through much of their history, medicine and religion were intertwined, with the earliest hospitals in Europe built by the Catholic Church. Although the ties between the two remained strong, the professional status of the physician compared to the cleric soared dramatically in the twentieth century as the science of medicine became secularized. The acceptance of germ theory, the advent of antibiotics, and advances in surgery increased dramatically the ability of physicians to save lives.[2] In the case of psychiatry, Sigmund Freud and many of his disciples saw a strong connection between religious beliefs and mental illnesses.[3]

Until the twentieth century, medicine could do little to stem the grievous loss of life of those serving in wartime. Disease killed more combatants than enemy bullets. Communicable diseases easily spread through encampments, fostered by the lack of adequate sanitation, poor hygiene, and the absence of vaccines capable of preventing such common maladies as the mumps, typhoid fever, and measles. Even in World War I, deaths from the influenza epidemic of 1918 and 1919 (the "Spanish flu" epidemic) rivaled the numbers of those lost in the trenches.[4] By World War II, however, these infections could be treated with sulfa drugs.

Chaplains still staffed army and navy hospitals in World War II and were generally welcomed by physicians, nurses, and patients. A good number of soldiers still prayed for recovery and healing and, with a few important exceptions, they put their trust in modern medicine. This confidence was not entirely misplaced, for while GIS faced a lethal battlefield, made even more perilous by combined arms warfare, their chances of survival if wounded were much greater than in earlier wars. Battle took the lives of 291,557 American GIS, but more than twice as many, 670,000, were listed as wounded. Building on administrative and logistical advances made in earlier conflicts, the army and navy developed sophisticated networks of medical care for the wounded and the sick. On the front line, army medics and navy corpsmen tended the wounded on the battlefield, often suffering high casualty rates in their attempts to treat them. At clearing stations close to the line, surgeons ensured patients were stabilized before their evacuation to field hospitals. For chronic cases evacuations were made to general army hospitals or hospital ships. Even before the war ended, the most serious cases were transported back to the United States for further medical care. Sulfa drugs and penicillin led to a dramatic decline in deaths from infection and allowed surgeons to observe and assess before intervening with limb amputation. To control malaria the military relied on Atabrine and sprayed DDT in locations where mosquitos would commonly breed.[5]

While many physicians and nurses prayed, attended chapel services, and looked for guidance from chaplains, when it came to the practice of medicine, they embraced a secular ethos that rested heavily on empiricism and scientific inquiry. Religious discourse was often completely absent in their writings related to the practice of medicine, even when considering issues regarding mental illness. With the support of military authorities, the medical establishment favored several policies that upset some religious leaders, chaplains, and average GIs. The most vocal dissent would center on the increasing medicalization of the problem of venereal disease in a period when germ theory had firmly established the causes of the spread of syphilis and gonorrhea and the military could provide an effective prevention (condoms) and cure (penicillin). Although the military continued to use moral suasion to discourage sexual promiscuity outside of heterosexual marriage, over the objections of Roman Catholic and other religious leaders, they freely dispensed condoms and later used penicillin to cure the infected without mandating court martials or other disciplinary actions. More muted conflict emerged over how to deal with mental illness, especially for those who broke down as a result of battle and became neuropsychiatric casualties. At various stages in the war, "combat fatigue"—the term favored over "shell shock," which had arisen in the First World War—reached epidemic proportions, rivaling the incidence of physical wounds. To cope with unseen wounds, military psychiatrists had to implement new treatment regimes that caused consternation in some religions. Although most religious leaders and military chaplains deferred to medical personnel in this area, the Roman Catholic hierarchy retained serious misgivings about the ideas embedded in modern psychiatry.

Chaplains were ubiquitous at all levels of the medical system. In training, they were instructed to view regular visitation of the wounded and sick as one of their main duties, emphasizing the need to help alleviate the fear and alienation of young GIs in recuperation. Chaplains deployed on the line often assisted medics in aid stations and even retrieved the wounded that lay in harm's way. Chaplains were part of the Table of Organization for army and navy hospitals. In training, chaplains were advised that a GI suffering severe illness or recovering from a wound should, ideally, have access to a chaplain of his faith. Chaplains often earned the gratitude of many GIs for offering spiritual guidance and countless acts of individual kindness: writing a letter on behalf of a recover-

20. Medics, chaplain, and driver. Esther Crowe Collection, Institute on World War II and the Human Experience.

ing soldier, providing a cigarette to a wounded sailor, or offering counseling to a troubled marine. Chaplains assigned to hospitals and other medical units also played an important role in ministering to the spiritual needs of the physicians, nurses, and other affiliated personnel.

Chaplains and physicians had some important commonalities. They were both part of the military, and both physicians and civilians had to possess professional credentials from civilian institutions. A chaplain could gain a commission only if a religious denomination endorsed him. Similarly, military or naval physicians were trained in accredited medical schools and their licenses to practice medicine issued by state government. Like chaplains, physicians could not bear arms or engage in combat under international law.

While pious physicians, nurses, and other medical personnel served, their religious and moral outlooks often differed substantially from those of chaplains. Chaplain Renwick C. Kennedy, a Presbyterian minister stationed with the army's 102nd Field Hospital, found that only half of the members of the unit attended his chapel services. Although Kennedy imbibed he was alarmed by the heavy drinking of many medical personnel and, in one case, while the unit was deployed to a combat zone, he saw three off-duty physicians stagger into a patient's ward drunk. The senior leadership's unwillingness to rein in physicians and exert discipline, even when the unit was deployed overseas, distressed Kennedy. At one point enlisted personnel came to Kennedy, when the unit was deployed to France, complaining of the double standard that allowed officers to drink to excess, sleep with nurses, and use them as "personal lackeys." Under these circumstances Kennedy did his best to minister to the needs of the medical personnel and the stream of patients receiving medical care.[6]

The wounded often turned to prayer for comfort. Sagie Nishioka, fighting in Italy during the final weeks of the war in Europe, was reading the Bible when shellfire forced him to dive headfirst into his foxhole, saving his life. Although he had taken cover, the force of the explosion blew him out of the slit trench, severely wounded his feet, and punctured his heart and stomach. While he lay on the ground waiting for evacuation, he prayed that he would survive to see his family again.[7]

GIs often welcomed the comfort bestowed on them by chaplains. After the USS *Tennessee* was hit by a kamikaze during the battle for Okinawa, Harry Mehle suffered severe wounds and feared for his life. In an oral history, Mehle recorded that while he was being led to sick bay, a ship's chaplain came by and encouraged him to say a prayer, assuring him that everything would be "all right." In an interview years after the incident, Mehle recalled that the only prayer he remembered expressed ominous sentiments: "Now I lay me down to sleep. I pray the Lord my soul to keep. If I die before I wake. I pray the Lord my soul to take."[8]

Military service diminished individual autonomy, which was further attenuated for the wounded and sick, who were confined to bed and required the assistance of others to walk, eat, and wash. Complaints arose claiming chaplains sought to take advantage of this situation and chose not to respect sectarian differences. One Catholic chaplain, based in a naval hospital in New Zealand, bitterly denounced the Protestant chaplain at the naval operation base. He said that this "bastard" . . . had been "repeatedly marrying, burying Catholics and coercing our lads."[9] In early 1945 another Roman Catholic chaplain, stationed at a U.S. naval hospital, protested the practice of Protestant chaplains conducting "War Religious Services" that often consisted of "Hymns, Bible reading, . . . a sermonette on Scriptural exposition, Communion Service, and prayers." He complained to the medical officer, explaining that these services were held in a ward with ambulatory patients that included "Jews, Catholics, Protestants [and] Infidels." To exercise their constitutional rights, men should not have to be present during such services or suffer the inconvenience of "vacating their sack."[10]

In defending their conduct, the Protestant ministers at the naval hospital did not deny that they held ward services in the presence of Roman Catholics. They sought not to proselytize but simply to meet the needs of Protestants who could not physically attend chapel services. Not only had they received no complaints regarding this practice, but the patients who did not want to attend were free to leave or, if confined, "to interest themselves, in a book, magazine, or letter-writing."[11]

However, time in the hospital sometimes led to moments of reflection and even the embrace of a new faith. A Roman Catholic chaplain serving a stateside army base and hospital was incredulous when he received a letter from a patient of his faith who had decided to return his rosary and prayer book with the explanation that "God has called me" to religious service, but as a Baptist minister. Far from embracing this decision, the priest wrote to his sister about the incident, commenting that he thought "the guy's nuts."[12] Others were defiant even when suffering grievous injuries. One Catholic chaplain recalled, in his correspondence, his frustration with a GI who, because of an altercation with a priest back home, refused his entreaties to accept one of the sacraments. Even after suffering severe wounds falling from a truck, this individual refused confession.[13] This reaction was not unique. U.S. Navy chaplain George W. Wickersham II, serving a U.S. Marine regiment, described ministering to the wounded during the campaign for Okinawa. "There were men who cursed and swore, men whose only desire was for a cigarette, men who kept insisting that you write them up for a medal and men who had no use for preachers."[14]

Christian Science and Modern Medicine

By the same token, not all soldiers and sailors found comfort in medicine. For some, like Christian Scientists, true healing remained the work of God. They insisted on the efficacy of prayer and the special role of Christian practitioners who facilitated the intervention of the divine. Faith healing was not unique to Christian Science; in fact, chaplains of all major faiths embraced petitionary prayers for the sick and wounded. There were Protestants, often from rural regions, engaged in faith healing, but they lacked the prestige of the First Church of Christ, Scientist, which offered such a sophisticated challenge to modern medicine. By World War II Christian Science, founded by Mary Baker Eddy in the late nineteenth century, shared many of the attributes of mainline Protestant churches. Headquartered in Boston the church's most distinctive means of proselytizing was reading rooms that dotted the nation, where individuals could read and purchase Bibles and other Christian Science publications. For many Americans the public face of the church was the highly regarded nonsectarian weekly newspaper the *Christian Science Monitor*. Their theological position regarding modern medicine would make the Christian Scientists distinctive among denominations granted the right to recommend chaplains to the U.S. Army.

At its founding Mary Baker Eddy's teachings called on followers to reject modern medicine as ineffective and a contradiction to the spiritual nature of God and man. Discounting the physical world, Christian Scientists stressed the importance of prayer to overcome maladies, diseases, and even open wounds. Christian Science practitioners took the place of physicians for members and others in need of healing. Practitioners, like physicians, charged for their services, but they completely eschewed any attention to physical treatments or pharmacological interventions. Instead, they encouraged individuals to rely on scripture, the writings of the church's founder, and prayer. For the army, male Christian Science practitioners who had performed this calling for three years and held a college degree were prime candidates for the chaplaincy.[15]

Resisting the demands of authority in a hierarchical institution could be difficult for all but the most determined. Theodore

C. Mason, a Christian Scientist who joined the navy in 1940, took the opportunity to attend local church services of his denomination when ashore and on leave. In his memoir he also noted that in pre–Pearl Harbor America not all churches welcomed sailors; he had encountered at least one congregation that was less than inviting. As a result of church teachings, Mason recorded in his memoir that he remained "suspicious and a little fearful of doctors." At boot camp this young sailor quickly realized that the navy would not change its "routines to accommodate esoteric religious beliefs" and that it appeared pointless to resist the "stipulated inoculations, inspections, and treatments." Over time Mason's attitudes toward medicine changed, and he eventually found the navy health care system admirable.[16]

In contrast, Walter Denise, who served in the U.S. Army, never reconciled himself to army medicine. The tension between duty to country and faith was heightened when the army sent him to the medical corps. Administering vaccinations and participating in other medical procedures troubled his conscience. Eager to escape this duty, Denise gladly accepted a transfer to the infantry where, during the war, he never fired his weapon in anger.[17]

The leadership of the Christian Science movement sought to avoid direct conflict with the armed forces and urged its members in uniform to follow the dictates of the military to accept the inoculations and traditional medical care offered to them. This decision doubtlessly defused a major source of conflict and helped gain acceptance of Christian Science chaplains commissioned in the army.[18] Many chaplains also indicated in their reports to church officials that they sought to develop cordial, even friendly, relations with physicians and other medical personnel. For instance, Herbert Rieke's army air corps group commander deliberately had the Christian Scientist chaplain share a hotel room with the squadron surgeon. The two developed a great rapport, talking late into the night. The unnamed surgeon is reported to have said to Rieke that he was the first chaplain in the army to whom he had felt a personal connection. According to Rieke this surgeon described his concerns over the sanitary conditions at many squadron bases and said it was only "because of the grace of God that there had not been an epidemic there." In addition, Rieke described how every day he was helping the group dentist give up the tobacco habit.[19]

Christian Science chaplains, in their reports to Boston headquarters, indicated a strong belief in the efficacy of church teachings. One chaplain based in Texas described how, after learning that a Christian Scientist had "collapsed on the drill field with a hemorrhage of the brain," he rushed to the base hospital to begin his work aided by a civilian Christian Scientist minister from Michigan. So grave was this soldier's condition that the Red Cross sent the "lad's mother" to his bedside. In the end the soldier recovered, and this case was thought to demonstrate "further proofs of God's law" and that "so-called medical laws regarding that condition have been annulled." In another case Cecil F. Denton recounted how physicians expected an ingrown toenail to require one Christian Scientist to have an operation that would lay him up for over forty-five days; but with the aid of "Science" this condition was resolved in half the time.[20]

Given the unique role of Christian Science practitioners in meeting the medical needs of members, the church leadership petitioned the army chief of chaplains and the army surgeon general to allow the denomination to send civilian practitioners abroad to supplement the work of the chaplains. While it acknowledged twenty-three Christian Science chaplains were in service and fifteen were deployed overseas, most were attached to specific military units, which meant many GIs lacked access to them. While affirming that "those of our denomination shall render full and respectful obedience to all medical officers and authority," the petition asserted "there are many men in the armed services whose parents are Christian Scientists who have never known any other type of healing than that afforded through the teaching of Christian Science."[21]

In replying to this petition, Secretary of War Henry L. Stimson recognized that the current number of chaplains was "insufficient to allow all soldiers of that faith always to receive ministrations by Christian Science chaplains," but he insisted that this was always "unavoidably true of all denominations." Stimson insisted, due to the exigencies of war, the War Department could not permit civilian organizations to send civilian clergy abroad.[22]

For the leadership of Christian Scientists, it was particularly distressing when one of their chaplains became ill and was diagnosed and brought "under the observation of the division psychiatrist" and then deemed to be "unfit for combat service." This incident, at the 77th Division during the battle for Okinawa, "caused considerable comment and unfriendliness among the Division Staff and the Chaplains and Medical Corps" of the 77th division. It also proved an "embarrassment to Christian Scientists and their friends."[23] The division commander wrote in confidence to church officials about his astonishment when his division chaplain told him that the Christian Scientist chaplain had to be evacuated on the recommendation of the division medical officer. Maj. Gen. A. D. Bruce described his efforts to help this Christian Scientist chaplain, since the chaplain suffered from the "basic fear" common to many men when they first experienced combat. This chaplain's interactions with the wounded only heightened this anxiety, for "he had heard some fearful tales from them." Because his evacuation could not be carried out before V-J Day ended fighting, this chaplain remained within the division, but Bruce was eager to see him reassigned elsewhere to be given another chance."[24]

Moral Suasion Is Not Enough: The Clash over Venereal Disease

The policies adopted by the armed forces to deal with sexually transmitted disease led to conflict with the moral teachings of Roman Catholicism, Protestantism, and Judaism. The armed forces continued to try to tame GIs and limit illicit sex and did not abandon moral suasion, as chaplains regularly delivered lectures regarding sexual morality as part of this effort. By sanctioning the USO at home and abroad, army and navy officials hoped that providing an outlet for wholesome recreation would keep GIs away from brothels, bars, and gambling dens. In contrast to leaders of other countries, the U.S. government never officially embraced regulated prostitution for American troops. Within the continental United States, the military pressured local and state governments to take punitive measures to suppress prostitution.[25]

However, the armed forces remained much more pragmatic in supplementing moral suasion with the liberal distribution of condoms and treating the infected with penicillin when it became widely available. Many commanders overseas often tolerated prostitution and sought measures to regulate it. Some commanders even sanctioned official brothels staffed by indigenous populations with access regulated by the military police. American GIs, by the standards of the global economy, were well paid and were often deployed to parts of the world impoverished by the war. Many took full advantage of their position to purchase sex from women desperate to support themselves and their dependent children. In a series of letters to his wife, the recently married Gilbert Ketcham graphically described the prevalence of prostitution in North Africa and Italy. In Morocco, one of his men kept an "Arab" prostitute in his pup tent for several days until Ketcham got wind of the situation.[26] In another letter, he described a case of stark sexual exploitation, recounting how one of his men in North Africa bought a woman for five dollars. The difficulty emerged of how to get rid of her when he was deployed to Italy.[27]

Attending the problem of sexual promiscuity was that of sexually transmitted diseases; however, religious leaders often resisted the military's efforts to medicalize the problem of venereal disease, seeing it instead as a moral problem in need of a religious solution. Chief of Chaplains William R. Arnold, in writing to Bishop John F. O'Hara of the military ordinariate, described his "hammering at the authorities to treat the whole matter as a vice problem, not merely as a disease problem."[28] His efforts were less than successful.

Chaplains found the lack of morality distressing and often took issue with the military condoning such behavior, especially through distribution of free condoms, which they saw as encouraging sexual immorality. Despite official policies prohibiting the sanctioning of brothels, some commanders went beyond tolerating them and worked to establish them. The 29th Division, following the orders of their commander, gained the assistance of the French police and even a pimp to staff a brothel for GIs of the unit. By reporting these efforts to the provost marshal, the chaplain of this unit succeeded in getting this brothel shut down quickly, but not before at least seventy men were serviced.[29] Writing to his father provincial, Roman Catholic chaplain Joseph B. Murphy of the Holy Ghost Fathers described his efforts to halt the distribution of contraceptives to his fighter group, based in England. He complained about the advertising being promulgated by the medical staff and the series of front-page stories in *Stars and Stripes* that condoned the use of contraceptives. He preferred condemnation because by making it possible for men to "obtain freedom from the medical disease . . . these fools remove[d] the element of fear which God undoubtedly intended as a help to avoid the occasions of sin."[30]

The distribution of condoms distressed not only Roman Catholic chaplains in the field but also the hierarchy at home. But appeals to various army officials, such as chief of staff George Marshall and even President Roosevelt, to end the practice fell on deaf ears, in large measure out of the need to ensure venereal disease did not diminish the ranks of able-bodied soldiers. Outside of the United States, many commanders issued orders mandating that GIS use prophylactics. Writing from Italy one chaplain noted that a commander ordered men to take four sulfur tablets in the presence of a commanding officer, even though the chief surgeon for the SOS *Natousa* did not approve of this procedure and pledged he would put a stop to it.[31] Another Catholic chaplain believed his transfer to another unit stemmed from his objection to requiring men on leave to carry a "pro kit."[32]

Not all commanders condoned policies that promoted sexual activity with civilians. One chaplain recounted with pride that his commanding general had banned dances for French women and GIS. His commander's policies endeared him to the local French population for protecting their young women from vice. The chaplain expressed hope that it would remain in force. He also made it clear that promiscuity could not be blamed solely on GIS and, in the same letter to the military bishop, castigated the "girls in Italy" who looked for "any excuse, any time, etc., combined with drink, and a thorough[ly] communistic Italy put many [a] soldier in the hospital in disgrace."[33]

Despite the embrace of prophylactics by physicians and social hygienists, many commanders continued to advocate for conventional views of morality. For instance, the double standard regarding sexual morality remained quite pronounced and even embedded in official army and navy policies. The military issued contraception to male GIS while flatly denying it to women in the armed forces. Even promiscuous male GIS could express misgivings about the faithfulness of girlfriends and spouses. During group therapy for mental illness, one GI discussed how his girlfriend, Ruth, had been faithful to him, regularly writing and phoning him. Furthermore, this GI claimed that he had checked up on Ruth, and he had learned from friends and relatives that she had been faithful to him, even though he had often cheated on her while claiming to be a religious man.[34]

Some medical professionals publicly challenged conventional religious mores about sex. For instance Harry Benjamin, a European-trained physician, did not view distributing condoms as an unfortunate compromise with the sinful condition of men. Instead, Benjamin challenged the whole notion that men should be encouraged to be continent during their time in service. From his perspective venereal disease prevention contributed to a holistic view of health in which premarital sex was acceptable because it could improve troop morale and prevent a negative mental outlook among soldiers.[35]

In March 1943 William R. Arnold wrote to the commandant of the chaplain school at Harvard about the willingness of the American Social Hygiene Association to offer courses on "sex hygiene and morality" as part of the training curriculum.[36] M. J. Exner, who headed the Venereal Division of the Board of Health of Newark, New Jersey, had been tasked with giving the first of these lectures in April 1943. But the head of the chaplain school abruptly canceled his session, insisting that there simply was not enough time in the curriculum and that the medical staff sufficiently covered sexual hygiene in their lectures.[37]

Was this the real reason for the invitation's rescission? It is clear from the lecture's outline that Exner planned to emphasize the "normal sex impulse" and overcome the "misguided education" that many had received from their homes that characterized sex as a "forbidden subject, evaded as something secret, ignoble or even nasty." Exner also planned to denounce prostitution and the "menace" of "large numbers of young girls, who attracted by the uniform and misled by the general moral relaxation which war always fosters, become 'women of easy virtue.'"

While these views caused a few points of conflict with the teachings of the Catholic Church and other faiths involved in training the chaplaincy, Exner's views on masturbation were less than welcome by the Roman Catholic who headed the chaplain school. Exner would directly contradict the Roman Catholic teaching on sexuality by identifying masturbation as an acceptable alternative for men who were sexually mature but had to wait until "marriage and legitimate exercise of the sex function becomes feasible." While recognizing masturbation could be harmful in some cases, he firmly rejected the notion that it was a "terrible vice and sin" or that it robbed a man of his "sexual powers" and induced "insanity." He asserted that a "vast majority" of men engaged in masturbation and a "smaller majority of women." For men seeking to cope with the "strains and tensions of army life" during wartime, Exner argued masturbation may to many men serve a useful purpose of adjustment and of avoiding the dangers of physical, social and spiritual damage. If a choice must be made between masturbation and the prostitute, the preferable choice is masturbation."[38]

Religion and Psychiatry

Treatment of psychiatric casualties represented both one of the war's great challenges and one of its great successes. Initially, military psychiatrists sought to take a prophylactic approach by screening out those individuals who were thought likely to become psychiatric casualties. Although over one million volunteers and draftees were rejected, the psychiatric casualties were staggering. In the North Africa campaign, documented psychiatric casualties outnumbered those from physical wounds.[39]

The high rate of psychiatric casualties, especially for the most common condition, combat fatigue, led to a fundamental reordering of our understanding of courage, fear, and disease. Psychiatrists and social scientists began to recognize that the stress of modern warfare inevitably harmed all combatants. While green troops suffered high rates of psychiatric casualties, empirical studies commissioned by the army demonstrated that over time even battle-hardened GIs were likely to collapse under the strain.

In contrast to the earlier assumption that "shell shock" derived from actual physical injury to the brain, military psychiatrists stressed that environmental factors caused breakdowns on the battlefield. Fear, they determined, was a sensible intellectual and emotional reaction to the conditions of the battlefield that soldiers had to overcome. In addition, they determined that fear combined with lack of sleep, inadequate diet, and harsh living conditions contributed to the severity of the resulting mental response. Returning to earlier practices learned in the First World War, the military tried to treat men as close to the front as possible and approach the condition as an aberration. A period of sleep (often induced by narcotics), warm food, and the chance to discuss their experiences with medical professionals often enabled rehabilitated men to rejoin their units.

Although religious groups also had ideas about mental health, the army chaplain school instructed chaplains to defer to the expertise of the medical establishment, even in cases of neuropsychiatric casualties. While lecturing at the army chaplain school, Chaplain Charles Blakeney called on chaplains to embrace the role of counselor, emphasizing the skills necessary to succeed in this aspect of their duties. At the same time, Blakeney stressed the importance of avoiding the "mentally or physically desperate" and serving the "normal and near normal." For background Blakeney recommended not a religious text but *The Human Mind* written by Karl Menninger, one of the nation's leading psychiatrists.[40] At the front, chaplains frequently took on this counseling role, often without being asked, and some of their remedies were remarkably simple. Bernard Rice, an army combat medic, described how during one battle a group of dejected men on the verge of breaking down often congregated around aid stations. The chaplain did not offer words of comfort but did something even better. He stood in front of the stove cooking cheeseburgers to dispense to exhausted men, reviving their spirits enough to go out and fight.[41]

Medical personnel, at times, asked chaplains to take a proactive role in dealing with psychiatric casualties. Renwick Kennedy, a Protestant chaplain serving the 102nd Hospital during the fighting near St. Lo in September 1944, was assigned to offer assessments of the mental health of those hospitalized and to help determine those who were psychiatric casualties. As a chaplain who took an active interest in watching surgeons perform operations and autopsies, Kennedy embraced this task diligently. Based on his interviews with patients, he determined that half of all cases were combat exhaustion or related casualties, including several cases of self-inflicted wounds. As his biographer noted, Renwick described the ailments of these patients using medical terminology. He recorded one case of a private who claimed a knee injury even though the surgeon could find nothing wrong with him, noting: "It is a mental or psychogenic knee or hysterical knee (hysterical conversion) . . . set off by exhaustion."[42]

W. Edgar Gregory, an army chaplain who went on to earn a doctorate in sociology, discusses—in an early postwar article in the *American Journal of Sociology*—the role of the chaplain in mental hygiene. Observing that little had been written on the topic, he draws on his own experiences as well as anecdotal evidence to sketch out the place of chaplains in aiding psychiatric casualties. Chaplains fill an important role, in part because there are too few experienced psychiatrists to meet their needs. They play an "unconscious" role in helping men overcome their fears by their very presence. Because the chaplain is perceived as a "man of God," soldiers think no harm will come to him. Ironically, harm did come to many chaplains in the combat zone, with many grievously wounded or killed. Despite the risks to their personal safety, Gregory asserts that good chaplains recognize the importance of offering reassurance, and GIs expect them to "show no fear."[43]

The role of chaplain as counselor and confessor remained an important aid to reaching mentally distressed men. Given the "sanctity of the confessional," chaplains were the only officers in the army to whom a soldier could freely express himself without fear that his identity or what he said would be revealed without his consent. GIs were generally more willing to reveal concerns to chaplains than to medical officers, who could interfere with their assignments or duties. Moreover, the status of chaplain as officer often proved beneficial in allowing a good chaplain to seek the necessary assistance for men in distress.

Some chaplains strived to help men suffering from mental distress. In writing to a fellow chaplain and his wife, Chaplain Richard G. Hertz vented about the travails of two GIs he sought to assist. In one case a soldier, Joe Camhi, who had gained approval for a Section VIII discharge from a military psychiatrist, went up the chain of command only to be disapproved by the corps commander. He recounted how Camhi, on hearing the news, "broke down completely" in the chaplain's office, and Hertz had to "carry him bodily back to his barracks for shipment" to a new base. In another instance he described the poor care Mannie Silverman received from the base hospital's psychiatrist. In Hertz's view Silverman, who became violent and went on hunger strikes that led the psychiatrist to order force-feeding, would have "cracked up" even without joining the army. The military, however, did little to meet his healthcare needs.[44]

But chaplains had only so much training in psychology and psychiatry, and some of them could be insensitive as well. Bert Manoff, who had fought in France, recalled that the chaplain who greeted him and other neuropsychiatric casualties of combat when they arrived at a stateside hospital in Long Island, New York, did not give a good first impression:

> The chaplain getting on the bus and we were all grisly veterans. I mean we had been through a lot. The chaplain gets on with a smiling face. He says, "I'm going to give each one of you a TS slip." Which originally meant "tough shit," see, but his was a "theological service." [laughs] But when he said, "I'm going to give each one a TS slip," he was taking a chance that some of these guys would not have treated it as a big joke, you know. We had some real battle star veterans on that bus with us going out to the hospital there. In fact, one guy got in front of me in a cafeteria line and he saw milk, bottles and bottles of milk. And he hadn't seen milk in months and months and months. And he almost flipped out over the milk. That I will say. He started calling it in German, "Milch, milch," I said, "You're back here in Long Island. Knock it off!" Which was stupid of me, too, because he could have turned on me because he was a little bit off the beam, seeing all that milk. He hadn't seen it for so long. And he obviously came from a [dairy] state and he loved milk and all that kind of stuff and everything came back to him. But yes, this chaplain thought he was funny.[45]

In his discussion of the value of chaplains for mental hygiene, Gregory stresses their ability to assist medical professionals in cases where "religion plays a significant part." For some especially devout soldiers, their chances of recovery are improved if a sympathetic chaplain can have a medical diagnosis translated into appropriate "religious language." Gregory's point stands out against the solidly secular orientation of military psychiatry. For instance Grinker and Spiegel, in their case study *War Neuroses*, which appeared in 1945, offer no significant mention of religion in either their discussion of specific case studies or in outlining ways to treat psychological casualties. Among military psychiatrists there existed a strong ethos to medicalize issues that had been deemed by the faithful as moral questions.[46]

In her training notes for treating psychological casualties, Hildegard Peplau, an army nurse deployed to Europe, scarcely mentions religion or faith. One of the few explicit mentions is on a worksheet nurses used to assess the condition of neuropsychological patients. Nurses were to consider a patient's mood, activities, thinking, eating, and the condition of his bowel movements. Under the category of recreation, nurses were to take note of what a patient did in his spare time and whether he liked to do things with others. "Does he attend church?" was something implied to be positive, but too much religion was not a good thing. A nurse should also consider the question: "Does he appear over-religious (fanatical)?"[47]

Faith does emerge as a category of analysis when considering the truths revealed by a patient given sodium pentothal. This drug often allowed a patient to talk about his "ghosts" and recount the devastating experience of combat. To survive battle required "a certain amount of *faith*" not in a divine being but in the "belief that you can kill and not be killed—that you can watch your buddies come and go and remain *strong*." A patient who had "given-up" had lost confidence not in a Supreme Being, but in "himself."[48]

These conflicts between religion and psychiatry stemmed in part from the strong secular orientation of psychiatric medicine, with many of the pioneers being openly agnostic, even antagonistic toward organized religion. The army's embrace of psychiatry raised concern with Roman Catholic bishop John F. O'Hara, charged with appointing Catholic chaplains and supervising them ecclesiastically. O'Hara protested to army chief of staff George Marshall that some army psychiatrists were too freely classifying soldiers as "neuropathic" and claimed these GIs would be "regarded perfectly normal by other observers." Even more disturbing: "It is not only that men suffering from 'battle fatigue' are classed as neuropathic, but decent young soldiers who have given everything they had to their country." O'Hara claimed these men were told by "these unworthy practitioners that they are nervous because they are 'sex starved.'" O'Hara believed it was necessary to conduct a secret investigation "because the offenders, who are followers of Freud, recognize no moral law, and are invariably dishonest."[49]

The Catholic hierarchy was not alone in making these complaints to army leaders. Chaplain Louis J. Meyer wrote a detailed letter to the senior chaplain for Roman Catholic priests, John F. Monahan, describing how "soldier-patients, Catholic and Protestant" protested the use of the "needle" to induce the twilight sleep that forced patients to answer a range of deeply personal and unnerving questions that invariably centered around the question of "Sex." Furthermore, the results of these suspect examinations dealt irreparable damage. They resulted in the classification of GIS as "'nervous', 'criminally inclined' or 'homosexual.'" He described a tragic case of one young woman ("a saner person never lived") who, after one of these examinations, was classified as having "suicidal tendencies" and was sent home. This inappropriate diagnosis unnecessarily haunted this woman. For Meyer there were deeper theological problems with the use of sleep-induced examinations. These examinations were being improperly used by army physicians to substitute for "Confession, Communion, and a few heart-to-heart talks with the priest." An equally disturbing aspect of the practice of producing twilight sleep rested in the invasion of an individual's conscience without full consent.[50]

An aviator wrote to Chief of Chaplains William R. Arnold complaining about being branded "abnormal" and washed out from flight training because of the "pagan beliefs of a few psychiatrists." During a psychiatric examination, this army air force sergeant admitted that he had never "indulged in sexual relief in spite of strong passion." As a result of this admission, he was sent to another psychiatrist, who continued the discussion of his sexual history and required "the lowering of [his] trousers for examination." Holding firm to his "statements of non-relief" meant being sent off to "an Anthropology unit where I was forced to submit to sex pictures" and again was required to continue the "sex discussion."[51]

Arnold thought there was merit in White's claim and passed his letter to the senior chaplain serving under the commanding general of the army air force. In writing to Chaplain Charles I. Carpenter, Arnold challenged the psychological standards outlined in the technical manual governing aviation medicine. He maintained that neither "good psychology nor good psychiatry" required the "slurring question" . . . on the "validity of the moral law, . . . and on sound home training." Interrogating individuals about their sexuality in an accusatory manner might be effective for criminals, "but it provokes the average decent person and arouses in the less patient gentlemen the combative desire to bust the questioner in the nose." Unless something was done, Arnold believed, individual aggrieved soldiers and their supportive chaplains would start writing to the president, the secretary of war, and their church bodies about these affronts to morality.[52]

Religious leaders were not alone in challenging the authority of psychiatrists. Some within the military hierarchy were skeptical about how to treat and even define cases involving combat exhaustion. In 1942 George Marshall wondered whether many neuropsychiatric cases were merely cowards or malingerers. What is the line, he pondered, between cowardice and mental illness? For some old-school warriors, the line remained rigid. Perhaps the most famous and reviled incident is Gen. George Patton's twice assaulting a patient suffering from battle fatigue during tours of military hospitals.

Although Arnold was critical of some psychiatric practices, he also recognized the efficacy of others. In a letter written to a senior official in the military ordinariate, he explained the severe combat fatigue that afflicted many GIs. To bolster his point, he even forwarded them a classified study written by the preeminent combat psychiatrists Roy Grinker and John P. Spiegel. But there existed a grain of truth to the bill of indictment against Grinker and Spiegel and the general practice of psychiatry.[53]

Despite some tension between religious beliefs and psychiatric values, faith and medicine could also align. Both the religious and psychiatric establishments viewed homosexuality as a disordered condition that required a cure. In 1943 army chaplain Charles Dutton wrote to the chief of chaplains about his experiences in dealing with two homosexuals. In offering an overview of how to properly respond, Dutton thought it important to "take the attitude that a trained psychiatrist will take toward such a man." Far from keeping this matter confidential, a chaplain should discuss the issue with the company commander in order to make the necessary arrangements. In cases of homosexuality there were crucial questions that only a psychiatrist could answer: Is the man a bona fide case or is he simply trying to get out of the military? The chaplain should assist those with homosexual tendencies who were desperately trying to avoid committing an overt act. He should also stand ready to counsel a homosexual and be his advocate if called before a Section VIII board.[54]

Many chaplains who counseled GIs with a range of problems no doubt performed many of the roles of psychiatrists and other mental health professionals. Moreover, while the stigma attached to mental illness, to a certain extent, diminished during the war and in the immediate postwar era, there were men and women who undoubtedly sought out a chaplain but would never have voluntarily requested treatment from a psychiatrist. For many chaplains the experience of serving and counseling men on such a broad range of issues, often far astray from theology and religious practice, bolstered the pastoral counseling movement, which gained renewed strength after 1945. In fact, the postwar era saw a growing rapprochement between the psychiatric establishment and organized religion; even an erstwhile critic like Bishop Sheen eventually embraced it.

TEN

The Dead

During World War II, bullets and bombs carried out their deadly mission with brutal efficiency, yet many men and women died in various ways that attracted far less attention. For example, numerous GIS succumbed to fatal diseases such as meningitis and bacterial infections. And there were good reasons why aviators received extra flight pay; fatalities were a common occurrence, even in training. Automobile accidents were ubiquitous in training and later, after deployment, overseas. Other accidents could be equally deadly. One marine, traveling aboard the USS *West Point* off the coast of Australia, in January 1943, slipped and the side of beef he was carrying fell on him, fracturing his skull and causing fatal internal injuries.[1] Sailors drowned after being washed into the sea during storms, and scores lost their lives when whole vessels capsized during treacherous typhoons. Although there were many draftees in their thirties and many generals who were in their fifties and sixties, the death toll fell heavily on the young. Indeed, a significant number of draftees had not even reached the voting age of twenty-one when called up to fight.

Although no one was immune to the grim reaper, the death toll from combat fell disproportionally on those in the infantry. But often those in support units, even close to the lines, had few encounters with death. One army captain, who commanded a motor maintenance unit attached to a combat division, remembered coming under artillery fire during the push for Monte Cassino, but his unit never lost any men killed in action.[2] Combat on the high seas, even in the midst of a major battle, was capricious. It spared some ships and sank or severely damaged others. Ray Taub, a pharmacist's mate, recalled in an oral history interview how several destroyers in his squadron were hit by kamikazes during the battle for Okinawa, but his vessel was spared despite being in the thick of enemy action.[3] For those in the infantry who spent any length of time on the line, death proved the norm.[4] Even if a combat unit was lucky and experienced relatively few casualties in battle, GIs encountered the enemy dead, along with the bodies of hapless civilians caught in the crossfire. For almost everyone involved in the war, death was a constant companion.

Hollywood films played a prominent role in drumming up support for the war, but how to portray death posed a potential challenge. During the war Hollywood generally portrayed GIs dying in heroic circumstances, frequently giving their lives so others might live. Their deaths were clean with little hint of the trauma that war could inflict on the human body. Hollywood generally sought to invest death with a larger meaning. In many instances the dying offered stirring words, even if whispered, to comrades and even a chaplain standing nearby. In *Bataan*, a story focusing on a band of soldiers seeking to hold off the Japanese onslaught in 1942, the film allows for convenient lulls in the fighting so comrades can bury the dead. The last survivor of the unit fighting this hopeless battle digs his own grave and mounts a machine gun by it.[5] Even before Pearl Harbor, Hollywood films conformed to a private censorship body that restricted the depiction of graphic violence. America's entrance into the war only heightened this sensitivity and encouraged self-censorship, as many producers and directors wanted to produce pictures that supported the war effort while still turning a profit.

The Spiritual Dimension of Death and Dying

Cinematic depictions may have been comforting on the home front, but they seldom captured the agonizing and often lonely deaths of many GIs. GIs died alone in foxholes or in the middle of no man's land. In many cases death came so suddenly that the GI never had the opportunity to utter last thoughts or receive the comfort of friends or the ministrations of chaplains. There were, of course, cases where GIs suffered long and agonizing deaths that tested their faith. First Lieutenant Hershel G. Horton knew he was dying when he wrote a last letter home to his parents. Found in his prayer book, it described the agony of being wounded and alone on a jungle battlefield in New Guinea. Herschel recounted how he had the misfortune, on a mercy patrol, to be picking up the dog tags of the dead when he and several men with him came under fire. Wounded, the sergeant accompanying him escaped and promised that help would return—that help did not come for two days. But instead of evacuating him, a medic bandaged him and left him with the promise of help. Although he could see patrols trying to reach him, Herschel recognized that his health was steadily deteriorating without food or medical care. Digging a water hole to sustain himself, he noted that while the water was refreshing, "it was polluted by all the rotting bodies within 12 and 14 feet of me." He lacked the strength to crawl out, and when he managed enough energy to stand, he was shot again. This additional bullet did not kill him, and he contemplated an existential question, "wondering not why God has forsaken me, but rather why He is making me suffer this terrible end." Although he considered suicide and "nearly lost my faith a couple of days here" he retained his "faith in the Lord"; God must be "giving me the supreme test." Convinced of God's purpose, even if unknowable, Hershel confessed dying left him troubled about how much he would never experience. While this Illinois native hoped for a rescue, he told his parents he expected to meet them in the next world.[6]

Lest one think that the medics in Hershel's case were shirking their duty, this is not the case. In the heat of battle, especially during an assault, the army medics or navy corpsmen became responsible for the mortally wounded, an often overwhelming task in many senses. Death came in horrible ways, which left remains that were a distressing sight for the living. Artillery shells pulverized bodies into dozens of pieces and caused brains to ooze out of skulls, guts to hang out, and limbs to be torn off. Tankers unable to escape a burning Sherman tank would be roasted alive and the occupants' bodies turned into ash. Bodies not immediately recovered became bloated, especially in the tropics, and sometimes became food for animals. One GI recalled leaving behind the bodies of two German soldiers in a barn with pigs that had not been fed for days, and within a matter of hours these animals had consumed them.[7]

The ever presence of death was signified by the metallic tags GIs wore around their necks, widely nicknamed "dog tags." An innovation that caught on during World War I, these metal tags carrying individuals' names helped ensure their identities would be preserved if they became disfigured casualties. Those in the Second World War not only bore individuals' names but, in contrast to the ones issued in 1917, they listed GIs' religious preferences to facilitate proper burial. Accidents had been made in World War I, and crosses had been placed on the graves of Jewish soldiers.[8]

Other sobering actions required GIs to contemplate their mortality. The armed forces encouraged GIs to purchase government-sponsored life insurance to benefit their dependents. Before being deployed overseas, a GI was usually required by his commanders to write and sign his last will and testament. The Rabbinical Council of America encouraged each Orthodox Jewish GI to grant a *get* (divorce) to protect the war widow. In case a body could not be recovered, the Get could be used by a spouse in order to remarry. To facilitate the process the council developed and distributed preprinted forms that could be used for the duration of the war. Although the council encouraged each GI to appear before a tribunal of rabbis to signify his assent to the Get, it also made provisions for a Jewish chaplain or a body of three Jewish GIs to render a final decision.[9]

The question of what to do for the dying and the dead had profound religious implications. The National Conference of Christians and Jews issued a pamphlet aimed at those in the armed services, calling on GIs to notify a chaplain, ideally of the man's faith, when confronting a wounded soldier. If no chaplain was present, the pamphlet encouraged a comrade to "help the soldier to offer the prayer appropriate to his faith" and provided suitable Catholic, Protestant, and Jewish prayers.[10] E. B. Sledge described how, during the initial assault on Pelileu by the First Marine Division, one navy corpsman was grief stricken at his inability to save the life of one marine. Despite the chaos of exploding shells, small-arms fire, and smoke, this corpsman "held the dead Marine's chin tenderly between the thumb and fingers of his left hand and made the sign of the cross with his right hand."[11]

For the Catholic hierarchy, the prospect of a Catholic GI dying without access to a priest raised deep concerns. Not only would a devout Catholic fail to receive the sacraments and the opportunity to make a confession and receive absolution, but there also existed an undertone that a Protestant minister or others might lead the faithful astray at a perilous time. Some Protestant chaplains ignored the prohibition against offering last rites to dying or dead GIs. No doubt some of these Protestants did so out of compassion; others were motivated by a lack of respect for strictures of Roman Catholic doctrine. One Lutheran pastor, the only naval chaplain aboard his aircraft carrier, instinctively went to the body of a friend who had been killed when a Japanese kamikaze hit the *Sangamon*. Even though a member of the ship's company told him he should not be offering last rites, he took out his book and read the appropriate remarks.[12]

Chaplain Joseph T. O'Callahan received the Medal of Honor for his efforts to comfort the mortally wounded and properly mourn the dead. Some chaplains commented on their efforts to comfort the mortally wounded on the battlefield and in hospitals. In his postwar memoir, Roman Catholic chaplain Joseph T. O'Callahan sj, described the ghastly aftermath of a direct hit on the aircraft carrier *Franklin* during the battle of Okinawa. In the initial hours of the attack, O'Callahan offered absolution and anointed the wounded, but with decks ablaze, which caused further explosions of bombs and munitions, hundreds were immolated and could not be reached. O'Callahan joined the effort to rescue trapped men and even manned the fire line briefly. After the ship had been stabilized, O'Callahan and the crew went about the grim task of retrieving the dead. Many were incinerated below deck, and it proved a ghastly process to not only locate them but, even more disconcertingly, to carry them up steep ladders. Since many sailors avoided this duty, O'Callahan took it upon himself and carried dozens up to the deck for a brief prayer uttered by either him or the Protestant chaplain aboard the *Franklin*. His exhaustion led to an incident that produced years of nightmares for O'Callahan. While carrying one body up a ladder, he fell asleep briefly. As O'Callahan remembered in his memoir, "It is disconcerting to awake and find oneself clasping and facing a burned corpse."[13]

Even more frustrating for chaplains were commanders who

MASS FOR MARINE DEAD
ON TARAWA

21. Mass for Marine dead on Tarawa, 1943. Harry Johnston Collection, Institute on World War II and the Human Experience.

would not give them access to the war dead. One chaplain, writing to the military ordinariate, complained about the failure of commanders to notify him of the deaths of Catholic GIs. He described how in New Guinea he presided over the funeral of a Catholic, and afterward "a colonel had the nerve to tell me that he would consider it a 'token' funeral for whatever men from his battalion would be killed in the future."[14]

In considering the grief following the loss of a loved one in battle, we should not overlook the converse. The inability of many sons and daughters in the service and deployed abroad to properly mourn the passing of their parents and other loved ones was one of the most distressing elements of the war. GIs frequently wanted a chaplain of their own faith in their hour of grief. In the middle of battle in the Pacific, Roland Winter received an unexpected visitor in his foxhole. A Protestant chaplain brought him the sad news that his father had died. Winter lashed out at the chaplain and asked, "Where was the Jewish chaplain?" The Protestant chaplain informed Winter that, regrettably, one was not available and that he would do what he could to comfort Winter. Winter rejected this offer, but fortunately there were enough Jewish soldiers in his army unit to form a minyan, allowing him, for several days, to say kaddish in memory of his father. Despite being on the front lines, Winter and his fellow Jews stood up to recite the prayer that praised the majesty of the divine and actually said nothing about death or the afterlife. One can imagine the sight of grimy and tired soldiers intoning in Hebrew: "Glorified and celebrated, lauded and worshipped, acclaimed and honored, extolled and exalted may the Holy One be praised beyond all song and psalm, beyond all tributes which mortals can utter."[15]

The Burial of the Dead

The Field Manual for U.S. Army Graves Registration mandated that chaplains could be charged with the burial of the dead, including the process of verifying the identity of a deceased soldier in the absence of graves registration personnel. They were required to find a suitable terrain for graves and supervise the work party, which should ideally be headed by a reliable noncommissioned officer. Chaplains or their assistants were also tasked with searching the bodies of dead soldiers for objects that would be wanted by "those at home," and when dog tags were missing, providing clues for identification. The importance of keeping detailed records was emphasized in the field manual.[16]

At the army's chaplain school, the curriculum provided an overview of procedures for handling the war dead. As the war progressed, the curriculum expanded to include instruction in taking fingerprints for identification of the dead. Future chaplains were warned about the crucial role the proper handling of the dead played in sustaining unit morale. Otherwise, it could plummet like "quicksand" when fighting the enemy. Dead bodies should be removed with "all the respect due a comrade in arms fallen in battle—this is highly important!!!" and "any irreverent handling must be corrected at once." At the same time, chaplains were told to hide the fallen from view and take them off the battlefield, ideally by a back road to "avoid public gaze and troops observing." In confronting the dead, the chaplain was to remember to "*keep a sense of God's presence*" and "neither become soft and emotional or hard and caloused."[17]

Many army chaplains embraced the duties mandated by the field manual, and some took great risks in leading efforts to retrieve the dead. This could be a physically difficult—even dangerous—task, especially if taking place on an active battlefield. Chaplain Israel Yost, a Lutheran pastor serving with a Japanese American unit, formed ad hoc groups to retrieve the dead on several occasions. Yost found it difficult to prod exhausted men to go out, sometimes into no man's land, to find the war dead. Chaplain Hiro Higuchi, who served with the same unit in Italy, recalled having to lead a group to retrieve a GI lying in a minefield. Besides relying on the engineers to clear a path through the minefield, Higuchi recalled to his wife that the Germans had booby-trapped the body and the engineers had to disarm the explosives. The whole episode took several hours and, as the leader, Higuchi could not display any fear, to avoid sapping the morale of the men following him.[18]

Other perplexing questions arose about the war dead. Should the dead be privileged over the living, especially when a burial party came across German wounded? Chaplain Higuchi recalled, in a letter to his son, risking his life to retrieve the American wounded and dead in the midst of battle in October 1944. He recounted how the graves registration officer did not have the guts to go out on the battlefield to retrieve the American fallen. Higuchi decided to take on the task himself and ventured out with several men to retrieve four American bodies. In the midst of these efforts, Higuchi noticed that, among a group of German corpses, one enemy soldier was still alive when he moved his arm. Hiro did not come to this stricken man's aid since there were only enough stretchers for the American dead, and as he told his wife, "I wasn't going back and risk my neck for a wounded Jerry."[19] In further reflecting on his experiences on the battlefield, Hiro openly recalled the hate he had felt toward the enemy as a result of seeing men returned dead or wounded. Yet he also noted that his encounter with a captured German POW, once back in his lines, made him realize the essential humanity of the enemy. After he offered the German POW a cigarette and struck

22. Salute to the American dead on Kwajalein. Harry Johnston Collection, Institute on World War II and the Human Experience.

up a conversation with him, this prisoner started showing him pictures of his family.

Official army policies regarding the burial of the dead indicate great sensitivity on the part of the army toward religious pluralism. The U.S. Army Field Manual for Graves Registration issued in September 1941 called for a nonsectarian name peg to be used as a temporary grave marker. If the V-shaped wooden marker was unavailable, graves registration personnel and chaplains were instructed to use an ordinary stake. For more permanent burials, the field manual called for the use of crosses, when available, for those of the "Christian faith and the Star of David to mark the graves of those of the Jewish Faith." The field manual underscored that the cross should not be used as the default maker for all graves, mandating that in the event that "Hebrew markers are not available, the crosspiece of the cross will be removed prior to replacement thereof." It further acknowledged the pluralism of potential enemies. The manual made the provision that "in the case of burial of the dead of opposing forces of other religious faiths, the type of grave marker to be used will be determined by the commanding general, theater of operations, and procured by the Quartermaster Corps."[20]

The Enemy Dead

What of the enemy dead? The army field manual stressed that, unless impractical, the enemy dead should be buried apart from American and Allied graves, but their section should still be in the same cemetery. It mandated that the graves of the enemy dead be identified with markers that provided their identities but also their enemy status. The manual firmly declared that the "robbery and maltreatment of the wounded or dead on a battlefield are outrageous offenses against the laws of war." Commanders were tasked with making sure offenders were apprehended and brought before "competent military tribunals."[21]

In the war against Germany, most GIs followed the letter and spirit of the field manual with regard to the enemy dead. While the German dead were not always given proper burials, especially during major battles, seldom were they mutilated. During lulls in battles or when the front moved forward, American units were quite diligent in burying the dead. Following the mandates of the field manual, American units generally buried Germans in separate graves, properly marked. Gen. George Patton, who relished combat and the destruction of the enemy, reaffirmed to the graves registration units in his command the importance of properly burying the German war dead.[22]

American forces in the Pacific generally did not extend this same care to the Japanese war dead. Seldom would any effort be made to preserve the individual identities of the Japanese fallen, much less offer funeral rites. In fact, sanitation provided the motivation for American forces to bury the Japanese war dead, usually in mass graves. Sometimes this grim task was given to others. Serving with the marines, Abraham Felber described how, after one engagement on Guadalcanal, in August 1942, Korean prisoners of war were given the task of collecting and throwing into a pit between sixty and seventy "puffed up and bloated" bodies of dead Japanese combatants. As Felber recorded in his diary, some bodies had become so badly decomposed it proved impossible to move them.[23]

Despite the mandates of the laws of war, Americans, on occasion, mutilated the Japanese war dead. Racial animus certainly played a crucial part in promoting this illegal conduct. In what one historian deems a "War without Mercy," the Japanese committed similar atrocities to American war dead, often mutilating bodies and leaving them unburied.[24] Many soldiers and marines made souvenirs of Japanese skulls.[25] Serving with an army amphibious unit, John Gaitha Browning recounted the killing of two Japanese prisoners by a marine guard in the middle of the night. In the morning the marine colonel instructed this marine to get rid of the bodies. Before anything could be done, a "medical private" planned to salvage the gold teeth from one of them, but he made the mistake of going to breakfast. When he returned, he found another "guy had a trench pick and was picking them out." Instead of digging a grave on land, the marine decided it would be easier to put the two corpses on a boat and weight their necks down with rocks. He dropped them into the water and, as they sank, "the marine emptied his pistol at them."[26]

There were exceptions to the disrespect with which the Japanese war dead were treated. In a memoir issued by Chaplain W. Wyeth Willard before the war ended, he described the burial and funeral service accorded to a Japanese POW who had died in captivity from his wounds. This "Jap" prisoner was buried near a small cemetery for marines who had died in the Solomons. Willard described joining the Catholic chaplain in leading a general funeral service for this fallen enemy soldier, but he made no "reference to the dead Jap." Two Japanese POWs took part in the funeral, with a "Christian Jap prisoner" reading "from the Japanese Bible." Although the religious affiliation of the deceased Japanese soldier is not clear, the "other Jap prisoner placed a white wooden cross over his departed friend's grave." On the cross he had painted, in the Japanese language, the name of his fallen comrade."[27]

Willard, a Baptist chaplain, observed that a number of sailors and marines witnessed this burial service, and he recounted his discussion with a GI afterward, which indicated how seldom Japanese were accorded such rites and rituals. The GI asked the chaplain, with a degree of bewilderment, "Why all this kindness? They'd never do that for you." Willard asserted that, after a battle,

Christians should be kind when an "enemy has been disarmed and captured." Proper treatment of even the Japanese dead, for Willard, served as a marker separating Christians from pagans. He admonished this GI and the readers of his memoir, published in 1945, "Let us not lapse back into paganism because others, like the Japs, have not been brought out of paganism and barbarism because of the indifference and neglect of the Christian Church."[28]

However, Willard's views on how the Japanese dead should be treated were not the norm, even after the war ended. For example, American military authorities that occupied Iwo Jima did little for the Japanese war dead scattered throughout the island. Occupation officials did little to limit access to the caves and tunnels that contained the bones of thousands of Japanese dead. As a result, American souvenir hunters regularly collected skulls from among the dead as grisly souvenirs of the conflict. Not only did the military authorities undertake few efforts to bury or cremate the Japanese war dead; they also frustrated official and unofficial Japanese efforts to retrieve and mourn the dead. Wachi Tsunezo commanded the Iwo Jima garrison just prior to the American invasion and returned to Japan when he was replaced by Lt. Gen. Kiribayashi Tadamichi, who led Japanese forces against the American invasion. After V-J Day Tsunezo sought access to the dead in order to care for them. After Japan's crushing defeat, Tsunezo embraced Buddhism, became a priest of the Tendai School, and adopted a new name, Jushoan Koami. Koami dedicated the rest of his life to mourning the Japanese and American war dead. Some American GIs supported his quest to visit Iwo Jima, beginning with Lt. Col. Richard Hayward of the U.S. Marines, who met Koami when he took over his naval base during the surrender of Japan.[29] But not until Douglas MacArthur's departure from Japan did occupation authorities finally grant him limited access to Iwo Jima.

For many chaplains one of the most difficult duties was presiding over funeral services. Younger chaplains, especially those in the navy accepted into service immediately after graduation from seminary, had little significant civilian pastoral experience to draw upon. This was the case for Donald Mackay who, soon after arriving at the San Diego Naval Air Station, found himself tasked with organizing the funeral of his executive officer, who held the rank of captain. Having never before presided over one, civilian or military, this Methodist chaplain and recent Duke University Seminary graduate received mixed encouragement from the senior chaplain, who offered these comforting words prior to the somber ritual: "There is nothing in the Navy which can make or break a chaplain so fast (with an emphasis on *break*) as such a funeral."[30] The day before the funeral, the new executive officer asked him "in a rather gruff manner" for an accounting of the arrangements he had made. In the end, the service attracted an "impressive array of gold-braid, numerous captains and some admirals," which pleased the widow. The new executive commander complimented Mackay on the way he had handled the service and deemed it beautiful.[31]

For those on the battle lines, the chance to mourn could be fleeting as bodies were evacuated to the rear for burial. Ernie Pyle described the grief that befell one unit after the death of their beloved captain. He described how, one dark evening in Italy, members of his unit took great care to evacuate his body from their mountaintop battlefield to the valley. But although each member of the unit paused before the body of their beloved leader, the unit moved out before a funeral or burial service could be held. The best they could do for their captain was mutter words of remembrance as they walked by the body.[32]

Edward Elson, serving as corps chaplain in France during the Ardennes Offensive, wrote regular letters to his congregation about presiding over the funerals of all the dead from units that did not have their own chaplains. After conducting services into the night, on "one of the coldest" nights of the winter, he described his satisfaction that he had performed this "hallowed" task, which would provide assurance to folks back home that an "ordained clergyman had attended the body at the grave and given a fitting Christian service for an honored soldier." At the same time, without going into detail, Elson made it clear that many of the "niceties" of a civilian funeral were absent. He hinted that the audience was small and probably included the men, likely from quartermaster corps, who operated the heavy machines and a motley crew of German prisoners, who were "filthy, grimy, beastly looking creatures—subhuman appearing rather than the vaunted supermen."[33]

In other instances funerals evoked anger and fueled a quest for vengeance. Marine sergeant James P. Casey died from friendly fire, and his friend Joseph Kelly had his weapon taken away from him for "fear of what he might do" to the enlisted man responsible for this accidental killing. Just prior to the funeral, an astute chaplain deftly calmed down Kelly, diverting the grieving marine's anger by having him make a cross for Casey's grave. In recounting the funeral, a fellow NCO described the angst of his comrades when they placed his body, wrapped in blankets and a poncho, into a grave that did not fit. Initially, they thought the chaplain would not let them expand the grave to allow Casey to lie flat in it and they would have to live with the memory of him being in a "cramped position"—his "head and feet were against the wall of the grave." They were pleased to be allowed to widen the grave, letting Casey "lay straight and relaxed." After Casey's funeral his comrades filled in the grave and placed the recently-made cross over it.[34]

Most GIs who died on land were buried in graves, but this did not apply to those in the navy and marines who died on the high seas. The navy continued the time-honored tradition of burying the dead at sea after a ceremony presided over by a chaplain or, in a number of cases, by a commanding officer who read a funeral service provided for the occasion. A burial at sea could be an especially somber affair, where a significant portion of a ship's crew would gather to hear the service read by a chaplain or senior officer and the body was cast into the sea. Funerals offer opportunities to mourn and display emotions, in the hypermasculine world of the armed forces, which would be considered inappropriate in other circumstances. One naval chaplain recalled that when he presided over a funeral for forty officers and sailors killed in a kamikaze attack, the ship's captain cried "like a baby." This Lutheran pastor noted that this was the only time he ever saw the captain cry while he was under his command.[35]

On naval vessels the lack of Catholic chaplains precluded funeral Masses for those to be buried at sea. Ecumenical services were, in fact, forced upon many naval chaplains and crews because of the imperative to bury the dead as quickly as possible given the lack of facilities to store bodies for any length of time. But the navy was not alone in holding general services for the burial of the dead, even when casualties occurred in the United States. Charles F. LaCour, director of the National Catholic Community Service USO Club in Dalhart, Texas, queried the army chief of chaplains, William R. Arnold, about the decision, at the Army Air Forces Advanced School, near Dalhart, to hold a joint memorial service for five soldiers killed in a training accident. The post chaplain at the glider school refused to permit the local priest, Father James L. Daly, auxiliary chaplain of the post and affiliated with the USO club, to participate in the ceremony, even though three of the dead were Catholic. The post chaplain at first deemed the memorial service as nonreligious in character and dispensed with the priest. For LaCour this memorial service was certainly Protestant in character, since there would be the "singing of hymns, a short talk etc." LaCour found the lack of inclusion of a Catholic priest even more distressing because a protestant chaplain was coming to the base to assist with the funeral. Protests from Daly and LaCour would force the post's executive officer and chaplain to relent and include Daly. As part of the memorial service, Daly said a memorial Mass for the three Catholic GIs who had been killed.[36]

Even after the incident appeared settled, the executive officer wrote to express regret that a Mass had been said as part of the memorial service. In replying to this letter, Arnold made it implicitly clear that LaCour and Daly had acted appropriately, especially since the army had "no particular type of memorial service prescribed by regulations." He stressed that official policies called for a "Protestant service for Protestants, a Catholic Mass and Absolution for Catholics, and a Jewish service for Jews" and that care should be taken not to impose a service that the deceased person would object to if he were living.[37]

The right chaplain was not always present to preside over a burial of the dead and perform the rituals of his or her faith. Chaplain Selwyn D. Ruslander complained to the JWB that, while he had presided over a number of Protestant funerals during the invasion of southern France, he had not received timely information about Jewish casualties in his jurisdiction, despite being the only Jewish chaplain for the Mediterranean. During his entire tenure as fleet chaplain, Ruslander presided over the funeral of only one Jewish officer, Lt. Perry M. Phelps, who was buried in Oran. Ruslander wrote Phelps's sister about his death, giving her the "comfort that he did not suffer" and saying he was "grateful he [was] laid to rest by such friends and with the prayers of his faith."[38]

The topic of Jewish burials made its way to the top of the army hierarchy. In a May 1944 memorandum, army chief of staff George Marshall noted that the War Department had learned of many cases when Jewish men had been buried by non-Jewish chaplains and proper Jewish religious rites had not been held either coincident with or subsequent to the internment. Marshall ordered that a Jewish chaplain be tasked with engaging in systematic visits to every military cemetery to ensure that Jewish graves in each military theater were marked with a Star of David and that Jewish memorial services were conducted over these graves. To ensure accountability, Jewish chaplains were to record the names on all the Jewish war graves they located and indicate the dates services were held over them, with the final list going to the memorial branch of the quartermaster corps.[39]

GIS' religious preferences were registered and often indicated on their dog tags, but questions of which religious rite to perform were not always clear to surviving family members. For instance Edna, the widow of Roland Bullock, wrote to her late husband's unit chaplain to learn what funeral rites he had received.[40] Edna, a Roman Catholic, learned from Chaplain L. E. Cousins that her late husband had listed his religious affiliation as Protestant and had received Protestant funeral rites. Cousins had inquired with the unit's Catholic chaplain and reported to Bullock that he had never expressed an interest in conversion or attended Catholic services.

Cousins sought to comfort the widow by stressing the ecumenical nature of religious life among GIS. He implied that, before his death, Private Bullock would likely have heard the prayers of a Catholic chaplain: "Combat conditions are such that before the troops go into action it is customary for both the Catholic and Protestant chaplains to offer prayers for all of the soldiers' protection." Seeking to minimize the theological import of her husband not receiving the Catholic sacrament accorded to the dying and dead, he explained the difficulties chaplains faced in meeting the religious needs of the GI in this way: "I hope that you will understand that in war we have hundreds of boys to administer to and to look after their spiritual lives; consequently we must talk to them in large groups and pray for them likewise, and I am sure that God, Our Father, understands all the difficulties in a war and makes allowances for them."[41]

Naval chaplain W. Wyeth Willard, who served with the marines on Guadalcanal, recognized that men who never attended chapel could be found at funerals for fallen comrades. For Willard, the funeral represented an opportunity to preach the gospel to these men and proclaim the message, "I am the resurrection and the life, saith the Lord: he that believeth in me, though he were dead, yet shall he live; and whosoever liveth and believeth in me, shall never die."[42]

The end of major campaigns, significant lulls in the fighting, and Memorial Day usually prompted chaplains to organize memorial services. On March 14, 1945, Protestant chaplains organized a memorial service for those from the Fourth Marine Division who had died in the Battle of Iwo Jima. According to the one-page mimeographed program, no eulogy or memorial address was offered. The service consisted of scripture readings, the committal service, the recitation of the Lord's Prayer, and the singing of two hymns: "Rock of Ages" and "Faith of Our Father."[43]

Spouses and families seldom attended burial services of GIs who died overseas. Delays in reporting deaths meant that days and even weeks went by before loved ones learned the news of their loss, generally through a telegram delivered by Western Union. Conscientious chaplains wrote to next of kin offering condolences. Chaplain Harold Saperstein, a Reform rabbi with a congregation outside of New York City, strived to write personal letters to the next of kin, especially if he had known the soldier well. In his letters, Saperstein stressed that he had conducted a "service in accordance with the tradition of our faith" and emphasized the enduring legacy of an individual soldier's sacrifice. Writing to one Philadelphia mother, he declared that her son, Herman S. Perelman, had died "fighting for his country in its hour of trial" and had joined others who had laid down their lives to ensure "the ideals of democracy survive."[44] These letters meant a great deal to many survivors.

Many of those who had lost comrades made pilgrimages to World War II battlefields. In his postwar memoir Franklyn Johnson, who served as a young lieutenant with the army's First Divi-

23. *Two dungaree-clad Coast Guardsmen pay silent homage to the memory of a fellow Coast Guardsman who lost his life in action in the Ryukyu Islands* [ca. 1945]. Still Picture Branch, U.S. National Archives (26-G-4739).

sion, described how he and his fellow officers sought out the grave of one comrade after the fighting in Sicily ended in 1943. When they found the grave of Dick Koehler, they replaced the stick marking his grave with his dog tags attached to a cross they had made. To bring comfort to Koehler's family, they took a picture of the grave with its new grave marker. In his memoir Johnson did not mention offering any prayers and cited no biblical verses to offer comfort. Instead, he recalled the brotherly love among comrades and quoted from the funeral oration of Pericles: "Heroes have the whole earth for their tomb; and in lands far from their own, where the column with its epitaph declares it, there is enshrined in every breast a record unwritten with no tablet to preserve it, except that of the heart."[45] Viewing the graves forced GIs to ponder mortality and the essential meaning of the struggle. As one GI recorded in his journal:

"Each cross spoke like thunder through the coconut grove, across the pale tropic sky, loud sounds of broken bodies and broken hopes and leaving behind those who cared. What shall the harvest be? . . . Unborn of unborn shall see . . . What are we to believe—we who are left to look upon the rows of crosses?"[46]

Photojournalists and official photographers frequently took images of the gleaming wooden crosses and stars of David over the graves, interspersed with the official markers for unidentified dead. But the first cemeteries built after battle were usually ad hoc affairs, especially on the isolated islands of the Pacific. Mack Morriss, who served in the Pacific as an army journalist with *Yank* magazine, described in his diary the remarkable variety of grave markers and symbols of remembrance he found at the military cemetery on Tulagi. Some grave markers were made of "concrete blocks, with mess kits cemented into them and names, dates, and a few words scratched in on them." Marine aviators used "props" for gravestones and he even saw the "cowling of an F4F" for one grave. Sacred and profane memorials included [rifle] "stocks, bayonets, crosses cemented in by .45 caliber bullets." Many grave markers had "snapshots" attached to them that showed "grinning kids with garrison caps tilted on the back of their heads." Religious diversity was represented by the "Hebrew stars" on the graves of "Jewish boys," while Catholics' grave markers included rosaries or pictures of the Virgin Mary. Protestant graves tended to feature tributes "that were so simple and sincere that they have to be seen for what they are there to be appreciated." Morriss observed that this was sacred space and "nobody walks in there and speaks except in lowered voice."[47]

Those captured by the enemy faced a severe loss of autonomy in virtually every aspect of their lives; dying and death were no exception. Fortunately, while Americans died in German prisoner of war camps, their numbers were relatively few. Moreover, the German military generally adhered to the Geneva Convention. In fact, the Germans were quite diligent in ensuring those who died in captivity received proper burials and funeral services. Chaplain Sampson, who was captured at the Battle of the Bulge, outlined a string of grievances about the way the Germans treated him and his fellow captives, including a forced march in the bitter cold. But as he recorded in his postwar memoir, they acted surprisingly honorably in the way they treated the American war dead and allowed him to bury them in a local cemetery.

Once he arrived in Stalag II-A, Sampson presided over—on average—the funerals of two Americans and two British servicemen every week. For Roman Catholics a French priest provided him with oil to anoint the dying and the dead before their burial. The Germans provided a coffin and allowed eight pallbearers, along with an additional honor guard of twelve men, to carry the body from the hospital to the cemetery. During each funeral, men in the camp lined up inside the gate and offered a salute as the body passed them on the way to a cemetery. Sampson described how, along with offering the burial rituals, he sought to place each death into a broader context. He did not ignore the fact that the deceased was buried "thousands of miles from his home and unattended by his family and friends" and that he lay "naked" in a "crude coffin" with only a "crude marker over his grave," while stressing the "grace of a holy and Christian death," which offered liberation from the "prison of this life." In his memoir Sampson recalled that "Taps" was played after each funeral.[48]

Even American POWs consigned to the Berga concentration camp, who endured inhumane treatment from their captors, were accorded individual graves if they died from malnutrition, disease, or physical brutality. American prisoners were allowed to bury American POWs in a civilian cemetery outside the camp and, in some cases, a coffin was provided. In other cases bodies were wrapped in blankets. Although the graves of American Jewish soldiers were unmarked, those who were Christian had crude crosses erected over their graves with helmets hanging over them.[49]

For those held prisoner by the Japanese, the living witnessed indignities heaped upon those who had been murdered or had died from disease or malnutrition. During the Bataan Death March, stragglers or those who broke ranks to find food and water were summarily executed. Bodies were generally left along the side of the road or given, at best, a hasty burial. The situation did not improve much when prisoners settled into Fort O'Donnell and Catabaun. The death rate soared from diseases compounded by the lack of medicine and inadequate facilities. Weakened prisoners struggled to move the dead to burial grounds, and the Japanese resorted to mass burials to deal with the dead. No doubt some on burial detail offered prayers for the dead, but scenes recounted in memoirs and oral histories were ghastly. "They put twenty guys in at a time. So, when we would go there the next day, they didn't cover the holes that we put guys in, they wouldn't cover the holes that night and the dogs, wild dogs, would come and eat them."[50]

Not all the war dead were treated callously. Army colonel Paul D. Bunker described how the Japanese allowed an officer who died in Tarlac to receive a full Catholic service at his grave, led by a Filipino priest with even the camp commandant in attendance. But the Japanese did not provide a coffin, so his fellow prisoners had to fashion one from a partition in one of the camp lavatories. Moreover, the Japanese would not permit any American officers to accompany the body as pallbearers or hold a memorial service in the camp. Instead, a delegation of only six prisoners was allowed to attend the funeral.[51]

Mourning Delayed

While the war raged, it remained virtually impossible for next of kin to visit the graves of GIs buried overseas. The war dead would not rest even after victory had been achieved. As was the case after the First World War, next of kin were granted the opportunity to decide whether their son or daughter killed during the war would remain buried in an overseas cemetery or would be repatriated to the United States for final burial in a national or civilian cemetery. Following precedents from World War I, hundreds of small cemeteries were consolidated into a handful of larger cemeteries. Many bodies journeyed aboard naval vessels thousands of miles to find final resting places in permanent cemeteries established in Hawaii and the Philippines for the Pacific war dead. Except for the cemetery in Tunisia, the remaining overseas cemeteries were located in Europe, on the soil of countries that had been liberated. While a permanent cemetery was planted at Anzio, Italy, all the American war dead were removed from Germany.

At the end of July 1945, Chaplain Selwyn Ruslander joined a community roundtable discussion with fellow chaplains, including Protestants and Catholics, in Beaver Dam, Wisconsin. He stressed the brotherhood, religious tolerance, and religious freedom that he had found within the army and expressed his appreciation of the efforts Roman Catholic and Protestant chaplains had made on behalf of Jewish GIs. For Ruslander, the American military cemeteries served as an enduring symbol of a "Democratic Nation" that understands its "spiritual foundations rest upon the Hebrew-Christian Ethic and Law." For the men buried overseas, "whose symbols are the white cross and the star of David," these men remain united in death and death brought together "black man, yellow man, white man, rich and poor man, scholar, and dunce, youngster and oldster, Jew and Christian."[52]

Not all agreed that unity in death existed. Even with the sprouting of stars of David on foreign fields, some argued Jews had not borne their weight in the war. Chaplain Ruslander's papers include anti-Semitic doggerel titled "New Book of Revelations," accusing Jews of cowardice. Among the slurs directed at Jews: "And the Gentiles came up in great multitude from all the lands to fight for the Jews, and the Jews lifted up their voice and sang, 'Onward Christian Soldiers.'" This anti-Semitic poem ended with a plea to vote "the Republican Ticket."[53]

Ultimately, responsibility for maintaining the permanent overseas cemeteries would be given to the American Battle Monuments Commission. In building the first network of overseas cemeteries in World War I, the commission had altered the American pattern of commemorating the dead, mandating overtly sectarian grave makers, with the use of either a free-standing cross or star of David for the fallen. Although the U.S. Army had developed a nonsectarian grave marker, devoid of religious iconography, the American Battle Monuments Commission continued the precedent, established after World War I, of allowing next of kin to choose between a cross or a star of David for the graves of all fallen doughboys permanently buried in the overseas cemeteries. The bias toward Christian symbolism would be more pronounced after 1945, as the sectarian bias toward the cross led to a shift in policy on how to mark the graves of unidentified soldiers. After World War I the commission placed crosses and stars of David over the individual graves of the unidentified based on the percentage of members of each faith who had been killed in battle in this conflict. The commission decided after World War II to place crosses on all the unknown dead GIs out of fear an "unknown Christian" would have a star of David over his grave.[54]

Despite the emphasis on establishing overseas cemeteries, most GIs who died in the Second World War would not have their final resting places among their comrades on the field of battle. Mirroring the pattern in World War I, only 30 percent of next of kin elected to have the remains buried in overseas cemeteries; most opted for their loved ones to have their final resting places in either national or private cemeteries in the United States. Repatriation took years to accomplish, and for many families the funeral and burial services that accompanied the return of a body fostered renewed mourning and sparked profound grief.[55]

ELEVEN

Prisoners of War

More GIs spent time as prisoners of war in World War II than in any other conflict in the twentieth century. Over the course of the conflict, the enemy held 130,201 Americans captive; by comparison, the number of American POWs in World War I totaled 7,140; in Korea, 7,140; and Vietnam, 766.[1] To be a prisoner meant a life that bore little in common with a GI's experiences as a civilian or in the armed forces. All prisoners, whether held by the Germans or the Japanese, endured a severe loss of autonomy, usually combined with paralyzing fear. To be taken prisoner meant time out of combat, but certainly not time out of harm's way. Not only were prisoners at risk of harm from their captors; they often faced the possibility of friendly fire. Over the course of the war, POW camps were accidentally bombed, unmarked Japanese vessels carrying American prisoners in their holds were sunk, and German rail boxcars transporting captured soldiers were bombed and strafed.

The religious experiences of Americans in captivity varied. Many read scripture while others prayed and practiced other religious rituals to cope with the harsh conditions at even the best run camps. Although all religious groups faced challenges while in the hands of the enemy, one group felt particular burdens if captured: American Jewish GIs who had the misfortune of being captured by the Germans. Despite the vast outpouring of scholarship on the Holocaust, surprisingly little has been written about the experiences of Jewish GIs. Most survived their captivity, partly because international law made explicit the protections accorded to all prisoners of war. By the same token, there existed remarkable silence in the official record, including the records of the JWB, about the captivity of Jewish GIs and their religious life in German POW camps.

In considering the religious life of the American GI prisoner in World War II, it is important to examine his unique status under international law. One of the greatest accomplishments of the humanitarian movement—spurred on by peace movements in the late nineteenth and early twentieth centuries—was the effort to supplement customary law with explicit protections through a series of international treaties, most notably the Hague Convention of 1907 and the Geneva Convention of 1929. Under the Geneva Convention, prisoners were entitled to humane care and were monitored by protecting powers and the International Red Cross (IRC). Among the rights secured by the convention was the freedom of religion, including the right to attend services of their faith and for clergy to be allowed access to prison camps.[2]

Along with a strengthening of the legal protections for POWs, several international organizations marshaled considerable resources to aid prisoners of war on both sides of the conflict. The most significant was the International Committee of the Red Cross, headquartered in Geneva, Switzerland; under the terms of the Geneva Convention, this committee had the right to send official representatives to visit POW camps and even interview detainees to ensure humanitarian standards were being maintained. Equally vital to the survival of POWs, especially in camps run by Germany and Japan, was the distribution of Red Cross packages containing food and a host of items for personal grooming.

Less well studied is the role played by the International Committee of the YMCA. This organization, also based in Geneva, supplemented the efforts of the Red Cross and bore the principal responsibility for providing prisoners with resources to meet their spiritual, educational, and recreational needs. YMCA secretaries visited POW camps in Germany and Japan, but after the war, in reporting on its activities, the YMCA insisted it "never tried to be an inspecting semiofficial body" and deferred to the IRC in this regard.[3]

The Vatican took a strong interest in the treatment of prisoners of war, especially those from Italy. Vatican diplomats won the right to visit POW camps in several nations, including the United States. Pius XII even dispensed individual gifts to prisoners of war, and some American prisoners received them. For example, American prisoners held by the Japanese in Bilibid in 1944 received three hundred pesos as a papal gift.[4]

Among the responsibilities of the Vatican Information Office, established for the duration of the war, was facilitating communication between prisoners of war and their families. Although most American families learned about the imprisonment of family members from communications relayed through the International Committee of the Red Cross, the Vatican supplemented these efforts, especially for those held prisoner in Italy.[5] For instance, Private Henry J. Perner of Miami, Florida, completed a prisoner of war notification issued by the "Secretariat of State to His Holiness" that was transmitted to the Apostolic Delegate in the United States, who forwarded it to the Bishop of St. Augustine, who instructed a parish priest to deliver it personally to the prisoner's spouse.[6]

There were stark differences in how POWs fared under the Germans and the Japanese. Despite the genocidal nature of the Nazi regime, Germany generally adhered to the letter and spirit of the Geneva Convention with regard to American prisoners of war and those of the British Commonwealth. With some important exceptions, most Jewish American POWs survived German captivity. As one informational sheet issued to families of American POWs explained, in the closing days of the war, "most of the atrocities now being publicized are occurring in Concentration camps . . . not in military prison camps." It reassured Americans that American military prisoners were under the protection of the Geneva Treaty, while those in concentration camps, "held because of political and religious reasons," were "completely at the mercy of the enemy."[7]

German adherence to the Geneva Convention partly reflected the concern of Nazi leaders for the treatment of their own prisoners held by the Americans and the British. The fact that American and British soldiers were deemed to have a higher place in the racial hierarchy than Slavs can also explain the better treatment afforded them. Bureaucratically, German POW camps, for most of the war, came under the jurisdiction of the armed forces, while concentration camps and death camps came under the authority of the SS and Gestapo. Of course, care should be taken not to make too firm a distinction between the "good" German army and the evils of the ss. Soviet prisoners in German POW camps suffered staggering casualties as a result of deliberate policies to starve them to death and deprive them of adequate medical care. Moreover, if Germany had prevailed against the Western Allies, there is a good chance that American and British Jews would have been liquidated as part of "the final solution."[8]

Things were drastically different for POWs held by the Japanese. Japan, which was party to the Hague Convention, announced shortly after the attack on Pearl Harbor that it would also adhere to the Geneva Convention. Despite this affirmation the Japanese military's treatment of American and other Allied POWs was abysmal, with thousands of deaths stemming from malnutrition, diseases, mistreatment, and friendly fire. Even in the best circumstances, the Japanese military generally violated the norms of the Hague and Geneva Conventions. International inspections by the Red Cross occurred only sporadically, and Red Cross delegates were only granted authority to visit some camps on a limited basis.

Throughout the war the Red Cross and the YMCA struggled to send vitally necessary food, medicine, and other aid to Japanese camps. Even at camps where American prisoners were reasonably well treated, they suffered from malnutrition, inadequate medical care, and wretched living conditions. Prisoners, even officers, found themselves compelled to work on dangerous jobs that directly supported the Japanese war effort in direct violation of the Geneva Convention.

The Japanese inhumanity toward prisoners was at times inexplicable. The rise of Japanese militarism and the embrace of the principal of Bushido influenced official policies and the attitude of the military and individual Japanese soldiers about how American and other POWs should be treated. Japanese political and military leaders stressed that obedience to the emperor must be absolute, given his semidivine status. Japanese discourse allowed no room within military culture to disavow an order that violated international laws and norms. Within the military, Japanese officers regularly used corporal punishment on their own soldiers, and this brutality would also be visited on American captives. The Japanese army's attitudes toward sick and wounded soldiers were callous. The army devoted few resources to their care, especially in comparison to the medical care the U.S. Army and Navy provided for American GIs.[9]

A chasm existed between the Japanese and the Americans regarding the notion of surrender. American culture celebrated incidents where soldiers opted for death over capitulation, recounting the siege of the Alamo and George Armstrong Custer's last stand. But even American military leaders recognized that surrender was a necessary, perhaps honorable, option when further combat would only lead to senseless loss of life and all other paths of survival, much less victory, proved impossible. Although Gen. Douglas MacArthur railed against Jonathan Wainwright's decision to surrender in the Philippines, President Roosevelt and army chief of staff George Marshall recognized there existed no other viable option. Wainwright's decision to surrender would be affirmed after V-J Day, when he was promoted to the rank of four-star general and awarded the Congressional Medal of Honor.[10]

This illustrated a huge distinction between American and Japanese culture. It would have been inconceivable for a Japanese general or soldier to be decorated for surrendering his forces in order to end the senseless loss of life. Japanese soldiers, under the precepts of the codes of Bushido, were instructed never to surrender. While a significant number of Japanese soldiers departed from this mandate, it is striking how many refused to capitulate even when further resistance proved hopeless. American defenders of Bataan in 1942 were stunned when Japanese forces caught in an unsuccessful amphibious assault chose to fight to the death rather than give up. Even when the tide of war shifted, Japanese troops had little inclination to surrender. Moreover, the atrocities the Japanese visited on surrendering American troops initiated a round of counteratrocities by American units who, in many cases, simply refused to take prisoners. A number of Japanese prisoners who did surrender expressed great remorse and shame, ironically making them pliable captives once they were in prison camps.[11]

Guests of the Emperor

The opening months of World War II were disastrous for the United States and its Allies, with American defenders on Guam, Wake

Island, the Dutch East Indies, and the Philippines forced to surrender. Memoirs, diaries, and oral histories painted a grim tale of life under Japanese cruelty and neglect. Their veracity is confirmed by the stark fact that 10,650 of the 27,000 Americans imprisoned by the Japanese died before the war ended. The fates of captured chaplains were even worse. Despite their protected status under the Geneva Convention as clergy and as officers, chaplains died at a greater rate than other GIs. Of the thirty-seven chaplains who surrendered to the Japanese, only seventeen lived to see V-J Day.[12]

The first weeks of captivity for most American troops who surrendered were especially dangerous and bleak. After heroically defending Wake Island, the exhausted American marines and defense contractors were herded onto the sun-drenched airfield, on December 23, and remained there for several days. Discipline frayed despite the presence of officers; initially, a stampede of men sought access to the contaminated water dispensed by the Japanese. The next day, Christmas Eve, a small group began to sing carols in the evening, but they were hushed by others who were too demoralized to hear them and feared the Japanese would be alarmed.[13]

The fates of defenders of the Philippines were even worse, especially for the twenty-five thousand soldiers who surrendered at Bataan in April 1942. Exhausted, hungry, and often sick, most GIs were forced to march sixty-five miles to Camp O'Donnell. Japanese soldiers guarding the column provided little in the way of water or nourishment and frequently bayonetted those who dropped from the columns. Officers, including chaplains, joined the enlisted men in this march, which resulted in the deaths of at least several hundred Americans.

The experiences of army and naval chaplains held in captivity reads like a life of modern-day martyrs. Many strived to continue to hold religious services, conduct Bible studies, counsel prisoners, and bury the dead. One can only imagine the agony of a dying Roman Catholic chaplain trying to say Mass with no wine and scarcely any host. Some priests and Protestant ministers sacrificed their own food, cared for the sick, and labored to ameliorate the suffering of their fellow prisoners. The absence of rabbis in the peacetime establishment of regular army and navy chaplains meant that there were none in Japanese POW camps. At one camp a cantor who served as an enlisted man took a special role in organizing services for Jewish POWs.

Not all actions of chaplains were so welcome or meritorious. One navy physician, Thomas Hayes, attending the sick at Bilibid Prison, was critical of his encounter with a resident chaplain who undermined the efforts of officers to maintain discipline and a chain of command within the compound. In his diary Hayes described how the chaplain had come to the defense of a naval corpsman who had assaulted an officer, resulting in the complete exoneration of the corpsman before the camp's disciplinary board, despite "damning evidence" brought against him. Hayes, without naming the chaplain, criticized his poor judgment and expressed his frustration at trying to maintain unit cohesion under such trying circumstances. Another incident involved a Roman Catholic chaplain who made disparaging remarks about an amateur musical group formed by the prisoners, which Hayes found simply "ridiculous." While admitting, in his diary, that the "Bilibid Players" did not have much talent and their humor was a "little lusty," Haynes believed they gave a badly needed boost to morale. Hayes's assessment of the chaplain was harsh, and he insisted that if this Roman Catholic priest "was as wide open, aboveboard, and constructive as our Bilibid Theater he would serve a much more useful purpose around here." Furthermore, this chaplain rejected the offer of the Bilibid Players to stage a Christmas show under his auspices, and despite a tirade by the chaplain, the players put on their show anyway.[14]

Conditions at Japanese camps varied significantly, often stemming from the discretion of individual commanders. The marines who surrendered at Wake Island had a higher-than-average survival rate because of a strong sense of cohesion and the ability of officers to maintain discipline. But their survival also rested with the fact that when this group was transferred to Shanghai, they entered a prison that treated them humanely. They were fortunate that the Japanese leadership wanted to create a "model" prison camp for propaganda purposes. As a result they allowed Red Cross officials access to the camp and, even more importantly, prisoners received food and other supplies from this organization and from the international community in Shanghai, including substantial amounts of reading material.

Even before the surrender, the marines at Wake Island had no access to a chaplain. In captivity, religious services remained the domain of lay leaders who organized small groups of men for worship, prayer, and scripture study. Groups of Baptists, members of the Church of Latter-day Saints, and Roman Catholics regularly met while the marines were imprisoned in Shanghai. Although the executive officer that led the Catholics in prayer had managed to keep his rosary after his surrender, no Book of Mormon was available for members of the Church of Latter-day Saints to study. Distinctively, for this group of prisoners of war, the Japanese commander even arranged for a Protestant minister from Japan to lead weekly services in the camp beginning July 12, 1942. [15]

There were other instances when non-American clergy had access to American POWs. At a prison camp in Taiwan, one officer recorded in his diary that at the funeral for an American officer, the Japanese made arrangements for a local priest to offer Mass. In his prison diary, Thomas Hayes described how a German Catholic priest in Manila had regular access to the Bilibid Prison during the early months of his imprisonment. He reported in his diary that "Father B" took it upon himself to arrange for local women in Manila to collect supplies for American prisoners and considered saying Mass at the prison. Ultimately, mention of "Father B" disappeared from Hayes's diary, although he later described his interactions with several naval chaplains sent to Bilibid from other camps.

Brig. Gen. W.E. Brougher spent most of his captivity in the company of a bevy of senior American and other Allied officers, including a number of British colonial officials, in Taiwan and later Manchuria. Conditions were certainly better than in most other camps, but even the most senior officer was not immune to physical abuse. One senior British general, who regularly took the role of acting chaplain, died as a result of a beating from a Japanese guard. Moreover, the Japanese would, on occasion, forbid the holding of services. One Sunday it "interfered" with "Nip. work program in preparation for an expected visit by C.G., Taiwan Army." Later, in his captivity in a prison camp in Manchuria, Brougher described his inability to hold services for several Sundays because there was no place or means of having one. In one instance, when the Japanese did permit a service to be held, they restricted the chaplain, an Australian, from offering a sermon and only permitted him to read from the prayer book or Bible. Brougher expressed pleasure with the service because of the beauty of the chaplain's voice and his selection of texts. In his diary entry, Brougher noted that the Japanese guard at the service had to be awakened to take a salute in order for the congregation to leave. Brougher described how, on the eve of v-j Day, the chaplain had "to do obeisance" to the Japanese commander because their captors could "change Sunday to Monday at will," and on Sunday, August 5, 1945, they did so with church services being held the next day. The last Sunday before the Japanese surrender was announced, services were canceled.[16]

The relatively small number of chaplains, and the regular dependence on lay leaders for services, produced an ecumenical quality to many religious observances. Brougher described how, in the Tamazato camp in Taiwan in 1943, religious services were conducted by the British and they used a "High Church Order of service and hymns," unfamiliar to this Southern Baptist. Later in the year, Brougher was moved to a new camp, and several different American, British, and Dutch prisoners led services. One Sunday Brougher preached a sermon on Matthew 5:5, using the text, "Blessed are the meek for they shall inherit the earth." On another memorable Sunday, Brougher recorded a service where an American general spoke on prayer and talked about the need for "cooperation, in Christian Churches, and forgetting minor differences in creeds and other non-vital bars of unity to spirit and action." To provide "a practical demonstration of international-interdenominational cooperation," both British and Dutch prisoners took part in the scripture readings.[17]

The high casualty rate and the recurring suppression of religion by the Japanese make it difficult to fully reconstitute the religious life of GIs. For instance, members of the Church of Latter-day Saints managed to coalesce into an unofficial branch of the church while held in a prison camp in Davao, Philippines, in 1943 and early 1944. Army lieutenant George Robin (Bobby) Brown played a pivotal role in forming this branch and provided the group with a Book of Mormon and a Church of Latter-day Saints songbook that he had managed to hide from the Japanese after his surrender at Bataan. Unlike many Americans, who were forced to walk, Brown drove a U.S. Army truck from Bataan to the Cabanatuan prison camp; this allowed him the opportunity to hide these religious texts. At Davao, Brown and Sgt. Nels Hansen, an LDS high priest, regularly met for services that included singing hymns and offering testimony.

Most of the LDS members of this group would perish aboard a Japanese hell ship, the *Shinyo Maru*, which sank off the coast of the Philippines. Much of what we know about this group would be through a nonmember, army major Morris L. Shoss, a West Point graduate and a Jew, who often attended services led by Brown. Shoss, who often engaged in religious discussions with Brown, greatly admired this LDS group, especially for their willingness to adhere to the tenets of their faith under difficult conditions. In one instance Shoss informed the group of an ill LDS member; this group came to his aid and most likely offered a patriarchal blessing in response to his condition.[18]

Not all GIs held as captives turned to religion as a source of inspiration. Col. Paul D. Bunker kept a meticulous diary of his role in the defense of Corregidor and his life as a Japanese prisoner, first in the Philippines and later in Taiwan. This West Pointer, who had started his army career in 1915, recorded the days of the week and noted when Sundays fell, as well as the Christmas and Easter holidays. At the same time Bunker seldom mentioned his own religiosity, even though he commented on a range of issues, including some unflattering assessments of his fellow officers. While fighting, Bunker appreciated the visit of the unit chaplain to his artillery battery one Sunday, but he never mentioned attending chapel services, except for the funeral of a fellow officer. In fact, Bunker described how a Japanese guard expressed surprise to see him working on a Sunday while a Protestant chapel service was being held. When he outlined his reading list for 1942, Bunker did not list a single religious work. He offered trenchant observations about how faith sustained many of his fellow prisoners at a camp in Taiwan, where it became customary, on Sundays, to sing hymns after breakfast. Every Sunday the group ended with "God Bless America," and Bunker said to observe the "poor devils singing it so fervently and feelingly cannot but bring a lump in your throat to think of their condition and what has happened to them, and yet see that, in spite of all, their faith is in America."[19]

The most significant mention of religion in Bunker's diary was his glum feelings on Christmas Eve, 1942. He described listening to the choir touring the camp singing carols and remembering singing with his wife and children when they were younger. Their rendition of "O Little Town of Bethlehem" brought back memories of his late son who had graduated from West Point and died in an aviation accident before Pearl Harbor. Bunker, who would die the following year, expressed hope that this would be his second and last Christmas away from his wife, lamenting, "'Merry Christmas' is a hollow mockery."[20] Even when Bunker's health declined as a result of malnutrition and disease, he made no mention of prayer or Bible reading.[21]

After his liberation Frank "Foo" Fujita, who served with a Texas National Guard unit, remembered an upbeat chaplain who befriended other POWs recuperating in a stateside hospital. This chaplain's positive assessment of the role of foxhole religion caused Foo to reflect on the lack of spirituality he had witnessed among the American and British prisoners he had encountered in Singapore and, later, Japan. As he recorded in his diary and memoir, while a prisoner he had never "seen or heard a man pray or evoke God's name except in cussing." During part of his imprisonment, Fujita had the good fortune to have access to a large library and the chance to read scores of books on religion "to find a replacement for the concept of God and religion that I had lost in the trenches of Java." Despite his agnosticism Fujita bristled when an English POW ripped a page from the New Testament, used it as rolling paper for a cigarette, and started reading the genealogy of Jesus as a "joke." Fujita told this "Englishman" to "knock it off, that to make fun of the Bible was to make fun of my mother, who was very religious, and I wasn't standing still for that."[22]

Conditions for many POWs, which had stabilized and even improved as the Japanese had consolidated their gains in late 1942 and early 1943, deteriorated in 1944 as American forces advanced to the Philippines and throughout the Pacific. Eager to forestall possible liberation and to draw on their labor, their captors transported thousands of American prisoners, in the holds of Japanese merchant ships, to the home islands. Conditions aboard these vessels defy imagination; men were packed in the hold so tightly that they could scarcely move. Slop buckets fell to the deck, spreading feces and urine throughout the area. Only sporadically would the Japanese permit the removal of the dead for hasty burials at sea.

One Roman Catholic chaplain, William P. Cummings, was among the 1,631 Americans aboard the *Oryoku Maru* when it sailed from Manila to Manchuria. A GI who survived the voyage described Cummings's continual efforts to comfort his fellow passengers. Besides regularly leading men in prayer, he spent hours consoling the anguished and the dying. At one point a dying GI begged to be baptized. Cummings had no water available, and it would be hours before more was dispensed. Desperate to find a solution and unwilling to plead for a drop of water given the dire circumstances, Cummings had to rely on spittle to perform the sacrament of baptism.

Cummings died from starvation, dehydration, and disease, but his death was at least a peaceful one. For others death came as the result of a Hobbesian struggle for survival as men fought each other for water and food. In his postwar memoir, James Stewart remembers that while he retained his faith in God, his faith in man began to fail, and he even began to doubt and fear his closest friend. He witnessed several horrific incidents during the voyage; one was especially tragic: two West Pointers, father and son and both officers, engaged in fierce mortal combat. As he recalls: "I remembered how they had protected and cared for each other in the years past. . . . The son was killing his father. I could see the look in the father's eye. A look of compassion and pity for the son who was a maniac."[23]

German POW Camps and Rule of Law

The decisions by Germany and the British Commonwealth, in 1939, and the United States, in 1941, to adhere to the Geneva Convention saved the lives of countless Allied POWs. Most GIs received regular access to Red Cross packages, which proved essential in the closing years of the war in supplementing the increasingly spartan provisions offered by the Germans. Injured and sick prisoners generally received proper medical care, either from fellow prisoners who were medical professionals or the German military. American POWs regularly received correspondence from their families and packages of goods, which proved vital to sustaining their morale. The international YMCA, also based in Switzerland, would undertake major efforts to provide American and other POWs with goods and services that met their spiritual, religious, and recreational needs.

Official regulations promulgated by the German army recognized the right of prisoners to hold religious services and gain access to chaplains, in conformity to the requirements of the Geneva Convention. German captors placed relatively few restrictions on religious services; chaplains were required to avoid using the pulpit as a platform to make political statements, and their sermons had to be approved by camp authorities. Although some camp authorities required that sermons be cleared in advance, at several camps this policy was not enforced. Under the Geneva Convention, chaplains and medical officers were technically not prisoners of war. This provision did not offer escape from confinement, but chaplains and physicians were generally accorded the privilege of receiving extra shipments from home and were able to send more correspondence. Chaplains were also the only prisoners allowed transit between different prisoner of war camps, as well as a legal right—when practical—to visit enlisted men working outside camps.[24]

Despite the German adherence to the Geneva Convention, how 94,000 American POWs were treated depended on when and where they were captured. Initially, most held captive by the Germans were aviators shot down over Europe and were often well treated, aided by the fact that most were either officers or noncommissioned officers (NCOs), entitling them, under the Geneva Convention, to better conditions. Although rations were never generous, they were often adequate in the early years because of the overall strength of the German war effort. Angelo Spinelli, an army combat photographer captured in North Africa in 1943, even managed to barter for a camera and film to document life in his stalag. In his memoir Spinelli recalled that until the closing months of the war, American prisoners were fortunate to have adequate living conditions, regular access to Red Cross packages, and substantial autonomy to forge a rich array of social, cultural, and educational activities. This included the opportunity to build a chapel largely using materials from Red Cross boxes and other scraps of wood. The International YMCA provided hymnals, Bibles, candlesticks, vestments, and other ritual items.[25]

Although no Protestant chaplain was available to lead services, Spinelli noted that in his camp a divinity student who went on to become an Episcopal priest led weekly services. For Roman Catholics, a Polish priest regularly came to the camp to say Mass. While Spinelli did not recollect the status of the priest, he likely was a prisoner of war accorded the privilege of saying Mass at the American camp.

Helping to sustain the religious lives of GIs was the relatively free access to books and magazines. Both the Red Cross and the International YMCA undertook a massive effort to facilitate the movement of books to American and British Commonwealth prison camps. These efforts were so sophisticated that prisoners could request specific books, on an individual basis, from the Red Cross and they would often be sent to them. Estimates vary regarding how many books were sent to British and American POWs, but they conservatively numbered over one million books, provided by nonprofit organizations and individuals. For instance, the American Bible Society sent over fifty thousand Bibles to Americans in German camps through the YMCA.[26]

There were prisoners who took advantage of the enforced idleness to devour Bibles and religious books. For instance, some POWs read their Bibles, as well as a range of other religious works, from cover to cover. *The Robe*, a best-selling fictional account of a Roman soldier's conversion to Christianity, remained popular at many camps. One GI, not noted for often attending chapel, recorded in his diary that he found reading this work inspirational. Did GIs believe that this was the end times? In one Protestant study group in Stalag 17, they debated whether the swastika represented the mark of the beast prophesied in Revelations.[27]

At the same time, while religious books were significant, they never composed the majority of books sent by the YMCA and the IRC to inmates. Donors sent a wide range of books, works of fiction and nonfiction in a variety of other fields, including history, social sciences, business, and the sciences. The list of book requests by Spinelli survives, and they feature a range of books and magazines focusing on photography, Dante's *Divine Comedy* in the original Italian, and several academic works on sociology.[28]

As the war progressed the number of captured Americans soared, and their treatment by the Germans deteriorated. The growing destruction brought on by Allied campaigns led Nazi propagandists to demonize aircrews as gangsters, often empowering mobs of civilians to attack downed aircrews. During the Battle of the Bulge, which was fought from December 1944 to January 1945, the Germans captured over twelve thousand GIs and, in one instance, a Waffen SS unit massacred a group of unarmed American troops. Others endured harsh conditions as their captors struggled to move them to camps in Germany.

Those captured at the Bulge vividly remembered the starkness of their Christmas celebrations. One prisoner recalled spending this Christmas aboard a freezing German railcar while he observed the Germans celebrating with food, drink, and candles. While a German woman gave some of his fellow prisoners some beer, the guards waited until Christmas Day to let them out briefly to relieve themselves. A Roman Catholic chaplain found himself on a forced march from Bastogne—in the German city of Prum—on Christmas Eve, where he, along with eight hundred prisoners, was herded into an overcrowded building while American planes bombed the city where they were staying. At the suggestion of the senior officer, Francis Sampson held services and preached a sermon stressing the presence of Christ in the holiday. Christmas Day would be even bleaker as the American column suffered scores of friendly-fire casualties.

Conditions improved for Sampson when he arrived at his stalag. Although he was an officer, Sampson was allowed to remain in an enlisted men's camp, where he said Mass daily and offered Communion every Sunday. He recalled how they traded with the guards for the necessary supplies to build a chapel and relied on the labor of American prisoners and those in other compounds. For instance, an Italian POW carved the crucifix and a "Serbian artist did a magnificent job on the Stations of the Cross." There existed an ecumenical element to these efforts, Sampson noted in his postwar memoir, as an "American Jewish boy painted a lovely Madonna and picture of St. Joseph for the sides of the altar."[29]

Jewish GIs in the Stalag

In June 1944 the *New York Times* ran a short article about a forum held in New York City, by American Red Cross officials, for over a thousand next of kin to prisoners of war and internees. At this event, Red Cross officials outlined efforts to send critical supplies to American POWs held by Germany and Japan and responded to the relatives' major concerns. When one official was asked, "Do Germans discriminate against Jewish prisoners of war?" she declared, "They do not."[30] Aside from this small news report, which was also buried in the *Times*, there was no discussion of the lives of Jewish POWs in the American Red Cross *Prisoner of War Bulletin*, aimed at next of kin.

When this newsletter reported on the religious life of Americans in a German camp, no mention was made of religious observances by Jewish GIs. For instance, a detailed report on the conditions of Stalag VII-A, in the January 1944 bulletin, described how a Protestant minister had complete freedom to minister to his "American compatriots" and to two work detachments outside the camps. In offering a religious census of the camp, it described the prisoners as evenly divided between Roman Catholics and Protestants.[31] In the December 1944 issue, it described how religious interest in Stalag Luft III was "reasonably strong," with attendance averaging around 20 percent, with both Protestant and Roman Catholic chaplains leading services, but it offered no mention of Jewish services.[32]

Considering the publicity given to efforts by the Roosevelt administration and the armed forces to implement religious pluralism, the absence of any discussion regarding the fate of Jewish POWs is striking. Moreover, most Jews who became prisoners of war in Germany were treated in accord with the letter and spirit of the Geneva Convention. Like other prisoners of war, American Jewish prisoners were registered with the IRC and housed in camps that were regularly inspected by this organization. German authorities permitted them to correspond with their families and receive packages.

There exists no religious census for American prisoner of war camps in Germany, with the exception of Stalag XVII-B (January–October 1944), where the breakdown indicated that Jews made up 1.8 percent of the population of this camp, which held 4,172 Americans. Nearly two-thirds of this camp claimed to be Protestant, slightly less than one-third were Roman Catholic, and the non-religious and Orthodox represented less than 1 percent. Because no Jewish chaplain was ever captured, no American Jewish POW appears to have had access to a rabbi. This absence did not prevent Jews in Stalag I from holding regular services, joining similar ones for Roman Catholics, Protestants, Mormons, and Christian Scientists. In other camps, religious services were possibly held covertly, or Jews drifted over into the services of other faiths.[33]

Although the American and British governments engaged in a number of diplomatic exchanges with the German government over issues related to captivity of Allied prisoners of war, the Jewish question received no significant attention. At the end of the war, the YMCA issued a report outlining the assistance it had provided POWs around the world, describing at length the religious materials it had distributed and its efforts to arrange for clergy to attend those held captive, but it makes no mention of specific efforts to meet the needs of imprisoned Jews for matzo on Passover, prayer books for services, or rabbis to lead services. It minimized the German restrictions placed on the distribution of literature to POWs by stating that only exiled German Jewish authors were excluded, when in fact the restrictions were much more constraining. For instance, German censors would reject a book of poetry because a Jew wrote one poem.

The fate of Jewish POWs provoked relatively little discussion among the senior leadership of the JWB. At one point the executive committee discussed whether Jewish GIs should no longer indicate their identity through dog tags but wondered whether the mezuzah should be substituted. They rejected the mezuzah as unsuitable for identifying Jewish identity, because many British soldiers with Bernard Montgomery's Eighth Army wore the mezuzah as a good-luck charm in battle.[34]

After the war the official silence regarding the fate and religious life of Jewish POWs was striking. The general board's comprehensive examination of the army chaplain in the European theater, issued in 1949, offered an extensive discussion of the efforts of chaplains held prisoner in German POW camps to meet the religious needs of American GIs. The report offered varying degrees to which the Germans facilitated religious life in camps and other places where prisoners were held. In this section of the report, there was no mention of Protestant or Roman Catholic chaplains seeking to meet the needs of Jewish GIs. There was only one oblique reference to the treatment of Jewish GIs. A footnote to the report noted the service of Chaplain Alan F. Malden, who recounted that "while located at Stalag IX-B, a former concentration camp for Jews, German guards counseled . . . [him] to warn Jewish soldiers not to reveal their religion."[35]

Given the extensive coverage, in this general board report, of the Jewish chaplains and meeting the religious needs of Jews in the ranks, the silence of the report about anti-Semitism is surprising. Part of the silence may reflect the fact that most American Jewish GIs captured by the Germans survived their captivity, compared to most European Jews caught up in Hitler's network of concentration and extermination camps. But at the time, Jewish GIs feared their fates if they fell into the hands of the Germans. Jewish POWs captured by the Nazis grappled with whether or not to reveal their religious identities. When facing capture many Jewish GIs threw away their dog tags and sought to pass as Gentiles. One aviator took an even more proactive stance and, as described in an oral history, flew with three sets of dog tags: "Whenever I flew over northern Germany, I was a Protestant. If we were flying over France, I was a Catholic. Otherwise I wore my regular tags." Shot down over Germany and badly injured, he was the only POW patient in a civilian hospital run by Roman Catholic nuns, who never discovered his identity. Recounting the superb care he had been given and the gestures of humanity extended to him, including his receiving a packed lunch for his journey to a prison camp, he observed, "These people were Catholics first and then Germans."[36]

For German Jews serving with the American army, fear of German capture was even more pronounced. Hugo Lang, who had barely escaped Germany for the United States prior to the outbreak of the Second World War, fell into enemy hands at St. Vith during the Battle of the Bulge. Fearing that if he revealed his German Jewish identity it would mean immediate execution, he survived a three-hour interrogation and convinced his captors that he was born in Jersey City, New Jersey. Lang was fortunate; while one of the elderly guards was from his German hometown and recognized him, he did not report him to the commandant. On the eve of liberation, this guard spoke with Lang and told him that he had known his identity as soon as he arrived in the camp but did not turn him in. After liberation, Lang returned to the United States and later married an Auschwitz survivor. Although one brother managed to escape to the United States, the rest of his immediate family were murdered by the Nazis.[37]

In his memoir army air force pilot Leonard Winograd described his decision to reveal his identity during interrogation upon being captured. However, after the questioning, he later refused to divulge his religious faith to an NCO who queried him about it in a prison cell in Yugoslavia. For this rebuff Winograd, who often passed as Italian, was slapped by this NCO. The prison commander investigating the incident queried his friend, Bob Corbett, about Winograd's identity. Corbett told the prison commander that "he honestly did not know, and since Bob and the German officer were wearing the same saint's medal, they had a basis for rapport." To be an officer, even an enemy officer, had its privileges, and the NCO returned to his cell with orders to apologize to Winograd for slapping him. Despite the order to apologize for striking an officer, the NCO refused, "because he was a German and I was a Jew, and, he told me he could *see* that I was a Jew, because of my face."

During his interrogation at Frankfurt, Winograd was not physically beaten, but he did have to endure isolation and the constantly shifting temperatures of his cell. Determined to give only his name, rank, and serial number, Winograd was threatened with being turned over to the Gestapo if he did not cooperate. At the same time, Winograd was surprised at how much the interrogators knew, not only about his unit but also the army air force in general, even possessing copies of several top-secret technical manuals. Winograd expressed the feeling that his German interrogators were the true professionals in the business of war, and he was a rank amateur.[38]

To be a Jewish POW in captivity in a German camp meant isolation in ways that made it difficult to follow even basic religious practices. During his journey to a permanent camp, Winograd realized that he wanted to observe Passover, but he was unsure when the holiday fell. In the permanent prison camp, after hearing the name "Captain Goldberg" called, Winograd queried him on the day, but Goldberg only gave him the season it fell. With this limited information, Winograd selected seven days around the Easter holiday.

Winograd also wrote about another challenge facing POWs: friendly fire. That led to his decision to become a rabbi. Although Allied bombers made great efforts not to bomb prison camps, the problem of accuracy resulted in friendly-fire incidents. Winograd remembered the dread one night when bombers dropped flares into his prison camp. As an aviator he surmised that they had been targeted. (Later he learned the flares had been dropped to mark the camp, to divert bombers away from it and toward the railyard a mile away.) Fearing imminent death, Winograd prayed for individual family members, "as was his custom." "[I thought] I must not be selfish or God would ignore me altogether." For Winograd this experience ultimately proved to be a spiritual turning point: "And I lay in that filth on my belly on the floor of the barracks and told God that if He could get me out of that mess I would dedicate my life to Him. That was when I decided to become a rabbi. . . . I joke a lot especially in anxiety-laden situations, but I am serious about this moment and the rabbinate."

For Harry Glixson throwing his dog tags away made perfect sense. He said it would have been a travesty for the designation to "acknowledge G-d was used in my demise." Glixon's knowledge of Yiddish allowed him to converse with his captors in the prison camp, who were pleased; some thought his dialect meant he was of Dutch descent. As one of the few German speakers, Glixon was selected to speak with the camp commandant to convey to his fellow prisoners the chores to be completed each day of the week. Glixon would state the day in German, and the major would specify the chore. In this conversation Glixon, with a careless slip of the tongue, almost revealed his identity. When he finished with Friday, he continued with the word "Shabbos." Realizing quickly what he had said, Glixon immediately noted that his German was not very good.[39]

Glixon later felt an estrangement from some of the guards and fellow POWs as a result of being a Jew. Although captivity was fraught with anxiety, it also afforded the time to contemplate and read. It offered him the chance to read the New Testament from the Christian Bible, and he found it enlightening. While Glixon rejected the divinity of Jesus, he came away impressed with many of Jesus's teachings that challenged the power elite of his day.

Glixon's captivity, combined with his experiences on the battlefield, left him traumatized. Before his capture he had found himself alone in a minefield confronting a German soldier, only to discover the soldier was dead. Certain sounds triggered flashbacks about the fear that any sudden movement would kill or maim him, and he would lose sensation in his right foot. He also recalled his crisis of faith and fear that G-d had abandoned him or, worse yet, was "saving me for another and more horrible event."[40]

Daniel S. Abeles did not have the opportunity to throw away his dog tags as he narrowly escaped when his plane was shot down over Germany. He was captured, along with the bombardier, by local civilians before being turned over to soldiers, but not before the bombardier had been hit in the face by a rifle butt, breaking his nose. The German officer taking charge hit the bombardier again before coming over to Abeles, inspecting his dog tags, and declaring, "Ach Jude." The German officer "took out his gun," leading this radio operator and gunner from Philadelphia to fear he was going to be shot, but instead "he just wacked me alongside the head." A similar pattern of physical abuse occurred at the interrogation center at Frankfurt; at one point they asked Abeles the rhetorical question, "You know what is done with Jews here?"[41]

Abeles was fearful during his interrogation, and with good reason; he was sent to Stalag 17, where his identity card would contain a "big red 'J'" for Jude. While Jews in this camp were not segregated, as a Jew, Abeles remained uncertain of his fate and went to the American chaplain in the camp to express his concerns. Father Kane offered the following observations and advice regarding the fate of Jewish POWs: "It all depends how the war goes. If you were a Gentile and you escaped and were caught, you would be brought back. But if you escaped, nobody would ever hear from you again."

For some Jews, like Glixon, their doubts about the Gentile POWs magnified their fear of their German captors. But other Jews witnessed remarkable acts of solidarity that offer an opportunity to gauge the degree to which average GIs embraced religious tolerance and pluralism under extreme conditions. Toward the end of the war, when many camp commanders ordered the segregation of Jewish GIs, many Gentiles protested German actions. At Stalag Luft I, Col. Hub Zemke, the senior Allied ranking officer, lodged a formal complaint not only with the German camp commandant but also with the IRC.[42] The New Zealand army chaplain on the base regularly visited the Jewish POWs at their segregated compound. In his memoir Father Sampson recalls the anti-Semitic character of the German administration of his prison camp. The Germans "carried their Jew-hatred to such ridiculous extremes" that they smashed virtually every record in his compound because Jews were listed as composers, musicians, or manufacturers. Even Irving Berlin's "White Christmas" would fall victim to German censorship.

Although a small minority, some Jews and Gentiles were swallowed up by the Nazi system of concentration camps. In the closing months of the war, several hundred Jews, those deemed to have the physical characteristics of Jews, and supposed troublemakers, were sent off to the Berga concentration camp. Sandford "Sandy" Lubinsky described how, several days after his capture during the Battle of the Bulge, the Germans systematically separated "Hebrews" from the rest of his group of POWs. In his oral memoir, Lubinsky recounted how several non-Jews understood the gravity of the situation he and his fellow Jewish GIs faced. He noted that some Christian GIs were willing to give their dog tags to Jewish prisoners, but they were turned away for fear that without them they would be shot. Both an American colonel and a chaplain wanted to journey with the group headed for Berga, but German officials refused their request.[43]

Would more Jewish GIs have suffered Lubinsky's fate and joined millions of other Jews and victims of the Holocaust if the Germans had prevailed in World War II? Most likely, although the disappearance and murder of Jewish GIs would have been noticed due to their registration with the IRC. Of course, would a victorious Germany have allowed Switzerland, which served as headquarters for the IRC, YMCA, and World Jewish Congress, to remain independent? Many POWs, especially Jews, were well aware of the fate of European Jews. In his memoir about his experiences, "Kriege," David Howard wrote that he witnessed no mistreatment of Jewish POWs in Stalag Luft Three. But the fate of European Jewry was entirely different. Although captivity allowed him little contact with life outside the gates, he recalled one disturbing incident that occurred just outside of his camp:

> I saw two workers carrying away recently cut pine logs and piling them on a nearby wagon. The workers wore the six-pointed Star of David on the backs of their ragged-Jackets. As the two stooped to pick up a log, one of them, a young, husky looking man, picked up his end with no difficulty. The other man, a stooped, gray-haired oldster, struggled with his end, but was unable to lift it to his shoulder. The guard then walked over, unslung the rifle from his back, and proceeded to beat the old man about the head and chest with the butt of his gun.[44]

In the closing weeks of the war, the Germans forced Abeles and his fellow prisoners at Stalag Luft Three to march to another camp to prevent their liberation by advancing Allied forces. As Daniel Abeles remembered, "On our forced march . . . we saw these prisoners with stars of David on their arms. They were on work gangs and had been sleeping in the fields. Some were dead, and others couldn't get up. The rest could barely walk. The Germans just threw the bodies into these big wagons."[45]

International law had contributed to protecting most American Jewish GIs captured by German forces. As Howard's and Abeles's recollections underscore, the laws of war had failed to protect European Jewry. As GIs advanced into Germany in the closing months of the war, they encountered even more chilling cases of inhumanity as they liberated concentration camps. In the next chapter, we will consider how religious faith and identity served to condition the responses of American GIs to the Holocaust and the German people.

TWELVE

Religion and Reconciliation with Enemies

E ven before the fighting ended, American GIs had an inkling of the war crimes committed by Imperial Japan and Nazi Germany. American prisoners of war who had managed to escape captivity told grim stories when debriefed by American military and civilian leaders. Civilians liberated in New Guinea, the Philippines, and elsewhere in the Pacific and Asia recounted the pillaging of homes, the summary execution of civilians, and sexual violence perpetrated against women. The liberation of Jewish communities in North Africa, Italy, and France certainly gave GIs, especially Jewish soldiers, a better grasp of the full extent of Nazi anti-Semitism and glimpses into the nature of the final solution. After American troops liberated the first concentration camp in Germany, SHAEF commander Dwight Eisenhower was so distressed at what he had witnessed that he mandated that the crimes committed by the Nazis be widely publicized among American GIs. He wanted the GIs to have a full understanding of the enemy they fought and the righteousness of their cause. American commanders sought to drive home the nature of the Nazi atrocities to the defeated. In a number of instances commanders required local German civilians to bury the victims who had died just before liberation.[1]

Religious beliefs, the terrible nature of combat, and official policies shaped how GIs responded to the defeated Germans and Japanese after they surrendered, especially in the closing months of the war. GIs' emotions toward the vanquished enemy ran the gamut from anger, rage, numbness, apathy, pity, and even sometimes empathy. There were voices for reconciliation with and forgiveness of the enemy after v-e Day in Europe and v-j Day in the Pacific. Chaplains frequently joined civilian religious leaders in calling for charity toward former enemies. In the case of Germany, many Christian chaplains bristled at official policies that mandated nonfraternization as they wanted to rekindle connections with their co-religionists. Many Jewish GIs, often first-generation Americans, prioritized the desire to save the remnant of European Jewry over the quest for revenge.

The desire for reconciliation was aided in both Germany and Japan by the abject nature of defeat. Even the most hardened heart melted in encounters with children. The fact that no serious guerilla movement emerged in either Germany or Japan also aided reconciliation. Given the stark racialization of the war and the sheer brutality of the Pacific conflict, there remained significant animosity toward the former enemy by some occupation troops in Japan.[2] But most battle-grizzled combatants assigned to the occupation army, especially citizen soldiers, spent a relatively brief time in either Germany or Japan before being rotated home.

Memories, even of enemy atrocities, could be fleeting. For instance, when George Patton toured his first liberated concentration camp with Eisenhower, he was so disturbed at what he witnessed that he vomited. After his tour Patton ordered men in the Third Army to view the concentration camps to reinforce nonfraternization policies. But in a matter of months, Patton sprinkled his diaries and correspondence with anti-Semitic comments about the displaced persons under his jurisdiction. For Patton reconciliation with Germany would be promoted by his perceptions of the racial affinity between Americans and Germans combined with a growing fear of the Soviet Union. In Patton's mind the Asiatic hordes that made up the Soviet Union were prepared to descend on Germany and the rest of Western Europe.[3]

As GIs waited impatiently in both Europe and the Pacific, many gambled and drank. They sought female companionship and were quite willing to fornicate with former enemies. To the consternation of many chaplains and religious leaders at home, many GIs took full advantage of their status as conquerors. They possessed food and cigarettes that many German and Japanese women were desperate to obtain for their survival and often for the support of their families. While many GIs were compassionate, a fair number were uncaring about the plight of civilians and willing to exploit their position to lord over the vulnerable. Venereal disease and prostitution flourished in Japan, the American occupation zone in Germany, and even in China. Serving with the Sixth Marine Division in Tsingtao (Qingdao), China, marine sergeant Louis J. Maloof described the situation in a letter to a friend who, in turn, passed it on to the senior leadership of the National Catholic Community Service. In this letter Maloof described the moral debauchery permitted by the Chinese government and the Sixth Division commander. Despite the protests of Catholic chaplains, the "cat houses" had the divisional seal of approval, and men who had spent years "in the Pacific Islands in a hell of loneliness" were said to have "literally . . . [gone] wild" once they arrived in the Chinese port. Despite Maloof's pleas and those of Catholic priests, the command chaplain refused to press the issue, with the division commander, of making these brothels out of bounds for American marines.[4]

Evil: Anti-Semitism, the Holocaust, and the German Question

American propaganda issued during the Second World War has been criticized for being silent about the destruction of European Jewry. Critics have faulted Franklin Roosevelt and his administration, along with the Congress, for bowing to the anti-Semitism prevalent in American society and not taking more aggressive actions to admit more refugees into the United States. FDR and his administration have also been criticized for not using military force more decisively to halt the Holocaust.[5] How does one assess the extent of anti-Semitism in American society and the role it played in the nation's response to Nazi Germany?

In making the case for war, President Roosevelt had maintained that freedom of religion remained a core value that distinguished the United States from its enemies. Advocates of religious tolerance, including the National Conference of Christians and Jews, the Federal Council of Churches, the JWB, and countless individual military chaplains, officers, and enlisted personnel, recognized that America's entry into the war against Germany had not ended all anti-Semitism. During the war these organizations and individuals drew upon patriotic appeals by maintaining that anti-Semitic views and practices offered aid and comfort to the enemy.

At the behest of Rabbi Stephen Wise, one of the nation's preeminent Jewish leaders, Roosevelt issued such a statement, which forthrightly condemned anti-Semitism, to be read at the National Conference to Combat Anti-Semitism in February 1944. Roosevelt's letter contributed to a program that included such prominent Protestant, Roman Catholic, and Jewish leaders as New York mayor Fiorella LaGuardia and Supreme Court justice Frank Murphy. The statement, drafted by Elmer Davis, the head of the Office of War Information, and revised by FDR, was sent to Wise. In the letter FDR stressed that in their quest to rule the Western world, Hitler and the Nazi Party relied on "organized terror and organized anti-[S]emitism." Victory required Americans to not only "defeat Hitler's armies" but also "defeat his poisonous propaganda." To be an anti-Semite, FDR bluntly declared, "plays Hitler's game." The president ended with an unequivocal statement: "There is no place in the lives or thoughts of true Americans for anti-[S]emitism."[6]

Other voices also condemned anti-Semitism. In a letter to his home congregation, navy chaplain Rabbi Jacob Shankman described the actions of a fellow chaplain, a Southern Presbyterian minister, whom he had first met in chaplain school at the College of William and Mary. Bob Stamper impressed Shankman because he possessed an endearing personality mixed with a "passion for fair play and justice" and, without providing details, Shankman even characterized him as the "Negro's friend." Shankman provided several specific examples of Stamper's confrontations with bigotry. In one instance Shankman described how his colleague lambasted a "Christian lady" over the telephone for discriminating against a potential Jewish tenant. To the rabbi's surprise, he even declared, "What you do hurts me. My ancestry was Jewish!" At first Shankman was incredulous about this statement from an individual who embodied the traditions of "Virginia, Georgia, and Alabama" but, when queried, Stamper explained to Shankman that "If the Good Lord should choose a Jew (Jesus) through whom to reveal Himself, certainly it is no lie for me to appropriate Jewish ancestry for myself." This moral courage was also exercised on other occasions, such as when Stamper ordered a naval officer making "slurring remarks about the Jews" to get out of the car he was driving. In the presence of an admiral attending one of his services, Stamper called attention to "anti-Semitic propaganda" typed on navy stationary and circulating on his base. In his sermon he declared, "I held up that paper to the light and I saw the water-mark of the American eagle. Small people may stoop to mean and vicious prejudice, but they will never blot out or obscure the symbol of our American democracy!"[7]

Without question significant pockets of anti-Semitism existed within the American military and society in World War II. When soldiers in the European theater were surveyed about attitudes toward different groups in American society, in April 1945, 11 percent thought Jews had taken selfish advantage of the war. However, it should be added that a higher percentage, 19 percent, thought businesses had done the same. And 8 percent indicated they personally disliked Jews. By way of context, this survey also revealed much animosity toward African Africans.[8]

A significant amount of information was available on the plight of European Jewry. Navy chaplain Roger Warren Barney, an Episcopalian priest deployed to the Pacific, kept among his wartime papers a bulletin issued by the Federal Council of Churches' information service focusing on "The Mass Murder of the Jews in Europe." Issued in 1943 this depressing document outlined the deadly evolution of Nazi anti-Semitic policies, from systematically stripping Jews of their legal rights in the 1930s to the mass murder of Jews in gas chambers.[9]

GIs and journalists on the front line on occasion encountered evidence of Nazi atrocities, including the persecution of European Jewry. American and Allied troops liberated Jewish communities throughout the war, beginning in the North African campaigns of 1942 and 1943. Don Whitehead, an Associated Press journalist, recalled in his diary the tumultuous reception he received in the Jewish quarter of Tripoli after that city had been liberated by British forces. One GI, in a letter to a Jewish chaplain based in the continental United States, described how—while fighting the Germans in France since D-Day, in 1944—he had seen "and heard a great deal of the atrocities that the Germans had committed against not only our people but also the loyal French."[10]

In May 1944 Chaplain Harold Saperstein sent his wife a copy of a short article he had sent to JWB describing his first interactions with German prisoners of war being treated at an army hospital. He could not help thinking of the irony of a hospital filled with Jewish GI physicians and nurses giving these wounded Germans the "best of care, food and medical attention." Normally, visits to a military hospital evoked great empathy from Saperstein, but seeing wounded German soldiers only produced "hatred and loathing." Saperstein did not blame the Germans for their actions on the battlefield, since the rules of "sportsmanship" demanded one be a "good winner or good loser" when the fighting ended. But for these German soldiers, Saperstein could only think "how these men, or others like them, slaughtered an entire people, men[,] women, and children, how killing unarmed and defenseless Jews to them had been a pleasant diversion."[11]

Even before the victory had been achieved by Allied forces, some GIs relished teaching captured German POWs lessons on the question of blood, race, and survival. Army staff officer James Parton described, in a letter to his family, an incident that underscored both the humiliation of an arrogant German officer and the racism endemic in the U.S. Army, which countenanced the segregation of blood by race. He recalled the irritation of several soldiers at a German soldier who, despite receiving medical care, was quite obstinate. It began while they were giving him plasma. "What's that?" murmured the German, who apparently had quite a command of English. "This is good American blood we're giving you, Joe," replied the corpsman. "Might even be Jewish blood or [a] n—. Yeah. . . . says here on the label it's n—blood. How do you like that, you Aryan bastard."[12]

Lieutenant Peter F. Bank described, in a letter to a stateside Jewish chaplain, his experiences interrogating German POWs during the closing months of the war. Sending Chaplain H. E. Snyder a partial copy of a letter he had written in February 1945, Banks noted that, in defeat, German captives ran the gamut of emotions. Many expressed resignation to their fate; others remained defiant. Bank expressed amazement at how ill-informed the "German people" were about what was happening in their own country, noting the problem of relying only on information "approved by Dr. Goebbels."[13]

Throughout the war, but especially during the battles for France and Germany, American GIs encountered Jewish survivors, who were usually destitute and adrift. Many Jewish chaplains and GIs organized the earliest ad hoc efforts to meet their desperate need for material and spiritual sustenance. Chaplain David Eichhorn recorded repeated instances when GIs, both Jews and Gentiles, contributed to the relief of liberated French Jews. In his August 1944 report to the JWB, Eichhorn described his efforts on behalf of a group of over one hundred Jewish children and adults near Bonnetable, France. GIs attending his services raised one hundred dollars for their relief, and the Civil Affairs detachment found food and clothing that Eichhorn could distribute to them. These efforts were supplemented by "men in the. . . . [Advanced Section Communication Zone] . . . who collected two boxes full of food and candy for the refugees" and a "platoon of Negro soldiers in this barracks contributed its entire week's ration of candy to this collection."[14]

Jewish army and navy chaplains had sanctioned ties with the JWB, which offered them an authorized channel to report on conditions facing European Jewry and to arrange for assistance. After liberating Jewish communities, chaplains—in a number of cases—aided in restoring synagogues and reviving religious life. GIs sometimes provided the labor and frequently pressed German prisoners of war into cleaning desecrated synagogues. The absence of civilian rabbis—who had either been killed by the Nazis or fled persecution—meant that Jewish chaplains often took it upon themselves to lead services, especially on such significant holidays as Rosh Hashanah and Yom Kippur. The reopening of synagogues drew in not only Jewish GIs and recently liberated Jews. Often, as a show of solidarity, senior military leaders attended or sent their designated representatives.

The German Question

Even before victory had been achieved, American policymakers grappled with the German question and the problem of evil. Before strategic balance had tipped toward the Allies, the United States, in December 1942, had joined eleven other Allied nations in publicly condemning the extermination of European Jewry and threatening retribution against those responsible after the "overthrow of the Barbarous Hitlerite tyranny."[15] At the Casablanca Conference in 1943, FDR publicly proclaimed that the Western Allies would only accept the unconditional surrender of the Axis powers. This policy, adopted unilaterally by FDR, served to assure the Soviet Union that Britain and the United States would not seek a negotiated settlement. During his rise to power in the early 1930s, Hitler had asserted that Germany, in November 1918, had not been defeated but rather stabbed in the back by the civilian government. Unconditional surrender ensured that no such lie would emerge after this conflict. American critics, including some religious leaders and peace groups, protested the requirement of unconditional surrender because it threatened to prolong the war. Despite murmurings of dissent, this became the official policy of the Grand Alliance, and Germany ultimately did surrender unconditionally.

How should a defeated Germany be ruled? Some supported a quick reintegration and reconciliation with Germany. There existed strong sentiment, especially among many Protestant and Roman Catholic leaders, that the mistakes of Versailles should not be repeated and a victor's peace should be eschewed. In 1944, when Gen. Dwight Eisenhower sought guidelines for the eventual occupation of Germany, the War Department developed policy guidelines that called for the speedy revival of the German industrial base and economy. This benign policy would run into resistance from Secretary of Treasury Henry Morgenthau and FDR. In the summer of 1944 Morgenthau developed a proposal to prevent a resurgence of Germany by denuding it of all heavy industry and politically dismembering it into a series of small agricultural states. FDR embraced the plan and, at the Quebec Conference in September 1944, pressured a reluctant Winston Churchill to accept the Morgenthau Plan as the official policy of the Western alliance.

But within weeks of the Quebec Conference, FDR would be forced to reverse course after facing significant public opposition and dissent within his own cabinet. Secretary of War Henry Stimson and many other policymakers believed that turning Germany into a cluster of weak agricultural states was politically and economically unrealistic. An agricultural Germany stripped of industry simply would not be economically sustainable and threatened to sow the seeds of poverty and misery that would lead to more conflict. Humanitarian considerations were joined with realistic assumptions, as many opponents of the Morgenthau Plan foresaw a need for a united Germany to counter the Soviet Union in the postwar era.[16]

Even after the Morgenthau Plan was reversed, the Roosevelt administration mandated that the occupation of Germany would not be a soft one. Occupying forces received instructions to identify and detain war criminals for postwar trials. To build a divide between occupier and occupied, the U.S. Army adopted a policy of nonfraternization between GIs and the German population. Ideally, relations between GIs and Germans would be formal and limited to official matters to emphasize to the conquered nation its collective responsibility for the regime's crimes.[17]

In the closing months of the war, the full extent of Nazi war crimes was revealed as American GIs fought their way to the Elbe and Czechoslovakia. Even before liberating concentration camps, GIs encountered thousands of displaced persons, frequently escaped slave workers, wandering the German countryside. Chaplain Ben Rose, a Presbyterian minister serving with an infantry unit, described in a letter home the sight of hundreds of recently liberated foreign workers he encountered. This North Carolina native observed that this mass of humanity added to the chaotic situation within Germany, with many exploited workers showing few inhibitions about taking food, clothing, and other items needed for survival or exacting revenge against their former captors.[18]

An even worse sight would greet American combat units that liberated concentration camps in the closing weeks of the war. Desperate to carry out the final solution until the very end and unwilling to free those held captive, the SS evacuated death and concentration camps in the East and West before they could be liberated. This consolidation of the SS network of camps meant that the few waiting for liberation in the last days of the war were grossly overcrowded and access to food and water deteriorated grievously. Adding to these horrors, the shortage of fuel meant that Nazis could no longer fire up the crematorium. Many of the bodies of the final victims of Nazi tyranny were literally piled up inside and outside of the final camps liberated by the Allies.

Many Jews and Gentiles were shaken to the core at what they witnessed when they liberated camps. Lloyd Klaugin, one of only two Jews in his infantry unit, recalled in an oral history interview the shock his comrades experienced at the liberation of Ohrdruf concentration camp. He described how one big sergeant with whom he had been friendly simply broke down in tears calling out, "How could people be so cruel?"[19] Chaplain Gustave Schellhase, a Lutheran pastor, was so stunned by what he had witnessed at Dachau that he struggled to keep hate from his heart, declaring to his wife in a letter home, "I don't want to hate anyone but God help me to keep from hating these Germans!"[20]

One GI, a Gentile, recalled in a letter to his parents a ghastly site where six hundred slave laborers and political prisoners had been herded into a barn before it was set ablaze. In another instance four hundred slaves were placed in front of a ditch and machine gunned. After firing had stopped, German medics called out for survivors only to have them shot in the head. Americans discovered this atrocity because of the odor of decomposing bodies that had been inadequately buried. After learning the full extent of the crimes committed, the American commander ordered the nearby German community to dig proper graves for the victims of this regime. This GI expressed his outrage at the amnesia of the town residents, who claimed complete ignorance of the crimes committed by the Nazis and insisted they had not been supporters of the toppled regime. After recounting these horrible crimes, the GI expressed the sentiment that the Germans "don't deserve to live."[21]

Sorrow mixed with triumph, leavened with measured revenge, is reflected in the correspondence of one army chaplain writing to the JWB on the stationary of the Augsburg branch of the Nazi Party. He described his satisfaction at seeing SS troops being made to clean out a desecrated synagogue at bayonet point, guarded by Jewish GIs. For this chaplain the underlying root of this unspeakable evil was the godless nature of the Nazis. By rejecting the divine, the Nazis had dropped below the level of wild animals. For the text that marked the reopening of the synagogue, the chaplain read from the 94th Psalm: "Our Lord is a God of vengeance. . . . He bringeth back upon them their own iniquity, and for their evil shall cut them off."[22]

Concentration camp survivors of other religious faiths also needed sustenance. Army chaplain Sixtus "Richard" O'Connor, a Roman Catholic priest serving with the Eleventh Armored Division, described in his official report for May 1945 his efforts at Mauthausen and Gusen. He conducted nearly three thousand burials and administered last rites to two thousand patients.[23]

Rage at the Nazi war crimes led, in some instances, to extrajudicial violence. In the best-documented case, one American lieutenant sanctioned the execution of disarmed German guards during the liberation of Dachau. American troops often stood by while recently liberated inmates assaulted their captors. Chaplain David Eichhorn described how "combat hardened soldiers, Gentile and Jew, black and white, cried tears of hate" after witnessing the horrors of a liberated Dachau. Numbed and angry, Eichhorn described in a report to the JWB how American GIs stood by and did nothing while "guards were beaten to death, beaten so badly that their bodies were ripped open and innards protruded." He recounted the sentiment that "these evil people, it seemed to us, were being treated exactly as they deserved to be treated. To such depths does human nature sink in the presence of human depravity."[24]

Since Nazi leadership had placed the extermination camps in Eastern Europe and the Soviet Union, American and British troops liberated only concentration camps. By V-E Day most Jews held captive by the Nazis had already been killed, and the majority of inmates liberated in the concentration camps were non-Germans. As a result American GIs often had to intervene to protect Jewish victims from other survivors of the concentration camp system. At Dachau efforts to hold an outdoor Jewish service were initially stymied by the threat of violent disruption by Polish inmates. As a result Chaplain David Eichhorn held his first service in a laundry area with a recently liberated Czech rabbi. This situation improved when Signal Corps producer George Stevens was dispatched to the camp to record the liberation on film. Stevens declared this situation was intolerable. He protested to the American commandant of the camp, who provided a military guard to ensure an outdoor service could be held without incident.

What to say to those just liberated and to the liberators? For his sermon Chaplain Eichhorn had an ideal text to explicate. The Torah portion included a passage engraved on the Liberty Bell in Philadelphia: "Proclaim freedom through the world to all the inhabitants thereof; a day of celebration shall this be for you, a day when every man shall return to his family and to his rightful place in society."[25]

A number of GIs expressed deep hatred toward the Germans for the crimes they had committed. One NCO, a Gentile, offered a vivid description of the war crimes committed against political prisoners and Jews, including a vivid description of the scene of a grisly massacre. He wanted to ensure that people knew the culpability of German civilians so that soldiers would not let their guard down.[26] One Jewish GI recounted how he was able to use an army vehicle to drive around Germany on V-E Day. He contrasted the beauty of the countryside with the unimaginable destruction of German cities, but he described how "difficult" it was to look at Germans and "realize the evil in them." He hoped that no American would be "fooled" and that everyone "follows the nonfraternization policy."[27]

In the closing weeks of the war, Burton C. Andrus, an army colonel serving in the European theater, wrote to his Masonic brothers lambasting the hypocrisy of the Germans for "trying to pose as Christians." He noted that many had "religious statues and pictures around their houses" while "still launching robot bombs on the women and children in England." For Andrus the Germans were making war on "Christian religion and all it stands for."[28] Others had different reactions to what they encountered. Earl "Bill" Bailey, upon entering the homes of German civilians in January 1945, wrote home expressing his skepticism about the veracity of American propaganda about the Nazis attacking Christianity. The infantryman confided to his legal guardian, "Maybe it's just this area of Germany but I've a feeling the U.S. was fed a lot of hooey about lack of religion here & revival of Wodin, etc." More disturbing for Bailey was the degree to which German Christians supported the Nazis. He observed, "In about every Jerry house I've been in (&

that's hundreds) there are religious figures, statues, crosses & many papers that show religious backing of the Nazi war."[29]

In his letters to his wife, Chaplain Ben Rose, a Presbyterian minister, painted a complex portrait of the last days of the German Reich. Rose was aware that there were strident Nazis among the defeated. In one community the older residents sought to be "buddy buddy" with the new American conquerors, but a Jewish soldier in the unit who had fled Germany in 1936 informed Rose that this place had been a hotbed of Nazism.[30] But Rose shared the belief, widely held by Roman Catholic and Protestant chaplains and their churches, that there were good Christians to be found among the German people. For Rose, the imprisoned Niemoller represented the archetype of a good German. In early April he described finding a Protestant church in Cologne that had been spared significant destruction. He learned that the pastor of this congregation had been imprisoned in the same concentration camp as Niemoller, which raised his estimation of the church. Later, in April 1945, Rose saw what he deemed as promising signs that Germans would recognize their sins and return to the Christian fold. He told his wife and father of a sermon recently delivered in a German church by a pastor who had fought on the Russian front and had resumed the pulpit because of war injuries. This pastor explained to his German congregation that hatred of Germany existed among nations of the world. He preached that his countrymen must work to dispel this hatred in Europe and elsewhere. Rose remained optimistic about Germany's future since it was more "ready to acknowledge her sin and be reconciled" than France, because that "proud nation" refused to acknowledge "her corruptness."[31]

Nonfraternization also applied to chaplains, who were to maintain only limited contact with their German counterparts and were banned from participation in joint services with German clergy. American GIs could attend German services only if no other options existed and ideally only when civilians were not present. Nonfraternization had several aims, beginning with the need to ensure the security of American forces participating in the occupation, as well as to promote their morale and fighting effectiveness. Army air force chaplains were informed that nonfraternization would "bring to the German people a full realization of their defeat" and ensure compliance with the occupation. While deference should be shown to the German clergy, American chaplains were instructed that there should be no "intimacy or familiarity" in their interactions.[32]

Despite official policy, fraternization did occur between American chaplains and Germans, even before the fighting stopped. Chaplain William G. Mehringer, a Lutheran pastor stationed with his unit in the German city of Honningen in the closing days of the war, wrote with empathy about the plight of German civilians who had to give up their homes to the American occupiers. He described in detail the severe battle damage visited on the Lutheran church and his efforts to aid with its restoration, as well as his attempt to forge a close relationship with the local Lutheran pastor.

In his account Mehringer described at length the plight of German Christians and efforts by Nazi authorities to circumscribe their influence through the end of religious instruction in the schools and the removal of crucifixes from these and other public buildings. Tellingly, Mehringer said nothing about the plight of the Jews from this community or in Germany in general, even though he acknowledged the racist character of the regime. He noted that the son of the town's pastor died in a concentration camp for preaching against Nazi racial doctrines. It was not his defense of the Jews or other persecuted "racial" groups that got him in trouble. His expression of disappointment that German church mission work to Africa had stopped had attracted the attention of authorities, and "from the Nazi point of view [meant] a direct denial of their theory of race superiority."[33]

Violating nonfraternization policies, American GIs who had been Church of Latter-day Saints missionaries to Germany sought out their German brethren. Two former mission secretaries, Majors Donald C. Corbett and John Barnes, used their status as U.S. Army officers to circumvent the restrictions that denied Germans the right to receive packages mailed from abroad. They received relief packages mailed from relatives living in the United States and distributed them using army vehicles. Corbett, a member of Gen. Lucius Clay's staff, charged with overseeing the occupation, used his position to facilitate efforts by German LDS leaders to secure a cache of genealogical records assembled by the Nazis and discovered in a castle in the Thuringia zone. German leaders could not communicate with LDS officials in Utah, but Corbett managed to gain authorization from the American military government to use German church funds to pay transportation costs.[34]

After the fighting many chaplains had reached out to their religious brethren in Germany. In the case of Jewish chaplains, the nonfraternization policy, if strictly adhered to, would have prevented them from aiding German Jews. As one chaplain noted, the policy failed to take into account such nuances as a German Jew who had, during the Nazi era, passed as a Gentile by acquiring Aryan Papers.[35] One GI protested, in a letter to a friend that made its way to the JWB, that Jewish GIs wanted to help German Jewry, but not at the cost of a sixty-five-dollar fine and possibly three months in jail for violating the nonfraternization order. He found the policy unjust, since it prevented "fraternization with people who have suffered twelve years from the Nazis."[36]

The nonfraternization policy failed on another front as other chaplains, during the occupation, had become German apologists. In February 1946 Chaplain William Addison wrote a detailed letter to the Executive Committee of the Federal Council of Churches outlining his indictment of the American occupation of Germany. To begin Addison complained that Roman Catholic dominance of the army chaplaincy meant that German Catholic interests were favored over those Protestant. He outlined in detail the discrimination faced by German Protestants in the American and French zones. Addison also described at length his efforts to help Bishop Wurm free his son, incarcerated for his false replies on a questionnaire (Fragebogen). Addison wanted to leave the army and remain in Germany to aid the revival of his Christian Science brethren, but his request was denied by the theater chaplain.[37]

The quest for sexual partners, not religiosity, motivated the majority of GIs to fraternize with German civilians. American GIs had little difficulty securing the companionship of German women who were desperate to find means to survive in a shattered economy, especially those who lived in bombed-out urban centers. Germany, especially in the early years of the occupation, had been denuded of young men, who had been killed or held in

24. *Three American Jewish GIS celebrate Passover.* Rabbi Eli A. Bohnen Photograph Collection, United States Holocaust Museum.

captivity.[38] Ultimately, the senior army leadership felt compelled to bow to the reality of fraternization and ended the enforced separation between GIS and Germans.

Did fraternization encourage Americans to develop empathy for an enemy that had engaged in unspeakably barbaric acts? Lloyd Kalguin, a Jewish liberator after V-E Day, found himself stationed in Vienna, where he had the opportunity to enroll as a student in the University of Vienna. He also acquired an Austrian girlfriend, who one day asked whether he was actually a Jew. Kalguin had never denied his identity and asked why this young woman doubted he was Jewish. Eventually the young woman showed this GI some of her Nazi-era textbooks from her school days, which offered unflattering stereotypical images of Jews.[39]

Other Jewish GIS were determined to maintain a distance from Germans during the occupation. Lewis Bloom, an infantry officer, strived to maintain only the most formal of relationships with German civilians and, in an oral history interview, he described an incident involving two women whom he encountered while in

Germany. One day, after he left his living quarters, these young women called to him in German and he ignored them. But on the next day, these two women spoke to him in Yiddish, and he went over to learn their story and soon offered his assistance.[40]

Bloom was not the only GI to sublimate his anger toward Germans by aiding Holocaust survivors. Reopening of synagogues, saving cultural treasures from decimated communities, aiding survivors, and supporting the Zionist cause helped channel the anger many Jews felt while stationed in Germany. One Jewish chaplain in the Pacific found himself taking on responsibility for aiding Nazi victims. Stationed in Tokyo, on his own initiative, he opened a religious school for refugee children. Anger was not always easy to sublimate. Chaplain Morris Frank declared to the JWB, when he participated in services marking the reopening of the synagogue at Ansbach, Germany, on June 10, 1945, that it was an event he would always cherish, but "it doesn't counter-balance the scenes & experiences I've had at Dachau and other camps I visited."[41]

Fraternization with the Germans created a disturbing empathy on the part of some GIs stationed in the country. In a survey of GIs deployed there in August 1945, 51 percent thought Hitler had been "wrong" in leading Germany into war but had done a lot of good for his country. And 20 percent agreed there was "some truth" in the argument they needed more land to feed themselves. Perhaps most disturbing, 22 percent thought Germans "had some good reasons 'for being down on the Jews.'"[42]

Japan and the Mission Impulse

American policies diverged sharply depending on the enemy. For example, American propaganda generally made a subtle distinction between misguided Germans and the evil Nazis. In sharp contrast, the Japanese were portrayed as a monolithic people who differed in every respect from Americans. They spoke an alien tongue, worshiped a god-emperor, and fought tenaciously for their overlords. During the war a few American denominations acknowledged that, prior to the attack at Pearl Harbor, Japan had been an important venue for their mission work, but these voices became muted.

The sudden collapse of Japan in August 1945, as a result of the Soviet entry into the war, the dropping of two atomic bombs, and the Allied decision to relent on unconditional surrender, certainly helped speed reconciliation as American forces and a smattering of British Commonwealth troops moved to occupy the defeated nation. There were some remarkable gestures of goodwill prompted by Christian charity. For instance, three Roman Catholic chaplains, soon after the surrender ceremonies aboard the USS *Missouri* ended, gathered food and other relief supplies for the Jesuit community at Sophia University in Tokyo. For one of the naval chaplains, the trip to Sophia was a homecoming. Chaplain Robinson had been taught English at this Japanese institution before returning to the United States to teach Japanese at St. Louis University.[43]

American GIs who started streaming into Japan in the early months of the occupation expressed trepidation at what to expect. One sailor recounted that when he went on shore leave at Yokoyama, he had to stay with a group of sailors led by two officers who carried side arms. But any fear for the personal safety of those granted shore leave quickly dissipated when, to their surprise, they encountered a Japanese church.[44]

In contrast to the division of Germany into four occupied zones administered by the United States, the Soviet Union, Great Britain and France, Japan was under the control of Gen. Douglas MacArthur with only limited influence from the other victorious allies. MacArthur and his American advisors played an influential role in reshaping Japanese society, especially in promulgating a new constitution firmly disestablishing state Shintoism and providing solid guarantees for freedom of religion.[45]

An Episcopalian who seldom attended church services and had few close friends among chaplains, MacArthur wanted Christianity to play a major role in reshaping Japan into a democratic nation. Thousands of missionaries gained entrance into Japan despite strict travel restrictions that excluded most Americans and other foreign civilians from entering the defeated country. To further promote the cause of Christianity, MacArthur lent his name to the fundraising for the International Christian University.[46]

MacArthur welcomed scores of religious leaders from the United States and feted them in order to win their goodwill and support for his project. During his visit to Japan in 1949, Daniel Poling, editor of the *Christian Herald*, was invited by MacArthur to lead

Easter sunrise services for both American troops and Japanese civilians in the plaza in front of his headquarters. By Poling's estimate ten thousand American and Japanese people attended this service, which included a choir of three hundred Japanese youth singing the "Hallelujah Chorus." In his memoir Poling wrote that this service signified the growth of Christianity in occupied Japan, cultivated by Protestant and Roman Catholic missionaries, which promised to serve as a "great positive force in the resistance to the Kremlin's designs on Asia.["]47

Despite official occupation policies that promoted the separation of church and state, MacArthur encouraged his chaplains and military commanders to aid Japanese churches and clerics. For instance, in a report from 1946, Bishop John O'Hara—a prelate visiting Japan—not only praised Catholic chaplains for assisting Japanese priests and religious orders but also singled out an army officer, "Lieutenant de Faucundio of New York, who had surveyed every religious establishment in Sendia, and had done what he could do to meet these needs."48

For many chaplains and GIs, the impulse to aid Japanese Christians and non-Christians in need required little encouragement. In his memoir marine chaplain George Wickersham described in detail his empathy for the Japanese, especially the young, the sick, and the aged. Although his divisional commander was cool toward the idea of chaplains proselytizing to the Japanese, he was granted latitude in forming relations with Japanese Christians. Although his commander decided against Wickersham taking up a collection to aid a local Lutheran-sponsored orphanage, he did arrange for several truckloads, commandeered from the Japanese military, to be sent to this institution.

On one level Wickersham showed great sensitivity to the plight of Japanese Christians, especially their marginal status during the war. To highlight the equality of all believers, Wickersham arranged for Rev. Tamezo Harada, a graduate of Drew University Seminary, to preach on the last Sunday of Advent at his chapel service. Harada's participation in the service not only attracted a large turnout among the marines but also precipitated a favorable news story, penned by the town's mayor, in the local newspaper. It ended with the declaration: "Blessed be the Christian soldiers

25. "Camp Drew Service Club" at work in Japan. Jean Crosby Olsen Collection, Institute on World War II and the Human Experience.

who are to listen to the preacher from the defeated nation!"[49] On Christmas Day, Wickersham arranged for the youth minister and the Japanese choir from the local Lutheran School to participate in a chapel service for his marines. Even though the choir sang the hymns in Japanese, the tunes were well known and were welcomed by marines attending the service. Much to Wickersham's surprise, the Japanese youth minister interrupted the concluding benediction to give a short talk about his conversion to Christianity while studying in the States before the war. The youth minister then called on his choir to perform one last song in English, which they sang to the tune of "Happy Birthday": "Merry Christmas, dear Americans, Merry Christmas to you!" This gesture brought the marines at this Christmas Day service to their feet in applause.[50]

Christians were not the only ones who wanted to promote reconciliation with former enemies in the Pacific. In early 1947 Rabbi Moshe Sachs used the approaching holiday of Tu Bishvat to help reforest the denuded island of Okinawa by planting trees at the local Maebaru High School. The ceremony included music and speeches by Jewish GIs and Okinawan students. The Okinawans and GIs worked together in ten teams of three to plant trees and install signs in English, Hebrew, and Japanese with the Hebrew Bible quote, "Thou Shalt Plant Trees."[51]

The speeches offered by the high school students and superintendent of the school must have struck a responsive chord with the presiding rabbi and army authorities. Tanaka Koei described how, historically, Okinawans had maintained peaceful relations with their neighbors in Asia. Okinawans, according to Koei, had been forced to fight because of Japanese militarists. He expressed his gratitude for the American presence, especially their "sublime minds that can love their enemies" and declared his belief that "Jehovah who created the universe and all things in it must have given those pure hearts to you Americans." Superintendent Hokama described the Jews of the diaspora returning to their fatherland and reconstructing their dislocated country, noting efforts to plant trees in Palestine or the Holy Land. Superintendent Seisho Hokama described the rich stands of trees that had been planted by the rulers of Okinawa over two hundred years ago and the reckless destruction of these ancestral trees by the Japanese armies.[52]

For some GIs the religious impulse, no doubt, contributed to reconciliation with Japan. But MacArthur's vision of a Christian Japan would come to naught despite the influx of missionaries and the distribution of scores of Bibles. A reborn Buddhism, which embraced pacifism and cut its formal ties with the Japanese government, emerged as the dominant religion in postwar Japan. Shintoism, no longer a state religion, still attracted adherents with many Japanese people taking their children to Shinto shrines for blessing by a priest. While the Japanese, in promulgating a new constitution after 1945, formally renounced war, the Cold War ensured that American GIs remained in Japan long past the formal end of occupation.

MacArthur's vision was further complicated by the scores of GIs who sought illicit sex from Japanese women. Even before the formal surrender ceremonies, on September 2, 1945, a defeated Japanese government began to create a system of state-sanctioned brothels and actively recruited Japanese women to staff them. Prostitutes were called upon to patriotically sacrifice their bodies to protect the majority of Japanese women. The occupation authorities gave their blessing to this enterprise with the result that venereal disease rates soared during the occupation.[53]

Sanctioning prostitution earned the occupation authorities the ire of many chaplains. Less than two weeks after the surrender ceremonies on the battleship *Missouri*, Chaplain James Arthur Walther, a Presbyterian minister, wrote a senior Presbyterian official about the grave moral concerns of both Protestant and Roman Catholic naval chaplains. Walther noted that thirty-seven chaplains had gathered for social hour and discussed the issue. Although the gathering was not a formal conference, Walther reported unanimity regarding the official tolerance of prostitution by the armed forces stationed in Tokyo Bay. He described how sanctioned houses of prostitution were segregated, with separate ones for officers and enlisted personnel. Moreover, "Information, directions, and medical details are officially disseminated in a manner which practically amounts to open service sanction and advertisement."[54]

Chaplain George W. Wickersham expressed his dismay when he visited the command chaplain of the Second Division in Nagasaki on an errand. Characterizing himself as an "old China Marine," this chaplain told Wickersham how he enthusiastically embraced distributing condoms. In his memoir, Wickersham recounts how all the other chaplains based in Nagasaki signed a formal protest against sanctioning houses of prostitution. Others disregarded the chain of command and made their protests public. Naval chaplain Lawrence L. Lacour published a letter in the *Des Moines Register* protesting the sanctioning of vice by his superiors in Tokyo.

The battle against sexual immorality was not a new one for chaplains. In protesting officially sanctioned brothels, chaplains were primarily concerned with preserving the moral virtue of GIs and gave only passing attention to the plight of women, who were often forced into prostitution by poverty or, even worse, violence. The American public's view on this issue followed remarkably similar sentiments. In response to Chaplain Lacour's protests, the *Christian Century* reported that the public insisted that young men under twenty-one not be sent to perform occupational duties lest they be morally tainted.[55]

It can be argued that concern over sexual morality represented a misplaced emphasis on the part of the faithful. Should chaplains and religious leaders have placed greater emphasis on protecting the vulnerable from exploitation by American occupation forces? In any case the protests voiced by chaplains challenge the interpretation that all Americans participating in the occupation condoned prostitution as a necessary evil.

Conclusion

Legacies of War

For all of the armed services, one of the most important legacies of the Second World War was further institutionalizing religious pluralism as a dominant ethos. Rabbis had served in uniform after World War I but had not remained in the ranks of the regular army or navy after the Armistice. But after V-J Day, rabbis remained a permanent fixture in both the army and navy.[1] Over time this religious pluralism would extend to the appointment of Buddhist and Muslim chaplains in the army. After the Armistice of 1918, the Commission on Training Camps Activities quickly disbanded, but the USO never dissolved. It went on to serve servicemen and servicewomen who fought in Korea, Vietnam, Iraq, and Afghanistan. The peace that followed the Second World War would not last long, and the Cold War that followed soon turned into a hot war in the Korean Peninsula, in 1950. In the struggle against "atheistic" Communism, Pres. Harry S. Truman and his successor, Dwight Eisenhower, stressed that America's embrace of religion placed the nation on the side of good against the forces of darkness.

In September 1946, a full year after retiring as chief of chaplains, Workman wrote an overdue valedictory letter to the religious leaders who had supported his efforts to secure chaplains for the navy. Workman began this letter by expressing his gratitude for all these churches' support in helping the chaplain corps promote the "spiritual welfare of men and women who served in uniform during the war." During the Second World War, the chaplaincy had grown from only 150 regular enlisted personnel and reservists, in 1939, to over 2800 by V-J Day. Despite these gains in numbers, the secretary of navy failed to act upon Workman's retirement recommendation, made in June 1945, to amend the U.S. Navy and U.S. Marine Corps regulations, making it explicit that commanding officers must promote the religious life of all navy personnel or marines under their authority. Without such a regulation, the status of chaplains and his efforts to promote religious life would be subject to the whim of a commander. Workman also expressed his disappointment that the chaplain corps was still subsumed under the Bureau of Naval Personnel. As a result the chief of chaplains continued to lack the professional autonomy accorded to the other professional branches in the navy, such as physicians and engineers. Thus, a line officer that headed the personnel bureau had ultimate authority on religious and spiritual matters in the navy even though, as a layman, he had no training in theology and did not have to be "a professing religionist" or even "a [C]hristian." In expressing this concern, Workman used the same form letter he had used when writing to the JWB.

More than structural reforms in navy organization were needed, and Workman stressed the need for religious leaders—Catholic, Jewish, Protestant, and independent—to take an active interest in promoting religious life in the navy. Recruitment of chaplains had been difficult during the war, and Workman observed that four hundred Protestant clergymen never came forward to fill this quota. He also recommended that "a systematic study be made of the character of the youth who served in the U.S. Navy." How prepared were America's youth, morally and spiritually, for what they encountered in the war? Such a study would be helpful not only to the navy but also to parents, churches, and educators.[2]

Workman's departure as chief of chaplains could not have come soon enough for one of his subordinates: Chaplain E. W. Scott. In a letter to the head of the Federal Council of Churches, Scott expressed amazement that Workman had remained in this position longer than anyone else and at the honors bestowed upon him, including promotion to rear admiral. Scott expressed dismay "that my fellow clergymen, in the Navy & out of it, should apparently have so little concern over such personal conduct on the part of any minister, especially in one with whom we are directly associated."[3]

In contrast to the navy, the future of the chaplaincy was bright in the army. Chief of chaplains William R. Arnold had risen to the rank of major general, and after his retirement, Pius XII elevated him to an honorific bishopric in recognition of his wartime service.[4] In the postwar era, the role of army chaplains continued to be held in high regard, and their mission expanded to serve not only active-duty personnel but also their families, especially when stationed on overseas bases. Under the character guidance program, chaplains were explicitly tasked with indoctrinating soldiers ideologically and bolstering morale, especially among young draftees.[5]

Religious sectarianism persisted in the postwar era, especially lingering suspicions among Protestant leaders over Roman Catholic power. Although senior army leaders in late 1944 applauded the service of William R. Arnold as chief of chaplains, they expressed misgivings over what they viewed as the disproportionate influence of Roman Catholics within the chaplain corps. Both secretary of war Henry Stimson and army chief of staff George Marshall were determined that the Catholic Arnold be replaced with a Protestant chaplain. Within the broader society, mainline and fundamentalist Protestants doubted the willingness of the Catholic Church to abide by the democratic norms of American society, and they fiercely battled efforts to provide government aid to Catholic schools and the establishment of diplomatic relations with the Vatican.[6]

Other tensions persisted among groups that did not fit neatly into a Protestant–Roman Catholic–Jewish model. Buddhists continued to seek recognition of their faith and eventually pressured the army to allow adherents to their faith to place a *B* on their dog tags. Orthodox Christians and several members of other religious traditions made similar demands, to not only be recognized on their dog tags but also for chaplains to serve their adherents. Fundamentalists continued to protest the dominance by mainline Protestant denominations of the army chaplaincy and the official policies that continued to minimize significant theological differences among branches of Protestantism.

From War to Peace

Franklin D. Roosevelt would not live to see the final victory against Nazi Germany and Imperial Japan. On April 12, 1945, after months of declining health, a gaunt FDR succumbed to a brain hemorrhage while in residence at his Warm Springs, Georgia, retreat. Harry S. Truman of Missouri ascended to the position of commander in chief, tasked with leading the United States through the transition from war to peace. Truman, who had only joined the Roosevelt administration in January 1945, owed his elevation to the vice presidency to FDR bowing to pressure from conservative factions within his party demanding he drop the more liberal Vice Pres. Henry Wallace from the ticket at the 1944 Democratic Convention. In contrast to the patrician Harvard-educated Roosevelt, Truman had never attended college and had failed as a farmer and small businessman before embarking on a political career under the tutelage of the Prendergast political machine of Kansas City. In temperament there were other differences. While the mercurial FDR was often guarded about his opinions and had a strong opportunistic streak, Truman prided himself on being a decisive chief executive with a plain-speaking style. FDR seldom bared his soul, even to his close friends, while Truman often revealed his innermost thoughts in letters to his wife and expressed himself freely to close subordinates.[7]

While FDR had been a low-church Episcopalian, Truman was a proud Baptist. Theologically and liturgically there were important differences between these two religious traditions, but Truman's religious worldview had much in common with FDR's, especially his embrace of pluralism and ecumenicalism. Like his predecessor Truman appointed a significant number of Roman Catholics and Jews to senior positions in his administration. Like FDR Truman maintained good relations with the mainline Protestants and offered regular access to the White House to the Federal Council of Churches and its successor organization, the National Council of Churches. He remained solicitous of the Roman Catholic hierarchy and developed good relations with the Jewish community, especially after he recognized the state of Israel in 1948. Despite criticism from Protestant leaders, Truman continued diplomatic relations with the Vatican through a presidential representative.

Although Truman frequently attended Baptist services while president and remained close to Baptist clerics, most notably Daniel Pruden and Daniel Poling, his relationship with the evangelist Billy Graham was strained. Part of this stemmed from Graham's failure to keep a private conversation off the public record; it also resulted from disagreements on matters of faith. When asked by Graham to summarize his religious faith, Truman declared that he tried "to live by the Sermon on the Mount and the Golden Rule." During that White House meeting, Graham stressed to Truman that more was needed and that in order to gain salvation, one must accept Jesus Christ and his sacrifice on the cross.[8]

Truman was the first combat veteran to assume the presidency since Theodore Roosevelt. Commanding an artillery battery in France during the First World War, Truman had led a religiously diverse unit of Protestants, Roman Catholics, and Jews. One Jewish veteran ended up as Truman's business partner in an ill-fated clothing store and remained a lifelong friend, even lobbying his former comrade successfully on behalf of the Zionist cause when he served in the White House. While fighting in France, Truman came to know and admire his unit's chaplain, Father, later Monsignor, L. Curtis Tiernan, a Roman Catholic priest who, during the Second World War, rose to the rank of command chaplain for the European theater. When Truman attended the Potsdam Conference, he arranged for his friend to join him for several days at the Little White House in Potsdam, Germany. In his memoir Truman wrote of his affection for Monsignor Tiernan and the pleasure he took in recounting their wartime comradeship. Truman demonstrated his embrace of ecumenicalism through the religious services he attended on Sundays while in residence at Potsdam. He not only joined the general service for GIs led by a Protestant chaplain but also attended the Mass offered by his good friend and former comrade Chaplain Tiernan.

Truman, who fatefully ordered the atomic bombing of Hiroshima and Nagasaki, had the privilege of announcing the defeat of Japan on August 14, 1945. Victory against Japan sparked several days of pandemonium in the United States and wherever GIs were stationed. While some Americans, including GIs, marked the end of the war with prayer and attended religious services, most engaged in revelry, often involving drinking and carousing with the opposite sex. In the U.S. many GIs joined civilians in boisterous celebrations, flocking to city centers such as New York's Times Square. In fact, the most enduring image of V-J Day for Americans would be a sailor embracing a young woman in an intimate kiss in Times Square.

As the youngest GIs who served in the Second World War entered retirement age in the 1990s, a warm glow fell over them. Nostalgia mixed with a desire by politicians, journalists, and even some historians to create a useable past led to increasing lionization of the "Greatest Generation"[9] This canonization of those who served in the Second World War differed from the deep anxiety expressed by many Americans, in 1945, about the homecoming of the 16 million men who had fought in the war. Would a generation conditioned to kill and break many other taboos be able to make the transition from warrior to civilian? Even First Lady Eleanor Roosevelt had doubts and expressed publicly the sentiment that those who had been in combat would need significant rehabilitation before being reintegrated into society. Several high-profile murders and other crimes perpetrated by returning GIs fueled this societal unease.[10]

In religious circles there were murmurs of discontent over how the war had changed the young men who had taken part in it. In an article for *Christian Century*, Renwick Kennedy—who served as a chaplain with the army's 102nd Hospital Unit—lambasted the conduct of the GIs in Europe. While praising the GIs' fighting ability and courage on the battlefield, he criticized their attitude and treatment of European civilians, allied and enemy. Kennedy found their sense of superiority grating and condescending, like tenant farmers from the states "scoffing at the rock houses of European peasants" or the army medical officer who complained that "the dirty little bastards are not like American children." Often they were loud and boisterous; at worst they were thieves, rapists, and murderers. Both officers and enlisted men had no inhibitions about propositioning any woman they encountered.[11]

In 1945 Rev. Roy A. Burkhart described, in *The Church and the Returning Soldier*, the strong element of religious indifference that marked the World War II generation. While public opinion polls suggested a strong belief in God and indicated only a small percentage of Americans were atheists, church attendance among the GIs was fairly lackluster. He believed that part of this stemmed from the "pressures of paganism" of army life, which led young people astray. Burkhart also placed responsibility on the churches for this situation. To right matters, his work offers a range of practical theology, including sample liturgies for reaching GIS.[12]

Church-state cooperation during the Second World War was remarkable and instrumental in recruiting several thousand chaplains. Protestant denominations that had flirted strongly with pacifism during the interwar years were among the most ardent supporters of the war effort. Even the historic peace churches cooperated with the war effort by creating a network of public service camps for conscientious objectors. Victory did lead to a divergence of attitudes between military and religious leaders. For army chief of staff George Marshall, the great lesson of the world wars was the need for military preparedness, and thus he called for Universal Military Training (UMT).

Yet despite President Truman's support of UMT, opposition remained so strong that it died in Congress. A chorus of opposition to UMT spanned across the religious spectrum, uniting Roman Catholic clerics, evangelical preachers, mainline ministers, and rabbis. Religious leaders united in seeing UMT as unnecessary and an affront to traditional personal liberties Americans enjoyed in peacetime. They also stressed the deleterious moral impact of military service on young men. Why expose innocents to a military culture that embraced alcohol, tobacco, and promiscuous sex? The generally quiet and subdued misgiving among religious leaders during the Second World War regarding the moral environment of military culture burst forth with renewed vigor in the immediate postwar era. Only when Cold War tensions heightened in the late 1940s and at the outbreak of the Korean War would religious leaders close ranks again behind the military.[13]

What about the chaplaincy? Institutionally, the war had witnessed an unprecedented expansion of the army chaplaincy, and the stature of the army chief of chaplains had risen accordingly. While Congress debated whether the naval chief of chaplains warranted the rank of rear admiral, Chaplain William R. Arnold was awarded a second star before leaving the post, in 1945, to serve with the inspector general before his retirement from the army. Privately, senior leaders of the War Department and U.S. Army harbored lingering suspicions about the Roman Catholic presence in the chaplaincy. In December 1944 army chief of staff George Marshall sent a memorandum to secretary of war Henry Stimson regarding the chaplaincy. Marshall praised Arnold as an excellent administrator of strong character who, despite the "terrific pressures under which he has been forced to operate," had maintained a "united front in the Chaplain Corps." Despite Marshall's high regard for Arnold, the chief of staff saw too much mediocrity in the leadership ranks of the chaplain corps, and this resulted in Arnold having to rely too much on Catholic chaplains, partly because of the inadequacies of their Protestant counterparts. Marshall concluded, from his own observations, that Protestant churches had not given the army their best clergy, and were "too kindhearted in their admission of lame ducks," and the Catholic system had tapped "a much higher average of experience."[14]

Concern over what was perceived as the inordinate power of Catholics within the army chaplaincy would lead Protestant leaders to make sure a priest did not succeed Arnold. One of Henry Stimson's former law partners passed on the sentiments of Episcopal bishop Henry Sherrill regarding the state of the chaplaincy. In a memorandum summarizing Sherrill's views, Stimson's former legal colleague observed that Catholic chaplains held the key posts of chief of chaplains, director of personnel, theater operations chaplain of the European theater, and head of the chaplain school. The memorandum acknowledged that Protestants headed billets in North Africa, Alaska, the South West Pacific, and the Air Chaplaincy. This memorandum reiterated the sentiments expressed by some Protestant leaders and chaplains that Roman Catholic chaplains were insensitive to their needs. Moreover, followers of the Church of Rome often failed to appreciate "the point of view of the Protestant Church, e.g. there are continual complaints about the distribution of literature by Roman Catholic Chaplains which attacks the Protestant Church and faith."[15]

Marshall and Sherrill were not alone in questioning the quality of Protestant chaplains. In September 1945 Gen. Harry Vaughn, President Truman's military aide and crony, gave a talk to the women's auxiliary of the Westminster Presbyterian Church in Alexandria, Virginia. As reported by *Time* magazine in the "Inside Dope" column, Vaughn, a Presbyterian elder, spoke on a wide variety of topics, including the recent Potsdam Conference. Although he walked back derogatory comments he had made about the WAC, he ignited a new firestorm of criticism in Protestant circles for his critique of chaplains from this tradition: "I don't know why a minister can't be a regular guy, but unfortunately some of them are not. You have to give the Roman Church credit. When the War Department requests a bishop to supply 20 priests for chaplains, he looks over his diocese and picks out the 20 best men. But it is different in the Protestant Church. Frequently a Protestant [minister] does not have a church at the moment or is willing to go on a vacation for about three years."[16]

The General Commission of Army and Navy Chaplains publicly denounced his remarks. The *Christian Century* wrote stern editorials criticizing the original remarks and Truman's failure to properly reprimand Vaughn.[17] One naval chaplain on terminal leave sent, through official channels, a detailed memorandum protesting to the commander in chief of the army and navy the unwarranted insult to Protestant chaplains. While Lt. Commander Charles I. Stephenson had no objection to the aspersion that Protestant chaplains were not "regular guys," he bristled at the assertion that they were unemployed clergy seeking a paid vacation. Stephenson protested that Vaughn's comments besmirched the memory of the "327 Army and Navy Chaplains killed, wounded, missing, prisoners of war or chaplains who died in the line of duty, the majority of whom were Protestants." For Stephenson, who had served in naval hospitals as a base chaplain and with U.S. troops stationed in New Zealand, Vaughn had insulted not only him and other surviving chaplains but also the Catholic clergy not called into service by their bishops, the church that had granted him leave to serve in the navy, and his family, who had endured his years away from home.[18]

Not all Protestant chaplains disagreed with Vaughn's critique. Former chaplain Renwick Kennedy, who had been critical of the conduct of GIs, offered an indictment of the effectiveness of the army chaplaincy. In a *Christian Century* article, "How Good Were the Army Chaplains?," which appeared on June 5, 1946, Kennedy offered a stinging critique. He observed that while there were many good chaplains who ministered to the troops, the war had produced no religious revival. There were mediocre chaplains who had served in the war and were lured to remain chaplains in peacetime by the security of a regular paycheck, more freedom of the pulpit than many had with their civilian congregations, and the resources to carry out their job: an assistant and a Jeep. Even more disconcerting than the low caliber of many Protestant chaplains was their desire to cling to narrow sectarian divisions. In this regard he saved his harshest criticism for the Roman Catholic Church and its failure to embrace ecumenicalism. To buttress his case, Kennedy recalled that he had frequently sought to encourage and arrange for Roman Catholics in his hospital unit to attend Mass. Only once had a Roman Catholic colleague reciprocated and sought to bring Protestants to his services.[19]

Some line officers joined the chorus critical of Protestant chaplains. Paul Howe, who had served as battalion commander in the European theater, wrote to a senior Presbyterian church official in April 1946 in response to the debate. He bluntly stated that most Protestant chaplains he encountered in the field were mediocre and expressed a wish that more competent ministers had joined up. A significant number of both Protestant and Catholic chaplains relished being "officers" more than being God's ministers to men who were in need. Howe also criticized the political outlook of ministers who did not volunteer, convinced they were isolationists and that "some hated Roosevelt more than the Nazis!" Moreover, there were some Protestant and Catholic chaplains who "hated Russia and even England more than they did our enemy the Nazi fascists."[20]

Many wartime chaplains wanted to go home. Indeed, after V-J Day, they were eager to separate themselves from military culture. Even though still a bachelor, Chaplain Donald Mackay, who had been overseas for fifteen months, wrote to his family after V-J Day about how he had spurned efforts to become part of the regular navy. He told them the "social life would not interest me, and the general philosophy of life that dominates is foreign to my backgrounds and interests." He could not imagine a career that centered around attending countless cocktail parties and being constantly on guard, fearful of violating naval customs. In one letter while in Manila, Mackay related to his parents how he had managed to violate naval etiquette at a party hosted by his commanding general in honor of a visiting dignitary, Cardinal Spellman. Mackay's grave breach of decorum was turning down an offer of a drink; the proper protocol called for him to accept it and hold it for a time before setting it down.[21]

Not all embraced a vision that saw organized religion as an integral part of civic life. There were dissenting voices, even before the war ended, over efforts of the armed forces to promote a civil religion centered around the "Three Great Faiths." During the election season in 1944, the National Committee for The Non-Church People of America called on presidential candidates to take measures that conferred special recognition on non-church people and to include them in "Brotherhood Week" programs. They also sought a presidential proclamation that would recognize the week of Thanksgiving as "The National Week of the Non-Church People of America." In a more substantive statement, the group called for ending all public support and tax exemptions for religious organizations and schools. It called for an end to using a religious test as the deciding factor on where to send ambassadors, frequently delegating Protestant ambassadors to Protestant countries and Roman Catholics to Catholic countries. The organization denounced Ambassador William Bullitt's efforts to incorporate the Vatican's fierce anti-Communism into American foreign policy. In their indictment they charged Bullitt with calling for "a religious war between Roman Catholicism and Communist Russia."

In a letter to President Roosevelt, the Non-Church People of America, looking to the future, stressed the pernicious link between religion and war. In their view if there should be "a World War III, the soil from which it will grow will be well fertilized with ancient bigotries and fanaticisms miscalled 'religion.'" They also stressed the service and sacrifice of the non-church people who joined their "brothers-in-arms who are the Churchmen of whatever faith." The non-church had stormed the "beaches at Guadalcanal, at Salerno, and in Normandy," and many had made the ultimate sacrifice and lay in heroes' graves.

The Roosevelt administration never replied to this missive and simply filed the group's letter and resolutions in the president's official office file under "Church Matters." Edna Riley had earlier protested the role of religion in the public sphere, clashing with Roman Catholic Cardinal Haynes on the alleged role he had played in suppressing one of the plays she co-wrote with her husband and preventing it from being made into a Hollywood film. While there were indeed atheists in the armed forces and the wider society, they were a distinct minority and a besieged one, especially in the postwar embrace of civil religion.[22]

One Nation Under God . . .

After it all ended, many GIs had regrets about their wartime experiences. In November 1945, when the Samuel Stouffer team of social scientists surveyed soldiers who would soon be veterans, the majority thought the army had hurt them more than it helped. Although a higher number of veterans under twenty-five came away with a more positive outlook, even among this group, 55 percent thought military service had been detrimental. In sharp contrast, 60 percent of soldiers, in this same survey, recorded their agreement with the statement that their army experiences "had increased their faith in God." Only a minority, 18 percent, declared their faith had been weakened. Many who had served in World War II had come away from war with stronger faith.[23]

While many Protestant leaders had misgivings about the religiosity promoted in the armed forces, several rabbis who had served as chaplains in the war came out of the conflict more optimistic. When asked to reflect on his experiences during the war, Rabbi Albert Baum offered a more positive assessment of the influence of religion within the armed forces. In his view the war had been a watershed for the rabbinate, and for "the first time in American life, the Rabbi became an influential personality." Rabbis garnered the trust of GIs because "they rightly believed that the Chaplain would not only use his influence and prestige to uphold the rights and privileges of his men but would seek to better their lot."[24]

Were the GIs as lackluster about religion as their critics claimed? Naval chaplain Selwyn D. Ruslander, a Reform rabbi, in a speech probably given in 1945 in the Chicago area, stressed the strong religiosity of the American GI by beginning his talk with this anecdote:

The Father Superior of a Monastery in a small town in Algeria once commented to Chaplain David Griffith, USNR, a Presbyterian minister, and to me that he was amazed and gratified at the true religious attitudes of the Americans with whom he came into contact. I, too, with an opportunity to contrast our American Jewish youth with those in Europe, was thrilled to discover that our youth's attitudes to organized religion was to a great . . . exten[t] positive— whereas the European youth, and many Palestinian young people, were either in revolt or indifferent to religion.[25]

There were also Protestant chaplains who came out of the war enthusiastic about the prospects for the postwar years. Navy chaplain Hansel H. Tower argued that America must not simply return to prewar ways of doing things if there were to be a flowering of a "religious conscience" across the land. After all "in 1936 less than fifty-six million of the people of this country were even nominally affiliated with the two hundred fifty-six religious bodies." Moreover, several major denominations lost membership in this period even though the country "increased by several million." During the war Hansell and his fellow chaplains from different faiths and denominations enjoyed great success in meeting the religious needs of the U.S. Marines. In his view the legacy of the war should be an application of the naval chaplain's motto, "Cooperation without Compromise." Tower wanted the ecumenical cooperation between Protestant denominations, Roman Catholics, and Jews to continue in victory. He laid out a vision for the postwar era that imagined a community uniting to build a common house of worship that had a sanctuary with a rotating altar so that it could serve Protestants, Catholics, and Jews. No single denomination would own this house of worship, and it would be open to such civic groups as the Boy Scouts.[26]

These sentiments were shared not only by former chaplains, but they can also be found in memoirs and autobiographies of those who served. Reading postwar memoirs and oral histories, one can find countless examples of GIs speaking of their interactions with men and women of other faiths. William Chambers, a member of the Church of Latter-day Saints, wrote with affection of men of different religious faiths and temperaments, including one avowed atheist. Proud of his religious heritage and thankful for the Patriarchal Blessing he had received before the war, Chambers saw no contradiction in recognizing the efforts of others to find the divine.[27]

In *Protestant, Catholic, Jew*, William Herberg makes a compelling case that ethnic cleavages and religious sectarianism had diminished in American society. Most Americans embraced a national ethos that saw Protestantism, Roman Catholicism, and Judaism as part of a distinctive national identity. A good American could embrace any of these strands of the Judeo-Christian tradition. Moreover, Herberg sees a belief in a distinctive American way of life that spanned all three religious traditions. Herberg, who discusses the process of acculturation and is attentive to change over time, documenting the struggle of the Roman Catholic Church against nativist sentiment, says little about the legacy of World War II. In one of the few references to the Second World War in this book, Herberg offers an anecdote to describe how Roman Catholics within the United States have embraced a pluralistic view regarding religion, which stands in contrast with other societies. He draws upon Evelyn Waugh's insights into how American Catholics and those in Europe had very different reactions to the Italian film *Paisan*. Evelyn Waugh recounts how audiences in London and Chicago responded to a scene in the film where three American chaplains arrive at a remote Franciscan monastery. Quoting Waugh: "It transpires that only one is Catholic, the other two being respectively a Protestant and a Jew. The friars are disconcerted and impose a fast on themselves for the conversion of their non-Catholic guests. In London, the audience was mainly non-Catholic, but its sympathy was plainly with the friars. In Chicago, the audience was composed mainly of Italian speakers, presumably Catholics of a sort, and to them the friars seemed purely comic." In commenting on this anecdote, Herberg says, "Like to all Americans, it would have seemed right and proper that there should be *three* chaplains—one Catholic, the other Protestant, and the third Jewish—and to them too the conversion of the non-Catholic clergymen to Catholicism, while no doubt eminently desirable religiously, would have appeared slightly absurd in terms of American reality."[28]

To what degree did the Second World War serve to forge the tri-faith ethos described by Herberg? Did the increased membership in churches and synagogues, along with increased attendance at weekly services, stem from the experiences of World War II? Perhaps the most prominent example of a veteran who embraced this vision is Dwight D. Eisenhower. On the eve of his inauguration as president, General Eisenhower announced that he and his family would become members of the National Presbyterian Church, located a short distance from the White House. His pastor, Rev. Edward L. R. Elson, was an army chaplain who had risen to the rank of colonel before leaving active duty to accept a call to one of the most prestigious pulpits in the Presbyterian Church. When Rev. John Duggan, a former army chaplain serving a Roman Catholic parish in Buffalo, New York, learned the news of Eisenhower's decision, he wrote Elson of his full support. Duggan described his thrill at knowing someone famous but, on a more serious note, he expressed his full confidence in Elson's ability to serve as the spiritual guide for the former SHAEF commander. "If he takes your advise [*sic*], he will not make any mistakes of a spiritual nature, I can assure the world of that."[29] Elson was touched by these sentiments and later annotated the letter by writing "one of my most treasured letters from the R. C. Catholic who succeeded me as 75th Division Chaplain."[30]

The first veteran of the Second World War to win the presidency, Dwight D. Eisenhower would also be the only sitting president to be baptized in office. During his time in office, he developed a close relationship with Elson, marked by frequent meetings and correspondence. Besides advising the president on matters of faith he, on occasion, offered political advice during the 1956 presidential campaign. As the nation's chief executive, Eisenhower regularly proclaimed that religion remained the bedrock of American society as a free people. Like Roosevelt, Ike had little interest in the fine points of theological discourse and embraced a strong ecumenical outlook. In fact, critics derided Ike for declaring that Americans must have faith; it really did not matter which one.[31]

The arrival of the Cold War played an equally important part in sustaining the tri-faith vision of a religious America. For Cold Warriors the overt embrace of religion served to highlight the sharp

26. Army veteran Alan Wold and his bride, Rita Feld, sign the marriage ketubah (contract) under the watchful eye of Rabbi Louis Engelberg, who served as a U.S. Army chaplain in World War II (1949). Alan and Rita Wold Collection, Institute on World War II and the Human Experience.

contrast between the United States as a God-fearing nation and the atheistic character of the Soviet Union and world communism. Many religious leaders added their voices to the crusade against Communism. Billy Graham, who drew a wide following among Christians throughout the United States, staging massive rallies throughout the country, regularly lashed out against the atheistic Soviet regime. But the Christian realist Reinhold Niebuhr also made the case against Soviet totalitarianism.

The army formally expanded the role of the chaplain to ideologically indoctrinate enlisted personnel through the Character Education Program, which deliberately sought to integrate, in the words of the historian Anne Loveland, "moral, religious, and citizenship instruction." It was started as an experimental program for new recruits at Fort Knox, Kentucky, in 1947. Army chaplains offered a series of lectures, as part of the basic training curriculum, on such varied topics as "The Ten Commandments," "Grounds for

Moral Conduct," "Purity in Thought, Word, and Deed," "Marriage as a Sacred Institution," "The Citizen and Morality," and "The Citizen and Honesty." The success of this experiment led the army to extend this program, renamed "Character Guidance," to all basic training units. The reach of the program extended even further, with all units required to schedule a monthly Character Guidance lecture by an army chaplain. In contrast to the "sexual morality lectures" mandated during the Second World War, the Character Guidance lessons emanated from the army chief of chaplains.[32]

The first president to be baptized while still in office would be succeeded, in 1961, by the first Roman Catholic to serve as the nation's chief executive. John F. Kennedy, a navy veteran who commanded a PT boat in the Pacific theater, did not suffer the same fate as Al Smith and managed to overcome sectarian opposition that questioned whether a Roman Catholic could adhere to the constitutional separation of church and state. Kennedy, who emphasized his military service and youthful vigor, sought in the 1960 campaign to portray himself as the voice of a new generation, ready to take the reins of power from the older one.

Can the election of Kennedy to the presidency in 1960 be considered a triumph of the religious pluralism promoted by Franklin D. Roosevelt during World War II? Kennedy's election certainly marked a watershed in the status of Roman Catholics within the American polity. It would be comforting to write a triumphalist narrative of Kennedy that saw the GIs' religious ethos as playing a central role in overcoming narrow-minded bigoted sectarians.[33] But, in fact, some prominent Protestant leaders openly expressed their reservations, most notably Daniel Poling, who was uneasy with Kennedy's potential subservience to the Roman Catholic hierarchy if elected to the presidency. Paradoxically, Kennedy came under fire from Poling for distancing himself from a memorial project—the Chapel of the Four Chaplains—that the latter envisioned as commemorating the spirit of ecumenicalism and religious pluralism present within the army chaplaincy during the Second World War.

The Four Chaplains

Despite a steady stream of press releases highlighting the service and sacrifices of those who served in the army and navy, the chaplaincy had a relatively low profile. In the hundreds of movies made during and after the war by Hollywood, chaplains were usually only minor characters or completely absent. When they did appear their roles were generally consigned, like in *Guadalcanal Diary*, to leading an inspiring service for men on the eve of battle or presiding over a funeral. In *Battleground* a Lutheran chaplain leads a short service for paratroopers at Bastogne and makes it clear that he is there to serve all GIs. He starts his short sermon by recalling that earlier in the month he had led Hannukah services for some of the men present. His sermon is light on theology, emphasizing why men must fight Nazi tyranny and sacrifice in their defense of Bastogne. In *Twelve O'Clock High* the only scene that features a chaplain is when he sneaks aboard a B-17 on the group's first bombing raid to Germany.[34]

The most prominent symbol of the chaplaincy that emerged out of the Second World War was the service and sacrifice of the four chaplains—Rev. George L. Fox, a Methodist minister; Rabbi Alexander Goode of the Reform Movement; Rev. Clark V. Poling, a Reformed Church minister; and Rev. John P. Washington, a Roman Catholic priest—who lost their lives on the evening of February 3, 1943 when their troopship, *Dorchester*, bound for Europe, took a direct hit from a torpedo launched from a German submarine. All four chaplains could probably have escaped the sinking vessel, but instead they all stayed aboard trying to bring order to the pandemonium that broke out as disoriented young soldiers, who had never seen combat, scrambled to find life belts and board lifeboats. Survivors reported that when they looked back at the sinking *Dorchester* they saw the four chaplains reassuring panicked GIs and even offering their life belts to soldiers without them. Over eight hundred GIs died in the sinking of the *Dorchester*. The loss of the four chaplains, while traumatic to their families and close friends, may have gained little notice but for the accounts of survivors that reported seeing them gathered together on the sinking ship, locked arm-in-arm in prayer, as the sea eventually swallowed them.[35] For the JWB, the death of Rabbi Alexander Goode had special significance, as he was the first Jewish chaplain to die in service during World War II. The Rev. Daniel Poling, a Baptist minister, editor of the *Christian Herald*, and leading Protestant leader, ensured that his son, Clark V. Poling, and his fellow chaplains would be remembered as icons of ecumenicalism.

Within a year of his son's death, Poling published a biography of his son, *Your Daddy Did Not Die*, recounting his short life and selfless sacrifice.[36] In December 1944 Lt. Gen. Brehon Somervell presented the Distinguished Service Cross to all four men posthumously in a ceremony attended by the widows of Fox, Goode, and Poling and the sister of John Washington.[37] Warner Brothers started planning to produce a feature film, *Four Men of God*, that would tell the story of these courageous chaplains.[38] Poling would not be alone in honoring the memory of the four chaplains. In a major address to the Protestant Council of the City of New York, John D. Rockefeller Jr, calling for greater ecumenical cooperation, cited their action as a model of sacrifice and as a model for the living.[39] In 1948, at a White House ceremony, Pres. Harry S. Truman unveiled a postage stamp memorializing the sacrifice of Fox, Goode, Poling, and Washington. They were deemed ineligible for the Congressional Medal of Honor, but Congress, in 1960, voted to bestow on the four chaplains a Congressional Gold Medal. In one of his last acts as president, Eisenhower awarded this medal to them posthumously in a White House ceremony.

One of the first memorials commissioned to the four chaplains was a mural in their memory for the chapel of the army's Halloran Hospital on Staten Island. It was dedicated on October 22, 1945, and the program featured the participation of both military chaplains and prominent civilian religious leaders, including Poling, the Rt. Rev. Francis W. Walsh of the military ordinariate, and Rabbi Louis M. Levistsky representing the J W B.[40] On July 22, 1947 New York Veterans Hospital in the Bronx dedicated a living memorial, built with private funds, honoring the four chaplains. New York radio stations broadcast the ceremonies, which included remarks from the city's mayor and the U.S. attorney general and a statement from Pres. Harry S. Truman.[41] In 1950 four memorial trees planted in New York's Riverside Park were dedicated to the memory of the four chaplains. Stained glass windows were eventually dedicated to their memory at the chapel at the U.S. Military Academy, the Pentagon, and the National Cathedral in Washington D C. Scattered across the country were other memorials, including a mural in York, Pennsylvania, a statue in Ann Arbor, Michigan, an abstract sculpture at National Memorial Park in Fairfax, Virginia, and a memorial plaque at Belmont Raceway in New York.

The memorial project that gained the most significant public attention centered around Poling's proposal to build a Four Chaplains Chapel as part of his own church in Philadelphia. Poling served as minister of the Baptist temple that housed his congregation but also served as a center for college life at Temple University, frequently hosting a range of university functions, including commencements, public lectures, and presidential inaugurations. Poling's vision for the memorial called for the creation of an ecumenical chapel in the basement of his church, highlighting three altars built in accordance with the Protestant, Roman Catholic, and Jewish traditions. Like a World War II army chapel, this space could provide a spiritual home to any of the tri-faith religions. These three altars would rotate to symbolically highlight the ecumenical nature of the chapel and to convert the chapel into a suitable space for Protestant, Catholic, and Jewish clergy to conduct services. Poling's connections garnered, in a short time, several significant financial contributions from philanthropic individuals, the Kresge Foundation, and the B'Nai B'rith, which paid for the Jewish altar, allowing this memorial chapel to be completed by 1951.[42]

Although conceived as a memorial to ecumenicalism, the Four Chaplains Chapel proved problematic. The Roman Catholic Diocese of Philadelphia, headed by Cardinal Dennis Dougherty, refused to lend its support because the chapel would be part of a Baptist church. Under canon law the Roman Catholic altar could not be consecrated, and Dougherty prohibited priests from celebrating Mass in the chapel. Cardinal Dougherty pressured Roman Catholic priests and laymen to distance themselves from the chapel project. However, some prominent Roman Catholics continued to support Poling's initiative, most notably First World War veteran William "Wild Bill" Donovan, who had headed the oss in World War II. A young congressman from Massachusetts, John F. Kennedy, decided at the last minute not to speak at a fundraising dinner in 1947 because of Cardinal Doherty's objections. Later, when the chapel was dedicated, Dougherty pressured the army's deputy chief of chaplains, Brigadier Chaplain James O'Neil, to pull out of the dedication ceremonies at the last minute.

Despite the opposition of the Roman Catholic hierarchy to the ceremonies marking the dedication of the chapel, Poling secured a number of prominent political, military, and religious leaders. Pres. Harry S. Truman, Gen. George Marshall, and the chiefs of chaplains of the army, navy, and air force were all in attendance. Bill Donovan, the most prominent Roman Catholic in attendance at the dedication, spoke, at the last minute, in place of Chaplain O'Neil. In his dedication speech, Truman spoke of the selfless sacrifice of the four chaplains, who lived up to the "moral standard that declares: 'Greater love hath no man than this, that man lay down his life for his friends.'" Faith and the "word of God" united these four chaplains and was emblematic of an "old faith in our country."[43]

Absent from the dedication ceremonies were not only Roman Catholic clerics but also the family of Rev. John P. Washington. In fact, the sectarian tension over commemorating the four chaplains was undermined by the Diocese of Newark, New Jersey, holding a solemn high memorial Mass on behalf of Washington, at St. Stephen's Catholic Church in Arlington, New Jersey, two days after the dedication of the chapel in Philadelphia.[44] Eventually, a memorial to Washington and to the four chaplains would be erected by the Roman Catholic Church outside of his hometown church in Kearney, New Jersey.

The successful campaign to build the Four Chaplains Chapel represented one of the most important memorialization efforts in the immediate postwar years. In most communities living memorials, such as parks, highways, hospitals, community centers, and stadiums, became the dominant form of remembrance. While the U.S. Marine Corps eventually dedicated a monument immortalizing the flag raising at Iwo Jima in bronze, few monuments were erected locally or nationally until the 1980s. The monuments to soldiers built after the Civil War and the doughboy statues that followed the Armistice of 1918 were seldom joined by statues to honor GI Joe after V-J Day. Even the burial of an Unknown Soldier from World War II at Arlington National Cemetery was delayed because of the Korean War.[45]

The Four Chaplains Chapel gained additional prominence during the presidential campaign of 1960. Daniel Poling used his editorship of the *Christian Herald* to publicize John F. Kennedy's decision not to attend a fundraising dinner for the chapel in 1947. There existed a disagreement on the reasons behind Kennedy's decision to miss the dinner. For Poling and others concerned about the subservience of a Catholic politician to the church hierarchy, Kennedy's decision not to participate in the fundraising dinner was problematic. Kennedy asserted that Poling had misrepresented his reasons for refusing to take part, arguing that he had been pressed by the sponsors of the dinner to attend not as a veteran of the Second World War and U.S. Congressman but as a representative of the Roman Catholic Church. Kennedy also claimed that the plans for the Four Chaplains Chapel had been misrepresented to him. Making the Four Chaplains Memorial part of a Protestant church breached canon law and remained an unacceptable place for a Roman Catholic to worship. Poling countered that Kennedy had been invited in his capacity as U.S. Representative in Congress and that the program for the dinner did not list the religious affiliation of any of the speakers. Poling kept pressing JFK to disavow his version of events and viewed his actions as reflective of subservience to the Catholic hierarchy.[46]

The sectarian controversies over the Four Chaplains reflected the tension inherent in the Rooseveltian promotion of the free exercise of religion and the embrace of religious pluralism. To promote religious life within the armed forces during the Second World War, the Roosevelt administration devoted significant resources to expanding the chaplaincy, building chapels, and supporting the creation of the faith-based USO. The established religion of the armed forces embraced an ethos that called for ecumenicalism and tolerance that, on many occasions, clashed with sectarian sentiment based on consequential theological differences, especially between Roman Catholics and Protestants.

In the end the four chaplains remain, at best, a flickering light in the American memory of the Second World War. Efforts to make a motion picture floundered soon after V-J Day and *Four Men of God* became a victim of Hollywood's cutback in the number of war films they produced. Relatively few textbooks tell the story of the four chaplains, Hollywood still has not made a film about them, and the Four Chaplains Chapel moved from the Baptist temple to the former chapel of the Philadelphia Navy Yard.

If the memory of the four chaplains has faded, remembrance of the religious and ethnic pluralism that existed in the armed forces during World War II has been more enduring. Hollywood films have transformed it into a cliché, but their image of the ethnically and religiously diverse platoon bears a strong resemblance to reality. If GIs of different faiths and ethnic backgrounds could fight and die together in war, why could they not live together in harmony once they returned home.

NOTES

Introduction

1. Cahn, *For God and Country*. Scholars examining Reagan's military service in World War II have offered no analysis for this film; see Eliot, *Reagan: The Hollywood Years*, 166; Morris, *Dutch*, 209, 210.

2. This study builds on the pioneering study by Moore, *GI Jews*. My study will confirm many of its key arguments with regard to the degree to which the wartime service of Jews fostered their acceptance into American society. Wartime service also fostered increased unity among Jews who served in the armed forces although, in my assessment, Moore minimizes the tension between the predominantly Reform rabbinate that served in the chaplaincy and the rank-and-file Jewish GI who came from Orthodox traditions.

3. Pioneering studies of American civil religion, beginning with Herberg's *Protestant-Catholic-Jew*, give only fleeting attention to military chaplaincy or the religious life of American servicemen/women. More recent scholarship has seen World War II as bolstering the emergence of the tri-faith tradition described by Herberg; see Hutchison, *Religious Pluralism in America* and Schultz, *Tri-Faith America*.

4. The role of religion in shaping FDR's worldview and diplomacy is considered by Preston, *Sword of the Spirit, Shield of Faith*.

5. Alpers, "Democratic Military," 129–63.

6. Marshall, *The Papers of George Marshall* 3: 411, 449–50.

7. Tobin, *Ernie Pyle's War*.

8. Manchester, *Goodbye Darkness*; Sledge, *With the Old Breed*.

9. Fussell, *Wartime*, 138.

10. Ryan, *Samuel Stouffer*.

11. For influential works examining the experiences of the American GI that make only passing reference to religion, see Ambrose, *Band of Brothers*; Cameron, *First Marine Division*; Wells, *Allied Aircrew Experience*; Doubler, *Closing with the Enemy*; Atkinson, *An Army at Dawn*.

12. Stouffer, *The American Soldier* 2: 172–91.

13. The forging of a more inclusive identity among white ethnic groups is explored by Gerstle, *American Crucible*; Bruscino, *Nation Forged in War*.

14. Ngai, *Impossible Subjects*, chap. 1.

15. Baker, *Gospel According to the Klan*.

16. Schultz, *Tri-Faith America*.

17. Coffman, *The Old Army*.

18. Budd, *Serving Two Masters*, 13, chaps. 4–5.

19. Chambers, *Raise an Army*.

20. On the effort to accommodate immigrants and first-generation Americans during the war, see Ford, *Foreign-Born Soldiers*. For a discussion of anti-Semitism in the officer corps of the U.S. Army, see Bendersky, *The "Jewish Threat"*.

21. Goldman, "Chaplains' Experiences," 395–426.

22. Stahl, *Enlisting Faith*, 24–27.

23. Goldman, "Chaplains' Experiences," 395–426.

24. Bristow, *Making Men Moral*; Lukasik, "Doughboys, the YMCA," 774–97; Cooperman, *Making Judaism Safe for America*. For a broad overview of the policy considerations in the founding of the USO, see Knapp, "The United Service Organizations (USO)," 321–38. The existing scholarship on the USO has largely focused on the indispensable role of women in the organization's success in World War II; see Winchell, *USO Hostesses* and Vuic, *The Girls Next Door*.

25. Budd, *Serving Two Masters*, 157.

26. Stahl, *Enlisting Faith*, chaps. 2–4.

27. Sittser, *Cautious Patriotism*.

28. Krehbiel, *General Lewis B. Hershey*.

29. Until recently those seeking to understand the military chaplaincy were dependent on official histories. Among the most important for the Second World War are Clifford Drury's pioneering work on the naval chaplaincy, *The History of the Chaplain Corps, Vol. 1*, and Gushwa, *Army Chaplaincy*. This study compliments the excellent study of the military chaplaincy by Stahl, *Military Chaplaincy*. In contrast to Stahl's study, this work focuses specifically on the Second World War and also seeks to examine the lived religion of the American GI. Snape's *God and Uncle Sam* is the first major study to seek to document religious life in the armed forces in the Second World War. The study draws heavily upon the extensive records of the army chaplaincy held by the U.S. National Archives. To document the lived religion of GIs, Snape draws largely on published memoirs and oral histories. My study draws on a broader range of sources for understanding the experiences of chaplains and the average GI by drawing on archival holdings, including the American Jewish Archives (AJA), Bentley Historical Library at the University of Michigan (UMB), Center for Jewish History (CJH), Mary Baker Eddy Library (MBE), Presbyterian Historical Society (PHS), Princeton Theological Seminary Library (PTS), Rutgers University Special Collections and University Archives (RUL), Schlesinger Library at Harvard University (HUS), University of Notre Dame Library (UNDA), and the United Methodist Archives at Drew University (UMA). It also draws extensively on the oral histories of the World War II generation conducted by the Rutgers Oral History Archives (ROHA).

30. For an overview of the advances in American military medicine during war, see Cowdrey, *Fighting for Life*.

31. On the futile efforts of German captors to propagandize American POWs, see "Copy of Pamphlet Goons Distributed on Feb. 20, '45: Soldiers of the British Commonwealth, Soldiers of the United States of America" in an unpublished scrapbook maintained by Lt. Robert H. Jacks, "Kriegsgefangenenlager nr. 3," Albert P. Clark Collection, USAFA.

32. Rable, *God's Almost Chosen Peoples*.

33. Fussell, *Wartime*, 232–36.

34. Ebel, *Faith in the Fight*.

35. Daddis, *Fighting in the Great Crusade*.

36. My views on understanding the role and practice of religion in American society draw heavily on Butler, *Awash in a Sea of Faith* and Orsi, *Madonna of 115th Street*.

1. Mobilizing a Faithful Nation

1. For a comprehensive account of the noninterventionist movement prior to Pearl Harbor, see Doenecke, *American Intervention, 1939–1941*. For a concise overview of the peace movement, see DeBenedetti, *The Peace Reform*.

2. On support of Roman Catholic and Protestant churches for nonintervention during the interwar years, see Preston, *Religion in American War and Diplomacy*, chap. 16. On the ambivalence of the Protestant churches toward the war effort, see Sittser, *Cautious Patriotism*. Charles R. Gallagher's biography of Bishop Joseph B. Hurley underscores the significant opposition within the church hierarchy to intervention; see Gallagher, *Hurley and Pope Pius XII*.

3. For a critical assessment of FDR's foreign policy, see Offner, *American Appeasement* and Marks, *Diplomacy of Franklin Roosevelt*. A revisionist movement after World War II maintained that FDR engineered a confrontation with Japan to provoke this country into attacking the United States, permitting America's entrance into the fight against Germany; see Beard, *American Foreign Policy* and Tansill, *Back Door to War*. For an assessment of revisionist historiography, see Darnton, "Archives and Inference," 84–126.

4. Bolt, "Franklin Delano Roosevelt, Senior Warden," 91–99.

5. Smith, *Faith and the Presidency*, 191–220. My assessment of Roosevelt also draws upon the classic biography by Burns, *Roosevelt: The Lion and the Fox*, Burns, *Roosevelt: The Soldier of Freedom*, and the more recent Brands, "*Traitor to His Class*." For a primary source assessing FDR's temperament, especially useful is Perkins, *Roosevelt I Knew*.

6. Stephen Early to Miss [LeHand], September 19, 1934, includes a newspaper clipping from an unidentified newspaper, "President Attacked as Non-Church Goer," file OF 310: Sabbath Observance, Official file, RNY.

7. Sutton, "Was FDR the Antichrist?" 1052–74. For a pioneering study on religion and the right in this era, see Ribuffo, *The Old Christian Right*.

8. On Coughlin, see Brinkley, *Voices of Protest*. For a recent study which argues Coughlin received significant support from Protestant and Catholic elites, see Wells, "Better Dead Than Red."

9. Franklin D. Roosevelt to Dr. Robert A. Ashworth, National Council of Jews and Christians, April 18, 1934, Copy, PPF-1426, National Conference of Christians and Jews, 1933–39, President's Personal file, RNY.

10. Franklin D. Roosevelt, "Radio Address on Brotherhood Day," February 13, 1936, UCSB. Also see Everett R. Clinchy to President Franklin D. Roosevelt, February 13, 1936, PPF-1426, National Conference of Christians and Jews, 1933–39, President's Personal file, RNY.

11. Blum, *From the Morgenthau Diaries*, 3 vols. Also valuable is Morgenthau, *Mostly Morgenthaus*.

12. Hand, *Samuel I. Rosenman* and Rowley, *Franklin and Eleanor*, 149–50, 157.

13. Many of these anti-Semitic missives came from cranks with little influence or power. But not all who expressed anti-Semitic sentiments can be dismissed as marginal men and women. The cartoonist Chuck Thorndike, whose books are still in print, wrote on December 5, 1938: "Dear Franklin Roosevelt: For the last ten years I have worked for you . . . If you doubt it refer to your files . . . I am enclosing one of my latest books . . . any, I am sure, will not take offense . . . However we old line gentile American families will NOT tolerate the JEWS . . . You may make sure of that . . . We would first rather give up our lives . . . The Jews of America today owe me over $56000 and I can prove it . . . I am a college graduate a former U.S. Marine . . . Today I owe nobody a dime . . . Jews are proselytes and blood suckers, this has been proven since the days of the Mesopotamians no [Je]w, anywhere is any bargain . . . they own too much already through subterfuge! and I can prove it! if you don't believe it . . . call my turn!" Chuck Thorndike to Franklin Roosevelt, December 5, 1938, file OF76c: Jewish, 1938, official file, RNY.

14. Franklin D. Roosevelt, "Address at Chicago," October 5, 1937, UCSB.

15. On American immigration policy and the refugee crisis, see Wyman, *Abandonment of the Jews* and Breitman and Kraut, *American Refugee Policy*. For a revisionist account claiming a greater willingness by Western democracies to aid Jewish refugees, see Rubinstein, *The Myth of Rescue*. On the efforts of one key Roosevelt official to aid refugees, see Zuker, "Frances Perkins and German Jewish Refugees," 35–59.

16. For instance, the *Christian Century* criticized the head of the Federal Council for lending his support for the Bundles for Britain campaign; see "Editorial: The Federal Council and the Propagandists," *Christian Century* 57, no. 41 (October 9, 1940): 1235–36.

17. Editorial, "Why Did Mr. Roosevelt Demand Conscription?" *Christian Century* 57, no. 39 (September 25, 1940): 1165; Editorial: "No Third Term!" *Christian Century* 57, no. 42 (October 16, 1940): 1270–73.

18. Editorial: "The Attack on Lindbergh," *Christian Century* 57, no. 34 (August 21, 1940): 1022–23.

19. Preston, *Religion in American War and Diplomacy*, chap. 16.

20. Nasaw, *Joseph P. Kennedy*.

21. Ventresca, *Pius XII*.

22. Franklin D. Roosevelt, Annual Message to Congress, January 4, 1939, UCSB.

23. Divine, *Roosevelt and World War II*; Burns, *Roosevelt: The Soldier of Freedom*; Heinrichs, *Threshold of War*.

24. FDR and Four Freedoms Speech, Franklin D. Roosevelt Library, Hyde Park, New York, https://www.fdrlibrary.org/four-freedoms.

25. Wilson, *The First Summit*, 99.

26. Franklin D. Roosevelt, Press Conference on the USS *Potomac*, August 16, 1941, UCSB.

27. Franklin D. Roosevelt, Address for Navy and Total Defense Day, October 27, 1941, USCB.

28. F. L. LaGuardia, U.S. Director of Civilian Defense, Circular Letter, November 3, 1941, box 2, RG10, PHS.

29. "'Canned Sermon': of Mayor Scorned," *New York Times*, November 9, 1941, 1.

30. Franklin D. Roosevelt, Radio Address for the Drawing Under Selective Service Act of 1940, October 29, 1940, USCB.

31. Cole, *Roosevelt and the Isolationists, 1932–1945*; Doenecke, *The Challenge to American Intervention, 1939–1941*.

32. Sirgiovanni, *An Undercurrent of Suspicion*, chap. 7; older works are still useful: MacCarthy, "War and Peace, 1914–1946," and Magden, "American Religious Press."

33. Flynn, *The Draft*.

34. Chambers, *To Raise an Army*.

35. Krehbiel, *General Lewis B. Hershey*.

36. Bennett, "American Pacifism," 259–92.

37. On the heroic service of conscientious objectors on the home front, see Matthews, *Smoke Jumping on the Western Fire Line* and Tucker, *The Great Starvation Experiment*.

38. Both scholars of the peace movement and military historians have neglected the story of conscientious objectors who served within the armed forces. For two biographies examining the noncombatant military services of conscientious objectors, see Coffin, *Lew Ayres* and Doss, *Desmond Doss*.

39. On the role of frontline medical personnel and the experience of combat, see Linderman, *World Within War*.

40. Roy Bullard Chamberlin to Roger Warren Barney, March 20, 1941, file C, box 1, Roger Warren Barney Papers, UMB.

41. "Statement Concerning Non-Registration" Section of "An Affidavit to Conscientious Objection to the Selective Service Act of 1940" [November?] 1940, C.O. Papers, 1940, file 1, bMS 551/1 (19), Schomer Papers, HUD.

42. Peters, *Judging Jehovah's Witnesses*, 272.

43. Murray, "Blacks and the Draft," 57–76,

44. Peters, *Judging Jehovah's Witnesses*, 272.

45. Fisher, "Law of Conscientious Objection," 447–74.

46. "The Army and Navy Chaplaincy, Unofficial Progress Report on the Current Study Presented by F. Ernest Johnson at the Biennial Meeting of the Federal Council," Dayton, Ohio, December 4, 1934, file 24, box 4, RG18, PHS.

47. E. Clarendon Hyde to Roger Warren Barney, May 30, 1941, file H, box 1, Roger Warren Barney Papers, UMB.

48. Edward W. Blakeman, "Peace War Discussion by Students in Religious Education, Radio Forum (W.J.R.)," Transcript, file Radio Scripts, 1939–45, box 1, Blakeman Papers, UMB.

49. "Plymouth to Hear Rabbi: His Thanksgiving Sermon Will Break a Precedent of 317 Years," *New York Times*, November 16, 1938, 14.

50. George F. Rixey, Chaplain, U.S. Army, Executive, to Rev. Paul Moody, General Committee on Army and Navy Chaplains, December 2, 1940, file 080: General Committee, February 14, 1923–December 31, 1941, box 69, RG247, NACP.

51. Hiro Higuchi to Hisako Higuchi, January 7, 1943 [4], Higuchi Papers, UHM.

52. Sittser, *A Cautious Patriotism*. Despite the cautious patriotism of many Protestants, a significant number of Quakers decided to bear arms in World War II; see Hamm et. al, "The Decline of Quaker Pacifism," 45–71.

53. Stouffer et al., *American Soldier* 1: 462.

54. "Prelude to War, Report on Experimental Study of the First Film in the 'Why We Fight' Series, Based on Studies Conducted at Three Replacement Training Centers in November, 1942." Special Service Division Research Branch Report No. B-46, Army Service Forces, War Department, Washington DC, Fol. "Prelude to War," Orientation Film #1 (Experimental Film Study), box 1, Reports and Analysis of Attitude Research Surveys, Index, Misc. Studies, Entry A1 92, RG330, NACP.

2. Mobilizing and Building

1. Budd, *Serving Two Masters*.

2. Stahl, *Enlisting Faith*, chaps. 2–3.

3. Builder, *The Masks of War*.

4. Bergsma, *The Pioneers*.

5. William R. Arnold, Chief of Chaplains, to Chaplain Marion B. Harris, July 10, 1941, folder 27, box 1, William R. Arnold Papers, GML.

6. William R. Arnold to Reginald W. Hover, September 11, 1942, file 32, box 2, Papers of William R. Arnold, GML.

7. William R. Arnold to Abe Murdock, June 13, 1941, Copy, file 032: Letters to Congress and Related Matters, box 44, Office Management Division, Decimal file, 1920–45, RG247, NACP.

8. William R. Arnold to Miss Delia Ridge, December 29, 1944, folder 4, box 5, Arnold Papers, GML.

9. William R. Arnold to Donald R. Sanger, March 13, 1940, folder 14, box 1; J. J. Ganey to William R. Arnold, October 26, 1940, folder 18, box 1, GML.

10. For a sense of his ecumenical sensitivity, see William R. Arnold to Mr. Irwin Greenberg, Chairman, Religious Committee, United Service Organizations, Inc., March 23, 1945, folder 13, box 5, Arnold Papers, GML. In this letter, Arnold declines an invitation to attend a community seder for GIs at the Mayflower Hotel, noting that the date falls on Holy Week. But he also adds, "You and the members of the local Jewish community are kind indeed to remember me. Would that all the men

in the world would devote themselves zealously to their religious duties at frequent intervals. If all men would pray more there would be less need of the punishment of war to keep us humble and chaste of heart."

11. "Admiral Robert Workman, 92, Ex-Chief of Navy Chaplains," *New York Times*, June 22, 1977, 28.

12. Joshua Lewis Goldberg, Interview with Commander H. Lawrence Martin, 1980, Washington DC: Chaplain Corps History Branch, Office of the Chief of Chaplains, Department of the Navy, 17–21, UNCW.

13. For the navy's inability to secure funding for chapels, see Drury, *The History of the Chaplains Corps, United States Navy* 2: 4–9.

14. William R. Arnold to James Dalton, February 13, 1941, folder 21, box 1, Arnold Papers, GML.

15. William R. Arnold, Chief of Chaplains, to Representative J. Buell Snyder, November 21, 1941, file 032, Letters to Congress and Related Matters, box 44, Office Management Division, Decimal file, 1920–45, RG247, NACP.

16. "Army to Open Arlington Chapel," *New York Times*, July 21, 1941, 4.

17. Robert D. Workman, Captain, Chaplain Corps, USN, Head of Chaplains' Division, to Rear Admiral John Downes, Commandant, Ninth Naval District, April 5, 1941, file Detail (1 of 2), Navy, Coast Guard, etc., 1917–41, box 3, RG24, General Correspondence, Records of the Chaplains Division, 1804–1946, NADC.

18. Robert D. Workman to Rear Admiral John Downes, April 5, 1941, file Detail, Navy, Coast Guard, etc., 1917–41, General Correspondence, box 3, Records of the Chaplains Division, 1804–1946, RG24, NADC.

19. John F. O'Hara to The Honorable David I. Walsh, Chairman, Committee on Naval Affairs, February 5, 1943, Copy, M folder: Chaplain Division, 1936–45, box 33, Official file, RNY.

20. FDR, Memorandum for the Secretary of the Navy, February 16, 1943, copy, file Department of the Navy: Chaplain's Division, box 33, official files, RNY.

21. Frank Knox to the President [Franklin D. Roosevelt], February 17, 1943, file Department of the Navy, Chaplain's Division, box 33, official files, RNY.

22. Frank Knox to the President [Franklin D. Roosevelt], February 25, 1943, file Department of the Navy, Chaplain's Division, box 33, official files, RNY.

23. Randall Jacobs, Memorandum for the Secretary [Frank Knox], February 20, 1943, with Two-Page Appendix by Robert Workman, file Department of the Navy, Chaplain's Division, box 33, official files, RNY.

24. "Memorandum, Helpful Hints, and Other Information," War Department Service of Supply, Office of the Chief of Chaplains, Mary 1942, 21 in file Military Service, Office Corps Chaplain (1), 1928–45, box 2, Warner Papers, UMB.

25. Abbot Peterson Jr., Chaplain, to Rev. Everett Moore, American Unitarian Association, July 5, 1942, file AUA, War Services Correspondence, file D, American Unitarian Association, War Services Council Administrative Subject files, bMS 11130-1, HUD.

26. Minutes of the Minister and Chaplains, Friday, June 5, 1942, 10:30 a.m., Park Hotel, Los Angeles, file 080: Congregational and Christian Churches, January 1921–May 18, 1943, box 64, Central Decimal file, 1920–45, RG247, NACP.

27. Rev. Giles N. Knight, DD, LLD, Vice President, Secretary, International Church of the Foursquare Gospel, to War Department, Services of Supply, Office of the Chief of Chaplains, Washington DC, Attention: Chief-of-Chaplains Arnold, November 12, 1942, file 80: International Foursquare Gospel Evangelism, August 1942–October 1945, box 71, Central Decimal file, 1920–45, RG247, NACP.

28. Carroll C. Roberts, Committee on Chaplaincy Endorsement of the International Convention of Disciples of Christ, to Lt. Col. Walter B. Zimmerman, March 4, 1942, file 080: Disciples of Christ, Nov. 1930–July 10, 1943, box 64, Central Decimal file, 1920–45. For another case of a woman automatically denied an appointment, see William R. Arnold, Chief of Chaplains, to Honorable Carroll Reece, House of Representatives, August 8, 1942, file 032: Letters to Congress and Related Matters, Vol, 1, July 15, 1921–August 31, 1942, box 44, Central Decimal file, 1920–45, RG247, NACP.

29. William R. Arnold to Captain Ralph E. Riordan, August 15, 1940, folder 16, box 1, William R. Arnold Papers, GML.

30. William R. Arnold, Chief of Chaplains, to Rev. J. J. Ganey, October 30, 1940, folder 18, box 1, William R. Arnold, GML.

31. Frederick C. Fromhagen, Chaplain, Res-USA Assistant, to Herbert W. Beck, December 11, 1940, folder 14666, box 1621, MBE.

32. William R. Arnold to Arthur W. Eckman, November 22, 1943, file 14666, box 1621, MBE.

33. Miriam D. Gaarbrick, C.S., to Arthur W. Exkman, Committee on Publication, First Church of Christ, Scientist, August 27, 1942, folder 16142/322355, MBE.

34. Emily Ziegler to Miss Myrthena Taylor, March 15, 1943, file 16142/322355, MBE.

35. Frank F. Bunker to Arthur W. Eckman, February 23, 1943, folder 14666/1581, MBE.

36. R. D. Workman, Chief of Chaplains, USN, "Information Concerning Pre-Theological and Theological Training Under the Navy College Training Program, V-12" n.d., file 1-32, box 1, RG10, PHS.

37. Joseph Martin Dawson, "Baptists Hit Navy Chaplain Training: Southern Denomination Heads Protest V-12 Plan—Claim Largest Number of Free Church Members," *Christian Century* 60, no. 23 (June 9, 1943): 701 and Editorial: "Navy's V-12 Program Will Debase College Education," *Christian Century* 60, no. 24 (June 16, 1943): 709.

38. Carl McIntire to Ernest Fisk, September 12, 1944, folder: World War II Letters from Church Members in Military and Responses, box 27, Carl McIntire Papers, PTS.

39. Samuel McCrea Cavert, General Secretary, to Chaplain Edwin R. Carter, Chief of Chaplains Office, January 19, 1945, file 1, box 5, RG18, PHS.

40. Reinhold Niebuhr to Samuel McCreat Cavert, February 13, 1945, file 1, box 5, RG18, PHS.

41. Wm. D. Cameron to Rev. Samuel Cavert, Secretary, January 24, 1945, file 1, box 5, RG18, PHS.

42. Frank F. Bunker to the Christian Science Board of Directors, March 18, 1943, folder/box: 14666/1522, MBE.

43. Wm R. Arnold, Chief of Chaplains, to the Most Reverend Philip G. Scher, December 11, 1941, Copy, file 000.3: Catholic Denominations, June 1939–July 42, box 3, Central Decimal file, 1920–45, RG247, Chief of Chaplains, NACP.

44. Rev. Francis E. Wallace to Very Rev. Msgr. Wm. Arnold, April [1942], file 000.3: Catholic Denominations, July 1942–April 1943, box 3, Decimal file, 1920–45, RG 247, NACP.

45. Wm. R. Arnold, Chief of Chaplains, to Reverend Francis E. Wallace, April 22, 1943, file 000.3: Catholic Denominations, July 1942–April 1943, box 3, Central Decimal file, 1920–45, RG 247, NACP.

46. Rt. Reverend F. J. Pokluda, Administrator of the Diocese, to War Department, Chief of Chaplains, July 22, 1941, Copy, file 000.3: Catholic Denominations, June 1939–July 1942, box 3, Central Decimal file, 1920–45, Office Management Division, RG 247, NACP.

47. Wm. R. Arnold, Chief of Chaplains, to Rev. John R. Schmidt, July 28, 1941, file 000.3: Catholic Denominations, June 1939–July 1942, Copy, box 3, Central Decimal file, 1920–45, RG 247, NACP.

48. S. Arthur Devan, Director, to Chaplain Kurt W. Schalk, March 24, 1942, file General Commission on Army and Navy Chaplains, November 1941–August 6, 1942, box 63, Central Decimal file, RG 247, NACP.

49. Roger W. Barney to Father, February 22, 1943, file Navy, World War II Souvenir, box 3, Barney Papers, UMB.

50. Rev. Frederick Barnhill to Roger Warren Barney, May 6, 1941, file B, box 1, Barney Papers, UMB.

51. Paul Howe to Stewart M. Robinson, April 18, 1946, file 45, box 1, RG 10, PHS.

52. William R. Arnold to Chaplain Howard McKnight Wilson, October 3, 1942, box 4, RG 774, PHS.

53. Yost, *Combat Chaplain*, 35.

54. Yost, *Combat Chaplain*, 34.

55. Herbert Gross, Interview with G. Kurt Piehler and Travis Richards, October 26, 1993, ROHA.

56. Satterfield, *Saving Big Ben: The USS Franklin*.

57. Yost, *Combat Chaplain*, 35.

58. W. Marlborough Addison to Arthur W. Eckman, Manager of Committees on Publication, February 27, 1944, folder/box: 16142/322353, MBE.

59. "Dear Folks," July 31, August 7, 1943, folder 14, box 8, Saperstein Papers, AJA.

60. Howard M. Wilson, The Second Section of Notes on Practical Duties, [1942], box 1, RG 774, PHS.

61. R.W. Barney, Chaplain USNR, file Navy Notebooks, Temporary Duty Log, August 1943. For the case of the cheating sailor, see the entry for Joseph Dinghan, August 7, box 4, Roger Barney Papers, UMB.

62. Kertzer, *With an H*, 10–12.

3. Turning Civilians into GIS

1. Joseph W. Katz, Interview with G. Kurt Piehler and Darren Purtlebaugh, February 17, 1995, ROHA.

2. Kennett, *The American Soldier*, 42–109; Kindsvatter, *Ground Combat*, 17–29.

3. Braddock, *Dog Tags*.

4. S. Arthur Devan to Reverend E. Edward Dowdy, October 22, 1943, file 25, box 4, RG18, PHS.

5. J.E. Tilford to Richard C. Boys, May 16, 1943, file World War II Correspondence, January–June 1943, box 1, Boys Papers, UMB.

6. Richard G. Shea, "Monthly Report of the Chaplain," September 1943, file Monthly Report of Chaplains, file 1943–54, box 1, Papers of Richard G. Shea, BC.

7. Joshua Louis Goldberg, Interview with H. Lawrence Martin, Transcript, 9–11, Washington DC: Chaplain Corps History Branch, Office of Chief of Chaplains, Department of Navy, 1980, UNCG.

8. Responsa, Prepared by the Committee on Army and Navy Religious Activities of the Jewish Welfare Board, August 18, 1942, folder 1, box 1, I-249, CJH.

9. Albert G. Baum to Rabbi Jacob K. Shankman, December 4, 1947, folder: General Correspondence, box 1, Albert Baum Papers, AJA.

10. Edward H. Bohn Jr. to Carl McIntire, October 10, 1944, folder: Armed Forces Letters from Men in Armed Services #2, box 27, Carl McIntire Papers, PTS.

11. John R. Bradstreet to Consuelo Bradstreet, April 25, 1943, file MSS 020 0002 0003, box 1, Bradstreet Papers, SLL.

12. John R. Bradstreet to Consuelo Bradstreet, May 1, 1943, file MSS 020 0002 0003, box 1, Bradstreet Papers, SLL.

13. George J. Flanigen to Most Rev. William T. McCarty, July 29, 1943, Military Delegate, file Southwest Pacific, box 11, O'Hara Papers, UNDA.

14. W. Roy Bradley, Chaplain (Col.), U.S. Army, IX Corps Chaplain, to Chaplain Edward L. Elson, September 25, 1942, folder 12, box 1, RG253, PHS.

15. Arthur W. Eckman, Manager of Committee on Publication, Re: Chaplain Willard Walter Janes, Camp Edwards, Massachusetts, June 4, 1942, Memorandum, f 322304/16142, MBE.

16. Sam Zipkin to Rabbi Phineas Smoller, June 24, 1942, file 5, box 1, Smoller Papers, AJA.

17. Ernest L. Loomis (?), Chaplain (Lt. Col.), U.S.A., to "Dear Friends," April 30, 1945, file bMS /1 (20), General Correspondence, April 1945, bMS 392 (20), UCA-Chaplain Records, HUD.

18. Lee U. Klierall (?), Office of the Chaplain, 56th Air Depot Group, Tinker Field, to "Dear Friends," May 1944, file 1-34, box 1, RG10, PHS.

19. Aquila, *Home Front Soldier*, 61–69.

20. Bob (?) to Roger Barney Warren, May 14, 1964, folder B, box 1, Barney Papers, UMB.

21. Carl B. Montgomery to John Pedicord, January 9, 1942, file Letters to and from John Pedicord, 1935–78, box 4, Montgomery Papers, USAHEC.

22. Stouffer, *American Soldier* 1: 140.

23. Robert Fishkin, Interview with G. Kurt Piehler and Tara Kraenzlin, November 8, 1995, ROHA.

24. Rabbi Albert G. Baum, Kasruth, n.d. [late 1940s?], folder 6, box 1, Baum Papers, AJA.

25. DeSalvo, *Chasing Ghosts*, 173.

26. Joseph Hunter, President, Bloomfield College, to William Barrow Pugh, June 3, 1944, file 1-34, box 10, RG10, PHS.

27. Leonard (?), Fort McClellan, Alabama to Dr. Robert Cummins, October 7, 1942, file bMS /392/1 (5), General Correspondence, October 1942, bMS 392, UCA–Chaplains, HUD.

28. Military Ordinariate, Circular Letter No. 37, June 1, 1944, Circular Letters to Chaplains, box 9, O'Hara Papers, UNDA.

29. Chaplain E. T. "Earnest" Marble, USNR, 87th Naval Construction Battalion, August 13, 1943, file bMS /392/1 (15), General Correspondence, August 1943, bMS 392 UCA—Chaplains, HUD.

30. Eichhorn, *The GI's Rabbi*, 50–51.

31. Andrew MacCormick, Minister, First Presbyterian Church, to Chaplain Elson, Headquarters Ninth Service Command, Fort Douglas, Utah, December 16, 1942, folder 12, box 1, RG253, PHS.

32. Edward L. R. Elson, Chaplain, to Reverend Andrew W. McCormick, First Presbyterian Church, December 21, 1942, folder 12, box 1, RG253, PHS.

33. William E. Chapple, Depot Chaplain, to Commanding Officer, 12th Replacement Depot, August 19, 1945, file 250.1: Morals and Conduct (Miscellaneous), box 195, Central Decimal file, 1920–45, RG247, NACP.

34. Clifford Ingle, Chaplain, Major, Post Chaplain, to Dr. T. W. Medearis, Missouri Baptist General Association, April 19, 1946, file 2.36: Chaplain Clifford Ingle, box 2, Medearis Papers, SBH.

35. For an example of a sexual morality lecture, see Michael C. Elliott to Chaplain Alva J. Brasted, August 2, 1943, with Attachment, "Sex Morality Lecture," Decimal file 726, box 336, Decimal file, Office Management Central files, RG247, NACP.

36. Herman Berenson, Interview with Shaun Illingworth and Rodolfo Medini, October 31, 2005, ROHA.

37. Frederick Osborn, "Personal Narrative and Autobiography, Part II," Osborn Papers, USAHEC.

38. Principles and Policies for the Conduct of Religious Activities in U.S.O. Local Operations, Exhibit C, Minutes, Conference of Executives, Hotel Roosevelt, October 13, 1942, folder 2, box 24, Weil Papers, AJA.

39. Chester I. Barnard, President, to Members of the General Policy Committee, November 10, 1942, folder 1, box 21, Weil Papers, AJA.

40. Chester Barnard to Arthur W. Page, Chairman, Joint Army and Navy Committee, November 12, 1942, Copy, folder 1, box 21, Weil Papers, AJA.

41. Chester I. Barnard, President, to Members of the General Policy Committee (USO), Confidential Memo, Subject: Special Services of Particular Agencies, August 20, 1942, folder NCCS: Board of Trustees Correspondence (1942), box 7, NCWC/USCC: NCCS Collection, CUA.

42. John D. Rockefeller Jr. to Walter Hoving, August 7, 1942, Copy, folder 571, box 51, P-Welfare Interests-General, III OMR, Rockefeller Family Collection, RAC.

43. R B. Fosdick, Memorandum on the U.S.O, April 23, 1942, folder 571, box 51, P—Welfare Interest-Groups, Record Group III OMR, RAC.

44. Howard M. Wilson, Chaplain, BCT #8, to Chaplain Wm. R. Arnold, Office of Chief of Chaplains, February 18, 1943, box 4, RG774, PHS.

45. Herbert A. Johnston, Manager, Camp Welfare Activities, to All Chaplains, June 7, 1944, folder 14666/1561, MBE.

46. Harvey Swanson, Post Chaplain, Camp Elliott, to Robert Cummins, August 14, 1943, Superintendent, Universalist Church, file BMS /392/1 (15), General Correspondence, August 1943, BMS 392, UCA—Chaplains, HUD.

47. Memorial Sunday, May 25, 1941, 110th Infantry, Indiantown Gap Military Reservation, Pennsylvania, Regimental Service, Order of Worship, file Church Bulletins, box 1, Carl B. Montgomery Papers, USAHEC.

48. Chapel Services, Gen. Fox Conner Aud., Frank B. Crandall, Chaplain, September 13, 1942, file BMS 392/1 (5), General Correspondence, October 1942, BMS 392, UCA-Chaplains, HUD.

49. For a list of some of the titles circulated, see the short pamphlet put out by the Church Peace Union, "Religious Literature for Chaplains and Service Men: A Checklist" (New York: Church Peace Union, 1943). A copy of this pamphlet can be found in the Board of Directors Meeting Records, War Service Council, 1944-Chaplain's Retreat file, American Unitarian Association, Board of Directors, Meeting Records, 1942–46, BMS /11043, HUD.

50. Unitarian War Service Council, "What We Are Fighting For," Boston: American Unitarian Association, 1942, in: Mr. Murray Scrapbook file, War Service Council: Administrative files, 1942–43, American Unitarian Association, War Service Council Administrative Subject files, 1942–43, BMS 11130-2, HUD.

51. John F. Schwanhausser, Interview with G. Kurt Piehler, April 29, 1995, ROHA.

52. Private Bernard Silverstein to Rabbi Albert Baum, September 22, 1942; Rabbi Albert Baum to Pvt. Bernard Silverstein, September 23, 1942, file 3, box 1, Baum Papers, AJA.

4. Pilgrims to the World

1. Edward Culwick, Interview with G. Kurt Piehler and Troy Dayton, November 6, 1995, ROHA.

2. Captain John David Zimmerman, Interview with Lawrence Martin, Oral History Program, Chaplain Corps, U.S. Navy, July 27–29, 1981, 25–30, UNCW.

3. O' Brien, "Blackrobe in Blue," 173, 175.

4. Rev. Francis J. McGarry to Most. Rev. John F. O'Hara, September 17, 1944, file USS Sampson, box 11, O'Hara Papers, UNDA.

5. Crosby, Battlefield Chaplains, 228–29.

6. Kernan, Crossing the Line, 48–50.

7. Tower, Fighting the Devil, 31–32.

8. George K. Davies, Lt. (ChC), USNR, Chaplain, to Dr. William B. Pugh, June 14, 1944, file 1-37, box 1, RG10, PHS.

9. R. D. Workman, Chaplain, to William B. Pugh, D.D., Office of the General Assembly, July 13, 1944, file 1-37, box 1, RG10, PHS.

10. Father Paul Hatch to John F. O'Hara, September 15, 1944, file USS Otus, box 10, O'Hara Papers, UNDA.

11. Lt. (j.g.) Davis W. McCarthy, [Nov. 1942], file USS Perth Amboy, O'Hara Papers, box 11, UNDA.

12. Donald Mackay to "Dear Mother," September 4, 1944, folder 2, box 10, Mackay Family Papers, EU.

13. Father Telpern (?) To Military Ordinariate, New York, NY, November 5, 1942, file Africa, box 10, John F. O'Hara Papers, UNDA.

14. William Frame Llewellyn, Interview with Stewart Holyoak, February 7, 2004, ROHA.

15. Eugene Lipman, "Memoirs of World War II Chaplaincy Duty and Work as a Liaison Between the U.S. Army and the Jewish Agency," Lipman Papers, AJA.

16. Lawrence A. Mott to Irving [Murray], Unitarian War Service Council, August 23, 1942, file BMS 11130-1, American Unitarian Association, AUA War Service Council, Administrative Subject files, 1942–43, Chaplains Correspondence, Andover Unitarian Association, HUD.

17. Aloysius H. Lasche, 1st Battalion, 354th Infantry Regiment, 89th Division, Army Service Experiences Questionnaire, #5-3318, USAHEC.

18. Mathew P. Landers, 353rd Regiment, 89th Division, "Army Service Experiences Questionnaire" # 3506, Army Service Experiences Questionnaire, USAHEC.

19. Richard McGowan Lee, 89th Division Headquarters, "Army Service Experiences Questionnaire" #5015, 89th Division Headquarters, USAHEC.

20. Everett W. Anderson, 89th Division Headquarters, Army Service Experiences Questionnaire #3269, USAHEC.

21. Dario Antonucci, Interview with G. Kurt Piehler and Jamie Murray, April 6, 2004, 51, UTCWS.

22. "Excerpt from Chaplain Curry's letters," Sent by Mrs. Sietske L. Curry, Copy, England, May 27, box ID 322162/16142, MBE.

23. Samuel Frankel, Interview with Kurt Piehler and Jonathan Diaz, March 23, 1995, 32, ROHA.

24. William E. Capron to William Arnold, Chief of Chaplains, October 27, 194[2], Copy; William R. Arnold to William E. Capron, November 16, 1942, Copy; William R. Arnold to Most Rev. John F. O'Hara, Military Ordinariate, November 16, 1942, Copy, file 080: Catholic Denomination, July 1942–April 1943, box 3, Central Decimal file, 1920–45, RG247, NACP.

25. David M. Ogden, Division HQ, 89th Division, Army Service Experiences Questionnaire, USAHEC.

26. L. C. Lemons to Dr. T. W. Medearis, August 21, 1943, file 2.43: Chaplain L. C. Lemons, box 2, T. W. Medearis Papers, SBH.

27. Kenneth Vance to "Dear Aunt Martha," March 25, 1944, file January–March 1944, Vance Papers, UMB; Kenneth Vance to "Dear Betty & Jim," November 5, 1945, file October–December 1945, Vance Papers, UMB.

28. Father Kilian Dowling (?), 1112th Engineers Combat Corps to Your Excellency, January 22, 1944, folder: New Guinea, box 11, O'Hara Papers, UNDA.

29. Becker and Thobaben, *Common Warfare,* 72.

30. Alfred V. Sloan, Interview with Shaun Illingworth and Peter Asch, July 6, 2005, 12, ROHA.

31. Rev. Charles W. Kolek to Your Excellency, November 11, 1942, file Naval Air Station, Palymara Island, box 11, O'Hara Papers, UNDA.

32. Gilbert Ketcham to Jean Ketcham, October 10, 1943, file WWII: Vol. 4, box 2 Ketcham Papers, UMB.

33. Memoir, 23, box 16, Engel Papers, UMB.

34. U.S. War Department, *Short Guide to Iraq.*

35. Paschal Kinsel to John F. O'Hara, July 7, 1942, file Palestine, box 11, O'Hara Papers, UNDA.

36. Capt. Francis L. Ware, M.C., "Family Doctor to 2nd Battalion, 12th Infantry, 4th Infantry Division, June 6–November 29, 1944, Vol. 1: New Orleans to Paris, Unpublished Memoir, 48, World War II Veterans Survey, USAHEC.

37. Henry Francis Buinicky to Priscilla Buinicky, September 19, 1945, folder 1, box 3, Buinicky Papers, HUS.

38. James Parton to Family [after May 1944] folder 165, box 7, Parton Papers, HUH.

39. James Parton to "Dear Auntie," March 2, 1944, folder 164, box 7, Parton Papers, HUH.

40. Press Release, Air Service Command, United States Strategic Air Forces in Europe, Public Relations Workshop Tours, [1945?], box 3, RG774, PHS.

41. Harriette Gould Myerson to "Dear Folks," October 27, 1944, folder 1, box 2, Harriette Myerson Papers, HUS.

42. "Bread Upon Waters," Headquarters, Army Services Forces, Office of the Chief of Chaplains, Circular Letter No. 283, April 1, 1944, 3–4, file Circular Letters, box 2, Warner Papers, UMB.

43. "Dedication of Sugana Tareie (House of Worship), Fourth Base Depot, V Amphibious Corps, 1944, Program, folder 4, Austin Collection, FSU.

44. Walter F. Junk to John F. O'Hara, September 8, 1944, file Italy I, O'Hara Papers, UNDA.

45. Tull, "A Chaplain's War."

46. Chris C. Leahey to Most Reverend John F. O'Hara, October 1, 1944, folder: New Guinea, box 11, O'Hara Papers, UNDA.

47. Robert J. White to Bishop O'Hara, May 23, 1943, file Italy 1, box 10, O'Hara Papers, UNDA.

48. Bennett, *Army GI, Pacifist CO,* 186–87.

49. Bennett, *Army GI, Pacifist CO,* 238–40.

50. For an example of this correspondence, see box 4, Papers of Howard M. Wilson, RG774, PHS.

51. Florence Julie Lillibridge to Don Lillibridge, August 8, 1943, file 20:5, box 20, HUS.

52. Edward Bradley to "Dear Jim," Personal, January 5, 1944, file Edward Bradley, box 9, O'Hara Papers, UNDA.

53. Hazel Peters to Samuel Sandmel, Chaplain, USNR, October 4, 1944, folder 6, box 1, Sandmel Collection, AJA.

54. Lucas, *Every Other Day*, 2, 95.

55. Stahl, *Enlisting Faith*, 109–17.

56. "Lutheran Chaplain in Aleutians Commemorates Reformation Sunday," December 9, 1943, Press Release, file Releases Sent 1943 "B" box 18, General Correspondence, 1916–40, Records of the Chaplains Division, 1804–1946, RG24, NADC.

57. "Seaman Conducts Religious Services Aboard Freighter," June 3, 1943, file Public Relations Material, box 18, General Correspondence, 1916–40, Records of the Chaplains Division, 1804–1946, RG24, NADC.

58. "Press Release," Air Service Command, United States Strategic Air Forces in Europe, Public Relations Section, For Immediate Release, To: Dr. Jacob S. Payton, Publicity Dept., Gen. Com. On Army and Navy Chaplains [1945?], box 3, RG774, PHS.

5. Religion and the Conduct of War

1. Marshall, *Men Against Fire*.

2. For two of the earliest critiques of Marshall's assertion, see Spiller, "S. L. A. Marshall and the Ratio of Fire," and Blumenson, "Fire Ratios," 16–21.

3. George Schroeder to Lieutenant Jim [unidentified], October (?), 1944, Copy, folder 7 [Aboard SS *Young America*], box 3, Burks Papers, RUL.

4. Franklin D. Roosevelt: "An Appeal to Great Britain, France, Italy, Germany, and Poland to Refrain from Air Bombing of Civilians," September 1, 1939, UCSB.

5. Franklin D. Roosevelt to Pius XII, July 10, 1943, Quoted in Combined Chief of Staff to CG NATO [Henry Maitland] Wilson, January 21, 1944, MR 000.3, Section 1, Religion, Churches, Denominations, Services, 1942–44, box 46, Series 2, Military files, Map Room files, RNY.

6. Franklin D. Roosevelt: "Statement on the Nazis' Using Rome," March 14, 1944, UCSB.

7. Overy, *Allied Air War*, 344–46.

8. Letter, Gen. Dwight D. Eisenhower, Commander-in-Chief, AFH, to All Commanders, Subject: Historic Monuments, December 29, 1943, file CAD 000.4 (3-25-43) (1), Sec. 2, Security Classified General Correspondence, 1943–July 1949, General Records, Civil Affairs Division, Records of the War Department General and Special Staffs, RG165, NACP.

9. Bombing of Rome and Declaring Rome an "Open City," June 13–August 20, 1943, file Map Room Papers, RNY.

10. Reynolds, *Amazing Mr. Doolittle*, 262–64.

11. On the reaction of Pius XII to the bombing of Rome, see Ventresca, *Life of Pius XII*, 189–93 and Cooney, *Francis Cardinal Spellman*, 133–35.

12. Parker, *Monte Cassino*, 160–75.

13. Crosby, *Battlefield Chaplains*, 111–12.

14. Robert Steward Spencer, Memorandum to Colonel Bickenell, Subject: The Effect of an Attack on the Ise Shrine on Japanese Morale, May 22, 1942, folder 3, box 3, Burks Papers, RUL.

15. "Wants Shrines Bombed: Christian Church Group Denies Shinto System is Religion," *New York Times*, February 8, 1944, 3.

16. Crane, *Bombs, Cities, and Civilians*, 29–32.

17. Sittser, *Cautious Patriotism*, 220.

18. On the willingness to accept collateral damage, see Bourque, *Beyond the Beach*.

19. Ronald Schaffer is critical of the U.S. Army Air Force for not acknowledging the toll the air war took on civilians; see Schaffer, *Wings of Judgment*.

20. On the air war against Japan, see Crane, *Bombs, Cities, and Civilians*, 64–66. On the decision to spare Kyoto, see Stimson and Bundy, *On Active Service in Peace and War*.

21. Ginzberg, *Breakdown and Recovery*, 113–14.

22. Townsend, "Notes: Aerial Warfare," 516–27.

23. Weinberg, *A World at Arms*, 558–60.

24. The General Board, United States Forces, European Theater, "Report on the Army Chaplain in the European Theater," file 322.01/4: Study Number 68, 88–89, AFHA.

25. War Department, Services of Supply, Office of the Chief of Chaplains, "Memorandum, Helpful Hints, and Other Information," May 1942, 22, file Military Service, Office of Corps Chaplain (1), 1928–45, Warner Papers, UMB.

26. Yost, *Combat Chaplain*, 52.

27. Francis W. Read, 1st Lt., Chaplain, to Chaplain Curtis, July 6, 1945, Copy, file 52: Battle and Battle Reports, Vol. I: June 1943–March 1944, box 45, Central Decimal file, 1920–45, RG247, NACP.

28. Frederick A. Barnhill, Chaplain, 32nd Infantry, to Chaplain Reuben E. Curtis, July 7, 1943, file 052: Battle and Battle Reports, box 45, Central Decimal file, 1920–45, RG247, NACP.

29. Circular Letter, No. 29, January 12, 1943, folder 348, box 9, O'Hara Papers, UNDA.

30. Iwo Jima Diary, Typescript, 9, box 3, Barney Papers, UMB.

31. Alfred C. Oliver Jr., Monthly Report of Chaplains, February 1942, 201 file Oliver, Alfred C. Jr., 9678, RG237, NASL.

32. Edwin L. Kirtley, Major, Asst. Division Chaplain, 7th Division Chaplain, "Narrative Report, Kwajalein Operation [March 1944], file 052: Battles and Battle Reports, vol. 1, June 1943–March 1944, box 45, RG247, NACP.

33. Smith, *Tin Pan Alley Goes to War*, 16–17, 107.

34. Piehler, *The United States in World War II*, 46–56.

35. Crosby, *Battlefield Chaplains*, chap. 1.

36. McGuire, *The Captain Wears a Cross*, 8; Smith, "Tin Pan Alley" and "Chaplain Wrecks Legend of December 7," *New York Times*, November 1, 1942, 35.

37. Forgy, ". . . *And Pass the Ammunition*", 11.

38. Erenberg, "Swing Goes to War."

39. Frank Kneller, Interview by G. Kurt Piehler and Elizabeth McDonald, October 6, 1994, 21, ROHA.

40. Proehl, *Marching Side by Side*, 29.

41. Office of the Chief of Chaplains, Circular Letter No. 282, March 1, 1944, Warner Papers, UMB.

42. Chaplain Herman Dicker to Chaplain Richard G. Hertz, July 31, 1944, file 8, box 14, Hertz Papers, AJA.

43. Crosby, *Battlefield Chaplain*, 135.

44. Rose, *Sermons to Soldiers*.

45. Brengle, "Killing in Battle," 9–11.

46. Corpening, "No Such Commandment," 19–20.

47. Pastor Lester Westlund, Arthur, Iowa, Reference to General Commission of Army and Navy Chaplains for the Reverent Russell George Honeywell, June 13, 1944, 2620-6-1:33, UMA.

48. D. H. Gilliott, Homiletics and Practical Theology, Bonebrake Seminary, Dayton, Ohio, to General Commission of Army and Navy Chaplains for Reverend Lester Bierbaum Honderich, Decatur, Illinois, October 1, 1942, 2620-6-1:32, UMA.

49. H. B. Trimble, Dean, Emory University, to General Commission of Army and Navy Chaplains, for the Reverend Joseph Pryor McCluskey Jr. of Knoxville, Tennessee, June 29, 1944, 2620-6-1:8, UMA.

50. Victoria, *Zen at War*; Skya, *Japan's Holy War*.

51. On the dehumanization of the enemy in the Pacific War, see Dower, *War Without Mercy* and Linderman, *World Within War*.

52. Mark T. Warner, Diary, February 3, 1943, August 12, 1943, file Diary, 1943–44, box 3m, Warner Papers, UMB.

53. Morriss, *South Pacific Diary*, 62.

54. Toliver, *An Artist at War*, 5.

55. Toliver, *An Artist at War*, 52–53, 58–59, 162–64, 167, 234.

56. Toliver, *An Artist at War*, 216, 243.

57. Samuel Franklin to Dorothy Franklin, June 30, 1944, Series 3, box 2, Franklin Papers, UTS.

58. Joseph V. King to Military Ordinariate, August 8, 1944, file New Guinea, box 11, O'Hara Papers, UNDA.

59. Francis Bridenstine, Memorandum to Military Ordinariate, file Marshall Islands, March 9, 1944, box 10, O'Hara Papers, UNDA.

60. R. A. W. Farrell to Rev. Joseph J. Tennant, April 4, 1944, file USS Yorktown, box 10, O'Hara Papers, UNDA.

61. Captain John David Zimmerman, Interview with H. Lawrence Martin, Chaplain Corps, Oral History Program, Chaplains Corps, U.S. Navy July 27–29, 1981, 29, UNCW.

62. Reuben E. Curtis, Division Chaplain, to William Arnold, July 12, 1943, file 052, Vol. 1: Battles and Battle Reports, June 1943–March 1944, box 45, Central Decimal file, 1920–45, RG247, NACP.

6. Fear, Faith, and Will to Fight

1. Palmer, Wiley, and Keast, *Procurement and Training of Ground Combat Troops*.

2. Muth, *Command Culture*.

3. For a critical view of the combat performance of the American soldier and junior officer, see van Creveld, *Fighting Power*. For dissenting interpretations, see Doubler, *Closing with the Enemy* and Mansoor, *The GI Offensive in Europe*.

4. MacKenzie, *Superstition and Allied Aircrews*.

5. Glass, *The Deserters*.

6. Spector, *At War at Sea*.

7. Kindsvatter, *American Soldiers*; Schrijvers, *The Crash of Ruin*; Linderman, *World Within War*; Kennett, *G.I.*

8. Maj. Gen. Walter K. Wilson, "The Mission of the Chaplain," June 1941, file Office of the Corps Chaplain, 1928–45 (1), box 2, Warner Papers, UMB.

9. Stouffer, *The American Soldier* 2: 172–91.

10. Clipping from page 3, WD OCCH Circ. Letr. #250, 5/1/1942, file Records Relating to the History of the Chaplains of the U.S. Army, Entry 6A, box 7, RG247, NACP.

11. Gray, *Warriors*, 117.

12. Alfred C. Oliver Jr., Monthly Report of Chaplains, February 1942, 201 file Olive, Alfred G. Jr., 9678, December 1945, RG237, NASL.

13. Linderman, *Embattled Courage*.

14. U.S. War Department, Pamphlet 21-13, 159.

15. Felber, Felber, and Bartsch, *Old Breed of Marine*, 92.

16. Felber, Felber, and Bartsch, *Old Breed of Marine*, 76.

17. Morriss, *South Pacific Diary*, 64.

18. Felber, Felber, and Bartsch, *Old Breed of Marine*, 101.

19. Glass, *Deserters*.

20. Rontch, *Jewish Youth at War*, 225. On cowardice and war, see Walsh, *Cowardice: A Brief History*. Walsh offers no discussion of the connection between religious beliefs/practices and cowardice or how certain groups have been stereotyped as cowards.

21. Eichhorn, *The GI's Rabbi*, 106–12.

22. Harry Lee Virden, Chaplain (Lt. Col.) USA, Assistant to the Reverend Henry K. Sherrill, D.D., Chairman, Army and Navy Commission of the Episcopal Church, May 16, 1945, file Episcopal Protestant, Vol. V, January–December 1945, box 66, Central Decimal file, RG247, NACP.

23. Edmund C. Sliney, Department Chaplain, to Bishop John F. O'Hara, November 14, 1942, file Fort Shafter, Hawaii Department, box 10, O'Hara Papers, UNDA.

24. M. S. Chataignon to John F. O'Hara, September 2, 1943, file Sicily, Italy, box 11, O'Hara Papers, UNDA.

25. Edward Connolly to Most Rev. John F. O'Hara, March 10, 1943, file Edward Connolly, box 9, O'Hara Papers, UNDA.

26. Emmett T. Michaels to John F. O'Hara, file New Caledonia, box 10, O'Hara Papers, UNDA.

27. Mark T. Warner, Diary Entry, July 15, 26, 1943, file Diary, box 2, Warner Papers, UMB.

28. John B. Young, Regimental Chaplain, 162nd Infantry Regiment, to Chaplain William Arnold, October 8, 1943, file 052, Vol. 1: Battles and Battle Reports, June 1943–March 1944, box 45, Central Decimal file, 1920–45, RG247, NACP.

29. Kertzer, *With an H*, 12–13.

30. Bert R. Manhoff, Interview with G. Kurt Piehler and Jeff Schneider, April 19, 1995, ROHA.

31. Eichhorn, *The GI's Rabbi*, 109–10.

32. Felber, Felber, and Bartsch, *The Old Breed of Marine*, 86.

33. Morriss, *South Pacific Diary, 1942–1943*, 79.

34. Kelly, *Voices of My Comrades*, 258–59.

35. Iwo Jima Diary, Typescript, 17–18, box 3, Barney Papers, UMB.

36. Wickersham, *Marine Chaplain*, 120, 105–6.

37. Sampson, *Paratrooper Padre*, 50.

38. Raymond O' Connor to Bishop O'Hara, March 18, 1944, file USS Monterey, box 10, O'Hara Papers, UNDA.

39. Fr. [Francis J.] Keenan to Bishop John F. O'Hara, September 11, 1943, file Sicily, box 11, O'Hara Papers, UNDA.

40. George T. Quinlivan to John F. O'Hara, March 2, 1944, file Africa, box 10, O'Hara Papers, UNDA.

41. Paul J. Knapp to O'Hara, October 31, [1943], file Solomon Islands, box 11, O'Hara Papers, UNDA.

42. Paul Redmond to Bishop O'Hara, May 19, [1943], folder: Solomon Islands, May 19, [1943], box 11, O'Hara Papers, UNDA.

43. Stanley Mitchell Swinton to "Dear Stan, Gary and Nancy (and your father and mother, too)," April 1?, 1945, file 1945, box 1, Swinton Papers, UMB.

44. Rev. Francis J. McGarry to Most. Rev. O'Hara, September 17, 1944, folder: USS Sampson, box 11, O'Hara Papers, UNDA.

45. Louis J. Meyer to Bishop O'Hara, Jun 7, 1944, Somewhere in India, folder: India, box 10, COHA, O'Hara Papers, UNDA.

46. Margueritte Asbell, "Chaplains on Guadalcanal," August 7, 1944, box 3, file Guadalcanal, Entry 6A, RG257, NACP.

47. Name: Kennedy, Kenson R., Biography, "The following copied from information sent to Mrs. Ruth Kennedy, wife, in 1949," folder/box: 322311/16142, MBE.

48. D'Este, *Patton*, 685–86.

49. Eichhorn, *The GIs Rabbi*, 118.

50. MacKenzie, *Superstition and Allied Aircrews*, 92.

51. MacKenzie, *Superstition and Allied Aircrews*, 92–94.

52. MacKenzie, *Superstition and Allied Aircrews*, 96–97.

53. Fr. Keenan to Bishop O'Hara, September 11, 1943, folder: Sicily, box 11, O'Hara Papers, UNDA.

54. Donald M. Mackay to "Dear Folks," September 14, 1944, folder 2, box 10, Mackay Family Papers, EU.

55. Abraham Shafer, "Babe," to "Dear Folks," July 11, 1943, folder 1, Abraham Shafer box, Small Collections, AJA.

56. MacKenzie, *Superstition and Allied Aircrews*, 67–71.

57. Images in the Private Collection of Charles Wells, Tallahassee, Florida. Copies available in the files of the author.

58. Rutter, *Wreaking Havoc*, 100–102.

59. Rose, *Sermons to Soldiers in World War II*, 40.

60. Harry W. Webster to "Dear Loved Ones," Somewhere in the Philippines, June 11, 1945, file Records Relating to the History of the Chaplains of the U.S. Army, HI-58, Entry 6A, box 7, RG247, NACP.

61. Harry W. Webster to "Dear Loved Ones," February 15, 1945, Somewhere in the Philippines, file Records Relating to the History of the Chaplains of the U.S. Army, HI-58, Entry 6A, box 7, RG247, NACP.

62. William O. Moss to "Dear Friends," July 22, 1945, file 8.7: Meridian, Mississippi, Letters to Soldiers (World War II), box 8, Cox Papers, SBH.

63. Robert Earhart to Harriet Earhart, January 8, 1945, file January 1–31, 1945, box 2, Earhart Papers, HUS.

64. Atkins, "A Soldier's Second Thoughts," 102.

65. Atkins, "A Soldier's Second Thoughts," 101.

66. Atkins, "A Soldier's Second Thoughts, 108–9.

67. "Our Ladies of Lourdes Church, Today is the 13th Sunday After Pentecost," August 27, 1944, Unprocessed Collection, Eisold Papers, HUS.

68. Florence Lillibridge to Donald Lillibridge, July 18, 1943, file 20:5, box 20, Lillibridge Papers, HUS.

69. Donald Lillibridge to Florence Lillibridge, December 1, 1943, file 19.6, box 19, Lillibridge Papers, HUS.

70. Donald Lillibridge to Florence Lillibridge, December 18, 1943, file 19.6, box 19, Lillibridge Papers, HUS.

71. Blum, *V Was for Victory*.

7. Race and Religion

1. Takaki, *Double Victory*.

2. Stilwell, *The Golden Thirteen*.

3. Sandler, *Segregated Skies*.

4. McLaurin, *First Black Marines*.

5. McCaffrey, *Going for Broke*; Tamura, *Nisei Soldiers Break Their Silence*.

6. Bennett and Holm, "Indians in the Military," 11–18; Bernstein, *American Indians and World War II*.

7. U.S. Office of War Information, *The Negroes and the War*.

8. Cripps, *Making Movies Black*, 102–25.

9. Masuda, *Letters from the 442nd*, 16.

10. Nalty, *Strength for the Fight*.

11. Fletcher, *America's First Black General*.

12. "Army Seeks 235 Race Chaplains," *The Chicago Defender*, March 27, 1943, 2.

13. Harrod, *Manning the New Navy*, 11, 57–60.

14. Chester, "Doris Miller, Pearl Harbor," 31–61.

15. T. W. Medearis, General Superintendent, to Chief of Chaplains, Washington DC, July 20, 1942, file Chaplain, 2.28, William Edward Hall (Colored), box 2, T. W. Medearis Papers, SBH.

16. Drury, *Chaplains Corps, 1939–1949*, 43–44, 53–55.

17. Crosby, *Battlefield Chaplains*, 61–64.

18. 1st Sgt. Walter J. Pierre to Most Rev. Francis J. Spellman, July 18, 1945, file Africa, box 10, Papers of John F. O'Hara, UNDA.

19. Walter B. Zimmerman, Chaplain, USA, Assistant, to Rev. Frederick L. Fagley, Associate Secretary to the General Council, file 080: Congregational Church, Vol. II: May 27, 1943–Dec. 1945, box 64, Central Decimal file, 1920–45, RG247, NACP.

20. William R. Arnold, Chief of Chaplains, Memorandum to Commanding Officer, 158th Infantry Regiment, December 17, 1942, file 291.2: Indian, box 199, Central Decimal file, 1920–45, RG247, NACP.

21. Carl L. Wilberding, Chaplain, Assistant to Reverend George C. Lenington, January 13, 1943, file 291.2: Indian, box 199, Central Decimal file, 1920–45, RG247, NACP.

22. HQ, 79th CA (AA), Manchester, Connecticut, to Chief of Chaplains, December 24, 1942, file 291.2, box 199, Central Decimal file, 1920–45, RG247, NACP.

23. Stahl, *Enlisting Faith*, 95–97.

24. Harold J. Ockenga to George Marshall, December 26, 1944, Marshall Papers, Microfilm, Reel 26: 432, New York Public Library.

25. George Marshall to Harold J. Ockenga, January 6, 1945, Marshall Papers, Microfilm, Reel 26: 432, New York Public Library.

26. M. H. McIntyre, Secretary to the President, to Brig. Gen. William R. Arnold, May 22, 1943, file #80: Fraternal Council of Negro Churches in America, April 1943–December 1945, box B7, Central Decimal file, 1920–1945, RG247, NACP.

27. William R. Arnold, Chief of Chaplains, to the Chief of Staff [George Marshall], Attention: Lt. Col. McCarthy, May 27, 1943, file 80: Fraternal Council of Negro Churches in America, April 1943–December 1945, box 67, Central Decimal file, 1920–1945, RG247, NACP.

28. Gregg, *Of Men and of Arms*; McGuire, *Taps for a Jim Crow Army*, 134–39.

29. F. L. Fagley to Manager, Charlotte Hotel, Charlotte, North Carolina, October 29, 1942, file 080: Congregational and Christian Churches, January 1921–May 18, 1943, box 64, Central Decimal file, 1920–45, RG247, NACP.

30. Memorandum to All Army, Army Corps Chaplains, from William Arnold, Office of the Chief of Chaplains, January 15, 1942, file Office of the Corps Chaplains, 1939–42, box 2, Warner Papers, UMB.

31. William B. Zimmerman, "Memorandum on Telephone Conversation" [1943?] In the routing slip indicating this memorandum had been reviewed by Chaplain Arnold, the author of the memorandum wrote: "I have told Moody and Devan that the Chief of Chaplains has no desire to inject duty of [a] Negro officer in the War Dept. among the many problems C S has. That when the W.D. adopts such a policy, we will gladly conform." file 80: General Commission on Army and Navy Chaplains, August 7, 1942–June 30, 1943, box 68, Central Decimal file, 1920–1945, RG247, NACP.

32. "Army Bias Keeps Pastors Out of Chaplain Corps," *Chicago Defender*, June 2, 1945, 18.

33. Lee, *Employment of Negro Troops*, 230

34. McGuire, *Taps for a Jim Crow Army*, 132–33.

35. A. E. McWilliams to Rev. S. Arthur Devan, June 8, 1942, file 4/10 Chaplaincy-Ecclesiastical Endorsement, 1939–64, Requests: Ma-Mc, box 4, Henry C. Bunton Papers, NYPLS.

36. "Alcan Highway Chaplain Back in D.C. Tells of Work in the Wilds of Frozen North," *Chicago Defender*, February 6, 1943, 9.

37. Benjamin O. Davis, Brigadier General, U.S. Army, Memorandum of the Inspector General, August 7, 1943, folder 4, box 18, Benjamin O. Davis, Sr. Collection, USAHEC.

38. McGuire, *Taps for a Jim Crow Army*, 115.

39. "Protest Rally for Chaplain Fuller," *Chicago Defender*, March 4, 1944, 11. For the U.S. Army chief of chaplains' stance toward the court martial, see Walter B. Zimmerman, Chaplain, USA, Assistant to Edith Morris, August 26, 1943, file 250.4: Court Martials, box 195, Central Decimal file, 1920–45, RG247, NACP. For more on Fuller, see also Brandt, *Harlem at War*, 134

40. Beverly Ward, box 1863, Chaplains Reports and 201 files, 1920–45, RG247, NASL.

41. Henry C. Bryant, Captain, M.C., to General Dwight D. Eisenhower, February 5, 1945, Copy, box 1863, Chaplains Reports and 201 files, 1920–45, RG247, National Archives, NASL.

42. Dwight D. Eisenhower to Captain Harry C. Bryant, February 17, 1945, Copy, box 1863, Chaplains Reports and 201 files, 1920–45, RG247, NASL.

43. Benjamin O. Davis to Captain Harry C. Bryant, February 20, 1945, Copy, box 1863, Chaplains Reports and 201 files, 1920–45, RG247, NASL.

44. Roberts, *What Soldiers Do*, 223–29.

45. Carl Montgomery, "Felix Werpechowski" "Undated Memoir Post 1945" file Correspondence from Felix Werpechowski, Carl Montgomery Papers, USAHEC.

46. Captain Phillip L. Thayer to Robert Cummins, February 9, 1943, bMS 392/1 (9), UCA-Chaplains, HUD.

47. "Negro Soldiers in Northern Camps," Church Letter on War Commission, Christian Commission for Camp and Defense Communities, No. 2, December 1942, file 13, box 5, RG18, PHS.

48. Edwin R. Carter Jr., SOS Chaplain, U.S. Army, "The Racial Problem in Britain" [October? 1942?], folder 12, box 17, Benjamin O. Davis Sr. Collection, USHEC.

49. Morris Gordon, *Dare to Be: The Autobiography of Rabbi Morris Gordon*, box 1, Morris Gordon Papers, CJH.

50. Mary Robinson, Interview with G. Kurt Piehler, Linda Lasko, and Bruce Chadwick, October 28, 1994, 21, ROHA.

51. Hall, *Love, War, and the 96th Engineers (Colored)*, 60, 187, 232–37.

52. Charles Fisher, Chaplain, 366th Infantry, to Rev. Frederick L. Fagley, General Council of the Congregational Churches, September 1942, Copy, file 080: Congregational and Christian Churches, January 1921–May 18, 1943, box 64, Central Decimal file, 1920–45, RG247, NACP.

53. Biggs, *The Triple Nickels*, 5.

54. Alfred Nisnoff, Interview with G. Kurt Piehler, August 1, 1994, 23–24, ROHA.

55. "White Chaplain Blasts Bitter Hate on Navy Ship," *Chicago Defender*, December 22, 1945, 1.

56. Captain John David Zimmerman, Interview with Lawrence Martin, Oral History Program, Chaplain Corps, U.S. Navy, July 27–29, 1981, UNCW.

57. Daniel F. Meehan, "Brothers in Arms," *Bee Lines*, October 5, 1942, folder: Bee Lines: August 24, 1942–December 28, 1942, Kelly Collection, FSU.

58. Donald Mackay to "Mother," February 20, 1944, folder 7, box 9, Collection 691, Mackay Family Papers, EU.

59. Donald Mackay to "Dear Folks," May 1, 1944, folder 8, box 9, Collection 691, Mackay Family Papers, EU.

60. Church Activities, Naval Air Station Chapel, North Island, San Diego, California, [1944], Item No. 14, folder 7, box 9, MacKay Family Papers, EU.

61. Jacob D. Shankman to "Dear Friends," Chaplain Shankman's Letter, April 6, 1944, folder 3, box 10, Shankman Papers, AJA.

62. Dunn, *On Board the USS Mason*.

63. Minutes of the Board of Directors of the Booker T. Washington Center for Servicemen, Inc., May 14, 1945, 3, file 1, box 1, Booker T. Washington Center for Servicemen Papers, 1943–46, NYPLS.

64. On the image and lure of Hawaii, see Bailey and Farber, *The First Strange Place*.

65. Hiro Higuchi to Hisako Higuchi, April 19, 1944, Hiraoka Papers, UHM.

66. Hiro Higuchi to Hisako Higuchi, July 8, 1944, Hiraoka Papers, UHM.

67. Hiro Higuchi to Hisako Higuchi, December 30, 1944, Hiraoka Papers, UHM.

68. Minoru Masuda, *Letters from the 442nd*, 41, 45.

69. Yost, *Combat Chaplain*, 104–5.

70. Fujita, *Foo*.

71. Wong, *Americans First: Chinese Americans*.

72. "Confirmation," *Gung Ho*, January 14, 1944, 4.

73. "Echoes of the Xmas Party," *Gung Ho*, December 31, 1944, 4.

74. "A Matter of Time," *Gung Ho*, March 3, 1944, 6.

75. Yung, *The Adventures of Eddie Fung*, 157, 187.

76. Wenger, *We Have Religion*.

77. Meadows, *The Comanche Code Talkers*, 118.

78. U.S. Department of the Interior, *Indians in the War*.

79. Holiday and McPherson, *Navajo Code Talker*.

80. For some tribes, the return of Native American veterans from the war revitalized warrior traditions and rituals; see Meadows, *Kiowa, Apache* and Meadows, *Kiowa Military Societies*.

8. Religious Life of Military Women

1. Treadwell, *The Women's Army Corps in World War II*, 216–17.

2. Tilly Spetgang, Interview with Shaun Illingworth, January 12, 2012, ROHA.

3. Meyer, *Creating GI Jane*.

4. Meyer, *Creating GI Jane*, 139.

5. Treadwell, *Women's Army Corps*, 337.

6. MacKenzie, *Superstition and Allied Aircrews*, 62.

7. Pfau, GIS, *Gender, and Domesticity*.

8. Patterson, "Gender and Marine Corps Body."

9. Archer, *Women, Warfare and Representation*, 24–35.

10. Myers, "A Weapon Waiting to Be Used."

11. Campbell, "Women in Combat"; Pennington, *Wings, Soviet Airwomen*.

12. Treadwell, *Women's Army Corps*, 337.

13. Stahl, *Enlisting Faith*, 82–84.

14. For an excellent history of this unit, see Moore, *To Serve My Country, To Serve My Race*.

15. Earley, *One Woman's Army*, 157–59.

16. U.S. Army Recruiting Publicity Bureau, "Facts You Want to Know About the WAC," Pamphlet, 1944, UNCG.

17. Frederick G. Lamb, Monthly Report of the Chaplain to the Military Ordinariate, October 1944, file Italy II, box 10, O' Hara Papers, UNDA.

18. Nona Baldwin to Maria Rose, June 3, 1942, file 1.14, box 1, Brown Papers, HUS.

19. Naval War College, Newport, Rhode Island, Oral History Program, The History of the WAVES. Interviewee: Nona Baldwin Brown, December 27, 1997, Copy, "Military Oral History Transcript for National War College, 1997–1998" file, box 2, Brown Papers, HUS.

20. "True Confessions of Hazel M. Hitson," Anthropology C-8, February 20, 1951, Dr. F L. K. Hsu, file 6: Biographical Education, Northwestern, 1951, box 1, Weidman Papers, HUS.

21. "True Confessions of Hazel M. Hitson," Anthropology C-8, February 20, 1951, Dr. F L. K. Hsu, file 6: Biographical Education, Northwestern, 1951, box 1, Weidman Papers, 18, 25–26, HUS.

22. S. Caroline Levin, Interview with Chris Hillary and Laura Micheletti, April 1, 1998, 12–13, ROHA.

23. Katherine Keene, Unpublished Memoir, file 2.7, box 2, Keene Papers, 8, HUS.

24. Katherine Keene to "Folks," February 26, 1945, file 1.9, box 1, Keene Papers, HUS.

25. Ann Kaplowitz Goldberg, Interview with Herman J. Trojanowski, November 11, 2010, UNCG.

26. Bertha Marie Clark, "When WAC Was a Dirty Word," Unpublished Manuscript, 1979, 23–26, Bertha Marcie (Strittmatter) Clark Papers, HUS.

27. Dorothy H. Jordan, Interview with Eric Elliott, May 3, 1999, 18, UNCG.

28. Francis I. Holway to Brigadier General William R. Arnold, June 17, 1943, Copy, file 726: October 1938–December 1945, box 335, Decimal file, 1920–45, Office Management Division, RG247, NACP.

29. Katherine Keene, "Memoir," 42, file 2.7, box 2, Katherine Keene Papers, HUS.

30. Selwyn D. Ruslander, Chaplain, USNR to Pvt. J--A--S--, Barracks 245, Sqd. T, Chanute Field, Illinois, October 1945, file 6, box 24, Ruslander Papers, AJA.

31. Isador Signer, Chaplain, USA, to Chaplain Selwyn Ruslander, October 19, 1945, file 6, box 24, Ruslander Papers, AJA.

32. "North Island Chapel Choir," *San Diego Journal*, April 1, 1944, Press Clipping, folder 7, box 9, Mackay Family Papers, EU.

33. Donald MacKay to Parents, March 12, 1944, folder 7, box 9, MacKay Family Papers, EU.

34. Mary Robinson, Interview with G. Kurt Piehler, Linda Lasko, and Bruce Chadwick, October 28, 1994, 35, ROHA.

35. Katherine Keene, Memoir, file 2.7, box 2, Keene Papers, HUS.

9. The Wounded

1. In his oral history, Lionel Greer described the perfunctory screening he received when he sought to become an aviation cadet, noting that the psychiatrist asked only one question: "'Yeah you graduated from college in '42?' 'Yeah.' He said, 'Okay, you're done, you're okay.'" Although Greer was not asked whether or not he liked girls, he did learn that one G.I. was rejected because of concerns over homosexuality. See Lionel Greer, Interview with G. Kurt Piehler, November 13, 2003, 52, UTCWS.

2. Ferngren, *Medicine and Religion*.

3. Koenig, "Religion and Medicine I."

4. Byerly, *Fever of War*.

5. For a broad overview of military medicine in the Second World War, see Cowdrey, *Fighting for Life*.

6. McWilliams, *The Chaplain's Conflict*, 76–78.

7. Tamura, *Nisei Soldiers Break Their Silence*, 101–2.

8. Utley, USS *Tennessee*, 129.

9. Charles C. Reide (?) to Bishop O'Hara, April 19, 1943, file New Zealand, box 11, O'Hara Papers, UNDA.

10. To Medical Officer in Command from Chaplain Robert J. Cronin, Memorandum, Violation of Freedom of Conscience and Religious Liberty, Request for Discontinuance of, March 9, 1945, file 41, box 1, RG10, PHS.

11. Statement: "The following is a general summation of the reply of the Protestant Chaplains stationed at the Naval Hospital at Oakland, California," n.d., file 41, box 1, RG10, PHS.

12. John Bradstreet to Consuelo Bradstreet, November 6, 1943, box 1, Series 2, folder 3, Bradstreet Papers, STL.

13. Victor Dux to Father Stegman, August 9, 1944, file Italy 1, box 10, O'Hara Papers, UNDA.

14. Wickersham, *Marine Chaplain*, 91.

15. For an overview of the role of Christian Science during World War II, see Christian Science Board of Directors, *Christian Science Wartime Activities*.

16. Mason, *Battleship Sailor*, 41–42, 189–90.

17. Walter Denise, Interview by G. Kurt Piehler and Jennifer Lenkiewicz, March 25, 1997, ROHA. See also Coyne, *Marching Home*, 85–87.

18. Arthur W. Eckman, Manager of Committee on Publication, to Mr. Gardner M. Damon, Ft. Devens, September 2, 1942, 14666/1633, MBE. In the letter, Eckman affirmed that all "Christian Scientists in uniform are subject to Army and Navy

discipline, which includes proper medical and surgical treatment according to the standards of and practices of the armed forces." In Great Britain the church, in a published circular letter to Christian Scientists joining British forces, advised: "It would be unwise for a Christian Scientist, when serving in His Majesty's Forces, to refuse to go to hospital when ordered there, or to refuse to submit to medical treatment. A Christian Scientist is, however, at the same time free to get in touch with a Christian Science practitioner. If necessary he can do so through the Christian Science Minister. Office of the District Manager of the Christian Science Committee on Publications for Great Britain and Ireland. This circular letter has been prepared for the information of Christian Scientists joining or serving in His Majesty's Forces." August 1941, file 14666, box 1607, MBE.

19. Report of Activities of Chaplain Herbert E. Rieke, March 25, 1942–May 4, 1942, file 322322, box 16142, MBE.

20. Cecil F. Denton to Arthur W. Eckman, June 7, 1944, folder 322163, box 16142, MBE.

21. To Chaplain William R. Arnold and Maj. Gen. Norman T. Kirk, Surgeon General of the United States Army, Petition, folder 14699, box 14113, MBE.

22. Henry L. Stimson to Frank F. Bunker, August 22, 1944, Copy, file 14669, box 1413, MBE.

23. James H. Munn to Lt. Col. Herbert A. Johnson, Manager, Camp Welfare Activities, June 11, 1945, file 322305/16142, MBE.

24. A. D. Bruce, Major General, U.S. Army to [Herbert A.] Johnson, October 26, 1945, file 43405/16142, MBE.

25. The classic work examining efforts to control venereal disease in the first half of the twentieth century is Brandt, *No Magic Bullet*. See also Hegarty, *Victory Girls, Khaki-Wackies, and Patriotutes* and Byers, *The Sexual Economy of War*.

26. Gilbert Ketcham to Jean Ketcham, October 9, 1943, file WWII: Vol. 4, box 2, Ketcham Papers, UMB.

27. Gilbert Ketcham to Jean Ketcham, October 1, 1943, file WWII: Vol. 4, box 2, Ketcham Papers, UMB.

28. William R. Arnold to Most Reverend John F. O'Hara, June 23, 1943, file 720: Health and Prevention of Disease, box 355, Decimal file, 1920–45, RG247, NACP.

29. Roberts, "The Price of Discretion," 1002–30.

30. Joseph B. Murphy, C.S.P. to Very Rev. George J. Collins, C.S. Sp., June 4, 1943, file POW–England, box 11, O'Hara Papers, UNDA.

31. George Sherry to John F. O'Hara, October 5, 1944, file Italy II, box 10, O'Hara Papers, UNDA.

32. Raymond L. Talbot to Military Ordinariate, September 30, 1944, file France II, box 10, O'Hara Papers, UNDA.

33. R.E.R. Martin to Bishop John F. O'Hara, October 20, 1944, file France II, box 10, O'Hara Papers, UNDA.

34. Hildegard Peplau, "War Psychology Group Discussion," September 24, [1944], file 303, Carton 10, Hildegard Peplau Papers, HUS.

35. Benjamin, "Morals Versus Morale in Wartime."

36. M. J. Exner, M.D., Director, Venereal Division, City of Newark, Department of Health, to Brigadier General William R. Arnold, April 2, 1943, file 726: Vol. 1, October 1938–December 1945, box 335, Central Decimal file, 1920–45, RG247, NACP.

37. William D. Cleary to Walter Clarke, M.D., April 6, 1943, Telegram, Copy, file 726.8: Special Practices and Treatment, 1935–45 (?), Vol. 1, box 335, Entry 1, Central Decimal file, 1920–45, RG247, NACP.

38. [M. J. Exner], The Chaplain in Relation to the Sex-Social Problem of the Soldier, Three Lectures, General Outline [1943] file 726, Vol. 1, October 1938–December 1945, box 335, Central Decimal file, 1920–45, RG247, NACP. Initially chief of chaplains William R. Arnold gave a strong endorsement to having a short course on sexual hygiene and morality at the chaplain school. William R. Arnold, Memorandum to the Commandant, The Chaplain School, March 8, 1943.

39. For an understanding of military psychiatry in the Second World War, see Cowdrey, *Fighting for Life*; Grob, "World War II and American Psychiatry," 41–69; Hale, *The Rise and Crisis of Psychoanalysis*, 187–210; Gabriel, *Military Psychiatry*; Shephard, *A War of Nerves*; and Greene, *Breaking Point*.

40. Chaplain Blakeney, "Practical Duties," file 10, box 14, Hertz Papers, AJA.

41. Rice, "Combat Medic," 312–44.

42. McWilliams, *The Chaplain's Conflict*, 62.

43. Gregory, "The Chaplain and Mental Hygiene," 420–23.

44. Chaplain Richard G. Hertz to Morton and June Bauman, July 17, 1944, folder 5, box 14, Hertz Papers, AJA.

45. Bert Manhoff, Interview with G. Kurt Piehler and Jeff Schneider, April 19, 1995, 53, ROHA.

46. Burnham, "The Encounter of Christian Theology," 321–52.

47. "The following are suggestions of what to observe and report concerning an NP Patient," Memo, [1944], file 303: Psych Lectures, Carton 10, Hildegard Peplau Papers, HUS.

48. Hildegard Peplau, Lecture 3, 312th Psych Lectures, Notes, 1944, file 303: Psych Lectures, Carton 10, Peplau Papers, HUS.

49. John F. O'Hara, Military Ordinariate, to Gen. George Marshall, Chief of Staff, September 29, 1944, file Special Practices and Treatments, Schools of Healing and Medicine, box 335, Central Decimal file, 1920–45, RG247, NACP.

50. Louis J. Meyer to Chaplain John F. Monahan, [September 15, 1944], file 702: Medical Examination, April 1935–July 1945, box 335, Center Decimal file, 1920–45, RG247, NACP.

51. Av. S. Joseph Gordon White Jr. to Chief of Chaplains Arnold, August 5, 1943, file 726: Vol. 1, October 1938–December 1945, box 335, Central Decimal file, 1920–45, RG247, NACP.

52. William R. Arnold, Chief of Chaplains, to Chaplain Charles I. Carpenter, August 12, 1943, file 726: Vol. 1, October 1938–December 1945, Vol. 1, box 335, Central Decimal file, 1920–45, RG247, NACP.

53. William R. Arnold, Chief of Chaplains, to Most Reverend William T. McCarty, Military Delegate, October 28, 1944. The restricted study Arnold sent was "War

Neuroses in North Africa: The Tunisian Campaign (January–May 1943), file 730, Special Practices and Treatments, Schools of Healing and Medicine, box 335, Central Decimal file, 1920–45, RG247, NACP.

54. Charles C. Dutton, Captain, Post Chaplain, Fort Bliss, Texas, to Chief of Chaplains, August 9, 1943, with enclosure: "Homosexuality," file Morals and Conduct (250.1), box 195, Central Decimal file, 1920–45, RG247, NACP. The interaction of military chaplains with gay GIs is briefly discussed in Berube, *Coming Out Under Fire*, 165.

10. The Dead

1. Felber, Felber, and Bartsch, *The Old Breed of Marine*, 165.
2. Thomas A. Kindre, Interview with G. Kurt Piehler, June 28, 1994, 24, 30, ROHA.
3. Ray Taub, Interview with G. Kurt Piehler, June 29, 1994, 13–14, ROHA.
4. Linderman, *World Within War*.
5. Suid, *Guts and Glory*, 45–47.
6. 89 Cong. Rec. A 5115 (1943).
7. Carlson, *Each Other's Prisoners*, 6.
8. Budreau, *Bodies of War*, 120–21.
9. "For the Protection of the War-Widow, n.d., Rabbinical Council of America, folder 1, box 1: Chaplaincy Correspondence, box 1, Baum Papers, AJA.
10. Schultz, *Tri-Faith America*, 48.
11. Sledge, *With the Old Breed*, 64.
12. Lemuel Sparks interview with G. Kurt Piehler and Viviana Chaps, March 13, 2001, 31–32, UTCWS.
13. O'Callahan, *Chaplain on the Franklin*, 122.
14. Walter T. Hanley to John F. O'Hara, November 6, 1942, file New Guinea, box 11, O'Hara Papers, UNDA.
15. Roland A. Winter, Interview with G. Kurt Piehler and David Tsang Hou, September 15, 1995, 30, ROHA. The quote from Mourner's Kaddish is from Harlow, *Prayerbook*, 525.
16. U.S. War Department, Technical Manual 10-630: Graves Registration, September 23, 1941, 15–117.
17. Howard M. Wilson, Army Morale: Notes of Chaplain Howard M. Wilson, AUS, Section 8, Room 82, box 1, RG774, PHS.
18. Hiro Higuchi to Hisako Higuchi, September 4, 1944, Higuchi Papers, UHM.
19. Hiro Higuchi to Hisako Higuchi, October 20, 1944, Higuchi Papers, UHM.
20. U.S. War Department, Technical Manual 10-630: Graves Registration, September 23, 1941.
21. U.S. War Department, Technical Manual 10-630: Graves Registration, September 23, 1941.
22. Piehler, *Remembering War the American Way*, 214n3.
23. Felber, Felber, and Bartsch, *The Old Breed of Marine*, 79.
24. Dower, *War Without Mercy*, chaps. 2–3.
25. Sledge, *With the Old Breed*, 120.
26. Toliver, *An Artist at War*, 164–65.

27. Willard, *The Leathernecks Come Through*, 61.

28. Willard, *The Leathernecks Come Through*, 162.

29. Eldrige, *Iwo Jima and the Bonin Islands*, 349–55.

30. Donald Mackay to "Mother, Dad, and Betty," February 28, 1944, folder 7, box 9, Collection 691, Mackay Family Papers, EU.

31. Donald Mackay to "Dear Folks," March 1, 1944, folder 7, box 9, Collection 691, Mackay Family Papers, EU.

32. Ernie Pyle, *Brave Men*, 164–65.

33. Edward Elson, Letter, Copy, January 28, 1945, #60, folder 13, box 1, RG253, PHS.

34. Felber, Felber, and Bartsch, *The Old Breed of Marine*, 76–77.

35. Lemuel Sparks, Interview with G. Kurt Piehler and Viviana Chaps, March 13, 2001, 32, 35 UTCWS.

36. Charles F. LaCour to Brig. Gen. William R. Arnold, January 29, 1943, file 003: Catholic Denominations, vol. 1–3, July 1942–April 1943, box 3, Central Decimal file, 1920–45, RG247, NACP.

37. William R. Arnold to Charles F. LaCour, Director, National Catholic Community Service, Delhart, Texas, February 3, 1943, file 003: Catholic Denominations, vol. 1–3, July 1942–April 1943, box 3, Central Decimal file, 1920–45, RG247, NACP.

38. Selwyn D. Ruslander to S. C. Kohs, National Jewish Welfare Board, July 17, 1946, folder 9, box 24, and Dorothy Phelps Bultman to Chaplain Ruslander, April 30, 1945, folder 6, box 24, Ruslander Papers, AJA.

39. G. C. Marshall, Chief of Staff, Memorandum No. W 60–44, Jewish Memorial Services, May 18, 1944, Copy. In the case of England and Northern Europe, Chaplain Morris Ketzer was tasked with this assignment, in 1944, by Chaplain Judah Nadach, the deputy to the theater chaplain. Judah Nadach, Chaplain (Maj.) to Chaplain Morris Ketzer, December 13, 1944, folder 2, box 12, Kertzer Papers, AJA.

40. Mrs. Edna L. Bullock to L. E. Cousins, January 15, 1945, file Cousins, Mrs. L. E., box 6, BRU.

41. L. E. Cousins, Chaplain (Capt.), 314th Infantry Division, to Mrs. Edna L. Bullock, April 2, 1945, file Cousins, Mrs. L E., box 8, BRU.

42. Willard, *The Leathernecks Come Through*, 160.

43. "Protestant Memorial Service for Men of the 4th Marine Division Who Gave Their Lives on Iwo Jima," March 14, 1945, file Navy: World War II Souvenirs, box 3, Barney Papers, UMB.

44. Harold I. Saperstein to Mrs. Eva Perelman, March 14, 1945, file 8, box 8, Saperstein Papers, AJA.

45. Johnson, *One More Hill*, 122–23.

46. Toliver, *An Artist at War*, 232–33.

47. Morriss, *South Pacific Diary*, 147.

48. Sampson, *Paratrooper Padre*.

49. Bard, *Forgotten Victims*, 86–88.

50. Thomas G. Calderone, Interview with Shaun Illingworth, Erick Coccia, and Sarah Rice, February 24, 2006, 50, ROHA.

51. Barlow, *Bunker's War*, 207.

52. Address of Chaplain S. D. Ruslander, USNR, for "Meet the Chaplain" Meeting at Beaver Dam, Wisconsin, July 31, 1945, file 4, box 24, Ruslander Papers, AJA.

53. No Author, "New Book of Revelations," [March 1944], file 3, box 24, Ruslander Papers, AJA.

54. Piehler, *Remembering War*, 131.

55. On the delayed mourning, see Bodnar, *The "Good War" in American Memory*, 98–107.

11. Prisoners of War

1. Doyle, *Voices from Captivity*, 308.

2. Convention Between the United States of America and Other Powers, Relating to Prisoners of War, July 27, 1929 (Geneva Convention), Article 16, The Avalon Project: Documents in Law, History, and Diplomacy, Lillian Goldman Law Library, Yale Law School, http://avalon.law.yale.edu/20th_century/geneva02.asp.

3. Vulliet, *War Prisoners Aid*, 12.

4. Feuer, *Bilibid Diary*, 175.

5. Marchione, *Pius XII and POWs*.

6. "Prisoner of War" Form, Henry J. Perner, April 18, [1943], Joseph Hurley to The Rev. Father Francis Finnegan, Corpus Christi Rectory, Miami, Florida, May 20, 1943, Perner Papers, FSU.

7. "American Prisoners in Germany," [April or May 1945], Perner Papers, FSU.

8. For an overview of the German armed forces' policies toward British and American prisoners of war, see Vourkoutiotis, *Prisoners of War and the German High Command*. Anglo-American wartime diplomacy with Nazi Germany is considered in Kochavi, *Confronting Captivity*. The best discussion of the German policy regarding American and British Jewish POWs in German captivity can be found in MacKenzie, "The Treatment of Prisoners of War," 487–520.

9. Linderman, *The World Within War*, chaps. 4–5. For Japanese views regarding the prisoners of war, see Hata, "From Consideration to Contempt," 253–76.

10. James, *The Years of MacArthur*, 2: 148–51. For a biography of Wainwright, see Schultz, *Hero of Bataan*.

11. Linderman, *The World Within War*, chaps. 4–5.

12. Crosby, *Battlefield Chaplains*, 32.

13. Urwin, *Victory in Defeat*, 54–56, 57.

14. Feuer, *Bilibid Diary*, 123, 164–65.

15. Urwin, *Victory in Defeat*, 331–49, 167–68.

16. James, *Brigadier General W. E. Brougher*, 149–51, 179–82.

17. James, *Brigadier General W. E. Brougher*, 67, 78–79, 84.

18. Clark and Kowallis, "Davao Penal Colony," 109–39.

19. Barlow, *Bunker's War*, 210

20. Barlow, *Bunker's War*, 277.

21. Barlow, *Bunker's War*, 299–302.

22. Fujita, *Foo: A Japanese-American Prisoner*, 227, 346, 349.

23. Stewart, *Give Us This Day*, 162.

24. Vourkoutiotis, *Prisoners of War and the German High Command*.

25. Spinelli and Carlson, *Life Behind Barbed Wire*.

26. Shavit, "Books and Libraries," 113–34.

27. Hasselbring, "American Prisoners," 261.

28. Spinelli and Carlson, *Life Behind Barbed Wire*, 198–201.

29. Sampson, *Paratrooper Padre*, 97–98.

30. "Next of Kin Hear of Aid to Captives: Red Cross Goal is to Start Steady Flow of Relief Supplies to Orient," *New York Times*, June 26, 1944, 15.

31. J. Townsend Russell, "Prisoner of War Camps in Germany-Stalag VIIA," *Prisoner of War Bulletin* 2, no. 11 (January 1944): 3.

32. Report on German Camps: Stalag Luft III, *Prisoner of War Bulletin* 2, no. 12 (December 1944), 2–3.

33. Foy, "For You the War is Over," 173.

34. Philip S. Bernstein to Chaplain Aryeh Lev, May 12, 1943, folder 52, box 7; Charles S. Freeman, Chaplain, to Rabbi Philip S. Bernstein, April 28, 1943, folder 52, box 7; Chaplain Aryeh Lev to Rabbi Philip Bernstein, May 24, 1943, folder 52, box 7, I-249; Committee on Army and Navy Religious Activities, Minutes, May 3–9, 1943, folder 2, box 1, I-249, CJH.

35. The General Board, United States Forces, European Theater, "Report on the Army Chaplain in the European Theater," 88, file 322.01/4, Study Number 68, AFHA.

36. Carlson, *We Were Each Other's Prisoners*, 51.

37. Hugo Lang, Interview by G. Kurt Piehler, March 19, 2001, UTCWS.

38. Leonard Winograd, "Double Jeopardy," 3–17.

39. Harry Glixon, Chap. 7, Prisoner of War, 53, 59, 1997, box 2, Small Collections-Glixonson, AJA.

40. Harry Glixon, Chap. 7, Prisoner of War, 85, 1997, box 2, Small Collections-Glixson, AJA.

41. Carlson, *Each Other's Prisoners*, 46–49.

42. Zemke, *Zemke's Stalag*, 28–29.

43. Carlson, *Each Other's Prisoners*, 181–99. For a more detailed history of Berga, see Whitlock, *Given Up for Dead*.

44. David Howard, "A Kriege Log: Wartime Experiences, 1941–1945" Memoirs, folder 3, box 8, Clark Papers, USAFA.

45. Carlson, *We Were Each Other's Prisoners*, 48–49.

12. Religion and Reconciliation

1. McManus, *Hell Before Their Very Eyes*. Also useful is Abzug, *Inside the Vicious Heart*.

2. Roland Winter, Interview with G. Kurt Piehler and David Tsang Hou, September 15, 1995, 35–40, ROHA.

3. Patton, *Patton Papers*, vol. 2, 751.

4. Louis Maloof to William Fink, December 29, 1945, Copy; John F. Noll to H. J. Carroll, January 16, 1945, folder: NCCS: Overseas, Misc., 1942–46, box 8, Collection: NCWC/USCC, CUA.

5. For a critical account, see Wyman, *The Abandonment of the Jews*.

6. Stephen Wise to the president, February 3, 1944; William D. Hassett, Memorandum for the Honorable Elmer Davis, February 7, 1944, Statement Draft with FDR Corrections, [February 1944]; Franklin D. Roosevelt to Stephen Wise, February 9, 1944, Copy, file PPF: 5029-American Jewish Congress, box 5004, President's Personal file, RNY. The question of anti-Semitism mixed with apathy is important in assessing the American response to Nazi Germany and the Holocaust. The bill of indictment is extensive and often centers on the failure to admit refugees into the United States and the unwillingness to bomb Nazi death camps and the rail lines leading up to them. Anti-Semitism is often cited as one of the principal reasons for this failure, along with a lack of political will on the part of political, military, and religious leaders. Franklin D. Roosevelt has often come under intense scrutiny and criticism for his failures of action, but blame is also apportioned to a range of others, including the U.S. State Department, Congress, and the wider public. Scholars who have examined Roosevelt's response to Nazi Germany and the Holocaust have offered little discussion of official policies regarding religion and the armed forces. Even the recent comprehensive study of FDR and the Jews does not consider religion and the armed forces; see Breitman and Lichtman, *FDR and the Jews*.

7. Jacob K. Shankman, "Chaplain Shankman's Letter, February 8, 1945, folder 3, box 10, Shankman Collection, AJA.

8. Stouffer, *American Soldier*, 2: 585.

9. Information Service, Federal Council of the Churches of Christ in America, Vol. 22, No. 17, Saturday, April 24, 1943, file Navy, World War II, box 3, Barney Papers, UMB.

10. Whitehead, *Combat Reporter*, 98–100; T. Segt N. Oberman to Chaplain H. E. Snyder, Post Chapel, Camp J. H. Pendleton, February 24, 1945, file 5, box 18, Snyder Papers, AJA.

11. Harold Saperstein to Frances Saperstein, May 5, 1944, 2, folder 13, box 8, Harold Saperstein Papers, AJA.

12. James Parton to "Dear Family," September 27, 1944, folder 165, box 7, Parton Papers, HUH.

13. Peter F. Bank to Unknown Recipient, February 1945, Copy enclosed in a letter from Peter Bank to Chaplain H. E. Snyder, USNR, folder 5, box 18, Snyder Papers, AJA.

14. Eichhorn, *The GI's Rabbi*, 85.

15. "11 Allies Condemn Nazi War on Jews," *New York Times*, December 18, 1942, 1, 10.

16. For a documentary history of the Morgenthau Plan, see Kimball, *Swords or Ploughshares*.

17. McCreedy, "Planning the Peace," 713–39.

18. Ben Rose to Anne Rose and Charles Gradison Rose, April 16, 1945, file 4L: Correspondence, 1945, Rose Papers, UNC.

19. Lloyd Kalugin, Interview with G. Kurt Piehler and Jason Riley, March 3, 1996, 30, ROHA.

20. Eichhorn, *GIs Rabbi*, 194.

21. John Gray to Elizabeth Gray, April 30, 1945, folder 6: Overseas-Germany 1945, 11-2, box 192, Series VI: Overseas, by Country, Correspondent, and Subject, Undated, 1942–51, I-180, CJH.

22. [Jewish Chaplain, Name Illegible] to Phillip Bernstein (?), Executive Director, Jewish Welfare Board (?) and also addressed "Dear Folks," Augsburg, Germany, May 6, 1945, folder 6, 45–46, box 192, Germany Series VI: Overseas, by Country, Correspondent, and Subject, Undated, 1942–51, I-180, CJH.

23. Townsend, *Mission at Nuremberg*, 208.

24. Eichhorn, *GI's Rabbi*, 178.

25. Eichhorn, *GI's Rabbi*, 188.

26. John Gray to Elizabeth Gray, April 30, 1945, folder 6: Overseas-Germany 1945, Germany, 11, box 192, d Series VI: Overseas, by Country, Correspondent, and Subject, Undated, 1942–51, I-180, CJH.

27. Bob [Weil] to "Dear Mother and Father" [Jacob Weil], May 9, 1945, folder 6: Overseas-Germany 1945, Germany, 14, box 192, Series VI: Overseas, by Country, Correspondent, and Subject, Undated, 1942–51, I-180, CJH.

28. Burton S. Andrus, Col. Cav. to The Recorder, San Diego Commandery, No. 25, K.T., Masonic Temple, San Diego, March 15, 1945, Andrus to The Secretary, Rossville, Chapter No. 149, R.A.M., Rossville, Georgia, folder 29, box 3, Burton C. Andrus Collection, USAHEC.

29. Earl "Bill" Bailey to Polly and Ed, January 11 & 13, 1945, folder 7, box 1, Bailey Papers, FSU.

30. Ben Rose to Anne Rose and "Dear Father" April 2, 1945, Correspondence 1945, folder 4, Rose Papers, UNC.

31. Ben Rose to Anne Rose and "Dear Father" April 22, 1945, Correspondence 1945, folder 4, Rose Papers, UNC.

32. AGO 09-1 (Germany) to Commanding General, U.S. Strategic Air Forces in Europe, March 30, 1945, box 4, RG774, PHS.

33. Proehl, *Stories from Lutheran Chaplains*, 109–10.

34. Nelson, *Moroni and the Swastika*, 244–58.

35. Abraham Haskelton to Phil Bernstein, April 17, 1945, folder 6, box 192, Germany Series VI: Overseas, by Country, Correspondent, and Subject, Undated, 1942–51, I-180, CJH.

36. Harry to Anna, June 10, 1945, 62, folder 6, box 192, Germany Series VI: Overseas, by Country, Correspondent, and Subject, Undated, 1942–51, I-180, CJH.

37. W. M. Addison to Executive Committee, Federal Council of Churches, February 22, 1946, William M. Addison Papers, VMI.

38. Petra Goedde argues that reconciliation between Germany and the United States was promoted by the relationships, which were generally unequal, between German women and American GIs. See Goedde, *GIs and Germans*.

39. Lloyd Kalguin, Interview with G. Kurt Piehler and Jason Riley, March 3, 1996, 33–36, ROHA.

40. Lewis M. Bloom, Interview with G. Kurt Piehler, June 21, 1994, 28–29, ROHA.

41. Chaplain Morris A. Frank to Phillip Bernstein, June 18, 1945, folder 6: Overseas-Germany 1945, Germany, 73–75, box 192, d Series VI: Overseas, by Country, Correspondent, and Subject, Undated, 1942–51, I-180, CJH. National Jewish Welfare Board, "Chaplain Starts Jewish School in Tokyo with Materials from JWB," For Release January 3, 1948, folder 9, box 197, 173, I-180, CJH.

42. Stouffer, *American Soldier*, 2: 571.

43. Sophia University, "In Spite of Defeat of Japan, The Spirit of Sophia Could Prosper," No. 3, https://www.sophia.ac.jp/eng/aboutsophia/history/u9gsah00000007pn -att/websophia_e3.pdf; Crosby, *Battlefield Chaplains*, 249–50.

44. Donald Heilman, Interview with Shaun Illingworth, January 31, 2013, ROHA.

45. On the American occupation of Japan, see James, *The Years of MacArthur*, 3 and Dower, *Embracing Defeat*.

46. Wittner, "MacArthur and the Missionaries," 77–98.

47. Poling, *Mine Eyes Have Seen*, 235–36.

48. Report of the Visit of Bishop O'Hara of Buffalo and Bishop Ready of Columbus to Japan, to Reverend Amelto G. Cicognani, Apostolic Delegate to the United States, [July 1946], box 8, O'Hara Papers, UNDA.

49. Wickersham, *Marine Chaplain*, 140–41.

50. Wickersham, *Marine Chaplain*, 152.

51. Moshe Sachs, Dear Fran, February 9, 1947; "Ceremony," Maebaru High School, Okinawa, February 9, 1947, Moses B. Sachs, folder 7, box 1, Sachs Papers, AJA.

52. Tanaka Koei, Boy Student of the Maebaru High School, Okinawa, February 9, 1947; Seisho Hokama, Superintendent, Maebaru High School, February 1947, Sachs Papers, AJA.

53. Kovner, *Occupying Power*.

54. James Arthur Walther, Chaplain, USNR, to Dr. William Barrow Pugh, September 13, 1945; William Barrow Pugh to Chaplain W. N. Thomas, Chief of Chaplains, Navy Department, October 8, 1945; W. N. Thomas to William Barrow Pugh, October 16, 1945, file 1–45, box 1, RG10, PHS.

55. Wickersham, *Marine Chaplain*, 140–43; "Hit Immorality in Japan," *Christian Century*, 62, no. 51 (December 19, 1945), 1425.

Conclusion

1. Slomovitz, *Fighting Rabbi*, chap. 2.

2. Robert D. Workman to Dr. David De Sola Pool, September 12, 1946, box 8, folder 64, I-259 CJH.

3. E. W. Scott to [Samuel] Cavert, July 16, 1945, file 1, box 5, RG18, PHS.

4. "Ex-Chief Chaplain Becomes a Bishop," *New York Times*, October 12, 1945, 27.

5. Loveland, "Character Education," 795–818.

6. McGreevy, "Thinking on One's Own," 97–131.

7. McCullough, *Truman*.

8. Smith, *Religion in the Oval Office*, 228–59, 516.

9. Ambrose, *Band of Brothers*; Brokaw, *The Greatest Generation*.

10. There is a growing literature on the transition from war to peace experienced by Second World War veterans; see Gambone, *The Greatest Generation Comes Home*; Brooks, *Defining the Peace*; and Coyne, *Marching Home*.

11. Renwick C. Kennedy, "The Conquer," *Christian Century* 63, no. 16 (April 17, 1946): 495–97.

12. Burkhart, *Church and the Returning Soldier*, 27

13. Loveland, *American Evangelicals*, chap. 1.

14. George C. Marshall, Chief of Staff, Memorandum for the Secretary of War, December 18, 1944, file Chaplain, official file, 1940–45, box 2, Correspondence of Secretary of War, RG107, NACP.

15. Charles Burlingham to Honorable Henry L. Stimson, December 5, 1944, and Unsigned, "Memorandum Re: Army Chaplains, file Chaplin, official file, 1940–45, box 2, Correspondence of Secretary of War, RG107, NACP.

16. "Uncensored Dope," *Time* 46, no. 11 (September 10, 1945): 20.

17. "Repudiate Slur of Chaplains," *Christian Century* 62, no. 45 (November 7, 1945): 122.

18. Lt. Comdr. Charles I. Stephenson, CH USNR 295427, to The Commander in Chief of the Army and Navy, November 15, 1945, file 1, box 1, RG18, PHS.

19. Renwick Kennedy, "How Good Were the Army Chaplains? *Christian Century* 63, no. 23 (June 5, 1946): 716–17.

20. Paul Howe to Dr. Robinson, April 18, 1946, file 1–45, box 10, RG10, PHS.

21. Donald Mackay to Parents, September 9, 1945, folder 6, box 10, Mackay Family Papers, EU.

22. Mrs. Edna Riley, Chairman, Non-Church People of America, to Mr. Franklin D. Roosevelt, October 10, 1944, General Press Release, "Resolution Passed by the National Committee of the Non-Church People of America"; General Press Release, "Statement of the National Committee of the Non-Church People of America"; Elsa Maxwell, "Elsa Maxwell's Party Line: The Sacred Right of Skepticism," Clipping; Edna Riley, "A New Voice is Raised: The Case for the Non-Church People," *The Churchman*, Clipping; file Church Matters, 1942–45, box 1, official file, RNY; "Edna Goldsmith Riley, A Former Playwright," *New York Times*, May 5, 1962, 27.

23. Stouffer, *American Soldier*, 2: 611–12.

24. Rabbi Albert G. Baum to Rabbi Jacob K. Shankman, December 4, 1947, folder: General Correspondence, Baum Papers, AJA.

25. Selwyn D. Ruslander, Address, [1945], folder 4, box 24, Ruslander Papers, AJA.

26. Tower, *Fighting the Devil*, 166–72.

27. W. J. Chambers, "The Wasted Years, April 12, 1943–January 6, 1946," Unpublished Memoir, Chambers Collection, FSU.

28. Herberg, *Protestant, Catholic, Jew*, 152.

29. John D. Duggan to Rev. Edward Elson, December 22, 1952, folder 16, box 1, RG253, PHS.

30. John D. Duggan to Rev. Edward Elson, December 22, 1952, folder 16, box 1, RG253, PHS.

31. Smith, *Faith and the Presidency*, 221–58.

32. Loveland, "Character Education," 795–818.

33. Bruscino, *Nation Forged in War*, 206–11.

34. Suid, *Guts and Glory*, 107–8, 114.

35. Kurzman, *No Greater Glory*.

36. Poling, *Your Daddy Did Not Die*.

37. "Families Get the D.S.C. For Heroic Chaplains," *New York Times*, December 20, 1944, 12.

38. Fred Stanley, "Hollywood Reconverts" *New York Times*, January 6, 1946, 40.

39. "Text of Rockefeller Speech at Protestant Dinner," *New York Times*, February 1, 1945, 16.

40. "Dedication of Mural: Halloran General Hospital, Staten Island NY, Monday, October 22, 1945, Program, file Announcements of Memorial Day Exercises, box 3, Records of the Jewish War Veterans of the United States of America, 1-32, CJH.

41. "Pool is Dedicated to Four Chaplains" *New York Times*, July 28, 1948, 17.

42. Poling, *Mine Eyes Have Seen*, chap. 13.

43. Harry, S. Truman, "Address in Philadelphia at the Dedication of the Chapel of the Four Chaplains," February 3, 1951. For a news account of the dedication, see William G. Weart, "Donors View Rites Dedicating Chapel," *New York Times*, February 4, 1951, 61.

44. "Memorial Mass in Newark," *New York Times*, February 5, 1951, 22.

45. Piehler, *Remembering War the American Way*.

46. [John F. Kennedy], Statement, Thursday, January 14, 1960; Daniel A. Poling to John F. Kennedy, March 23, 1960; "The Kennedy Incident," Reprint from *Christian Herald*, Daniel A. Poling, "Editorially Speaking" and "Dr. Poling Answers Your Questions: The John F. Kennedy Incident; John F. Kennedy to Rev. Daniel A. Poling, April 11, 1960; Daniel Poling to John F. Kennedy, April 25, 1960; Daniel Poling to John F.1Kennedy, May 27, 1960; John F. Kennedy to Daniel Poling, July 23, 1960; Papers of John F. Kennedy, Pre-Presidential Papers, Presidential Campaign files, 1960, Religious Issue files of James Wine, 1960, Subject files: Chapel of Four Chaplains, Papers of John F. Kennedy, Pre-Presidential Papers, Presidential Campaign files, 1960, KMA.

Archives

AFHA. Air Force Historical Research Agency, Archives Branch. Maxwell Field, Montgomery, Alabama

    Charles I. Carpenter Papers

    General Board, United States Army, "Report of the Army Chaplain in the European Theater," file 322.01/4

AJA. Jacob Rader Marcus Center of the American Jewish Archives. Hebrew Union College, Cincinnati, Ohio

    Albert G. Baum Papers

    Solomon B. Freehof

    Harry R. Glixon, Small Collections

    Richard C. Hertz Papers

    Morris N. Kertzer Papers

    Bertram W. Korn Papers

    David Lefkowitz Papers

    Eugene J. Lipman Papers

    Judah Nadich Papers

    Selwyn D. Ruslander Papers

    Moses B. Sachs Papers

    Harold I. Saperstein Papers

    Samuel Sandmel Collection

    Jacob Shankman Papers

    Abraham Shafer box, Small Collections

    Phineas Smoller Papers

    Herman E. Snyder Papers

    Frank L. Weil Papers

BC. John J. Burns Library. Boston College, Chestnut Hill, Massachusetts

    Richard G. Shea Papers

BRU. Krupp Library. Bryant University, Smithfield, Rhode Island

    U.S. Women and World War II Letter Writing Project

CJH. Center for Jewish History. American Jewish Historical Society, New York City

1-32 Records of the Jewish War Veterans of the United States of America

1-180 National Jewish Welfare Board, Army-Navy Division Records

1-249 National Jewish Welfare Board Military Chaplaincy Records

1-337 National Jewish Welfare Board Records

P-34 Milton Weill Papers

P-910 Morris Gordon Papers

CUA. American Catholic History Research Center and University Archives. Catholic University of America, Washington DC

National Catholic Community Services, Board of Trustees, minutes and related materials, 1932–81

EU. Stuart A. Rose Manuscript Library, Archives and Rare Book Library. Emory University, Atlanta, Georgia

Edward George and Beulah Mason Mackay Family Papers

FSU. Institute on World War II and the Human Experience. Florida State University, Tallahassee

Jason M. Austin Collection

W. J. Chambers Collection

Earl L. Bailey Collection

Melvin James Kelly Collection

Henry John Perner Collection

GML. George C. Marshall Library. Lexington, Virginia

William R. Arnold Papers

HUD. Andover-Harvard Divinity School Library. Harvard University, Cambridge, Massachusetts

bMS 392: Universalist Church of America, Chaplain Records, 1921–56

bMS 11130: American Unitarian Association, War Service Council, Administrative Subject files, 1942–43, Chaplains Correspondence

bMS 11043: American Unitarian Association Board of Directors, Meeting Records, 1942–46

Howard Schomer Papers

HUH. Houghton, Houghton Library. Harvard University, Cambridge, Massachusetts

James Parton Papers

HUS. Schlesinger Library. Harvard University, Cambridge, Massachusetts

Nona Baldwin Brown Papers

Bertha Marie (Strittmatter) Clark Papers

Harriet Adams Earhart Papers

Helen Beggs Eisold Papers

Katherine Keene Papers

Florence Julie Lillibridge Papers

Harriette Gould Myerson Papers

Hildegard Peplau Papers

Hazel Hitson Weidman Papers

KMA. John F. Kennedy Library. Boston, Massachusetts

Papers of John F. Kennedy, Prepresidential Papers, https://www.jfklibrary
.org/asset-viewer/archives/JFKCAMP1960/1015/JFKCAMP1960-1015-003

MBE. Mary Baker Eddy Library. Boston, Massachusetts
    Organizational Records of the First Church of Christ, Scientist

NACP. U.S. National Archives. College Park, Maryland
    RG107 Records of the Office of Secretary of War
    RG165 Records of the War Department General and Special Staffs
    RG247 Records of the Office of Chief of Chaplains
    RG330 Records of the Office of Secretary of Defense

NADC. U.S. National Archives. Washington DC
    RG24 Records of the Bureau of Naval Personnel

NASL. U.S. National Archives. St. Louis, Missouri
    RG237 Records of the Office of Chief of Chaplains—201 Chaplain files

NYPLS. Manuscript, Archives, and Rare Book Division, Schomburg Center for
    Research in Black Culture, New York Public Library. New York City
        Henry C. Bunton Papers
        Booker T. Washington Center for Servicemen Papers

PHS. Presbyterian Historical Society. Philadelphia, Pennsylvania
    RG10 Presbyterian Church in the USA. Special Committee on Camp and
    Church Activities Records
    RG18 Federal Council of the Churches of Christ in America Records
    RG253 Edward L. Elson Papers
    RG774 Howard M. Wilson Papers

PTS. Princeton Theological Seminary Library. Princeton, New Jersey
    Carl McIntire Papers

RAC. Rockefeller Archive Center. Sleepy Hollow, New York
    Office of Messrs. Rockefeller Records
    John D. Rockefeller Jr. Personal Papers, Series P. Welfare Interests–General
    (FA335)

RNY. Franklin D. Roosevelt Library. Hyde Park, New York
    Map Room papers
    Official files
    President's personal files
    President's secretary's file

ROHA. Rutgers Oral History Archives. Rutgers University, New Brunswick, New
    Jersey, https://oralhistory.rutgers.edu/

RUL. Special Collections and University Archives, Alexander Library. Rutgers Uni-
    versity, New Brunswick, New Jersey
        Ardath W. Burks Papers

SBH. Southern Baptist Historical Library and Archives. Nashville, Tennessee
        Norman W. Cox Papers
        McCready-Orr Family Collection
        T. W. Medearis Papers

SLL. University Archives, St. Louis University Library. St. Louis, Missouri

John R. Bradstreet Manuscript Collection

UCSB. University of California, Santa Barbara

American Presidency Project, https://www.presidency.ucsb.edu/

UHM. Archives and Manuscript Department, University of Hawaii at Manoa Library

Hiro Higuchi Papers, https://manoa.hawaii.edu/library/research/collections/archives/manuscript-collections/japanese-american-veterans-collection/digital-resources-higuchi-wartime-correspondence/

UMA. United Methodist Archives. Drew University, Madison, New Jersey

Division of Chaplains and Related Ministries, Records of the United Methodist Church, General Board of Higher Education and Ministry

UMB. Bentley Historical Library, University of Michigan, Ann Arbor

Roger Warren Barney Papers

Edward W. Blakeman Papers

Richard Charles Boys Papers

Albert Joseph Engel Jr. Papers

Gilbert and Jean Seeley Ketcham Papers

Stanley M. Swinton Papers

Kenneth Vance Papers

Mark T. Warner Papers

UNC. Southern Historical Collection, The Wilson Library. University of North Carolina, Chapel Hill

Ben Lacy Rose Papers

UNCG. Martha Blakeney Hodges Special Collections and University Archives, UNCG Library. University of North Carolina, Greensboro

Women Veterans Historical Project, http://libcdm1.uncg.edu/cdm/landingpage/collection/WVHP/

UNCW. Special Collections, Randall Library. University of North Carolina, Wilmington

Centuries of Service: Military Chaplains, https://library.uncw.edu/chaplains/

UNDA. University of Notre Dame Archives, Hesburgh Libraries. South Bend, Indiana

John Francis O'Hara Papers

USAFA. Clark Special Collections Branch, McDermott Library. U.S. Air Force Academy, Colorado Springs, Colorado

Albert P. Clark Papers

USAHEC. U.S. Army Heritage and Education Center. Carlisle Barracks, Pennsylvania

Burton C. Andrus Collection

Sam J. Agent Collection

Benjamin O. Davis Sr. Collection

Chester B. Hansen Collection

Carl B. Montgomery Papers

Frederick Osborn Papers

World War II Veterans Survey

UTCWS. Center for the Study of War and Society. University of Tennessee, Knoxville

Oral History Project, https://csws.utk.edu/oral-history-project/read-an-interview/

UTS. Union Theological Seminary, Burke Library. New York City
    Sam and Dorothy Franklin Papers
VMI. VMI Archives, Preston Library. Virginia Military Institute, Lexington, Virginia
    William Addison Collection

Published Works

89 Cong. Rec. A5115 (November 24, 1943) (statement by Representative Reed).

Abzug, Robert H. *Inside the Vicious Heart: Americans and the Liberation of Nazi Concentration Camps*. New York: Oxford University Press, 1985.

Alpers, Benjamin L. "This Is the Army: Imagining a Democratic Military in World War II." *Journal of American History* 85 (June 1998): 129–63.

Ambrose, Stephen E. *Band of Brothers: E Company, 506th Regiment, 101st Airborne from Normandy to Hitler's Eagle's Nest*. New York: Simon and Schuster, 1992.

Aquila, Phillip L., ed. *Home Front Soldier: The Story of a GI and His Italian American Family During World War II*. Albany: State University of New York Press, 1999.

Archer, Emerald M. *Women, Warfare and Representation: American Servicewomen in the Twentieth Century*. London: Bloomsbury Academic, 2017.

Atkins, Elisha. "A Soldier's Second Thoughts." In *Religion of Soldier and Sailor*, edited by Willard L. Sperry, 99–115. Cambridge: Harvard University Press, 1945.

Atkinson, Rick. *An Army at Dawn: The War in North Africa, 1942–1943*. New York: Henry Holt, 2002.

———. *The Guns at Last Light: The War in Western Europe, 1944–1945*. New York: Henry Holt, 2013.

Bailey, Beth, and David Farber. *The First Strange Place: The Alchemy of Race and Sex in World War II Hawaii*. Baltimore: Johns Hopkins University Press, 1994.

Baker, Kelly J. *Gospel According to the Klan: The KKK's Appeal to Protestant America, 1915–1930*. Lawrence: University Press of Kansas, 2011.

Bard, Michael G. *Forgotten Victims: The Abandonment of Americans in Hitler's Camps*. Boulder: Westview, 1994.

Barlow, Keith, ed. *Bunker's War: The World War II Diary of Col. Paul D. Bunker*. Novato CA: Presidio, 1996.

Beard, Charles A. *American Foreign Policy in the Making, 1932–1940: A Study in Responsibilities*. New Haven: Yale University Press, 1946.

Becker, Carl M., and Robert G. Thobaben. *Common Warfare: Parallel Memoirs by Two World War II GIs in the Pacific*. Jefferson NC: McFarland, 1992.

Bendersky, Joseph W. *The "Jewish Threat": Anti-Semitic Politics of the U.S. Army*. New York: Basic Books, 2000.

Benjamin, Harry. "Morals Versus Morale in Wartime." In *Morals in Wartime* edited by Victor Robinson, 117–203. New York: Publishers Foundation, 1943.

Bennett, Pamela, and Tom Holm. "Indians in the Military." In *Indians in Contemporary Society*, edited by Garrick A. Bailey, 10–18. Washington DC: Smithsonian Institution Press, 2008.

Bennett, Scott H. "American Pacifism, 'the Greatest Generation,' and World War II." In *The United States and the Second World War: New Perspectives on Diplomacy,*

War, and the Home Front, edited by G. Kurt Piehler and Sidney Pash, 259–92. New York: Fordham University Press, 2010.

———. *Army GI, Pacifist CO: The World War II Letters of Frank and Albert Dietrich*. New York: Fordham University Press, 2005.

———. *Radical Pacifism: The War Resisters Leagues and Ghandian Nonviolence in America, 1915–1963*. Syracuse NY: Syracuse University Press, 2003.

Bergsma, H. L. *The Pioneers: A Monograph on the First Two Black Chaplains in the Chaplain Corps of the United States Navy*. Washington DC: Government Printing Office, 1980.

Bernstein, Alison R. *American Indians and World War II*. Norman: University of Oklahoma Press, 1991.

Berube, Allan. *Coming Out Under Fire: The History of Gay Men and Women in World War Two*. New York: Free Press, 1990.

Biggs, Bradley. *The Triple Nickels: America's First All-Black Paratroop Unit*. Hamden CT: Archon, 1986.

Blum, John Morton. *From the Morgenthau Diaries*. 3 vols. Boston: Houghton Mifflin, 1959–1967.

———. *V Was for Victory: Politics and the American Culture During World War II*. New York: Harcourt Brace, 1976.

Blumenson, Martin. "Did 'SLAM' Guess at Fire Ratios? Probably: A Legend Remembered." *Army* 39 (June 1989): 16–21.

Bodnar, John. *The "Good War" in American Memory*. Baltimore: Johns Hopkins University Press, 2010.

Bolt, Robert. "Franklin Delano Roosevelt, Senior Warden, St. James Church at Hyde Park, New York." *Historical Magazine of the Protestant Episcopal Church* 54, no. 1 (March 1985): 91–99.

Bourque, Stephen Alan. *Beyond the Beach: The Allied War Against France*. Annapolis MD: Naval Institute Press, 2018.

Braddock, Paul F. *Dog Tags: A History of the American Military Identification Tags, 1861–2002*. Chicora PA: Mechling, 2003.

Brands, H. W. *"Traitor to His Class": The Privileged Life and Radical Presidency of Franklin D. Roosevelt*. New York: Doubleday, 2008.

Brandt, Allan M. *No Magic Bullet: A Social History of Venereal Disease Since 1880*. New York: Oxford University Press, 1985.

Brandt, Nat. *Harlem at War: The Black Experience in WWII*. New York: Syracuse University Press, 1996.

Breitman, Richard, and Alan M. Kraut. *American Refugee Policy and European Jewry, 1933–1945*. Bloomington: Indiana University Press, 1987.

Breitman, Richard, and Allan J. Lichtman. *FDR and the Jews*. Cambridge MA: Belknap, 2013.

Brengle, Samuel Logan. "Killing in Battle: Is it Murder." *The Link* 1 (June 1943): 9–11.

Brinkley, Alan. *Voices of Protest: Huey Long, Father Coughlin, and the Great Depression*. New York: Knopf, 1982.

Bristow, Nancy K. *Making Men Moral: Social Engineering During the Great War.* New York: New York University Press, 1996.

Brokaw, Tom. *The Greatest Generation.* New York: Random House, 1998.

Brooks, Jennifer E. *Defining the Peace: World War II Veterans, Race, and the Remaking of Southern Political Tradition.* Chapel Hill: University of North Carolina Press, 2004.

Bruscino, Thomas A. *A Nation Forged in War: How World War II Taught Americans to Get Along.* Knoxville: University of Tennessee Press, 2010.

Budd, Richard M. *Serving Two Masters: The Development of American Military Chaplaincy, 1860–1920.* Lincoln: University of Nebraska Press, 2002.

Budreau, Lisa M. *Bodies of War: World War I and the Politics of Commemoration in America, 1919–1933.* New York: New York University Press, 2010.

Builder, Carl H. *The Mask of War: American Military Styles in Strategy and Analysis.* Baltimore: Johns Hopkins University Press, 1989.

Burkhart, Roy A. *The Church and the Returning Soldier.* New York: Harper & Brothers, 1945.

Burnham, John C. "The Encounter of Christian Theology with Deterministic Psychology and Psychoanalysis." *Bulletin of the Menninger Clinic* 49, no. 4 (1985): 321–52.

Burns, James MacGregor. *Roosevelt: The Lion and the Fox.* New York: Harcourt, Brace, Jovanovich, 1956.

———. *Roosevelt: The Soldier of Freedom, 1940–1945.* New York: Harcourt, Brace, Jovanovich, 1970.

Butler, Jon. *Awash in a Sea of Faith: Christianizing the American People.* Cambridge MA: Harvard University Press, 1990.

Byerly, Carol R. *Fever of War: The Influenza Epidemic in the U.S. Army during World War I.* New York: New York University Press, 2005.

Byers, Andrew. *The Sexual Economy of War: Discipline and Desire in the U.S. Army.* Ithaca NY: Cornell University Press, 2019.

Cameron, Craig M. *American Samurai: Myth, Imagination, and the Conduct of Battle in the First Marine Division, 1941–1951.* New York: Cambridge University Press, 1994.

Cahn, Edward L., dir. *For God and Country.* 1943. U.S. Army Air Force Production Unit. Online film posted by the Ronald Reagan Presidential Library. https://www.reaganlibrary.gov.

Campbell, D'Ann. "'Women in Combat': The World War II Experience in the United States, Great Britain, Germany, and the Soviet Union." *Journal of Military History* 57, no. 2 (April 1993): 301–23.

Cane, Lawrence. *Fighting Fascism in Europe: The World War II Letters of an American Veteran of the Spanish Civil War.* Edited by David E. Cane, Judy Barrett Litoff, and David C. Smith. New York: Fordham University Press, 2003.

Carlson, Lewis H. *We Were Each Other's Prisoners: An Oral History of World War II American and German Prisoners of War.* New York: Basic, 1997.

Chambers, John Whiteclay. *To Raise an Army: The Draft Comes to Modern America.* New York: Free Press, 1987.

Chester, Robert K. "'Negroes' Number One Hero': Doris Miller, Pearl Harbor and Retroactive Multiculturalism in World War II Remembrance." *American Quarterly* 65, no. 1 (March 2013): 31–61.

Christian Science Board of Directors. *The Story of the Christian Science Wartime Activities, 1939–1946.* Boston: Christian Science, 1947.

Clark, David L., and Bart J. Kowallis. "The Fate of Davao Penal Colony #502 'Branch' of the LDS Church, 1944." *BYU Studies Quarterly* 50, no. 4 (2011): 109–39.

Coffin, Lesley L. *Lew Ayres: Hollywood's Conscientious Objector.* Jackson: University Press of Mississippi, 2012.

Coffman, Edward M. *The Old Army: A Portrait of the American Army in Peacetime, 1784–1898.* New York: Oxford University Press, 1986.

———. *The Regulars: The American Army, 1898–1941.* Cambridge MA: Belknap, 2004.

Cole, Wayne S. *Roosevelt and the Isolationists, 1932–45.* Lincoln: University of Nebraska Press, 1983.

Cooney, John. *The American Pope: The Life and Times of Francis Cardinal Spellman.* New York: Times Books, 1984.

Cooperman, Jessica. *Making Judaism Safe for America: World War I and the Origins of Religious Pluralism.* New York: New York University Press, 2018.

Corpening, Albert N. "There Is No Such Commandment." *The Link* 2 (December 1944): 19–20.

Cowdrey, Albert E. *Fighting for Life: American Military Medicine in World War II.* New York: Free Press, 1994.

Coyne, Kevin. *Marching Home: To War and Back with the Men of One American Town.* New York: Penguin, 2003.

Crane, Conrad C. *Bombs, Cities, and Civilians: American Airpower Strategy in World War II.* Lawrence: University Press of Kansas, 1993.

Cripps, Thomas. *Making Movies Black: The Hollywood Message Movie from World War II to the Civil Rights Era.* New York: Oxford University Press, 1993.

Crosby, Donald F. *Battlefield Chaplains: Catholic Priests in World War II.* Lawrence: University Press of Kansas, 1994.

Daddis, Gregory A., ed. *Fighting in the Great Crusade: An 8th Infantry Artillery Officer in the Great Crusade in World War II.* Baton Rouge: Louisiana State University Press, 2002.

Darnton, Christopher. "Archives and Inference: Documentary Evidence in Case Study Research and Debate over U.S. Entry into World War II." *International Security* 42, no. 3 (Winter 2017–18): 84–126.

DeBenedetti, Charles. *The Peace Reform in American History.* Bloomington: Indiana University Press, 1980.

DeSalvo, Louise. *Chasing Ghosts: A Memoir of a Father, Gone to War.* New York: Fordham University Press, 2016.

D'Este, Carlo. *Patton: A Genius for War.* New York: Harper Perennial, 1996.

Divine, Robert. *Roosevelt and World War II.* Baltimore: Johns Hopkins University Press, 1969.

Doenecke, Justus. *Storm on the Horizon: The Challenge to American Intervention, 1939–1941*. Lanham MD: Rowman and Littlefield, 2000.

Doss, Frances May. *Desmond Doss, Conscientious Objector: The Story of an Unlikely Hero*. Nampa ID: Pacific, 2005.

Doubler, Michael D. *Closing with the Enemy: How GIs Fought the War in Europe, 1944–1945*. Lawrence: University Press of Kansas, 1994.

Dower, John W. *Embracing Defeat: Japan in the Wake of World War II*. New York: W. W. Norton, 1999.

———. *War without Mercy: Race and Power in the Pacific War*. New York: Pantheon, 1986.

Doyle, Robert C. *Voices from Captivity: Interpreting the American POW Narrative*. Lawrence: University Press of Kansas, 1994.

Drury, Clifford. *The History of the Chaplain Corps, United States Navy, Vol. 1, 1939–1949*. Washington DC: Government Printing Office, 1949.

———. *The History of the Chaplain Corps, United States Navy, Vol. 2, 1939–1949*. Washington DC: Government Printing Office, 1949.

———. *U.S. Navy Chaplains, 1778–1945: Biographical and Service-Record Sketches of 3,353 Chaplains*. Washington DC: Government Printing Office, 1948.

Dunn, James A. *On Board the USS Mason: The World War II Diary of James A. Dunn*. Edited by Mansel G. Blackford. Columbus: Ohio State University Press, 1996.

Earley, Charity Adams. *One Woman's Army: A Black Officer Remembers the WAC*. College Station: Texas A&M University, 1989.

Ebel, Jonathan. *Faith in the Fight: Religion and the American Soldier in the Great War*. Princeton NJ: Princeton University Press, 2010.

Eichhorn, David Max. *The GI's Rabbi: World War II Letters of David Max Eichhorn*. Edited by Greg Palmer and Mark S. Zaid. Lawrence: University Press of Kansas, 2004.

Eisenhower, Dwight D. *The Papers of Dwight David Eisenhower, Volume I, The War Years*. Baltimore: Johns Hopkins University Press, 1979.

Eldrige, Robert D. *Iwo Jima and the Bonin Islands in U.S. Japan Relations: American Strategy, Japanese Territory, and the Islanders In-Between*. Quantico VA: Marine Corps University Press, 2014.

Eliot, Marc. *Reagan: The Hollywood Years*. New York: Harmony, 2008.

Erenberg, Lewis A. "Swing Goes to War: Glenn Miller and the Popular Music of World War II." In *The War and American Culture: Society and Consciousness During World War II*, edited by Lewis A. Erenberg and Susan E. Hirsch, 144–68. Chicago: University of Chicago Press, 1996.

Felber, Abraham, Franklin S. Felber, and William H. Bartsch. *The Old Breed of Marine: A World War II Diary*. Jefferson NC: McFarland, 2003.

Ferngren, Gary B. *Medicine and Religion: A Historical Introduction*. Baltimore: Johns Hopkins University Press, 2014.

Feuer, A. B., ed. *Bilibid Diary: The Secret Notebooks of Commander Thomas Hayes POW, the Philippines, 1942–45*. Hamden CT: Archon/Shoestring, 1987.

Fisher, Jeremy. "A War for Liberty: On the Law of Conscientious Objection." In *The Cambridge History of the Second World War, Volume III: Total War: Economy, Society and Culture*, edited by Michael Geyer and Adam Tooze, 447–74. New York: Cambridge University Press, 2015.

Fletcher, Marvin. *America's First Black General: Benjamin O. Davis, Sr. 1880–1970*. Lawrence: University Press of Kansas, 1989.

Flynn, George Q. *The Draft, 1940–1973*. Lawrence: University Press of Kansas, 1993.

Ford, Nancy Gentile. *Americans All! Foreign-Born Soldiers in World War I*. College Station: Texas A&M University Press, 2001.

Forgy, Howell M. *". . . And Pass the Ammunition"*. Edited by Jack S. McDowell. New York: D. Appleton-Century, 1944.

Foy, David Alden. "'For You the War Is Over': The Treatment and Life of United States Army and Army Air Corps Personnel Interned in POW Camps in Germany, 1942–1945." PhD diss., University of Arkansas, 1981.

Fujita, Frank. *Foo: A Japanese-American Prisoner of the Rising Sun: The Secret Prison Diary of Frank "Foo" Fujita*. Denton: University of North Texas, 1993.

Fussell, Paul. *Wartime: Understanding and Behavior in the Second World War*. New York: Oxford University Press, 1989.

Gabriel, Richard A., ed. *Military Psychiatry: A Comparative Perspective*. New York: Greenwood Press, 1986.

Gallagher, Charles R.. *Vatican Secret Diplomacy: Joseph P. Hurley and Pope Pius XII*. New Haven CT: Yale University Press, 2008.

Gambone, Michael D. *The Greatest Generation Comes Home: The Veteran in American Society*. College Station: Texas A&M University Press, 2005.

Gerstle, Gary. *American Crucible: Race and Nation in the Twentieth Century*. Princeton NJ: Princeton University Press, 2001.

Ginzberg, Eli. *Breakdown and Recovery*. New York: Columbia University Press, 1959.

Glass, Charles. *The Deserters: A Hidden History of World War II*. New York: Penguin, 2013.

Goedde, Petra. *gis and Germans: Culture, Gender, and Foreign Relations, 1945–1949*. New Haven CT: Yale University Press, 2003.

Goldman, David I. "'Charlie' Chaplains in the Great War: Chaplains' Experiences in the U.S. Army, 1917–1919." *Journal of Military History* 84, no. 2 (April 2020): 395–426.

Gray, J. Glenn. *The Warriors: Reflections on Men in Battle*. New York: Harper and Row, 1970; rpt. Lincoln: University of Nebraska Press, 1998.

Greene, Rebecca. *Breaking Point: The Ironic Evolution of American Psychiatry in World War II*. New York: Fordham University Press, 2022.

Gregg, John A. *Of Men and of Arms: Chronological Travel Record of Bishop John A. Gregg With Messages of Cheer and Good Will to Negro Soldiers of All War Fronts*. Nashville: A.M.E. Sunday School Union Press, 1945.

Gregory, W. Edgar. "The Chaplain and Mental Hygiene." *American Journal of Sociology* 52, no. 5 (March 1947): 420–23.

Grob, Gerald R. "World War II and American Psychiatry." *The Psychohistory Review* 19, no. 1 (Fall 1990): 41–69.

Gushwa, Robert. *The Best and Worst of Times: The United States Army Chaplaincy, 1920–1945*. Washington DC: Office of the Chief of Chaplains, Department of the Army, 1977.

Hale, Nathan G. *The Rise and Crisis of Psychoanalysis in the United States: Freud and the Americans, 1917–1985*. New York: Oxford University Press, 1995.

Hall, Gwendolyn Midlo, ed. *Love, War, and the 96th Engineers (Colored): The World War II New Guinea Diaries of Captain Hyman Samuelson*. Urbana: University of Illinois Press, 1995.

Hamm, Thomas, Margaret Marconi, Gretchen Kleinhen Salinsas, and Benjamin Whitman. "The Decline of Quaker Pacifism in the Twentieth Century: Indiana Yearly Meeting of Friends as a Case Study." *Indiana Magazine of History* 96, no. 1 (March 2000): 44–71.

Hand, Samuel B. *Counsel and Advise: A Political Biography of Samuel I. Rosenman*. New York: Garland, 1979.

Harlow, Jules, ed. *A Prayerbook for Shabbat, Festivals, and Weekdays*. New York: Rabbinical Assembly and the United Synagogue of Conservative Judaism, 1985.

Harrod, Frederick S. *Manning the New Navy: The Development of a Modern Naval Enlisted Force, 1899–1940*. Westport CT: Greenwood, 1978.

Hasselbring, Andrew S. "American Prisoners in the Third Reich." PhD diss., Temple University, 1990.

Hata, Ikuhiko. "From Consideration to Contempt: The Changing Nature of Japanese Military and Popular Perceptions of Prisoners of War Through the Ages." In *Prisoners of War and their Captors in World War II*, edited by Bob Moore and Kent Fedorowich 253–76. Oxford: Berg, 1996.

Hegarty, Marilyn E. *Victory Girls, Khaki-Wackies, and Patriotutes: The Regulation of Female Sexuality During World War II*. New York: New York University Press, 2008.

Heinrichs, Waldo. *Threshold of War: Franklin D. Roosevelt and American Entry into World War II*. New York: Oxford University Press, 1988.

Hendrick, Charles. "Race Relations and the Contributions of Minority Troops in Alaska: A Challenge to the Status Quo." In *Alaska at War, 1941–1945: The Forgotten War Remembered*, edited by Fern Chandonnet, 277–83. Anchorage: Alaska at War Committee, 1995,

Herberg, Will. *Protestant, Catholic, Jew: An Essay in American Religious Sociology*. 1955. Reprint, Chicago: University of Chicago Press, 1983.

Holiday, Samuel, and Robert S. McPherson. *Under the Eagle: Samuel Holiday, Navajo Code Talker*. Norman: University of Oklahoma Press, 2013.

Honeywell, Roy John. *Chaplains of the United States Army*. Washington: Office of the Chief of Chaplains, Department of the Army, 1958.

Hutchison, William R. *Religious Pluralism in America: The Contentious History of a Founding Ideal*. New Haven CT: Yale University Press, 2003.

James, D. Clayton. *South to Bataan, North to Mukden: The Prison Diary of Brigadier General W. E. Brougher*. Athens: University of Georgia Press, 1971.

———. *The Years of MacArthur: Volume 2: 1941–1945*. Boston: Houghton Mifflin, 1975.

———. *The Years of MacArthur, Volume 3: Triumph and Disaster*. Boston: Houghton Mifflin, 1985.

Johnson, Franklyn A. *One More Hill*. New York: Funk and Wagnalls, 1949.

Kelly, Carol Adele, ed. *Voices of My Comrades: America's Reserve Officers Remember World War II*. New York: Fordham University Press, 2007.

Kennett, Lee. *G.I.: The American Soldier in World War II*. New York: Charles Scribner's Sons, 1987.

Kernan, Alvin. *Crossing the Line: A Bluejacket's World War II Odyssey*. Annapolis MD: Naval Institute Press, 1994.

Kertzer, Morris N. *With an H on my Dog Tag*. New York: Behrman House, 1947.

Kimball, Warren F. *Swords or Ploughshares? The Morgenthau Plan for Defeated Nazi Germany, 1943–1946*. Philadelphia: J. B. Lippincott, 1976.

Kindsvatter, Peter S. *American Soldiers: Ground Combat in the World Wars, Korea, and Vietnam*. Lawrence: University Press of Kansas, 2003.

Knapp, Gretchen. "Experimental Social Policymaking during World War II: The United Service Organizations (USO) and American War-Community Services (AWCS)." *Journal of Public Policy* 12, no. 3 (2000): 321–38.

Kochavi, Arieh J. *Confronting Captivity: Britain and the United States and Their POWs in Nazi Germany*. Chapel Hill: University of North Carolina Press, 2005.

Koenig, Harold G. "Religion and Medicine I: Historical Background and Reasons for Separation." *International Journal of Psychiatry in Medicine* 30, no. 4 (2000): 385.

Kovner, Sarah. *Occupying Power: Sex Workers and Servicemen in Postwar Japan*. Stanford CA: Stanford University Press, 2012.

Krehbiel, Nicholas A. *General Lewis B. Hershey and Conscientious Objection during World War II*. Columbia: University of Missouri Press, 2012.

Kurzman, Dan. *No Greater Glory: The Four Immortal Chaplains and the Sinking of the Dorchester in World War II*. New York: Random House, 2004.

Leab, Daniel J. "The Fighting 69th: An Ambiguous Portrait of Isolationism/Interventionism." In *Hollywood's World War I: Motion Picture Images*, edited by Peter C. Rollins and John E. O'Connor, 101–120. Bowling Green OH: Bowling Green State University Popular Press, 1997.

Lee, Ulysses. *The Employment of Negro Troops*. Washington DC: Office of the Chief of Military History, 19.

Linderman, Gerald F. *Embattled Courage: The Experience of the Civil War*. New York: Free Press, 1987.

———. *The World Within War: America's Combat Experience in World War II*. New York: Free Press, 1997.

Loveland, Anne C. *American Evangelicals and the U.S. Military, 1942–1993*. Baton Rouge: Louisiana State University Press, 1996.

———. "Character Education in the US Army, 1947–1977." *Journal of Military History* 64, no. 3 (July 2000): 795–818.

Lucas, George Blanchard. *Every Other Day: Letters from the Pacific.* Annapolis MD: Naval Institute Press, 1995.

Lukasik, Sebastian H. "Doughboys, the YMCA, and the Moral Economy of Sacrifice in the First World War." *Journal of Military History* 84 (July 2020): 774–97.

MacCarthy, Esther Josephine. "The Catholic Periodical Press and Issues of War and Peace, 1914–1946." PhD diss., Stanford University, 1977.

MacKenzie, S. P. *Flying Against Fate: Superstition and Allied Aircrews in World War II.* Lawrence: University Press of Kansas, 2017.

———. "The Treatment of Prisoners of War in World War II." *Journal of Modern History* 66, no. 3 (September 1994): 487–520.

Magden, Robert E. "Attitudes of the American Religious Press Toward the Soviet Union." PhD diss., University of Washington, 1964.

Manchester, William. *Goodbye Darkness: A Memoir of the Pacific War.* Boston: Little, Brown, 1980.

Mansoor, Peter. *The GI Offensive in Europe: The Triumph of American Infantry Divisions, 1943–1945.* Lawrence: University Press of Kansas, 1999.

Marchione, Margherita. *Crusade of Charity: Pius XII and POWs (1939–1945).* New York: Paulist, 2006.

Marks, Frederick. *Wind Over Sand: The Diplomacy of Franklin Roosevelt.* Athens: University of Georgia Press, 1988.

Marshall, George C. *The Papers of George C. Marshall: Selected World War II Correspondence.* Edited by Robert E. Lester. Bethesda MD: University Publications of America, 1992.

———. *The Papers of George Catlett Marshall, Volume 3, "The Right Man for the Job": December 7, 1941—May 31, 1943.* Edited by Larry I. Bland. Baltimore: Johns Hopkins University Press, 1991.

Marshall, S. L. A. *Men Against Fire: The Problem of Battle Command in Future War.* 1947; rpt. Norman: University of Oklahoma Press, 2000.

Mason, Theodore C. *Battleship Sailor.* Annapolis: Naval Institute Press, 1982.

Masuda, Minoru. *Letters from the 442nd: The World War II Correspondence of a Japanese American Medic.* Edited by Hana Masuda and Dianne Bridgman. Seattle: University of Washington Press, 2008.

Matthews, Mark. *Smoke Jumping on the Western Fire Line: Conscientious Objectors During World War II.* Norman: University of Oklahoma Press, 2006.

McCaffrey, James M. *Going for Broke: Japanese American Soldiers in the War against Nazi Germany.* Norman: University of Oklahoma Press, 2013.

McCreedy, Kenneth O. "Planning the Peace: Operation Eclipse and the Occupation of Germany." *Journal of Military History* 65, no. 3 (July 2001): 713–39.

McCullough, David. *Truman.* New York: Simon and Schuster, 1992.

McDannell, Colleen. *Picturing Faith: Photography and the Great Depression.* New Haven CT: Yale University Press, 2004.

McGreevy, John T. "Thinking on One's Own: Catholicism in the American Intellectual Imagination, 1928–1960." *Journal of American History* 84, no. 1 (June 1997): 97–131.

McGuire, Phillip. *Taps for a Jim Crow Army: Letters from Black Soldiers in World War II*. Santa Barbara CA: ABC-Clio, 1983.

McGuire, William A. *The Captain Wears A Cross*. New York: Macmillan, 1943.

McLaurin, Melton A. *The Marines of Montford Point: America's First Black Marines*. Chapel Hill: University of North Carolina Press, 2007.

McManus, John C. *Hell Before Their Very Eyes: American Soldiers Liberate Concentration Camps in Germany, April 1945*. Baltimore: Johns Hopkins University Press, 2015.

McWilliams, Tennant. *The Chaplain's Conflict: Good and Evil in a War Hospital, 1943–1945*. College Station: Texas A&M University Press, 2010.

Meadows, William C. *The Comanche Code Talkers of World War II*. Austin: University of Texas Press, 2002.

———. *Kiowa, Apache, and Comanche Military Societies: Enduring Veterans, 1800 to the Present* Austin: University of Texas Press, 1999.

———. *Kiowa Military Societies: Ethnohistory and Ritual*. Norman: University of Oklahoma Press, 2010.

Meyer, Leisa D. *Creating GI Jane: Sexuality and Power in the Women's Army Corps during World War II*. New York: Columbia University Press, 1996.

Moore, Brenda L. *To Serve My Country, To Serve My Race: The Story of the Only African American WACs Stationed Overseas during World War II*. New York: New York University Press, 1996.

Moore, Deborah Dash, *GI Jews: How World War II Changed a Generation*. Cambridge MA: Harvard University Press, 2004.

Morgenthau, Henry. *Mostly Morgenthaus: A Family History*. New York: Ticknor and Fields, 1991.

Morris, Edmund. *Dutch: A Memoir of Ronald Reagan*. New York: Random House, 1999.

Morriss, Mack. *South Pacific Diary, 1942–1943*. Edited by Ronnie Day. Lexington: University Press of Kentucky, 1996.

Murray, Paul. "Blacks and the Draft: A History of Institutional Racism." *Journal of Black Studies* 2, no. 1 (September 1971): 57–75.

Muth, Jorg. *Command Culture: Officer Education in the U.S. Army and the German Armed Forces, 1901–1940, and the Consequences for World War II*. Denton: University of North Texas, 2011.

Myers, Sarah. "'A Weapon Waiting to Be Used': The Women Airforce Service Pilots of World War II." PhD diss., Texas Tech University, 2014.

Nalty, Bernard C. *Strength for the Fight: A History of Black Americans in the Military*. New York: Free Press, 1986.

Nasaw, David. *The Patriarch: The Remarkable Life and Turbulent Times of Joseph P. Kennedy*. New York: Penguin, 2012.

Nelson, David C. *Moroni and the Swastika: Mormons in Nazi Germany*. Norman: University of Oklahoma Press, 2015.

Ngai, Mae M. *Impossible Subjects: Illegal Aliens and the Making of Modern America*. Princeton NJ: Princeton University Press, 2004.

O'Brien, Steven. "Blackrobe in Blue: Naval Chaplaincy of John P. Foley, 1942–1946." PhD diss., Boston College, 1999.

O'Callahan, Joseph T. *I Was Chaplain on the Franklin*. New York: Macmillan, 1956.

Offner, Arnold A. *American Appeasement: United States Foreign Policy and Germany, 1933–1938*. Cambridge MA: Belknap, 1969.

Orsi, Robert A. *The Madonna of 115th Street: Faith and Community in Italian Harlem, 1880–1950*. New Haven CT: Yale University Press, 2002.

Overy, Richard. *The Bombers and the Bombed: Allied Air War Over Europe, 1940–1945*. New York: Viking, 2013.

Palmer, Robert R., Bell I. Wiley, and William R. Keast. *The Army Ground Forces: The Procurement and Training of Ground Combat Troops*. Washington DC: Center of Military History, 1991.

Parker, Matthew. *Monte Cassino: The Hardest-Fought Battle of World War II*. New York: Anchor/Random House, 2004.

Patterson, Sarah E. "The Few, the Proud: Gender and Marine Corps Body." PhD diss., Florida State University, 2019.

Patton, George S. *The Patton Papers*. 2 vols. Edited by George Blumenson. Boston: Houghton Mifflin, 1972–74.

Pennington, Reina. *Wings, Women and War: Soviet Airwomen in World War II Combat*. Lawrence: University Press of Kansas, 2001.

Perkins, Frances. *The Roosevelt I Knew*. 1946. Reprint, New York: Penguin, 2011.

Peters, Shawn Francis. *Judging Jehovah's Witnesses: Religious Persecution and the Dawn of the Rights Revolution*. Lawrence: University Press of Kansas, 2000.

Pfau, Ann Elizabeth. *Miss Yourlovin: gis, Gender, and Domesticity during World War II*. New York: Columbia University Press, 2008.

Piehler, G. Kurt. *Remembering War the American Way*. Washington DC: Smithsonian Institution Press, 2004.

———. *The United States in World War II: A Documentary Reader*. Malden MA: Wiley-Blackwell, 2013.

Pinheiro, John C. *Missionaries of Republicanism: A Religious History of the Mexican-American War*. New York: Oxford University Press, 2014.

Poling, Daniel A. *Mine Eyes Have Seen*. New York: McGraw Hill, 1959.

———. *Your Daddy Did Not Die*. New York: Greenberg, 1944.

Preston, Andrew. *Sword of the Spirit, Shield of Faith: Religion in American War and Diplomacy*. New York: Alfred A. Knopf, 2012.

Proehl, Frederick. *Marching Side by Side: Stories from Lutheran Chaplains on the Far-Flung Battlefronts*. St. Louis: Concordia, 1945.

Pyle, Ernie. *Brave Men*. 1944. Reprint, Lincoln: University of Nebraska Press, 2001.

Rable, George C. *God's Almost Chosen Peoples: A Religious History of the American Civil War*. Chapel Hill: University of North Carolina Press, 2010.

Reynolds, Quentin. *The Amazing Mr. Doolittle: A Biography of Lieutenant General James H. Doolittle*. 1953; rpt. New York: Arno, 1972.

Ribuffo, Leo P. *The Old Christian Right: The Protestant Far Right from the Great Depression to the Cold War*. Philadelphia: Temple University Press, 1983.

Rice, Bernard L. "Recollections of a World War II Combat Medic." *Indiana Magazine of History* 93, no. 4 (December 1997): 312–44.

Roberts, Mary Louise. "The Price of Discretion: Prostitution, Venereal Disease, and the American Military in France, 1944–1946." *American Historical Review* 115, no. 4 (October 2010): 1002–30.

——. *What Soldiers Do: Sex and the American GI in World War II France*. University of Chicago Press, 2013.

Rontch, Isaac E., ed. *Jewish Youth at War: Letters from American Soldiers*. New York: Marstin, 1945.

Rose, Ben L. *Sermons to Soldiers During World War II*. Richmond VA: Self-published, 1990.

Ross, William F., and Charles Romanus. *The Quartermaster Corps: Operations in the War Against Germany*. Washington DC: Government Printing Office, 1965.

Rowley, Hazel. *Franklin and Eleanor: An Extraordinary Marriage*. New York: Farrar, Straus & Giroux, 2010.

Rubinstein , William D. *The Myth of Rescue: Why the Democracies Could Not Have Saved More Jews from the Nazis*. London: Routledge, 1997.

Rutter, Joseph W. *Wreaking Havoc: A Year in an A-20*. College Station: Texas A&M University Press, 2004.

Ryan, Joseph W. *Samuel Stouffer and the GI Survey: Sociologists and Soldiers during the Second World War*. Knoxville: University of Tennessee Press, 2013.

Sampson, Francis L. *Paratrooper Padre*. Washington DC: Catholic University of America Press, 1948.

Sandler, Stanley. *Segregated Skies: All-Black Combat Squadrons in World War II*. Washington DC: Smithsonian Institution Press, 1992.

Satterfield, John. *Saving Big Ben: The USS Franklin and Father Joseph T. O. Callahan*. Annapolis MD: Naval Institute Press, 2011.

Schaffer, Ronald. *Wings of Judgment: American Bombing in World War II*. New York: Oxford University Press, 1985.

Schrijvers, Peter. *The Crash of Ruin: American Combat Soldiers in Europe during World War II*. New York: New York University Press, 1998.

Schultz, Duane. *Hero of Bataan: The Story of General Jonathan M. Wainwright*. New York: St. Martin's, 1981.

Schultz, Kevin M. *Tri-Faith America: How Catholics and Jews Held Postwar America To Its Protestant Promise*. New York: Oxford University Press, 2012.

Shavit, David. "'The Greatest Morale Factor Next to the Red Army': Books and Libraries in American and British Prisoners of War Camps in Germany During World War II." *Libraries and Culture* 34, no. 2 (Spring 1999): 113–134.

Shephard, Ben. *A War of Nerves: Soldiers and Psychiatrists in the Twentieth Century*. Cambridge MA: Harvard University Press, 2001.

Sirgiovanni, George. *An Undercurrent of Suspicion: Anti-Communism in America during World War II*. New Brunswick NJ: Transaction, 1990.

Sittser, Gerald L. *A Cautious Patriotism: The American Churches and the Second World War*. Chapel Hill: University of North Carolina Press, 1997.

Skya, Walter A. *Japan's Holy War: The Ideology of Radical Shinto Ultranationalism*. Durham NC: Duke University Press, 2009.

Sledge, E. B. *With the Old Breed: At Peleliu and Okinawa.* 1981; rpt. New York: Oxford University Press, 1990.

Slomovitz, Albert Isaac. *The Fighting Rabbis: Jewish Military Chaplain and American History.* New York: New York University Press, 1999.

Smith, Gary Scott. *Faith and the Presidency from George Washington to George W. Bush.* New York: Oxford University Press, 2006.

———. *Religion in the Oval Office: The Religious Lives of American Presidents.* New York: Oxford University Press, 2015.

Smith, Kathleen E. R. *God Bless America: Tin Pan Alley Goes to War.* Lexington: University Press of Kentucky, 2003.

Snape, Michael. *God and Uncle Sam: Religion and America's Armed Forces in World War II.* Rochester NY: Boydell, 2015.

Spector, Ronald H. *At War at Sea: Sailors and Naval Combat in the Twentieth Century.* New York: Viking, 2001.

Spiller, Roger J. "S. L. A. Marshall and the Ratio of Fire." *RUSI Journal* 133, no. 4 (1988): 63–71.

Spinelli, Angelo M., and Lewis H. Carlson. *Life Behind Barbed Wire: The Secret World War II Photographs of Prisoner of War Angelo M. Spinelli.* New York: Fordham University Press, 2004.

Stahl, Ronit. *Enlisting Faith: How the Military Chaplaincy Shaped Religion and State in Modern America.* Cambridge MA: Harvard University Press, 2017.

Stewart, Sidney. *Give Us This Day.* New York: W. W. Norton, 1956..

Stilwell, Paul. *The Golden Thirteen: Recollections of the First Black Naval Officers.* Annapolis MD: Naval Institute Press, 1993.

Stimson, Henry L., and McGeorge Bundy. *On Active Service in Peace and War.* New York: Harper and Brothers, 1948.

Stouffer, Samuel A., Arthur A. Lumsdaine, Marion Harper Lumsdaine, Robin M. Williams Jr., M. Brewster Smith, Irving L. Janis, Shirley A. Star, and Leonard S. Cottrell Jr. *The American Soldier, Vol. 1: Combat and Its Aftermath.* Princeton NJ: Princeton University Press, 1949.

———. *The American Soldier, Vol. 2: Combat and Its Aftermath,* Princeton NJ: Princeton University Press, 1949.

Suid, Lawrence H. *Guts and Glory: The Making of the American Military Image in Film.* Revised Ed. Lexington: University Press of Kentucky, 2002.

Sutton, Matthew Avery. "Was FDR the Antichrist?: The Birth of Fundamentalist Antiliberalism in a Global Age." *Journal of American History* 98, no. 4 (March 2012): 1052–74.

Takaki, Ronald T. *Double Victory: A Multicultural History of America in World War II.* Boston: Little, Brown, 2000.

Tamura, Linda. *Nisei Soldiers Break Their Silence: Coming Home to Hood River.* Seattle: University of Washington Press, 2012.

Tansill, Charles C. *Back Door to War: The Roosevelt Foreign Policy, 1933–1941.* Chicago: H. Regnery, 1952.

Tobin, James. *Ernie Pyle's War: America's Eyewitness to World War II*. New York: Free Press, 1997.

Toliver, Oleta Stewart, ed. *An Artist at War: The Journal of John Gaitha Browning*. Denton: University of North Texas Press, 1994.

Tower, Hansel H. *Fighting the Devil with the Marines*. Philadelphia: Dorrance, 1945.

Townsend, K. V. R. "Notes: Aerial Warfare and International Law." *Virginia Law Review* 28, no. 4 (February 1942): 516–27.

Townsend, Tim. *Mission at Nuremberg: An American Army Chaplain and the Trial of the Nazis*. New York: William Morrow, 2014.

Treadwell, Mattie. *The Women's Army Corps in World War II*. Washington DC: Government Printing Office, 1954.

Tucker, Todd. *The Great Starvation Experiment: Ancel Keys and the Men Who Starved for Science*. Minneapolis: University of Minnesota Press, 2007.

Tull, James F. "A Chaplain's War: A Fighter Group Chaplain in Australia, India, and China, 1941–1943." Unpublished manuscript.

U.S. Department of the Interior, Office of Indian Affairs. *Indians in the War*. Chicago: Haskell, 1945.

U.S. Office of War Information. *The Negroes and the War*. Washington DC: Government Printing Office, 1942.

U.S. War Department. *A Short Guide to Iraq*. Washington DC: War and Navy Departments, 1943.

———. "Pamphlet 21–13." *Army Life*. Washington DC: Government Printing Office, 1944.

———. Technical Manual 10–630: Graves Registration, September 23, 1941.

Urwin, Gregory J. W. *Victory in Defeat: The Wake Island Defenders in Captivity, 1941–1945*. Annapolis MD: Naval Institute Press, 2010.

Utley, Jonathan G. *An American Battleship at Peace and War: The USS Tennessee*. Lawrence: University Press of Kansas, 1991.

van Creveld, Martin. *Fighting Power: German and U.S. Army Performances, 1939–1945*. Westport CT: Greenwood, 1982.

Vaughn, Stephen. "Ronald Reagan and the Struggle for Black Dignity in Cinema, 1937–1953." *Journal of African-American History* 87, no. 1 (Winter 2002): 83–87.

Ventresca, Robert. *Soldier of Christ: The Life of Pius XII*. Cambridge MA: Belknap, 2013.

Victoria, Brian Daizen. *Zen at War*. 2nd ed. Lanham MD: Rowman & Littlefield, 2006.

Vourkoutiotis, Vasilis. *Prisoners of War and the German High Command: The British and American Experience*. New York: Palgrave, 2003.

Vuic, Kara Dixon. *The Girls Next Door: Bringing the Home Front to the Front Lines*. Cambridge MA: Harvard University Press, 2019.

Vulliet, Andre. *Preliminary Report of the War Prisoners Aid Young Men's Christian Association During World War II*. Geneva: International Committee of the Young Men's Christian Association, 1946.

Walsh, Chris. *Cowardice: A Brief History*. Princeton NJ: Princeton University Press, 2014.

Weinberg, Gerhard L. *A World at Arms: A Global History of World War II*. New York: Cambridge University Press, 1994.

Wells, Daniel. "Better Dead Than Red: A History of the Christian Crusade Aesthetic." PhD diss., Florida State University, 2019.

Wells, Mark K. *Courage and Air Warfare: The Allied Aircrew Experience in the Second World War*. London: Frank Case, 1995.

Whitehead, Don. *Combat Reporter: Don Whitehead's World War II Diary and Memoirs*. Edited by John B. Romeiser. New York: Fordham University Press, 2006.

Whitlock, Flint. *Given Up for Dead: American gis in the Nazi Concentration Camp at Berga*. Cambridge MA: Westview, 2005.

Wickersham, George W. *Marine Chaplain, 1943–1946*. Bennington VT: Merriam, 1998.

Willard, W. Wyeth. *The Leathernecks Come Through*. New York: Fleming H. Revell, 1945.

Wilson, Theodore A. *The First Summit: Roosevelt and Churchill at Placentia Bay, 1941*. Revised ed. Lawrence: University Press of Kansas, 1991.

Winchell, Meghan K. *Good Girls, Good Food, Good Fun: The Story of USO Hostesses During World War II*. Chapel Hill: University of North Carolina Press, 2008.

Winograd, Leonard. "Double Jeopardy: What an American Army Officer, a Jew, Remembers of Prison Life in Germany." *American Jewish Archives* 28, no. 1 (April 1976): 3–17.

Wittner, Lawrence S. "MacArthur and the Missionaries: God and Man in Occupied Japan." *Pacific Historical Review* 40, no. 1 (February 1971): 77–98.

Wong, K. Scott. *Americans First: Chinese Americans and the Second World War*. Cambridge MA: Harvard University Press, 2005.

Woolner, David B., and Richard G. Kurial, eds. *FDR, the Vatican, and the Roman Catholic Church in America, 1933–1945*. New York: Palgrave Macmillan, 2003.

Wyman, David S. *The Abandonment of the Jews: America and the Holocaust, 1941–1945*. New York: Pantheon, 1984.

Yost, Israel A. S. *Combat Chaplain: The Personal Story of the World War II Chaplain of the Japanese American 100th Battalion*. Edited by Monica E. Yost and Michael Markrich. Honolulu: University of Hawaii Press, 2006.

Yung, Judy, ed. *The Adventures of Eddie Fung: Chinatown Kid, Texas Cowboy, Prisoner of War*. Seattle: University of Washington Press, 2007.

Zemke, Hubert. *Zemke's Stalag, The Final Days of World War II*. Washington DC: Smithsonian Institution Press, 1991.

Zuker, Bat-Ami. "Frances Perkins and German Jewish Refugees." *American Jewish History* 89, no. 1 (March 2001): 35–59.

Page numbers in italics indicate illustrations.

Manchuria, 259, 263

Manhoff, Bert, 147, 224

Manila, Philippines, 93, 259, 263, 308

USS *Marine Robin*, 99

Marines, U.S.: and burial of dead, 238–40, 242; chapel on Banika built by, 108; in combat, 140; grief of, in battle, 232; on Guadalcanal, 143–44; humanitarian actions of, 135; Navajo code talkers established by, 161, 188–91; and occupation of Japan, 293–94; as POWs of the Japanese, 257, 258–59; prostitution condoned by, 296; religious needs of, 7, 18, 90, 97, 101, 125, 146, 148, 150, 181, 245, 300, 311; women's service in, 195–96

marriage: and abstinence encouraged by chaplains, 16, 193–94, 210; between British women and GIs, 110–11; in Character Education Program, 315; counseling to support, 83–84, and *get* signing, 232; and infidelity, 85; interfaith, 206–7; interracial, 167, 170–71; and *ketubah* signing, 314; masturbation encouraged before, 221; and Roman Catholic priests, 77, 106; and unwanted pregnancy, 205–6; and wedding ceremonies, 65, 184, 212

Marshall, George: in dedication ceremonies, 52, 319; distribution of condoms supported by, 219; free exercise of religion promoted by, 4; and ideological commitment, 8–9, 44–45; proper burial services ordered by, 244; Protestant chief of chaplains sought by, 301, 306; and refusal to send preachers abroad, 168; UMT supported by, 305; Wainwright's decision to surrender accepted by, 256

Marshall, S. L. A., 116

Marshall Islands, 125–26

Mason, Theodore, 214–15

USS *Mason*, 181

Massachusetts, 318

McCarty, William T., 77

McCluskey, Joseph Pryor, Jr., 132

McGarry, Francis J., 96

McGuire, Thomas, 127–28

McIntire, Carl, 58–59, 76, 120, 121

McIntyre, Marvin H., 169

McNutt, Paul, 86

McPherson, Aimee Semple, 56

McWilliams, A. E., 173

Medearis, T. W., 165

medical care, 19–20, 40, 71, 97, 170, 208–28, 211, 280, 347n1, 347–48n18

Mehle, Harry, 212

Memorial Day, 90, 111, 187–88, 245

memorials, war, 317–19

Menninger, Karl, 222

Mennonites, 31, 39

Meridian MS, 157

Methodist Church, 55, 59, 61, 97, 119–20, 155, 192, 201

Mexican Americans, 167

Meyer, Louis J., 226

USS *Miami*, 96, 180

Miami FL, 254

Michaels, Emmett T., 146

Michigan, 216

Miller, Doris, 165

missionaries, 13, 94, 105, 119–20, 125, 186, 292

Mississippi USO, 184

USS *Missouri*, 292, 296

Monahan, John F., 226

Montclair NJ, 200

Monte Cassino, Italy, abbey at, 119, 130, 229

USS *Monterey*, 151

Monterrey-Fresno CA, Diocese of, 60

Montgomery, Bernard, 268

Montgomery, Carl, 79

Morgenthau, Henry, 29, 282

Morgenthau Plan, 282–83

Morocco, 218

Morrison, Charles Clayton, 37

Morriss, Mack, 132–33, 148, 247

Moss, Carlton, 162

Moss, William O., 157

Mother's Day, 111

motion pictures. *See* film

Mott, John, 32

Muhammad, Elijah, 42

Munda, 146

Munich Pact, 33

Murphy, Frank, 278

Musada, Minora, 185

Of Duty Well and Faithfully Done: A History of the Regular Army in the Civil War
Clayton R. Newell and Charles R. Shrader
With a foreword by Edward M. Coffman

The Militarization of Culture in the Dominican Republic, from the Captains General to General Trujillo
Valentina Peguero

A Religious History of the American GI in World War II
G. Kurt Piehler

Arabs at War: Military Effectiveness, 1948–1991
Kenneth M. Pollack

The Politics of Air Power: From Confrontation to Cooperation in Army Aviation Civil-Military Relations
Rondall R. Rice

Andean Tragedy: Fighting the War of the Pacific, 1879–1884
William F. Sater

The Grand Illusion: The Prussianization of the Chilean Army
William F. Sater and Holger H. Herwig

Sex Crimes under the Wehrmacht
David Raub Snyder

In the School of War
Roger J. Spiller
Foreword by John W. Shy

On the Trail of the Yellow Tiger: War, Trauma, and Social Dislocation in Southwest China during the Ming-Qing Transition
Kenneth M. Swope

Friendly Enemies: Soldier Fraternization throughout the American Civil War
Lauren K. Thompson

The Paraguayan War, Volume 1: Causes and Early Conduct
Thomas L. Whigham

Policing Sex and Marriage in the American Military: The Court-Martial and the Construction of Gender and Sexual Deviance, 1950–2000
Kellie Wilson-Buford

The Challenge of Change: Military Institutions and New Realities, 1918–1941
Edited by Harold R. Winton and David R. Mets

To order or obtain more information on these or other University of Nebraska Press titles, visit nebraskapress.unl.edu.